PHILOSOPHER-KINGS

<table>
<thead>
<tr><th></th><th>LINE</th><th></th><th>CAVE</th><th></th><th></th><th></th></tr>
</thead>
</table>

	Complete Power	Property Set Over	Analogue in Cave	Cave Person (Psychological Type)	Bound By (Ruled By)	Epistemic Power
INTELLIGIBLE (B–E)	Dialectical-Thought (Noēsis) (4)	Forms	The Sun	Unbound Daylight-Dwellers (Wisdom-Lovers)	Rational Desires	Knowledge
(E–C)	Scientific-Thought (Dianoia) (2)	Figures	The Things Themselves	Bound Daylight-Dwellers (Honour-Lovers)	Spirited Desires	True Opinion
VISIBLE (C–D)	Folk-Wisdom (Pistis) (2)	Modes	Models of the Things Themselves	Unbound Cave-Dwellers (Money-Lovers)	Necessary Appetites	Opinion
(D–A)	Perceptual-Thought (Eikasia) (1)	Qualities	Images of Models of the Things Themselves	Bound Cave-Dwellers (Food-, Drink-, Sex-Lovers)	Unnecessary Appetites	Opinion

PHILOSOPHER-KINGS

THE ARGUMENT OF PLATO'S *REPUBLIC*

C. D. C. REEVE

HACKETT PUBLISHING COMPANY, INC.
INDIANAPOLIS/CAMBRIDGE

21 20 19 18   3 4 5 6 7 8

For further information, please address:

     Hackett Publishing Company, Inc.
     P. O. Box 44937
     Indianapolis, IN 46244-0937

     www.hackettpublishing.com

Cover design by Abigail Coyle

Library of Congress Cataloging-in-Publication Data

Reeve, C.D.C., 1948–
  Philosopher-kings : the argument of Plato's Republic / C.D.C. Reeve
    p. cm.
  Originally published: Princeton, N.J. : Princeton University Press, c1988.
  Includes bibliographical references and indexes.
  ISBN 0-87220-815-X (cloth) — ISBN 0-87220-814-1 (paper)
    1. Plato. Republic. I. Title.

JC71.P6R43 2006
321'.07—dc22

                                     2005055057
ISBN-13: 978-0-87220-815-5 (cloth)
ISBN-13: 978-0-87220-814-8 (paper)

The quotation from Wallace Stevens on page vi is from *Collected Poems,* copyright 1954 by Wallace Stevens; reprinted by permission of the publishers, Alfred A. Knopf, Inc., New York, and Faber & Faber, London. Parts of Chapter 1.4–8 appeared in a different form in *Archiv für Geschichte der Philosophie* 67, Band 1985 Heft 3, pp. 246–65 (Walter de Gruyter & Co.).

For
Daddy and Mammy

Total grandeur of a total edifice,
Chosen by an inquisitor of structures
For himself.

WALLACE STEVENS

CONTENTS

PREFACE

One must then, in a single gesture, but doubled, read and write. And that person would have understood nothing of the game who, at this remark, would feel himself authorized merely to add on—that is, to add any old thing. He would add nothing: the seam wouldn't hold. Reciprocally, he who through "methodological prudence," "norms of objectivity," or "safeguards of knowledge" refrained from committing anything of himself would not read at all.

—JACQUES DERRIDA

The most prevalent and resilient interpretative myth about the *Republic*, found in almost every reference book and every encyclopaedia, is that it contains the metaphysical and epistemological doctrines we have learned to think of as archetypally Platonic. The transcendent forms are "separate" from the familiar, sensible world. They alone are completely real and knowable; it is neither completely real nor completely knowable. All knowledge is recollection—we gain it through prenatal direct contact with forms, forget it at birth, and recollect it in this life when our memories are appropriately jogged.

A second myth, almost as pervasive as the first, is that the *Republic* is neither a philosophically nor an artistically unified work. Book 1 belongs with Plato's earlier Socratic dialogues, not with the remaining books, and has no essential contribution to make to the defense of justice contained in them. The First Polis, described in Book 2 (369b5-372d3), lacks an intelligible place in the emerging argument, and may be simply an unexcised false start. The central analogies, the Sun, Line, and Cave, cannot be made to tell a single, philosophically coherent story. The views expressed in the body of the work, especially on the topic of poetry, are so radically at odds with those expressed in Book 10 that the latter can only have been written later and added as a sort of appendix to a work already substantially complete.

A third interpretative myth is that the *Republic* preaches totalitarianism, that the ideal city or Kallipolis it describes is a police state, closed to all innovation or freedom of thought, in which an alienated and brainwashed majority are forced by a brainwashed military police to obey social rules into whose purposes they have no insight, these being handed down by an elite group of overtrained intellectuals who systematically lie so that they can spend as much time as possible doing abstract philosophy. Few Plato scholars subscribe to this myth. But outside the ranks of specialists, it is as widespread and resilient as the other two.

A final interpretative myth is that the entire argument of the *Republic* is vitiated by equivocation, that Plato sets out to defend justice but ends up defending something else altogether. There have been many different attempts to explode this myth. But none seems to me to do full justice to its depth and power.

Now, if all or most of these interpretative myths are true, it is difficult to avoid the conclusion that, whatever the merits of some of its parts, the *Republic* as a whole is at best a seriously flawed masterpiece. Its metaphysics and epistemology are suspect, its major argument is fallacious, its political conclusions are obnoxious, its central analogies are incoherent, its composition is flawed. It is a book admitting of piecemeal interpretation only, a book philosophy has dissected, absorbed, and by and large transcended.

Are the myths true? In what follows, I develop a unified interpretation of the *Republic* which entails that they are not, that the orthodoxy they represent, if only by inclusion, constitutes a serious misunderstanding of Plato and should be rejected. Hence, by implication, and to some degree also by structure and intent, *Philosopher-Kings* is a revisionist work, a work which casts the *Republic* in a new and heterodox light.

I cannot summarize my interpretation here; I think, indeed, that a summary would do more harm than good, provoking skepticism without providing the detailed evidence that alone can lay it to rest. But I can at least sketch the broad outlines of my approach.

In Chapter 1 (and in 2.13 and 3.3), I argue that the *Republic*, especially its opening book, marks and explains Plato's decisive break with the definitive elements of what we think of as Socratism—the elenchus, the craft analogy, and the doctrine that virtue is knowledge, that weakness of will is impossible. However, this critique of Socrates leaves Plato with a problem about justice, and about philosophical method, which I try to characterize in 1.8-13.

The remaining four chapters are devoted to laying out Plato's solution to these problems. But they do not follow his order or style of exposition. What I have done, in effect, is to trace four different routes through the *Republic* each of which covers a different piece of philosophical territory. No doubt this conceals much that a sequential reading would reveal. But having tried the latter approach, and having seen what it revealed *to me*, I am persuaded that the benefits of the one I have adopted outweigh its costs. The order in which I follow these four routes is dictated by my sense of what presupposes what in the overall argument of the *Republic*.

For, as my subtitle indicates, it is Plato's argument that is my major theme.

Chapter 2 deals with foundations, with epistemology and metaphysics, with knowledge and reality. It is the most difficult chapter, and I ask the reader's patience with it. On the basis of a new interpretation of the Sun, Line, and Cave, and of the argument with the sightseers and craft-lovers in Book 5 (475c11-480a13), I argue that the *Republic* contains a theory of forms and a theory of our knowledge of them which are significantly different from, and vastly more plausible than, their predecessors in the *Meno, Phaedo, Symposium,* and *Phaedrus.* If I am right, the *Republic* marks a decisive break not only with the Socratic ethical theory of the early dialogues, but also with the doctrines of the middle dialogues with which it is commonly grouped.

Chapter 3 deals with psychology. It is the pivotal chapter. For, in my view, Plato's theory of the psyche, especially his account of the variety of desires, is the royal highroad to understanding his metaphysics and epistemology, and to seeing how the *Republic* as a whole is composed. That is why the initial sections of Chapter 2 are devoted to psychology.

Chapter 4 deals with Plato's politics, with his theory of the Kallipolis. Here his complex views on the producers, guardians, and philosopher-kings are analyzed and explained. Here we see why Plato puts so much emphasis on education, why he thinks that the laws governing it are the most fundamental, and why he is a defender of freedom properly understood, not of repression. In 4.13, I discuss Plato's much maligned account of poetry and defend its consistency.

With Plato's epistemology, metaphysics, psychology, and politics to hand, it is possible in Chapter 5 to exhibit his ethical theory, his solution to the problem about justice pinpointed in Chapter 1, as a single uninterrupted line of thought, and to see where on the map of ethical theories Plato's lies.

The evidence on which my interpretation ultimately rests is, of course, the text of the *Republic* as a whole. Hence I have relegated all discussion of secondary literature to the endnotes. Had I done otherwise, I would have created the impression that my interpretative argument depends on the success of my criticisms of rival views—and would also, I fear, have lost the reader, and no doubt myself as well, in a maze of often extraneous detail. The result is a text which can itself be read as a single sustained piece of philosophical argument, and a largely but not entirely independent subtext, which makes necessary, but idiosyncratic and nonencyclopaedic, connections to the work of other scholars and other philosophers.

I should say, too, that it is for philosophers that I have primarily written, so that some sections of *Philosopher-Kings,* like some parts of the *Re-*

public itself, are likely to be more readily accessible to those trained in philosophy. I have tried as far as possible, however, both to make what I have to say available to all readers of Plato who are willing to make an effort to understand him, and to give as vivid a sense as I can of the pleasures and insights that reward such effort.

I do not think that Plato's is the last word on any of the topics he discusses, and I have not tried to prove that it is. I defend him against common objections when these seem to me to rest on misunderstandings, or to presuppose questionable philosophy. But there are always other objections, including, no doubt, many I simply have not the wit to see. Nor do I think that my interpretation of the *Republic* is the last word on it. I have striven, certainly, for completeness and finality. But if I succeed in convincing the reader that my interpretation is one to be reckoned with and that, fully defensible or not, the theory it presents as Plato's is brilliant and compelling, I shall be well satisfied.

Line references following Stephanus page references are to Burnet, *Platonis Opera*. I have drawn freely on the available translations of the *Republic*, especially those of Bloom, Grube, and Shorey, emending and adapting them to suit my purposes.

I have translated the Greek terms *psuchē* (plural: *psuchai*) and *polis* (plural: *poleis*) as 'psyche' (plural: 'psyches') and 'polis' (plural: 'poleis'), to preserve the connections between these nouns and the corresponding adjectives, 'psychological' and 'political', and avoid the misleading connotations of 'soul' and 'city' or 'state'.

Parenthetical references in the text not to works of Plato or Aristotle are to this book. Full bibliographic information on works cited in the endnotes is given in the Bibliography.

I am grateful to George Bealer for insightful comments on the first three chapters and for much else; to Walter Englert for help with Greek and proofreading; to Frank Hunt for his exemplary editing; to Mitchell Miller and Alexander Nehamas (my readers at the Press) for their enthusiastic responses and useful suggestions; to audiences at Cornell and Florida State—especially Gail Fine, Terry Irwin, and Russ Dancy—for comments on 2.2-8; to (commentators) Alexander Nehamas and Nicholas White and (chairman) Gregory Vlastos for help with 3.2-3, which I presented as an invited address to the American Philosophical Association (San Francisco, March 1987); to John Simmons for his many good offices over the years since we were graduate students together; and to Reed College for two Vollum Fellowships, a sabbatical leave, and an Apple Macintosh.

PREFACE TO THE
HACKETT EDITION

When, fresh from graduate school in 1976, I went to Reed College, ostensibly to teach logic and the philosophy of science, I found myself having to lecture on Plato's *Republic* in the Freshman Humanities Course (Hum 110). The lectures I gave, polished and developed over a decade, became this book. More than twenty years later, I remain convinced—perhaps stubbornly—of much of what I wrote in it. I hope a new generation of readers will share my conviction or be provoked into vigorous disagreement. Of course, there are things that I would not now defend: for example, my interpretation of Glaucon's challenge, or my explanation of how forms are related to the form of the good. And there are other things that I would substantially revise, such as my characterization of Plato's eudaimonism. In the following papers, I have tried to do better on some of these fronts: "Philosophy, Craft, and Experience in the *Republic*," *The Southern Journal of Philosophy* 43 Supplement (2005): 1–21; "Plato's Metaphysics of Morals," *Oxford Studies in Ancient Philosophy* 25 (2003): 39–58, "The Role of *Technê* in Plato's Construction of Philosophy," *Proceedings of the Boston Area Colloquium in Ancient Philosophy* 16 (2000): 207–222.

Of the many reviewers of the original edition, I want especially to thank John Ferrari (*American Journal of Philology* 3 [1990]: 105–109), R.S.W. Hawtrey (*The Classical Review* 40 [1990]: 317–319), Richard Kraut (*Political Theory* 17 [1990]: 492–496), Michael Morgan (*The Review of Metaphysics* 43 [1989]: 417–418), and Paul Woodruff (*Ancient Philosophy* 2 [1991]: 173–178).

I renew my thanks to Reed College for supporting me and my work, and to George Bealer, Russ Dancy, Wally Englert, Gail Fine, Alison Gammie, Frank Hunt, Terry Irwin, Mitchell Miller, Alexander Nehamas, John Simmons, and Nick White.

I renew my thanks, too, to my beloved parents, now in their nineties, for all they have given me.

Finally, I thank Hackett Publishing Company for offering my first-born child a new home—Deborah and Jay, from the bottom of my heart, thank you.

Chapel Hill
September 2005

PHILOSOPHER-KINGS

ONE

A

PROBLEM
ABOUT JUSTICE

By opening our eyes we do not necessarily see what confronts us. We are anxiety-ridden animals. Our minds are continually active, fabricating an anxious, usually self-preoccupied, often falsifying *veil* which partially conceals the world. Our states of consciousness differ in quality, our fantasies and reveries are not trivial and unimportant, they are profoundly connected with our energies and our ability to choose and act. And if quality of consciousness matters, then anything which alters consciousness in the direction of unselfishness, objectivity and realism is to be connected with virtue. . . . The authority of morals is the authority of truth, that is of reality.

—IRIS MURDOCH

1.1 INTRODUCTION

Book 1 of the *Republic* differs markedly in philosophical style from its fellows. In it we find Socrates questioning all and sundry about what justice is, using the elenchus (1.2) to refute them, and refusing to provide any positive answers of his own. This should make us uncomfortable. For we know that Plato later proscribes this practice altogether; dialectic should be employed only among mature adults, who have mastered the mathematical sciences (537c9-539e2; 2.9, 2.11, 2.13). Why then does he begin the *Republic* with a lengthy example of Socrates violating this proscription?

Our discomfort should be increased by the fact that Socrates' arguments are portrayed as being unsatisfactory. Thrasymachus is dissatisfied with them, even though he cannot answer them (341a9-b2, 349a9-10, 350d9-e4, 352b3-4, 353e12, 354a10-11). Glaucon and Adeimantus are dissatisfied with them (358b1-4, 367b1-5). And, by implication, Plato is dissatisfied with them too; otherwise, why write nine more books?

Book 2 makes a new beginning, but it is a new beginning that harks back to the old one. For Glaucon argues in support of Thrasymachus' views about justice and injustice (358b1-d6). This raises an obvious question: If these views have already been defeated, or are, as some think, riddled with inconsistencies, why are they worth a nearly three-hundred-page response? If they merit such a response, why is Thrasymachus himself not permitted to defend them? Why are they defended at second hand by Glaucon? Why, for that matter, does Plato present Socrates with just these interlocutors, Cephalus and Polemarchus, Thrasymachus, Glaucon and Adeimantus, in the first place? Is this just an accident, or does it serve some purpose?

These questions deserve more attention than they have received. By answering them we shall discover not only how Book 1 fits into the overall design of the *Republic*, but also the precise nature of the problem about justice that Plato takes himself to be trying to solve.

1.2 SOCRATES

It is notoriously difficult to say anything uncontentious about the "Socrates" we meet in Plato's early dialogues. But it is essential to have some sense of his ethical method and doctrines before embarking on a reading of the *Republic*. For the latter, as we shall see, contains the arguments that led Plato to crucially modify his Socratic inheritance (a task with which he is already occupied in the *Meno, Phaedo, Phaedrus*, and *Symposium*), and to develop a new and more adequate ethical theory of his own.

Socrates' major stock in trade is the *elenchus*, which is primarily a search for an answer to the question of what justice is, or piety, or courage, or temperance, or wisdom, or friendship, or some other conventionally recognized virtue. The search usually takes the following form. An interlocutor puts forward an account of a virtue. Socrates then tries to refute him by constructing an argument for the falsity of his account using some of the interlocutor's other beliefs as premises. Moreover, these must be beliefs the interlocutor really holds; insincere beliefs are inadmissible (*Crito* 49c11-d2; *Gorgias* 500b5-c1; *Protagoras* 331c4-d1).

In addition to using the elenchus, Socrates routinely makes some of the following assumptions. First, the virtues are, or are exactly analogous to, crafts such as medicine or shepherding, so that if crafts have a particular feature, the virtues must have it as well. This is the *craft analogy* (*Charmides* 173a7-175a8; *Gorgias* 460a5-461b2). Second, a *genuine* virtue must be always good, fine, and beneficial to its possessor, guaranteeing him happiness (*Euthydemus* 278e5-282d3; *Meno* 88c2-5). Third, the conventionally recognized virtues are genuine virtues (*Charmides* 159c1; *Laches* 192c5-7; *Meno* 87e1-3; *Protagoras* 349e3-5, 359e4-7).

The elenchus, then, often takes the following form. (1) Socrates and his interlocutor assume that the conventionally recognized virtue under discussion is also a genuine virtue. (2) They conclude either that it is a craft or that it is good, admirable, and self-beneficial. (3) Socrates argues that if the virtue is what the interlocutor says it is, either it lacks some feature that the crafts possess, or it is not good, admirable, or self-beneficial. (4) The interlocutor is refuted.

So far, I have focused on the negative side of the elenchus. But in the course of refuting others, Socrates sometimes argues for positive theses of his own. He argues that only wisdom or knowledge is a genuine virtue on the grounds that it alone is always beneficial and advantageous to its possessor (*Meno* 87c10-89a5; *Protagoras* 351b4-362a4). This is his paradoxical doctrine that virtue is knowledge. It has as a consequence his doctrine of the unity of the virtues, according to which all the virtues are forms of wisdom. Socrates also argues that no one ever does what he knows or believes to be other than the best by arguing against the standard view that knowledge or belief can be overcome by desire (3.4). In this way he supports his equally paradoxical doctrine that *akrasia*, or weakness of will, is impossible.[1]

It is this man and these doctrines we meet in Book 1 of the *Republic*. But far from being an ordinary elenctic dialogue in which Socrates examines others and finds them wanting, it is a dialogue in which Socrates is himself under negative scrutiny.[2]

I.3 CEPHALUS AND POLEMARCHUS

Cephalus is an old man close to death. The lesson he has learned from his long experience is that a person's character influences the quality of his life more than anything else: "Both as regards sex, and in the matter of our relations with kinsmen and friends, there is one cause [of good or evil]—not old age, but the character of the man: if men are well balanced and easily contented, even old age is only moderately burdensome; if they are not, both old age and youth are hard to bear" (329d2-6). Socrates finds this conclusion congenial. However, he claims that most would not concede it. They think that it is not character that makes old age tolerable, but wealth (329e1-2). Cephalus responds that "A good man would not very easily bear old age in poverty, and a bad one, even if wealthy, would not be contented" (330a4-6). Money is important, in his view, but without character it does not guarantee happiness.

And this is not simply a view to which Cephalus pays lip service, it is something embodied in his life. For he possesses the type of character he has been praising. He has money, but he also has moderation:

> As a moneymaker I stand between my grandfather and my father. My grandfather and namesake inherited about the same amount of wealth that I possess but multiplied it many times. My father, Lysanias, however, diminished that amount to even less than I have now. As for me, I am satisfied to leave my sons here no less but a little more than I inherited. (330b1-7)

Indeed, his moderation is doubly exemplified in this self-portrait. He has been neither money-mad nor spendthrift. At the same time, he stands between his spendthrift father and acquisitive grandfather. The greatest benefit that his money has conferred on him is that by giving him the means to pay his debts to men and gods it has enabled him to avoid lies, injustice, and the fear of postmortal retribution.

From these closing reflections on the benefits of wealth, Socrates extracts an account of justice and argues that it is flawed:

> But speaking of this very thing, justice, should we say that it is simply telling the truth and paying one's debts? Or are these same actions sometimes just, sometimes unjust? I mean this sort of thing, for example: everyone would surely agree that if a friend has deposited weapons with you when he was sane, and he asks for them when he is out of his mind, you should not return them. The man who returns them is not acting justly, nor is the one who is willing to tell the whole truth to a man in such a state. (331c1-9)

Cephalus goes along with him. But before he can become grist for the elenctic mill, his son Polemarchus "inherits his rôle" (331d8-9), and Cephalus departs to attend to the sacrifice.

Cephalus is an attractive character, portrayed with delicacy and respect. He may not know what justice is, but his experience of life has given him a kind of wisdom that Plato by no means despises (620c3-d2).

The problem Cephalus poses to Socrates—and so to Plato (1.8, 2.13, 3.3)—is that he is to some degree moderate, just, pious, and wise without having studied philosophy or knowing what the virtues are. He is thus a sort of living counterexample to Socrates' claim that virtue is that kind of knowledge (1.2).

But the problem is sharper even than that. For, on Plato's view, Cephalus' life is not very different in character from Socrates'. Hence the striking similarities between the description of Cephalus and the description of Socrates given in the *Apology*, and later in the *Republic* itself. Both men have avoided injustice and impiety. Both face death with good hope (*Apology* 41c8-9; cf. 331a1-3). Neither knows what justice is (*Apology* 21b4-5).

> There remains but a very small group of those who deservedly consort with philosophy; perhaps some well-born and well-bred nature, caught up in exile, who remains with philosophy according to his nature because the corrupting influences are absent [cf. 493e2-496a9]. . . . Now those who have become members of this small group and have tasted how sweet and blessed a possession philosophy is, and have fully realized also the madness of the majority and that scarcely anyone ever acts sanely in public affairs, that there is no ally with whom they might go to the help of justice and live, but that, like

men who have fallen among wild beasts, being neither willing to join in wrongdoing nor strong enough to oppose the general savagery alone, they would perish before they have been of any benefit to polis or friends, useless both to themselves and to others—taking all this into account, they keep quiet and mind their own business [cf. *Apology* 31c4-33a1]. Like a man who takes refuge under a small wall from a storm of dust or hail driven by the wind, and seeing other men filled with lawlessness, the philosopher is satisfied if he can somehow lead his present life free from injustice and impiety, and depart from it with a beautiful hope, blameless and content. (496a11-e2)

The apparent implication is that the elenctically examined life is not guaranteed to be any better or more virtuous than the life of a traditionally brought up gentleman of means. It follows that Cephalus is an inappropriate subject for the elenchus. He is already of good character and disposed to virtue. That is why Plato has him depart before he can be examined.

Plato himself will resolve the problem Cephalus poses for intellectualist moral theories by a doctrine of degrees of virtue, and by making allowances for the inherent differences in people's characters, abilities, and interests. Not everyone either can, or should, lead the examined life (contrast *Apology* 38a5-6). But everyone can benefit by their rulers' leading such a life—a state of affairs which the Kallipolis is designed to achieve. Even for Plato, however, Cephalus will not count as completely virtuous: for complete virtue philosophical knowledge is required. But within the Kallipolis men of his natural type will reliably achieve the highest level of virtue of which they are capable.

Polemarchus inherits his father's place in the argument, as he will eventually inherit his place in life. On the authority of the poet Simonides, he is ready to uphold the account of justice that Socrates has extracted from his father's remarks, even though Socrates has already raised a problem for it: "He [Simonides] stated . . . that it is just to give to each the things that are due to him" (331e3-4). After a little preliminary clarification, this account yields the traditional view—championed by Solon among others—that "doing well by friends and badly by enemies is justice" (332d7-8). If Polemarchus is right, the property of being just is a property possessed primarily by *actions*. This will be of considerable importance later (1.12).

Now it is clear that neither Solon nor Simonides meant that it is just to *corrupt* one's enemies. No one wants enemies to be any more corrupt than they already are. What both poets mean is that it is just to destroy or disable one's enemies. And this is a view Plato himself endorses—provided that one knows who or what one's true enemies are (409e4-410a4). Yet Socrates takes the traditional view to mean that it is just to corrupt one's enemies (335b2-e5). Thus Socrates' refutation of Polemarchus is flagged by Plato as trading on a transparent misinterpretation, which Polemarchus is neither sharp enough nor well trained enough to detect.

Nor is this the only occasion on which Plato tips his hand. All of Socrates' arguments against Polemarchus, with the exception of one (334c1-335a10), make use of the craft analogy (332d2-3). But that analogy is suspect. And Plato indicates this by making one of Socrates' arguments (333e1-334b6) point us to its most glaring flaw. A craft is a capacity for opposites. It enables its possessor to do both good and bad things. The doctor knows how to cure, but *ipso facto* he knows how to kill as well. A virtue, on the other hand, can result only in good things. A virtuous person cannot perform vicious acts. Precisely on this ground Aristotle will later reject the idea that virtues are crafts (*Nicomachean Ethics* 1129a11-17). Once again, we are being given a subtle clue to what is really going on. Without showing the least awareness of the effect that he might be having on Polemarchus, Socrates is casually—notice how quickly he turns to Thrasymachus—sowing the seeds of skepticism about traditional values without providing a viable alternative to them.

Indeed, if Cephalus is an inappropriate subject for the elenchus because he is too old and set in his ways, Polemarchus is an inappropriate subject because he is too young and unformed. This is made clear in the account of the effects of the elenchus in Book 7:

> We hold from childhood certain convictions about what is just and fine, we grow up with them as with our parents, we follow them and honour them. . . . However, there are other ways of living opposite to those, which give pleasure, which pander to the psyche and attract it to themselves, but which do not convince decent men who continue to honour and follow the ways of their fathers. . . . And then, I said, a questioner comes along and asks a man of this kind, "What is the fine [*ti esti to kalon*]?" And when he answers what he has heard from the traditional lawgiver the argument refutes him [*exelegchēi ho logos*], and by refuting [*elegchōn*] him often and in many places shakes his conviction and makes him believe that these things are no more fine than shameful, and the same with just and good things and the things he honoured most. What do you think his attitude will be then to honouring and following his earlier convictions?—Of necessity, he [Glaucon] said, he will not honour and follow them in the same way.—Then, I said, when he no longer honours and follows those convictions, and cannot discover the true ones, will he be likely

to adopt any other way of life than that which panders to his desires? . . . And so from being a man of conviction he becomes lawless and unprincipled. (538c6-539a3)

Cephalus cannot benefit from the elenchus because his character is already as good as Socrates'; Polemarchus can only be harmed by it because his character is not yet fully formed.[3]

But Polemarchus not only serves to expose the dangers inherent in the elenchus, he also reveals an important weakness in traditional values, namely, their failure to provide the social and political institutions that will insure their successful transmission to the next generation. Cephalus grew up in a world relatively free from ethical skepticism, but he has neither passed on that world to Polemarchus nor equipped him to preserve his values in the new and skeptical world in which he actually lives. For whatever the quality of Socrates' arguments, or the adequacy of the account on which they are brought to bear, the fact remains that Polemarchus cannot defend that account against the elenchus, and may abandon his father's values as a result. The Kallipolis is in part Plato's solution to the problem of the transmission of the best values once they are found, and to the problem of how to insure that people who cannot defend their values against criticism, even when those values are the best ones, will yet hold securely to them.

Both Cephalus and Polemarchus show up the problematic nature of the Socratic elenchus. Cephalus shows that the elenchus is not necessary to produce a moral character like Socrates', and is of no use to someone like himself who already has such a character. Polemarchus shows that far from improving the youth, the elenchus is likely to corrupt them. As a father and son, they dramatize the crucial problem of how to preserve and transmit values and experience from one generation to the next.

It would be a mistake, however, to conclude that the elenctic examination of Polemarchus leaves his account of justice unscathed. For, as we shall see in 5.2, it is intended to expose, although not to adequately explain, the characteristic weakness in accounts that, like Polemarchus', represent the virtues as being primarily properties of actions.

I.4 THRASYMACHUS

No reader of the *Republic* soon forgets Thrasymachus. But the impression he makes is a mixed one. He is presented as a somewhat unattractive character full of bluster and contempt for the style of argument that Socrates has been employing against Polemarchus (336b7-d4, 337e1-3, 338b1-3, 338d3-4). Yet there is something refreshing about his irritation and his demand—repeated more politely by Glaucon and Adeimantus—that Socrates state his own views about justice:

> What nonsense have you two been talking, Socrates [and Polemarchus]? Why do you play the fool, giving way to each other? If you really want to know what justice is, don't only ask questions, and then score off anyone who answers them by refuting him. You know very well that it is much easier to ask questions than to answer them. Give us an answer yourself and tell us what you think justice is. And don't tell me that it is what ought to be, or what is beneficial, or the profitable, or the gainful, or the advantageous, but tell me clearly and precisely what you mean, for I won't take that sort of drivel from you. (336b8-d4)[4]

It is the cry of every substantive theorist against the destructive critic. But is Plato's Thrasymachus a substantive theorist? I think he is. Underneath the bluster there is a compelling theory of justice, which exposes some of the major philosophical weaknesses in Socratic ethical theory.

1.5 THRASYMACHUS' FIRST ARGUMENT

Having failed, despite his passionate appeal, to elicit an account of justice from Socrates, Thrasymachus is persuaded to give an account of his own (338c1-341a4).

> Do you not know, he said, that some poleis are tyrannies, some democracies, some aristocracies? . . . And are not these the things that are strong and rule in each? . . . And each ruling group makes laws advantageous to itself: a democracy makes democratic laws, a tyranny makes tyrannical laws, and so with the others, and when they have made these laws, they declare this to be just for their subjects, namely, what is advantageous to themselves, and they punish whoever breaks these laws as lawless and unjust. This then, my good man, is what I say justice is, the advantage of the established government. This I presume you will admit holds power and is strong, so that if one reasons correctly, it works out that justice is the same thing everywhere, the advantage of the stronger. (338d6-339a4)

His line of thought seems to be this:

(1) In every polis, some group is stronger than everyone else, and so rules. This group determines the constitutional character of the polis: if it consists of one man, the polis is a tyranny; if it consists of the wealthy few, it is an aristocracy; if it consists of the many, it is a democracy.

(2) In every polis, the rulers make laws advantageous to themselves: a democracy makes democratic laws, that is, laws advantageous to the *dēmos*, or many; an aristocracy makes laws advantageous to the wealthy few; and so on.

(3) In every polis, the rulers declare that justice for their subjects consists in obedience to those laws, and punish those who disobey them as unjust.

Therefore,

(4) In every polis, justice is the same thing, the advantage of the established government.

But, as has already been conceded at (1),

(5) In every polis, the established government is stronger than everyone else.

Therefore,

(6) In every polis, justice is the advantage of the stronger.

Thus Thrasymachus not only gives an account of justice, namely,

(A) Justice is the advantage of the ruler or stronger,

he also gives, and says that he gives (339a2-3), an argument for it.

If Thrasymachus is right, then being just is primarily a property of *laws* or *political institutions,* and only derivatively a property of the actions that are in accord with those laws. This, as we shall see, is the theoretically significant difference between Thrasymachus' account of justice and that of Polemarchus (1.12).

There follows a brief interlude (339b2-340c6) the purpose of which will emerge presently. Thrasymachus admits that, through error, rulers sometimes make laws that are not to their advantage (339c1-3). He also admits that it is just for their subjects to obey those laws (339c10-12). It follows at once that his argument for (A) is in trouble (339d1-3). For, given these admissions, it will sometimes be just for subjects to obey laws that are not advantageous to the ruler or stronger.

Now Thrasymachus could avoid this problem by taking the obvious way out—suggested by Cleitophon (340b6-8)—of identifying justice, not with what is actually advantageous to the ruler, but with what the ruler *believes* to be advantageous to him. This would still leave him with an interesting account of justice, supported by an interesting argument. Instead, Plato has him reject the obvious in favour of a defense which relies on the notorious notion of "the ruler insofar as he is a ruler" (the Ruler, as I shall call him). In effect, Thrasymachus claims that it was Rulers, not their loose and popular counterparts, he had in mind in his argument for (A), and run-of-the-mill rulers he had in mind when he admitted (339c1-3) that rulers sometimes make mistakes (340e7). Since Rulers, unlike rulers, cannot make errors in ruling, Socrates' criticism is undercut and Thrasymachus is back in business.

Because Thrasymachus is a character in a dialogue, there is no point in dismissing this maneuver as an illegitimate quibble—he is not, after all, writing his own lines.[5] The questions we must rather pursue are why Plato has him reject an obvious defense in favour of an arcane one, and why he takes such pains (in the Cleitophon episode) to advertise that rejection.

Thrasymachus does not produce Rulers out of thin air. He tries to legitimize them by appeal to a general principle about—of all things—*crafts*.

> Do you think I would call stronger a man who makes mistakes at the very moment he is making them? . . . Do you call someone a physician when he makes mistakes in the treatment of patients, at the moment of, and with respect to, that mistake? Or would you call a man an accountant when he makes a miscalculation, at the moment of, and with respect to, that miscalculation? I think that we use words which, taken literally, do say that the physician makes mistakes, or the accountant or the grammarian. But each of these, insofar as he is what we call him, never makes mistakes, so that if you speak precisely—and you are a stickler for precision—no craftsman makes mistakes. It is when the knowledge of his craft leaves him that he makes mistakes, and at that time he is not a craftsman. No craftsman, wise man, or ruler is mistaken at the time when he is a ruler in the precise sense. However, everyone will say that the physician or the ruler is in error. Take it then that this is now my answer to you; strictly speaking, the ruler, insofar as [*kath' hoson*] he is a ruler, does not make mistakes, and does not make mistakes about what it is best to decree, and this his subjects must do. The just is then, as I said from the start, to do what is advantageous to the stronger. (340c6-341a4)

Consequently, if we want to understand Rulers and their intellectual origins, it is the general principle we must interrogate.

Now, whatever we may think of this way of looking at crafts and craftsmen, Socrates is in no position to despise or reject it. For Socrates, as we have seen (1.2), routinely assumes that a genuine virtue must be always good, fine, and beneficial to its possessor, guaranteeing him happiness, and that virtues are crafts. But this identification would clearly collapse if a craft could sometimes result in things that were not beneficial or advantageous to its practitioner. Moreover, Socrates is quite aware of this. For he argues that only wisdom is a genuine virtue by appealing to the fact that it alone is always beneficial and advantageous to its possessor. Consequently, he too is committed to the claim that "no craftsman, wise man, or ruler is mistaken at the time when he is a ruler in the precise sense" (340e4-5). This explains the otherwise surprising fact that, unlike Thrasymachus' modern critics, Socrates does not attack the notion of strict and philosophical Craftsmen.[6]

I think we can now see what Plato is up to. By having Thrasymachus reject Cleitophon's easy solution in favour of a crucial Socratic principle, Plato is presenting him as a Socratic figure, albeit an inverted one. Thrasymachus is flamboyant, cocky, and blustery. Socrates is moderate, undogmatic, and patient. Socrates thinks that justice is a virtue (352d2-354a9). Thrasymachus argues that injustice is the genuine virtue, while justice is high-minded foolishness (348b8-349a2). However, Thrasymachus reaches his inverted Socratic conclusion by faithfully following a genuinely Socratic principle. And this exposes a weakness in the principle.

The question to which I now turn is whether Thrasymachus' first argument is indeed saved if it is about Rulers rather than rulers. For if it is not, he poses no real threat to Socrates.

That argument, uniformly recast in strict and philosophical idiom, and expanded to include the new material about Ruling, runs as follows:[7]

(1*) In every Polis, some group is Stronger than everyone else, and so Rules. This group determines the constitutional character of the Polis.

(2*) In every Polis, the Rulers are masters of the Craft of Ruling.

Therefore,

(3*) No Ruler ever makes a mistake in Ruling.

Therefore,

(4*) No Ruler ever makes a mistake about what Laws are advantageous to himself.[8]

(5*) In every Polis, the Rulers make Laws advantageous to themselves.

(6*) In every Polis, the Rulers declare that Justice for their subjects consists in obedience to those Laws, and punish those who disobey them as Unjust.

Therefore,

(7★) In every Polis, Justice is the same thing, the advantage of the established government.

But,

(8★) In every Polis, the established government is Stronger than everyone else.

Therefore,

(9★) In every Polis, Justice is the advantage of the Ruler or Stronger.

Since (9★) is (A), we now have an argument for (A) that is immune to the objection Socrates raises to its predecessor.[9]

This argument, however, will also fail unless it employs the same notion of Justice in its premises and its conclusion. Hence, Thrasymachus must convince us that by declaring that Justice *for their subjects* consists in obedience to their Laws, the Rulers somehow bring it about that Justice *simpliciter* consists in such obedience—note the lack of qualification in (7★).

One possible basis for such a view is:

(B) Justice is obedience to the Law.

For if (B) actually defines Justice, it follows immediately that simply by enacting particular Laws, the Rulers bring it about that Justice consists in obedience to them. But this cannot be Thrasymachus' route to (A). For he neither states nor argues for (B).[10] So we must look elsewhere.

Let us imagine a very powerful man, motivated entirely by self-interest, whom fate has made the guardian of a large group of infants (540e5–541a7). Not being self-sufficient, he needs the children (369b5-c4). Being self-interested, he wants to insure that when they are grown sufficiently they will act in ways advantageous to himself. Consequently, he works out a set of laws which will bring this about. Through his power to reward and punish, he then trains his young charges to obey those laws, to honour and respect them and those who follow or administer them. Those who learn well and obey the laws are rewarded with power and privileges, and have such terms of approbation as 'just', 'honourable', and 'fine' applied to them. Those who disobey are punished "as lawless and unjust" (338e4-6). In the polis which these children grow to inhabit and constitute, and over which the guardian presides as ruler, the behaviour that is described and praised as just, rewarded with power and privilege, and fostered and inculcated in others is behaviour advantageous to the stronger ruler.

What this means, in effect, is that control of behaviour includes control of *linguistic* behaviour, and with it, a kind of thought control.[11] The guardian controls the way in which the children will use the term 'just', how they will conceive of justice itself, how they will think about and evaluate both themselves and the world around them.

In my view, Thrasymachus derives (A) from (1*) and the rest, because he believes that all polis-dwellers are like these children in the relevant respect. Their rulers, through their power to reward and punish, and through their control of education and the flow of information generally, have trained them to praise as just the very behaviour that is to their—the rulers'—advantage. If we think for a moment of what that behaviour is likely to be, it is clear that it will be largely the kind of behaviour we ourselves think to be just.

On this showing, Thrasymachus' entire argument is based on a daring and insightful theory of the polis as a kind of exploitation machine in which *both social behaviour and the standards by which it is evaluated* are arranged by those who have the power to rule so as to benefit themselves.

This political theory seems itself to be ultimately rooted in a theory of the psyche. The latter is briefly characterized by Glaucon in Book 2 (358e1–361d3). According to it, people "by nature pursue pleonectic satisfaction [*pleonexian*] as the good" (359c3–5). That is to say, they want to have more and more, without limit, of the things they want (591d6–9).[12] Once we grant this theory, and accept that in every polis the ruling group has the power, Thrasymachus' argument is hard to resist. In every polis, the behaviour inculcated in the young, taught in the schools, sanctioned by the legal system, and rewarded and approved as just is behaviour advantageous to the ruler or stronger.

It should be obvious that whatever else it does, this powerful argument poses a serious challenge to the elenctic method, or indeed to any method of ethics that rests *au fond* on people's considered ethical judgements. For it suggests that all such judgements are tainted at the source, and so cannot be taken as providing reliable information about justice, or any other moral notion. The fact, for example, that (A) might conflict with the considered moral judgement that justice is a genuine virtue cannot possibly show by itself that (A) is false. A thoroughly manipulated consciousness will demonstrate to itself over and over again that it is not manipulated.

If I have represented Thrasymachus' line of thought correctly, it is clear that its force is scarcely diminished at all by the introduction of Rulers. For we can now see that the Polis with its Laws and Rulers is simply an idealization or theoretical model (472d9-473b2). It shows us what our rulers aim at being, what they would be if they were smarter or more powerful. Thrasymachus expresses this by saying "if they were masters of the Craft of Ruling." But his argument loses none of its force if we do not follow him in this.

To subvert this Thrasymachean argument it is necessary to show that the theories of psyche and polis it advances are inadequate, and that more nearly adequate theories do not support its conclusions. This is precisely what Plato will attempt in the remainder of the *Republic*.

1.6 THRASYMACHUS' SECOND ARGUMENT

Thrasymachus' first argument is based on a theory of the polis and a psychological theory. It makes no appeal to ethical judgements or principles. Its perspective is, one might say, conceptually external to any particular ethical point of view, including that of the assembled company. It reaches (A) by reflecting on the fact that constitutions are designed by self-interested people who seek their own advantage as far as their power or strength permits (358e1-360d7). His second argument (343a2-344c8) is quite different. It draws openly on the ethical judgements of the company, who must use their concept of justice both in judging that the tyrant acts unjustly (344a3-b6) and in assessing the evidence that Thrasymachus presents to support a key premise (343d1-e7). Its perspective is conceptually internal to their ethical point of view. It reaches (A) by reflecting on the advantages that subjects gain by breaking the laws (being unjust) rather than obeying them (being just).

Thrasymachus opens his second argument with an exhaustive list of the types of situations in which justice and injustice operate and in which their results can be compared—notice the generality of the conclusion stated at 343d1-3 (quoted below). The just and unjust man can have direct business with one another (343d3-6). They can have dealings with the polis to which both belong (343d6-e1). Finally, they can actually be officials in the polis conducting business on its behalf (343e1-6). In each of these cases, Thrasymachus claims, the unjust man overreaches or outdoes (*pleonektein*) the just one. He concludes that

(1) The just man is everywhere at a disadvantage in comparison to the unjust man (343d1-3).

It is important to notice that the evidence on which (1) is based does not include the case in which either man is the actual ruler (or Ruler) of the polis. And it follows, of course, that this restriction must apply also to any proposition derived from (1). Indeed, if this were not so, one of its consequences would actually be inconsistent with (A).

We might object, in any case, that it is only if the unjust man is undetected, or for some other reason goes unpunished, that he comes out ahead. Otherwise, he is "punished and faces great opprobrium" (344b1), giving the longer-term advantage to the just man. But this objection would miss its mark. For it is precisely cases in which injustice is practiced with impunity, of which tyranny is the most extreme example (343e7-344b6), that Thrasymachus has in mind (348d5-9). This explains, I think, why he is so certain that in each of the three cases he describes the unjust man outdoes the just one. For if, as is usually the case, the unjust portion exceeds the just one, and the injustice remains undetected or unpunished, so that no redistribution occurs, the unjust man must get more.

Having established (1), Thrasymachus concludes: "Therefore, I repeat what I said before, the man of great power outdoes [the just man]" (343e7-344a1). To assess the cogency of his conclusion we must inquire into the identity of "the man of great power." The fact that we have already met him—Thrasymachus is repeating himself—narrows the candidates to two. He could be the unjust man (343d1-3), or he could be the stronger (343c1-d1). But unless he is the latter, we can explain neither his name—why "great power"?—nor how Thrasymachus reaches the grand conclusion of his argument, which mentions the stronger again (344c4-8). In point of fact, however, the man in question is both. For, as we are about to discover, the unjust man is the stronger.

Assembling what we have already uncovered, together with what Thrasymachus derives from it, we arrive at the following argument.

(1) The just man is everywhere at a disadvantage in comparison to the unjust man (343d1-3). Conversely, the unjust man is everywhere at an advantage in comparison to the just man.

Therefore,

(2) The unjust man is, in the relevant sense (338c4-339a4), stronger than the just man.

But what makes him the stronger is precisely his injustice and the other's justice. Therefore,

(3) Injustice is stronger than justice (344c4-8).

From (2) and (3), Thrasymachus derives

(4) The stronger is everywhere at an advantage in comparison to the just man (343e7-344c1).

Since, again, it is the justice of the just man that gives the stronger his edge, he infers that

(5) Justice is the advantage of the stronger (344c4-8).

But because the relation of being stronger than something is irreflexive (nothing can be stronger than itself), (5) immediately entails

(6) Justice is the good (or advantage, 379b11) of another (343c3).

By contrast, injustice benefits the unjust man himself, so that

(7) Injustice is one's own advantage (344c8).

Thrasymachus concludes (348c7-8) that

(8) Injustice is virtue and wisdom (348e1-4).

For it, not justice, is genuinely advantageous and self-beneficial (1.5).

Look at (6) for a moment. If it is a general principle about justice, which applies to both rulers and subjects, it conflicts with (A). For if the ruler acts in a way advantageous to himself—that is to the stronger—he acts justly according to (A), but unjustly according to (6). It was with this in mind that I pointed out earlier that neither (1) nor any of its consequences apply to rulers (or Rulers).[13] Hence, no inconsistency.

Now look at (5). Since it too is derived from (1), the stronger it refers to cannot be the ruler (or Ruler). It follows that (5) is not (A). But nor does Thrasymachus suppose that it is. (5) is a vital step in his argument for (A), not its terminus.

The next move is made by means of the tyrant:

> You will see this [how much more it benefits the man of great power to be unjust rather than just] if you turn your thoughts to the most complete form of injustice, which brings the greatest happiness to the one who commits it, and the greatest misery to those who suffer it and are unwilling to do injustice. The most complete form is tyranny. (344a3-6)

At first, the tyrant's rôle in the argument seems to be merely illustrative, but, on closer inspection, he turns out to provide the necessary connective tissue between (5) and (A). Other unjust men are stronger than this or that just man, and are able to break this or that law with impunity (348d5-8). The tyrant, by contrast, is stronger than everyone else in the polis, is able to overthrow all the laws at once, seizing all property in one fell swoop, and simultaneously enslaving its owners as well (344b1-c8). In the process, he is revealed—if only for a moment—as an example of "the most complete form of injustice." Thus one kind of ruler (or Ruler) emerges as simply a more extreme version of the stronger unjust subjects referred to in (5). Since justice is their advantage, it is even more clearly his.

By breaking all the laws, the tyrant reveals himself as completely unjust. By simultaneously overthrowing them, and the power behind them, he destroys the standard by reference to which he is unjust. Justice is now his advantage, not that of the regime whose power he has usurped.

Thus whether we look at justice from outside our moral point of view, so to speak, by reflecting on the nature of psyche and polis, or from within it, by reflecting on how the just fare in comparison to the unjust, the conclusion is the same: Justice is the interest of the Stronger or Ruler.

Like the elenctic method, Thrasymachus' second argument draws on people's ethical judgements. But it does so in order to reveal a serious flaw in the craft analogy. For it shows that injustice as it is practiced by the tyrant is the craft that guarantees happiness. If we take the craft analogy seriously, therefore, we end up supporting not justice, but injustice. It is difficult to imagine a worse fate for a method of ethics. Once Book I is concluded, Plato will never employ the craft analogy again.

1.7 SOCRATES' RESPONSE AND ITS EFFECTS

In his first response to Thrasymachus, Socrates tries to establish that a Craft seeks not its own advantage but that of the weaker, who is subject to it (342c11-d1). Medicine aims to benefit the patient, not itself (341c4-343a2). From this he illicitly infers that a *Craftsman* practices his Craft not for his own advantage, but for the advantage of that on which he exercises it (342d2-e4). He concludes that the Ruler pursues, not his own advantage, but that of his Subject.[14] Thrasymachus contemptuously disposes of this argument by producing a counterexample to it. The Shepherd practices his Craft not for the sake of his sheep, but for his own or his master's advantage (343b1-c1).

Socrates' second argument is intended to show that Thrasymachus has misdescribed his counterexample (345b7-347d8). Shepherding, strictly conceived, benefits the sheep, not the Shepherd. If the Shepherd benefits, it is because he simultaneously exercises a second Craft, Wage-earning.[15] Thrasymachus is not given a chance to reply to this argument *in propria persona*, but that is because Socrates has himself revealed its fatal flaw. If it is to succeed, Wage-earning must benefit its practitioner. Consequently, Wage-earning is itself a counterexample to the claim that no Craft can do this. Thus Socrates' second argument itself undermines his first.

Stepping back from these two attempts to refute Thrasymachus we can see at once that if successful, they prove too much. For if a Craft benefits the object on which it is practiced, never the practitioner, or if Wage-earning alone is self-advantageous, the Craft of Justice will benefit not the Just man, but someone else. This not only conflicts with the view that Justice is a Socratic virtue (352d2-354a9), it is exactly what Thrasymachus claims when he argues that "justice is the good of another" (343c3). Hence, by arguing that Ruling benefits the Subjects, never the Ruler himself, Socrates may be, in Freud's phrase, wrecked by success.

Socrates' third argument concentrates on Thrasymachus' claim that complete Injustice is more advantageous and beneficial than complete Justice, making it, not Justice, the genuine Socratic virtue (348b8-350c11). Because Thrasymachus does not concede that Justice is a genuine virtue, Socrates cannot refute him in the usual way "by appeal to conventional principles [*kata ta nomizomena*]" (348e8-9), that is, by arguing from the view that the conventionally recognized virtues are genuine virtues (1.2). Instead he resorts to a grossly fallacious argument that Injustice cannot be a virtue because it is not a Craft. The true Craftsman does not try to "outdo" other practitioners of his Craft, only non-Craftsmen. The Unjust man, however, tries to "outdo" both Just and Unjust alike; therefore, he is no Craftsman, and Injustice is neither Craft nor virtue.

Now it is true that the Craftsman does not try to "outdo" his fellow Craftsmen in that he does not try to go beyond the principles of his (and their) Craft. But the Unjust man does not try to "outdo" his fellows in that way either. Instead, he tries to get the better of them by practicing the Craft of Injustice as well as possible. Moreover, the fact that the Unjust man tries to "outdo" everyone in the sense of trying to get the better of them does not in the least show that Injustice is not a Craft—practitioners of competitive Crafts, such as Generalship or Boxing, do it all the time. Hence Socrates has not succeeded in showing that Injustice is not a Craft, and, therefore, not a virtue.

In his fourth argument, Socrates wisely abandons craft analogies for political ones (351a6-352d2). Injustice causes factions, hatred, and quarrels in a polis, while justice causes friendship, cohesion, and a sense of common purpose. Therefore, no polis can succeed in a cooperative endeavour if its members treat each other unjustly. Similarly, Socrates claims, injustice causes dissension within the individual, rendering him incapable of coherent action. Although this argument has some promise, as Plato later shows (435a5-b2), it is not convincing as it stands. For, first, it is not clear that a polis cannot treat its members justly, thereby producing the desired cohesion, while treating nonmembers unjustly. If it can, the argument collapses. For someone could then treat himself justly (so to speak), while treating others unjustly. And, second, justice is not the only cause of political coherence. If the members of the polis believe that they are treated justly, that will usually be enough.

Socrates' final argument proceeds from the claim that Justice is a virtue, and Injustice a vice, to the conclusion that Justice is more advantageous and self-beneficial than Injustice (352d2-354a9). The intermediate steps make use of the view, later to find favour with Aristotle (*Nicomachean Ethics* 1.3), that the work or function (*ergon*) of the psyche is to live, and that its virtues are those states of it that enable it to live well or happily (5.2). However, the argument's weakest point lies not in that territory, but in the premise about Justice and Injustice. For the only support that has been offered for that premise, namely, Socrates' third argument, is not up to bearing that kind of weight.

Now *we* see what is wrong with all five of Socrates' arguments, but Thrasymachus is presented as having a response only to the first, and as not being able to defend even that. Yet he is also presented as being completely unconvinced that his views are mistaken (341a9-b2, 349a9-10, 350d9-e4, 352b3-4, 353e12, 354a10-11). And this is not sheer dogmatism on his part.

A key operating condition of the elenchus is that Socrates' interlocutor answer by stating beliefs that are really his own (1.2). And Socrates does indeed try to impose this condition on Thrasymachus: "Thrasymachus, you seem really not to be joking now, but to be speaking what seems to you to be the truth" (349a6-8; cf. 350e5). But Thrasymachus will have none of it: "What difference, he said, does it make to you whether *I* believe it or not? Isn't it *my account* you are refuting" (349a9-10). Because he drives a wedge between his theory and himself, he, like Cephalus and Polemarchus, is an unsuitable candidate for elenctic examination. He cannot defend his theory against the elenchus, but it does not follow that his theory is wrong (487b1-d5 is worth reading in this regard). If he were allowed to speak at length, he could defend it.

> Even what you [Socrates] are saying now doesn't satisfy me, and I have something to say about it. But if I speak, I know well that you would say that I am engaging in demagoguery. So either let me say as much as I want, or, if you want to keep on asking questions, go ahead, and just as with old wive's tales, I will say, "All right," and nod and shake my head.—Don't ever do that, I said, against what you believe yourself. (350d9-e5)

But if Thrasymachus is not permitted to defend his theory in this way, he is willing to answer only to please Socrates. To him, however, the proceedings have become no more than "a feast of words" (352b3-4, 354a10-11).

But whether or not Thrasymachus is right in thinking that he could defend his views, his refusal to identify his own strengths and weaknesses with those of his theory is obviously justified. And it reveals an important weakness in the elenchus. The latter can refute the man, but his theory, and even his rational commitment to his theory, may remain immune to it. This defect in the elenchus will be driven home more fully by Glaucon and Adeimantus. For they, too, will turn out to be unsuitable candidates for the elenchus.

As in the case of Cephalus and Polemarchus, however, it would be wrong to conclude that the elenchus cuts no ice against Thrasymachus' account of justice. For as we shall see in 5.2, it exposes, without adequately explaining, the characteristic defect in accounts of the virtues that identify them as being primarily properties of laws or political institutions.

1.8 PLATO'S PURPOSES

Both sides of the conversations we have been analyzing were—to reiterate an easily forgotten point—written by Plato. With the details before us, we must now try to determine their place in his argument.

Let us consider the pertinent facts. (1) The elenchus, the craft analogy, the assumption that the conventionally recognized virtues are genuine virtues, and the requirement that the interlocutor answer Socrates' question with what he himself believes are crucial components of Socrates' ethical theory. He makes use of all of them in the course of his arguments with Cephalus, Polemarchus, and Thrasymachus. (2) Each of these interlocutors is an unsuitable candidate for elenctic examination. Indeed, each reveals a different limitation of it. Cephalus shows that it is inappropriate for use on older people with settled characters. His son Polemarchus shows that it is unsuitable for use on the young. Thrasymachus shows that it is unsuitable for use on those who refuse to answer by stating their own beliefs, or who distinguish their own strengths and weaknesses in dialectical argument from the strengths and weaknesses of their theories. (3) Thrasymachus' first argument raises a serious doubt about the epistemic presuppositions of the elenchus (2.13). (4) His second exposes a crippling defect in the craft analogy, and puts into question the assumption that conventional virtues must be genuine ones. (5) None of Socrates' responses refutes Thrasymachus' account. (6) Thrasymachus rejects the negative elenchus in favour of positive theory, and develops such a theory himself. (7) Plato presents an explicit criticism of the negative elenchus, and abandons it after Book 1 in favour of a positive account, which, like Thrasymachus', rests on a theory of the psyche and a political theory. (8) He abandons the craft analogy, the assumption that the conventional virtues must be genuine ones, and the condition that interlocutors must state their own beliefs.

If we adopt the traditional view that Book 1 is an ordinary Socratic dialogue, we must suppose that these eight facts are largely a disconnected series of accidents. We must suppose that Plato shows Socratic ethical theory triumphing in Book 1, only to abandon it in the remainder of the *Republic* for reasons he never states. On this view, Book 1 certainly does emerge as an excrescence without any literary or philosophical justification.

But if we accept the interpretation suggested in the preceding sections, we have in (1)-(6) the explanation for (7) and (8), so that Book 1 emerges as a brilliant critique of Socrates, every aspect of which is designed to reveal a flaw in his theories. I shall have more to say about Book 1 in 1.11, but if even this much is accepted, Book 1 is clearly a cohesive and intelligible component of the *Republic* as a whole. For how could one more naturally begin a radical new departure in ethical theory than by showing that one is called for?

This interpretation, however, does leave one question unanswered. Why did Plato not simply come right out and tell us that he was abandoning Socrates' ethical theory, and give us his reasons for doing so? Why did he conceal his purposes in a drama that has proved so difficult to unravel? Insofar as this is a question about why Plato wrote dialogues in which transparency and directness are not the manifest virtues that they are in treatises, or in papers submitted to scholarly journals, it can be answered convincingly only by looking at all of Plato's dialogues. But I am confident that Plato's pedagogical aims and suspicion of writing lie behind it, that he conceals his purposes in order to make us confront in our own thought the problems and *aporiai* with which he himself is wrestling.[16] Insofar as the question is not this one, it is likely to rest on the false presupposition that Plato thought he was abandoning Socrates. For after all, Socrates is not killed off in Book 1, but reemerges, stripped of the elenchus and the craft analogy, and transformed into a positive theorist, who, having learned the lessons of that book, goes on to offer a much stronger response to Thrasymachus' arguments. Plato does not abandon him, or his theories; he transforms them. To those who cannot conceive of Socrates without the tools of his gadfly trade this will seem to be either filial piety or a deep betrayal on Plato's part. To Plato himself, I suspect, it is neither. For he thinks of Socrates as having had his philosophic nature "perverted and altered [*strephesthai te kai alloiousthai*]"

(497b1-3) by being brought up in the wrong kind of polis (496a11-497c3). What he gives us in Book 1 is that "perverted and altered" figure. What he gives us in subsequent books is that same man as he would have taught and theorized had he found the right kind of nurture (497a3-5).[17] The contingent and perverse features of Socrates and his teachings are thus rejected and condemned, but his essential nature, and the teachings that he would have produced if unperverted, are enthusiastically embraced. So it certainly is not mere filial piety that keeps Socrates center stage for the entire *Republic*, and prevents Plato from openly parading his criticisms. Whether keeping him there is an act of deep betrayal of Socrates, or one of deep insight into his character, is another, harder question.[18]

1.9 GLAUCON'S DIVISION OF GOODS

Book 2 marks a new beginning but not a discontinuity. For what Glaucon does is restate and defend the views of Thrasymachus in a philosophically sophisticated and precise way (357b4-8).

He begins by introducing a subtle and complex triadic classification of goods, which, like his discussion of Thrasymachus' theory, shows him to be familiar with philosophy (475a6-476a6, 504e7-505b4, 507a7-b10). Crucial to this triadic classification is a dyadic distinction between wanting something *for its own sake* and wanting it for the sake of its *apobainonta*, or, as I shall put it, for a reason that will become clear in 1.11, for the sake of its *Glauconic consequences* (or *G-consequences*).

> There is a kind of good which we would choose to possess not because we want its G-consequences [*apobainontōn*] but for its own sake [*auto hautou heneka*]. Enjoyment, for example, and those simple pleasures from which nothing else arises except enjoyment. . . . And again a kind we want both for its own sake and for its G-consequences—knowledge, for example, and sight and health. . . . And can you discern a third kind of good . . . such as physical training, being treated when ill, the art of healing, and other ways of making money? For we would say that these are painful and difficult, but beneficial, and for their own sake we would not want them, but only for the rewards and other benefits that result from them. (357b4-d2)

I shall call these A-goods, B-goods, and C-goods, respectively.[19]

According to Socrates justice is a B-good: "In my opinion justice belongs to the fairest class, that which a man who is to be happy or blessed must want for its own sake and for its G-consequences" (358a1-3). But according to most people it is only a C-good: "This is not the opinion of the many, they would put it in the wearisome class that must be done for the rewards and reputation based on opinion, but is to be avoided in itself as harsh" (358a4-6). Since both parties agree that justice is wanted for its G-consequences, and disagree only about whether it is also wanted for its own sake, it is natural to expect that debate will focus on the latter topic. And this is precisely what Glaucon seems to want: "I am eager to hear what each of them [justice and injustice] is, and what power each of them is, in and of itself [auto kath' hauto], in the psyche. I want to leave out of account the rewards and G-consequences of each" (358b4-7). The comparison of justice itself (justice stripped of its G-consequences) to injustice itself (injustice stripped of its G-consequences) remains the focus of discussion until the middle of Book 10:

> I granted your [Glaucon's] request that the just man should be reputed unjust and the unjust man reputed just, . . . so that justice itself [autē dikaiosunē] could be judged in comparison to injustice itself [adikian autēn]. . . . Since that judgement has now been made [see 612a8-b5], I ask on behalf of justice that the the reputation it in fact has among gods and men be returned to it. (612c7-d5)[20]

We shall see why this focus is not only natural, but also necessary. Given Glaucon's arguments, justice cannot be defended by appeal to its G-consequences alone (1.11).

Notice that unlike Polemarchus, who identifies being just as primarily a property of actions, or Thrasymachus, who identifies it as a property primarily of laws, Glaucon presupposes that being just is primarily a property of a *psyche*. This is the theoretically significant difference between his views about justice and theirs (1.12, 5.3).

I.10 GLAUCON'S DEFENSE OF INJUSTICE

In order to make clear to Socrates what he wants him to do, Glaucon proposes to defend injustice in precisely the way that he wants to hear justice defended: "I am going to speak at length in praise of the unjust life, and, in doing so, I will show you the way I want to hear you praising justice and denouncing injustice" (358d3-6).[21] Adeimantus then further specifies what Socrates must do by illustrating how he does *not* want to hear justice praised and injustice condemned (362e4-367e5). Glaucon says, in effect, "Do it this way." Adeimantus says, "Don't do it this way." The length and insistence of their speeches attest to the unprecedented nature of the defense of justice Plato is planning to give us:

> No one has ever blamed injustice or praised justice in any other way than by mentioning the reputations, honours, and rewards that are their G-consequences; no one has ever adequately described, either

in poetry or in private conversation,[22] what each of them is in itself
by its own power when it is within the psyche of its possessor even
if it remains hidden from gods and men, proving that the one is the
greatest evil that the psyche can have within itself, while justice is the
greatest good. (366e3-9)

Quite self-consciously, the *Republic*, like *Paradise Lost*, aims to accomplish
"feats unattempted yet in prose or rhyme."

Glaucon begins his defense of injustice with a preview of his overall
strategy:

So, if you agree, I will renew the arguments of Thrasymachus. First,
I will state what is said to be the nature and origin of justice; second,
that all who practice it do so unwillingly, as being necessary, but not
good; third, that they have good grounds for doing so, for according
to what is said the life of the unjust man is better than that of the just
man. (358b7-c6)

And this is exactly what he gives us—three arguments that support Thrasymachus' view that injustice itself is more choiceworthy than justice itself.

The first of these arguments provides a more explicit picture than
Thrasymachus himself does of the psychological and political underpin-
nings of his account of justice (358e3-359b2). People by nature pursue
pleonectic satisfaction of their desires as the good (359c3-5).[23] They want
to have as much as possible of the things they want, and they recognize
no limits on the pursuit of that end, of the sort for example that justice
might impose, except those which result from their own limited power.
Consequently, someone who was sufficiently powerful to take whatever
he wanted with impunity would have no motive to avoid injustice or to
agree with others to do so (359b1-4). The majority of people, however,
are not in this boat. They can neither do injustice with impunity nor avoid
suffering it at the hands of others. Hence they

decide that it is profitable to come to an agreement with each other
neither to do injustice nor to suffer it. And that is the beginning of
laws and covenants among men, and the law's command they call
lawful and just. This, they say, is the origin and essential nature of
justice; it stands between the best, which is to do injustice with impunity, and the worst, which is to suffer it without the power to
revenge oneself. (359a1-7)

If this account is accepted, the only reason to choose justice over injustice
is to avoid the bad G-consequences of the latter. It follows immediately

that injustice itself, stripped of its G-consequences, is more choiceworthy than justice itself.

This conclusion is further substantiated by Glaucon's second argument (359b6–360d7). If a just man could cancel the bad G-consequences of being unjust by using Gyges' ring to make himself invisible, even he would abandon justice for injustice. Hence, once again, injustice itself emerges as more choiceworthy than justice itself.[24]

Glaucon's third, and most important, argument suggests that those who choose injustice over justice make a wise choice.

> As for the choice between the lives we are discussing, we shall be able to make a correct judgement about it only if we put the most just man and the most unjust face to face. . . . We must subtract nothing of his injustice from the unjust man, nothing of his justice from the just one, but each must be complete in his own way of life. In the first place, the unjust man must act as clever craftsmen do—a first-rate pilot or physician, for example, distinguishes what his craft can do from what is impossible for it, attempting the one while letting the other go by, and when he blunders, he knows how to put things right. Hence the unjust man's successful acts of injustice must be supposed to escape discovery, if he is to be completely unjust, and we must regard the man who is caught as inept. For the extreme of injustice is to seem just without being so. To the completely unjust man, then, we must assign complete injustice, and withhold nothing of it, but we must allow him, while perpetrating the greatest injustices, to have secured the greatest reputation for justice. . . . Let us now put him beside the just man. . . . We must take away his reputation, for a reputation for justice would bring him honour, and it would then not be clear whether he is what he is for justice's sake or for the sake of rewards and honours. We must strip him of everything except justice and make him the complete opposite of the other. Though he does no injustice he must have the greatest reputation for it, so that he may be tested for justice by not weakening under ill repute and its consequences . . . so that our two men may reach the limits, one of justice, the other of injustice, and be judged as to which of the two is happier. (360e1–361d3)

Since the just man may live a wretched life, tortured and imprisoned, because of his reputation for injustice, while the unjust man benefits both from his undetected injustice and from his reputation for justice, the palm of happiness must surely go to the unjust man (361d7–e1). Again we arrive at the Thrasymachean conclusion that injustice itself is more choiceworthy than justice itself.

We can now see why it is crucial to Plato to be able to show that justice itself is more choiceworthy than injustice itself. For the latter includes the good G-consequences of justice, while the former does not exclude the bad G-consequences of injustice. Hence, justice cannot be successfully defended by appeal to G-consequences alone.

There are three important things to note about Glaucon's argument before we leave it. First, reputation and rewards, which are G-consequences of justice itself, are not G-consequences of injustice itself. If they were, Glaucon would not be praising injustice in the way that he wants Socrates to praise justice (358d3-6).[25] Second, happiness is not treated entirely as a G-consequence. For Glaucon supposes that when the just man has been stripped of the G-consequences of justice, and the unjust man has been stripped of the G-consequences of injustice, it is still possible to ask which of them is happier. This would not be so if happiness were itself one of the things entirely stripped away in both cases. Finally, the argument shows that Glaucon is supposing that the question of whether justice or injustice is more choiceworthy depends solely on which of them results in a happier life.

It follows from this final point that if Plato is to answer the argument he has put into the mouth of Glaucon (and why else put it there?), he must show that justice itself results in a happier life than injustice itself. Later he represents Socrates as seeing this quite clearly:

> After observing the most unjust of all we may oppose him to the most just; thus we can complete our inquiry into the relation between pure justice and pure injustice with regard to the happiness and wretchedness of the men who possess them, so that we may either be persuaded by Thrasymachus and pursue injustice or be persuaded by the argument that is now coming to light and pursue justice. (545a5-b1)

Consequently, there is little room for doubt about the rough nature of Plato's enterprise. He aims to defend justice by showing that it pays off in terms of happiness (4.9).[26]

1.11 GLAUCON'S CHALLENGE

Plato must show that a completely just person is happier than a completely unjust person, without appealing to G-consequences. But what exactly is it to show that? If happiness is not a G-consequence of complete justice, how are they related? To find out, we must interrogate the notion of a G-consequence, and the division of goods which relies on it.

Glaucon excludes having a reputation for justice from being a G-consequence of complete injustice. Not only is complete injustice a sufficient condition of being reputed just, but it is impossible to be completely unjust without being reputed just (361a5-b2; 1.10). At the same time, he includes having a reputation for justice among the G-consequences of being completely just. Being completely just is in fact a sufficient condition of being reputed just:

> I granted your request that the just man should be reputed unjust and the unjust man reputed just; you both demanded this, even though it isn't in fact possible for things to escape gods and men in this way; nonetheless it had to be granted for the sake of the argument, so that justice itself could be judged in comparison to injustice itself, or don't you remember? (612c7-d1)

However, it is logically possible both to be completely just without being reputed just and to be reputed just without being completely just.

Turning to an earlier passage (357b4-8), we find that Plato implicitly excludes the enjoyment of a simple pleasure from being a G-consequence of it. He could not otherwise consistently classify the simple pleasure itself as an A-good, since it would have a G-consequence, namely, enjoyment, which is also wanted (357b4-5). He does not explain why he proceeds in this fashion. But, given what we have already uncovered, it is surely because there is a noncontingent relation between enjoying a simple pleasure and experiencing it. If the simple pleasures in question are simply experiences, then it is impossible either to experience them without enjoying them or to enjoy them without experiencing them. If, as is more likely (3.6), they are activities, such as smelling a pleasant perfume (584b5-8), then it is possible to engage in the activity without enjoying it, but impossible to enjoy the activity without engaging in it. In either case, Plato seems to hold that if it is impossible to be G without being F, then being G cannot be a G-consequence of being F.

Together these passages suggest that

(1) Being G is a G-consequence of being F just in case (a) being F is a sufficient condition of being G, but (b) it is possible to be F without being G, and (c) it is possible to be G without being F.

But although (1) fits in well with the examples, it cannot be what Plato has in mind.

Glaucon wants to be shown that complete justice stripped of its G-consequences—justice itself—is more choiceworthy than injustice itself (1.9-10). Hence, if (1) captured the properties he wanted to exclude from the defense of justice, he would have to hold that people who want to be just solely for the sake of being G count as wanting to be just for its own sake even if G is a property one can have without being just, although not a property one can be just without having. And he would have to be satisfied with a defense of justice which appealed solely to such properties. But this conflicts with the claim that if justice is a B-good, it is something that "a man who is to be happy or blessed must want for its own sake and for its G-consequences" (358a1-3). For if it is possible to be happy without being just, then justice is not something "a man who is to be happy or blessed" must want. Moreover, this sort of view makes little philosophical sense. If someone wants to be just solely for the sake of being G, and it is possible to be G without being just, then he cannot count as wanting to be just for its own sake. He clearly wants to be just for the sake of something else. If both just and nonjust people can be G, justice cannot be shown to be more choiceworthy than injustice simply by appeal to G.

We seem to have reached an impasse. (1) is suggested by the examples, but it conflicts with other things we are told, and makes nonsense both of the division of goods and of Glaucon's challenge.

But suppose that part of what underlies those examples is a componential model of relations between properties. Being reputed just is not a G-consequence of being completely unjust because it is *an essential component* of it. Enjoying a simple pleasure is not a G-consequence of experiencing it because experiencing it is an essential component of enjoying it. But being reputed just is a G-consequence of being completely just because, even though being completely just is in fact a sufficient condition for being reputed just, the latter is not an essential component of the former, nor the former of the latter.

On this model, the notion of a G-consequence is to be understood in the following way:

(2) Being G is a G-consequence of being F just in case (a) being F is a sufficient condition of being G, but (b) being F is not an essential component of being G, and (c) being G is not an essential component of being F.

And (2) does seem to get us closer to what Glaucon has in mind. For, while (1) allowed justice itself to be defended solely by appealing to properties which a nonjust person could also have, (2) excludes this possibility. If being just is an essential component of being happy, it is not possible to be happy without being just.

However, even (2) does not seem to be quite right as it stands. For though it fits the examples, and avoids some of the difficulties to which (1) is exposed, it does not seem to sit well with the central metaphorical characterization of G-consequences as consequences that can be stripped away. If justice is an essential component of happiness, it is impossible to be happy without being just, but it seems to be possible to be just without being happy. If that is possible, however, it seems that happiness can be stripped away from justice, that happiness is merely a G-consequence of being just, and that it cannot be appealed to in the defense of justice.

To see our way past this objection we need to look more closely at justice and happiness. Justice and happiness admit of degrees. And when properties admit of degrees, essential components admit of varieties. In some cases, if being F is an essential component of being G, it is impossible to be to some degree F without being to some degree G. Having money is an essential component of being rich, and it is not possible to have any amount of money without being to some degree rich. In these cases, being F (or G) to some degree might be thought of as having some number of units or degrees of F (or G). For this reason, I shall call them *homoiomerous* essential components. For like the homoiomeries attributed to Anaxagoras, they are like one another, and like the whole they compose.[27] But in other cases this entailment does not hold; not all essential components are homoiomerous. Having a good ear for music is an essential component of being a good singer, but it is possible to have a good ear without being able to sing a note.

So (2) is ambiguous because the notion of an essential component is ambiguous. But this very ambiguity promises a solution to our problem. For if the essential components referred to in (2) are homoiomerous, it will not be possible to strip away happiness from justice. Happiness will not, then, be a mere G-consequence of being just, and it will be possible to defend justice by showing that it pays off in terms of happiness, without thereby violating the conditions for its defense set by Glaucon.

One thing in favour of homoiomerous essential components, then, is that they enable us to see the various examples given of G-consequences as illustrations of the metaphorical characterization of them as consequences that can be stripped away. But an equally important piece of evidence is provided by Plato's views about the relations between justice and happiness.

In Book 5, we are told that once we know how complete justice is related to happiness, we will know how degrees of justice are related to degrees of happiness:

It was then to have a model, I said, that we were seeking the nature of justice itself, and the completely just man, if he should come into being, and what kind of man he would be if he did, and likewise in regard to injustice and the most unjust man, so that by looking at

> how their relationship to happiness and its opposite seemed to us, we
> would also be compelled to agree about ourselves as well, that he
> who was most like them would have a portion [of happiness] most
> like theirs. (472c4-d1)

And the conclusion of the comparison between complete injustice and
complete justice in Book 9 substantiates this claim:

> Come, then, I said, and like the final arbiter, tell me who among the
> five, the king, the timocrat, the oligarch, the democrat, and the ty-
> rant, is first in happiness, who second, and so on in order.—That
> judgement is easy, he said. I rank them in virtue and vice, in happi-
> ness and its opposite, in the order of their appearance, as I might
> judge choruses.—Shall we, then, hire a herald, I said, or shall I my-
> self announce that the son of Ariston has given as his verdict that the
> best, the most just, and the most happy is the most kingly who rules
> like a king over himself, and that the worst, the most unjust, and the
> most wretched is the most tyrannical who most tyrannizes himself
> and the polis he rules? (580a9-c4)

But if this is so, if from the fact that the completely just must have a
certain share of happiness it is to follow that the more just we are the
larger our share of happiness must be, and the less just we are the smaller
our share must be, then every unit or degree of justice must be a unit or
degree of happiness. Which is to say, being just must be a homoiomerous
essential component of being happy.

Finally, and perhaps most importantly of all, the notion of a homoiomerous essential component enables us to make philosophical sense of the
division of goods. For that notion is exactly the one we need in order to
render intelligible the crucial distinction between wanting something for
its own sake and wanting it for the sake of something else. Put the other
way around, the technical notion of a G-consequence, unlike the ordinary
notion of a consequence, picks out precisely those consequences of being
F such that if someone wants to be F for the sake of them alone, he does
not want to be F for its own sake.

If we want to be F solely for the sake of being G, and being F is simply
a sufficient condition of being G, then it is clear that we do not want to
be F for its own sake.[28] But it is equally true, although it may not be
equally clear, that if we want to be F solely for the sake of being G, and
being F is simply an essential component of being G, it still does not
follow that we want to be F for its own sake. Knowing Greek is an essential component of knowing how to read Aeschylus. But someone can
want to read Aeschylus for its own sake without wanting to know Greek

for its own sake. He may loathe Greek and regret that Aeschylus wrote in such an impossible tongue, but find that being able to read the *Oresteia* compensates for it all. It is only if being F is a homoiomerous essential component of being G that wanting to be F solely for the sake of being G guarantees that we want to be F for its own sake. For in this case, to fail to do so is to fail to want to be G for its own sake.

Given this explication of wanting something for its own sake, and allowing that a good is a homoiomerous essential component of itself, we can characterize Glaucon's three kinds of goods as follows:

Being F is an *A-good* just in case it is wanted for the sake of something of which it is a homoiomerous essential component, and it has no G-consequences that are wanted.

Being F is a *B-good* just in case it is wanted for the sake of something of which it is a homoiomerous essential component, and it has some G-consequences that are also wanted.

Being F is a *C-good* just in case it is wanted for the sake of its G-consequences, and it is not a homoiomerous essential component of anything that is wanted.

On this showing, Glaucon's division of goods—which is really Plato's division of goods—is both cogent and well motivated. It is also a major intellectual achievement. For without it, it is impossible to see clearly what the alternative to defending justice by appealing to its consequences could conceivably be. And if we cannot see this clearly, Thrasymachus will win by default (1.10).

We are now in a position to state Glaucon's challenge with greater, albeit not yet complete, exactness (1.12). Glaucon wants to be shown that justice itself is a homoiomerous essential component of happiness. For this will establish each of the things on his agenda. First, it will establish that justice is wanted for its own sake. Second, it will establish that justice itself is more choiceworthy in terms of happiness than injustice itself. And, third, since no one disputes that justice is wanted for the sake of its G-consequences, it will establish that justice is a B-good (1.9).

I.12 WHY GLAUCON?

Why Glaucon? Two distinct but related questions are covered by this rubric. First, why does Plato have Glaucon rather than Thrasymachus, whose views he echoes and refines, pose the challenge about justice? Second, what are the reasons Plato gives him for posing it? The first will lead us naturally into the second.

To answer Glaucon, Plato must show how justice can be a homoiomerous essential component of happiness. But can Plato show this? There are two reasons to think that he cannot. One concerns happiness—I shall explore it first. The other concerns justice. Both are complex.

Glaucon is not himself convinced by Thrasymachus (358c6, 361e1-3, 368a7-b3), but for the sake of argument he is adopting Thrasymachus' position. Hence he cannot concede at the outset that justice is an essential component of happiness. But, surely, ends (like everything else) are actually identified by their essential components. It seems to follow that the end of which justice is an essential component cannot be what Glaucon is thinking of as happiness. Hence in undertaking to show Glaucon that justice is an essential component of what he thinks of as happiness Plato seems to have set himself an impossible task.

We can think of ends and their components, however, in two quite different ways, either *intensionally* or *extensionally*, and it makes a difference to the seriousness of the preceding problem which one of them is at issue. The intensional components of someone's ends are (roughly speaking) the things mentioned in his description or specification of them. Thus if someone orders bacon, egg, and sausage for breakfast, those three foodstuffs are the intensional components of what he wants. The extensional components of what he wants, on the other hand, are the essential components of the items in the world that his description or specification picks out (provided there are such things). Thus pig flesh, cholesterol, and albumen are among the extensional components of that particular breakfast. It is clear, I take it, that while a person must know the intensional components of his ends, there is no reason to think that he must know their extensional components. Indeed, it is often the case that when we discover the extensional components of one of our ends we cease to pursue it.

We may agree, therefore, that the attempt to prove to someone that his end has intensional components of which he is unaware is doomed to failure. But it does not follow that he cannot be shown that his end has extensional components of which he is ignorant. For all Glaucon knows, or is in a position to concede, justice might well be an extensional component of his ultimate end. Thus Plato can avoid the most difficult part of the present problem by undertaking only the latter task. But a very difficult part remains nonetheless. For once Plato abandons intensional components for extensional ones, he must also abandon tidy analytic arguments for messy explanatory ones. And these notoriously give the skeptic many places at which to dig in his heels.

A second, and much less tractable, problem about happiness must now be faced. Glaucon cannot allow that justice is an intensional component of his ultimate end. That much is clear. But if he is to follow Thrasymachus, he must go further than that. For Thrasymachus holds that happiness actually consists in pleonectic satisfaction of one's desires. And surely nothing picked out by this specification of happiness can have justice as a homoiomerous essential extensional component. For pleonectic satisfaction of one's desires, which involves having more and more without limit, must, as Thrasymachus and Glaucon both recognize, be unjust satisfaction of them (359c3-5, 348b8-349c6). In this case, the stratagem we employed to solve our first problem is clearly useless. Once again, Plato seems to have set himself an impossible task.

This brings us to the problem about justice. Plato presents Socrates with three groups of interlocutors: Cephalus and Polemarchus; Thrasymachus; Glaucon and Adeimantus. Each of them identifies justice, or being just, with a very different type of property. Cephalus and Polemarchus think that being just is identical to the property an action has provided it is a case of benefiting a friend or harming an enemy. In their view justice is primarily a property of actions (1.3). Thrasymachus, on the other hand, thinks that justice is a property exemplified primarily by laws or political institutions. In his view being just is a property laws or institutions have provided they are advantageous to the rulers (1.5). Finally, Glaucon and Adeimantus identify being just with a property possessed primarily by psyches (1.9). They do not know what property it is, but they have no doubt about what sort of property it is. It will emerge that these identifications are characteristic of the sort made by people of the different psychological types to which the interlocutors belong, and that Cephalus and Polemarchus, Thrasymachus, and Glaucon and Adeimantus are, in some respects at least, our introduction to the money-lovers, honour-lovers, and wisdom-lovers—the producers, guardians, and philosopher-kings—who are the true, if submerged, *dramatis personae* of the *Republic*.

It seems, then, that the justice Glaucon and Adeimantus want to be shown is an essential extensional component of happiness is neither the same as the justice Thrasymachus has in mind nor the same as the justice that Polemarchus and Cephalus have in mind. The entire argument of the *Republic* is, therefore, threatened with being irrelevant to some of the interlocutors. That is bad enough. But if, as some philosophers have argued, *our* conception of justice is significantly like that of Cephalus and Polemarchus, Plato's argument is also threatened with being irrelevant to the question *we* are interested in when we ask why we should be just.

Far from ignoring these problems, or tucking his answer to them away

35

in an obscure passage, Plato presents a solution to them that resounds through every aspect of the *Republic*, from the analogies of the Cave, Line, and Sun to the argument for the tripartite psyche, from the account of pleasure to the design of the Kallipolis, from the theory of forms to the structure of the dialogue itself. Here I will do no more than sketch that solution in broad dogmatic strokes, reserving detailed discussion and defense for subsequent chapters.

A person's needs, desires, and interests are in part determined by the natural lottery, in part by his education and upbringing, and in part by his actual social conditions. They also depend on his beliefs about what he is, and about what the world and its contents are, beliefs which themselves depend to a large extent on his needs, desires, and interests. For finding out about the world is itself a project set by desire. A person's *real interests* are those he would form under optimal conditions, in which his needs are satisfied, he is neither maltreated nor coerced nor the victim of false ideology (it is easier to specify these negatively), and his capacity to understand himself and the world is as fully developed as his nature permits.[29] *Real happiness* is stable optimal satisfaction of real interests throughout life.

But because people have different natures, they have different real interests, are made really happy by different things and have different degrees of insight into themselves and the world. These different natures are of three primary types: money-lovers, honour-lovers, and wisdom-lovers, or philosophers. Each is ruled, or has his ultimate goal determined by, the desires in one of the three parts of the psyche: appetite, aspiration, and reason. Each has his own distinctive pleasure, his own peculiar *Weltanschauung*.

A money-lover is ruled by the desires in appetite. He wants the pleasure of making a profit more than anything else, so that even under optimal conditions, he will develop his understanding of himself and the world only to the degree that doing so is profitable. He identifies things in the world as sources of his favourite pleasure, and justice with performing the kinds of actions, such as paying debts, which insure his real happiness—a condition he identifies with the stable acquisition of as much of the pleasure of making money as possible throughout life.

An honour-lover is ruled by the desires in aspiration. He wants the pleasures of victory, reputation, and being honoured more than anything else. Even under optimal conditions he will develop his understanding only to the degree that doing so brings him his favourite pleasure. He identifies things in the world as sources of honour. For him justice is a property exemplified by those political institutions within which people who are, for example, victorious in battle, are rewarded with honours and acclaim. He identifies real happiness with the stable acquisition of as much of the pleasure of being honoured as possible throughout life.

A philosopher is ruled by the desires in reason. He most wants the pleasure of learning and knowing the truth. Hence under optimal conditions he will come to understand the world as it really is. He identifies justice with justice itself, a property of psyches, and happiness with happiness itself, the stable acquisition of as much of the pleasure of learning and knowing the truth as possible throughout life.

Of these three types, even when each is raised and educated under optimal conditions, only the philosopher has knowledge of himself and the world, only his vision is undistorted by desire-induced fantasy. Included among the things he knows is how the world, which he sees clearly, looks to the other psychological types, who do not see it clearly. And in the light of this knowledge, he sees that their identifications of justice and happiness are the results of their inadequate attempts to get at the very properties with which he correctly identifies these things. The properties with which money-lovers and honour-lovers identify justice and happiness are, we might say, what justice itself and happiness itself "look like" to people with their characteristic desires and beliefs. Hence, even though money-lovers, honour-lovers, and philosophers identify justice and happiness with different things, these things are so related that the threat of irrelevance is avoided.

A person's actual interests may already coincide with his real interests. Plato's aim is to show such a person that only if he is ruled by a psyche of which justice itself is a homoiomerous essential extensional component can he achieve what is for him real justice and real happiness. If he is a philosopher, this psyche will be his own. But if he is a money-lover or honour-lover, it will not. And this is where the Kallipolis plays a crucial rôle. Money-lovers and honour-lovers can achieve what is for them real justice and real happiness only in a polis ruled by just philosophers. But then philosophers can themselves become reliably just and happy only in such a polis. So everyone is better off in the Kallipolis than out of it.

Most people, however, have interests that are to some degree pathological: their satisfaction could not possibly result in real happiness. This is the class to which Thrasymachus and, by proxy, Glaucon both belong. For it would not be in their real interests to strive for the pleonectic satisfaction with which they identify happiness. Indeed, the completely unjust tyrant who does strive after it will emerge as the most really wretched of people.

It is in this context that the Kallipolis is again crucial. For Plato's ingenious strategy is to engage people of this sort, as Socrates engages Glaucon and Adeimantus, in the task of designing a polis whose members are guaranteed as much real happiness as creatures who cannot survive outside a political community can possibly have. This will be the polis in which anyone guided by rational prudence would choose to have been brought up. But a polis shapes the desires, beliefs, aspirations, and interests of its members through training, education, and socialization. Hence anyone who selects a polis as the best kind in which to have been brought up is *ipso facto* selecting as his real interests those he would have had as his actual interests had he in fact been brought up there. In the process he will discover—if Plato is right in thinking that the polis such a person would select is the Kallipolis—that only if he is ruled by a psyche of which justice itself is a homoiomerous essential extensional component can he reliably achieve the end that would then have been his.[30]

Plato's approach to the problems about justice and happiness is, therefore, indirect in two quite different ways. First, he does not show directly that the property with which Thrasymachus identifies justice is essentially tied to the property with which he—and by proxy Glaucon—identifies happiness. Instead he shows that the property with which he would identify justice if he had been brought up under optimal conditions is essentially tied to the property with which he would then identify happiness. Second, he does even this indirectly by constructing a complex blueprint of the type of polis which (allegedly) provides that type of upbringing to its inhabitants.

The first kind of indirection raises a difficult question in the theory of rational motivation. Does someone's conviction that E is the end that would have been his ultimate end had he received the kind of upbringing he now judges best give him a motivating reason—conclusive or otherwise—to pursue E now? Surely the answer must depend on a host of factors. Is E very similar to his actual end or radically different from it? Is it within his power to make E his end now, or is it, for example, too late? Is E achievable within his actual social and historical circumstances? Is the argument that convinces him, and commands his intellectual assent, sufficiently vivid and persuasive to get a grip on his imagination or emotions? Is his actual life sufficiently unsatisfactory to make an alternative appealing? Since we cannot settle these questions in the abstract, there is no way to predict with certainty whether an argument of this kind will give a motivating reason or not.[31]

We have already glanced at the difficulties raised by the second kind of indirection in discussing the problem about happiness—but they are clearly raised by the first kind as well: complex arguments give a skeptic many opportunities to dig in his heels. And Plato's argument is as complex as they come. It includes, in addition to many hypotheses, analogies, and conjectures, a theory of the nature and origin of the polis, a psychological theory, a psychopathology, a theory of learning and education, a theory of knowledge, and, of course, a theory of forms, no one of which it purports to establish conclusively. It is not—and is admittedly not (435c9-d5, 504b1-504c4)—a demonstration from unhypothetical first principles, or even from widely shared premises (493e2-494a2). Hence there is no way to predict with certainty how someone, even someone rational (3.10), will react to it.

Plato's defense of justice is subject, then, to two kinds of indeterminacy of outcome. Even if it convinced the skeptic intellectually, there is no guarantee that it would give him a motive to be just. But, in addition, there is no guarantee that even a rational skeptic would be convinced by it.

Now Plato was, I think, perfectly aware of these limitations in his argument. He has Socrates explicitly acknowledge that Thrasymachus might not find it convincing: "Don't slander me and Thrasymachus just as we have become friends, not that we were enemies before. We will not relax our efforts until we either convince him and others or at any rate do something which may benefit them in a later incarnation when, born again, they happen on a similar discussion" (498c9-d4).[32] And, even more significantly, the argument is addressed not to Thrasymachus (who retires to the sidelines after Book 1), but to Glaucon.

Thrasymachus believes that injustice is better than justice, and has a theory of the psyche and polis to support his view. If he challenged Plato, it would surely be in these terms: "Show me that I'm wrong. Give me a motive to act justly that is stronger than my current motive to act unjustly." And Plato's argument, as we have seen, is not guaranteed to be able to do either of these things.

Glaucon, by carefully developed contrast, has not been persuaded by Thrasymachus to abandon his belief that justice is better and more choiceworthy than injustice (348a3, 358c6, 361e1-3, 368a7-b3). Consequently, he does not just want a proof or demonstration that justice is better. Adeimantus cautions Socrates to this effect more than once: "Do not merely give us a theoretical proof that justice is better than injustice" (367b2-3; cf. 367e2-3). Nor does Glaucon primarily seek a motive to be just. He already has a sufficient one, for he both lives and acts justly:

> You [Glaucon and Adeimantus] must be divinely inspired if you are not convinced that injustice is better than justice, and yet can speak on its behalf as you have done. And I do believe that you are not really convinced by your own words. I base this belief on my knowledge of the way you live, for if I had only your words to go by, I would not trust you. (368a7-b3)

Glaucon's challenge to Socrates is: "Show me that I'm right. Explain how, even in the face of Thrasymachus' arguments, it can still be true, as I believe, that justice itself, by its very presence in the psyche, makes one happier than injustice itself." Since showing someone that his moral beliefs can be true despite the skeptic's arguments is a very different task from that of refuting the skeptic, the challenge Glaucon poses is very different from the one that Thrasymachus poses—very different, and much more likely to be met by the type of argument Plato plans to give.[33]

In addition to wanting the kind of defense of justice that Plato can provide, Glaucon is himself a just man whose upbringing and education have made him an admirer of justice. Hence he will welcome a defense of it as corroborating what he believes and underwriting his values and way of life:

> The man who has been properly brought up in this area . . . will praise fine things, rejoice in them, receive them into his psyche, be nurtured by them, and become fine and good in character. He will rightly object to shameful things and hate them while still young before he can grasp the reason for it, and when the reason comes he who has been raised in this way will welcome it as something known with which his upbringing has made him familiar. (401e1–402a4)

To Thrasymachus, on the other hand, justice is "high-minded foolishness" (348c12), and the just are benighted weaklings. His upbringing has made him an admirer of tyrants and opportunists. Hence he will find a defense of justice hard to hear, for it will put in question his fundamental values and way of life.

However, the very fact that Glaucon wants what Plato can give him, and is the kind of person who will find it congenial, makes him a totally unsuitable candidate for the elenchus. Glaucon does not himself believe that injustice is more choiceworthy than justice. Consequently, *he* does not stand in need of refutation (1.2). So, while Thrasymachus is unsuitable because he distinguishes the strengths and weaknesses of his theory from his own strengths and weaknesses as a dialectician, Glaucon is unsuitable because the view he is troubled by is not his own.

Finally, Glaucon has a natural asset denied to the other interlocutors (his brother excepted). For Plato, as I intimated, has by design provided Socrates with three groups of interlocutors, one belonging to each of the three primary psychological types he recognizes (581c3–4), with which we will be later much occupied.

Cephalus and Polemarchus are presented as having the features characteristic of money-lovers who have been brought up in nonideal conditions outside the Kallipolis (2.2, 5.3). They focus on those aspects of justice—such as paying one's debts and keeping one's word—that are especially important to commerce (333b10). They cite poetry, which "imitates human beings performing compulsory or voluntary *actions*" (603c4-5; 4.13), to support their views about life (329b6-d1, 331a1-10, 331d4-5). They identify justice with a property of actions (5.3). Cephalus describes himself as a "moneymaker" (330b1-7). His moderation, which is the virtue having particularly to do with acquisition, is emphasized.

Thrasymachus is presented as having the features characteristic of an honour-lover. He identifies justice with a property primarily of laws and political institutions (5.3). He exhibits anger (336b1-6, 586c7-d2), and is described as being victory loving and eager for praise and admiration (338a5-8). However, he admires the appetitive tyrant, rather than the successful honour-lover, as we might expect, because, since he has not been brought up in the Kallipolis, his interests are pathological (548a5-c7, 549a9-550b7).

Glaucon and Adeimantus, alone of the interlocutors, are already familiar with, and sympathetic to, the theory of forms, which is the cornerstone of Plato's defense of justice (2.8-12, 5.3-4). Hence they are philosophic men. For only the latter are naturally qualified to understand and accept that theory (475b11-480a13).

Glaucon replaces Thrasymachus, then, not simply because what he wants is something that Plato's argument is exactly suited to give him, nor because his upbringing has made him likely to find the conclusion of the argument congenial, but because he is a philosophic man, the only kind naturally suited to be party to an investigation of justice.

Even the order of interlocutors is a part of the philosophical argument, then. Each interlocutor exposes a different weakness in the elenchus, each gives us an increasingly more adequate conception of justice. Thus, as we read, we are shown justice first as a money-lover sees it, then as an honour-lover sees it, then as a philosopher sees it, so that in our reading we follow a path of increasing enlightenment, analogous to the path that leads out of the Cave, up the Line, into the light of the Sun.

1.13 THE AIM OF THE *REPUBLIC*

The aim of the *Republic* is at once more limited and more realistic, therefore, than is generally recognized. For if 1.11-12 is right, Plato undertakes to do no more, and no less, than to show Glaucon and Adeimantus, and others relevantly like them, how justice can be a homoiomerous essential extensional component of happiness. It is a task for the nonskeptic's bureau of internal affairs rather than his foreign relations department. At the same time, however, Plato shows how ethics and politics could be freed from their dependence on shared judgements and intuitions, and set on a secure objective foundation. The path he takes in the *Republic* is a shortcut for friends of justice and the forms, but he describes a longer, exoteric path which, having reached the good itself, founds moral and political values, not on opinion and tradition, but on knowledge of the nature of things (435c9-d5, 504b1-7, 532d2-533a6; 2.8-12, 5.3).

EPISTEMOLOGY
AND
METAPHYSICS

To me, on the other hand, the most vital of questions for philosophy appears to be to what extent the character of the world is unalterable: so as, once this question has been answered, to set about *improving that part of it recognized as alterable* with the most ruthless courage. —NIETZSCHE

It is desire that engenders belief, and if we are not as a rule aware of this, it is because most belief-creating desires . . . end only with our own life.
—PROUST

2.1 INTRODUCTION

In the *Republic* Plato introduces epistemology and metaphysics piece-meal, exposing only as much as he needs at each stage in the dialogue. But we can better understand their structure and assess their cogency by treating them together as an epistemologico-metaphysical preface to the defense of justice which is the book's major topic. This does not mean that epistemology and metaphysics are less important than the defense of justice. Far from it. The defense of justice depends crucially on them; they are the key that renders it fully intelligible. Having considered them at the outset we will already be acquainted with the theory of forms—just as Glaucon and Adeimantus are—when we turn to the discussion of justice proper in Chapter 5.

I begin, however, not with epistemology and metaphysics, but with a strand of Plato's thought about the psyche, which leads, via his theory of education, to his views about knowledge and reality. By taking this less travelled road I hope to avoid some of the traffic of controversy that crowds the major highway, and throw new light on ancient problems.

2.2 THE DIVISIONS OF DESIRES

According to Book 9, "there are three primary types of people: philo-sophic, victory-loving [or honour-loving], and money-loving" (581c3-4). Each is ruled by a distinct psychic part. Each has its own characteristic desire, its own distinctive pleasure (3.2-7). The money-lover is ruled by appetite (*to epithumētikon*). His characteristic desire is for the money necessary to satisfy his desires for the pleasures of food, drink, and sex, which he values above all others (580d11-581a7). The honour-lover is ruled by aspiration (*to thumoeides*). His life is wholly dedicated to the pleasure of "power, victory, and high repute" (581a9-10). The philosopher, or wisdom-lover, is ruled by reason (*to logistikon*). He most values the pleasure of learning and knowing the truth about things (581b5-6).

Besides distributing desires among the three parts of the psyche, Plato also divides them into two fundamental kinds, necessary desires and unnecessary desires.[1] Necessary desires are "[a] those we are unable to deny . . . or [b] those whose satisfaction benefits us, for we are compelled by nature to satisfy them both" (558d11-e3). Unnecessary desires are those "one could avoid if one trained oneself from youth to do so, which lead to no good, or indeed to the opposite" (559a3-6). Hence there are potentially as many as six different classes of desires: necessary and unnecessary appetites; necessary and unnecessary spirited desires; and necessary and unnecessary rational desires. We shall see that these underlie the classification of psychological types.

But this sixfold classification is far from being the end of the story. The following passage, for example, shows that a desire does not have to belong to both (a) and (b) in order to be necessary:

> Is not the desire to eat to the point of health and well-being, the desire for bread and relishes, necessary? . . . The desire for bread is necessary on both counts, in that it is beneficial, and in that if it isn't satisfied, we die. . . . The desire for relishes is necessary too, insofar as it conduces to well-being. (559a11-b7)

The desire for bread is both necessary for life and beneficial. The desire for relishes is beneficial, but one does not die for want of them. Still, it is a necessary desire. For we necessarily pursue what benefits us, just as we necessarily pursue what is essential for life (505d11-506a2). Hence there are, in effect, two kinds of necessary appetites, those belonging to both (a) and (b), and those belonging to (b) alone.

A later passage makes it clear that there are also two subspecies of unnecessary appetitive desires, lawless ones and another, unnamed kind, which I shall call *nonlawless* appetitive desires:

> Some of our unnecessary pleasures and desires seem to me to be lawless [*paranomoi*]; these probably come to be in all of us, but when checked by the laws and the better desires in alliance with reason they are got rid of entirely by some men, or so nearly that only a few weak ones remain, while in others stronger and more numerous ones remain. . . . [I mean] those that are awakened in sleep when the rest of the psyche, the reasonable, gentle, and ruling part, slumbers; then

the beastly and savage part, full of food and drink, casts off sleep and seeks to find a way to gratify itself. You know that there is nothing it will not dare to do at such a time, free of all control by shame or reason. It doesn't shrink from trying to have sexual intercourse, as it supposes, with a mother or with anyone else at all, whether man, god, or beast; it will commit any foul murder, and there is no food from which it abstains. And, in a word, it omits no act of folly or shamelessness. (571b4-d4)

I suggest that appetitive desires are both lawless and unnecessary just in case they are so insatiable that someone in their grip will violate even such fundamental taboos as those forbidding parricide, incest, and cannibalism in order to try to satisfy them (575a1-4). The discussion which follows will expose the basis for this suggestion.

Nor does the complexity end with these subdivisions of necessary and unnecessary appetites. Money is harmful to guardians (416d3-417b8). Therefore, the desire for it is harmful to them too. But they can avoid the desire through training and education. Hence it is an unnecessary desire of theirs. However, money is necessary to producers. For their ruling necessary appetites are "best satisfied by means of money" (580e5-581a1; 4.4), and they need money in order to practice their crafts as well as possible.

Take the other craftsmen again, and consider whether these are the things that corrupt them and make them bad . . . [namely] wealth and poverty. . . . Do you think that a potter who has become wealthy will be willing to pay attention to his craft? . . . He will become idler and more careless than he was? . . . And therefore he becomes a worse potter? . . . And further, if because of poverty he is unable to provide himself with tools and the other requirements of his craft, the work he produces will be worse, and he will make worse craftsmen of his sons and any others he teaches. . . . And so both poverty and wealth make the work of the crafts worse and the craftsmen too. . . . Here, then, is a second group of things that our guardians must guard against and do all in their power to prevent from slipping into the polis without their knowledge . . . [namely] wealth and poverty: the former makes for luxury, idleness, and political change; the latter for mean-mindedness, bad work, and change as well. (421d1-422a3)

Hence a desire for money is a necessary desire of producers. This suggests that whether a desire is necessary to a person depends on his psychological type: philosopher-kings (wisdom-lovers), guardians (honour-lovers), and producers (money-lovers) draw the boundaries between necessary and unnecessary desires in different places.

They also draw the boundaries between the two subspecies of necessary desires in different places: "In fact he [the philosophic man] calls these pleasures [those of making money or being honoured] really necessary [*tōi onti anagkaias*] because he would not want them if they were not necessary for life" (581e2-4). The clear implication is that the philosophic man treats some pleasures, and hence the desires whose satisfaction results in them (3.7), as necessary solely because they are essential to sustain life, while the money-lover and honour-lover (by implied contrast) treat these pleasures and desires as necessary because they think them beneficial apart from their rôle in sustaining life. They would want these desires and pleasures even if they were not necessary to sustain life; the philosopher would not.

The explanation of this sort of relativity of the division of desires to character-type seems to be this. Each of the three psychological types believes that his own life, and his own distinctive pleasure, is the most pleasant (581c8-e4; 3.7). As a result, each has a different conception of the good, and of what is beneficial or harmful (2.12, 3.7-8). Given the definitions of necessary and unnecessary desires, it follows that each will have a different view of which desires, beyond those "we are unable to deny," are necessary, which unnecessary. The money-lover looks only to whether having (or acting on) a particular desire helps him acquire the pleasure of making money reliably throughout life. If it does, he classes it as necessary; if it does not, he classes it as unnecessary. The honour-lover looks only to whether having (or acting on) a desire helps him acquire the pleasure of being honoured reliably throughout life. If it does, he classes it as necessary; if it does not, he classes it as unnecessary. The philosopher looks only to whether having (or acting on) a desire helps him acquire the pleasure of knowing the truth reliably throughout life. If it does, he classes it as necessary; if it does not he classes it as unnecessary.

Finally, a desire can be either necessary or unnecessary depending on what it takes to satisfy it. Both wealth (too much money) and poverty (too little) harm a producer, as we have seen. However, he can avoid the desire for too much money and the desire for too little through training and education in a craft (4.4, 4.6). Thus they are unnecessary desires of his. But some amount of money, falling between excess and deficiency (618c4-619b1), is beneficial to a producer. A desire satisfied by that amount of money must therefore be one of his necessary desires.

We end up, then, with an eightfold division of desires: lawless and non-lawless unnecessary appetites; necessary appetites which are both beneficial and essential for life, and necessary appetites which are beneficial but not essential for life; necessary and unnecessary spirited desires; and necessary and unnecessary rational desires. But, as we shall see, only seven of these classes have members, for there are no unnecessary rational desires (5.4).

It is now clear that the theory of psychological types and the theory of the division of desires are intertwined. The basis of their relationship, however, has not yet been fully exposed.

Let us suppose that a person's psychological type is unknown. If his necessary appetites are so strong that he cannot be trained or educated to prefer any pleasure to that of making the money which is the best means to satisfying his desires for the pleasures of food, drink, and sex, he is a money-lover. If, on the other hand, his desires for the appetitive pleasures are weak enough that he can be trained to prefer the pleasure of being honoured to them, while his desire for that pleasure is so strong that he cannot be trained or educated to prefer any other pleasure to it, then he is an honour-lover. Finally, if both his appetitive and his spirited desires are sufficiently weak that he can be trained and educated to prefer the pleasure of learning and knowing the truth to either the appetitive or the spirited pleasures, he is a philosopher, or wisdom-lover. Thus the triadic division of desires into appetitive, spirited, and rational is the very basis both of the theory of psychological types and of the further divisions of desires into necessary and unnecessary desires (3.1-8). It is also, as we shall see in the next section, the basis of Plato's psychopathology.

2.3 PSYCHOPATHOLOGY

The account of the varieties of psychological types in Books 8 and 9 seems arbitrary and structureless. But once it is seen in the light of the division of desires, its underlying rationale emerges clearly.

The *tyrannical person* (571a1-576e2), who is the most pathological (3.8), is ruled by lawless unnecessary appetites: "Lust lives like a tyrant within him in complete anarchy and lawlessness [*anomiai*] as sole ruler" (575a1-2). He does not recognize even that external limit on his pursuit of more and more food, drink, and sex constituted by the taboos against homicide, cannibalism, and incest. In him, *pleonexia*, or the desire to have more and more without limit, rages unchecked. He is Thrasymachus' tyrant exposed for what he really is (343e7-344c8, 348b8-350c11, 545a2-b1, 571a1-592b6).

The *democratic person* (558c8-562a2) is ruled (at least part of the time) by his nonlawless unnecessary appetites, but never by lawless ones:

Such a man spends his money, effort, and time no less upon unnecessary than upon necessary pleasures. . . . He establishes his pleasures on an equal footing and so spends his life always surrendering the rule of himself to whichever of them happens along, as though it were chosen by lot, until it is satisfied, and then to another, dishonouring none, but fostering them all equally. (561a6-b5)

Thus he recognizes at least external limits on the satisfaction of his appetites. Because of this, pleonexia has a slightly weaker hold on him than it does on the tyrannical person.

The *oligarchic person* (553a6-555b1) is ruled by his necessary appetites. He is "thrifty and a worker, satisfying only his necessary appetites, and making no other expenditures, but enslaving his other desires as vain" (554a5-8). Hence, in addition to recognizing that there are external limits on his pursuit of food, drink, and sex, the oligarch also imposes some internal constraints on them. Thus he is less prone to pleonexia than the democrat.

The *timocratic person* (548d6-550d4), who is the first to escape from appetitive rule, is ruled by spirited desires. He has "surrendered the rule over himself to the middle part, the victory-loving and spirited part" (550b5-7). Thus he has moderated both his necessary and his unnecessary appetites. He is even less likely to succumb to pleonexia.

Finally, we reach the *philosopher* (473c11-541b5), who is ruled by rational desires and "is always straining to know where the truth lies" (581b5-6). He has moderated, not only his appetitive desires, but also his spirited ones. He is the least likely of all these types to succumb to pleonexia (442a4-443b2).

Each of these types, including the philosophic man who is not a philosopher-king (496d9-497c3), is pathological (we shall see why in 3.7). But in the Kallipolis a normal type corresponds to each of them. Corresponding to tyrannical, democratic, and oligarchic people are the producers (4.4);[2] corresponding to timocratic people are the guardians (4.6, 4.8); corresponding to philosophic people are the philosopher-kings (4.7, 4.9).

This correspondence is no accident. For within the Kallipolis money-lovers and honour-lovers, who would otherwise be ruled by appetite and aspiration respectively, are ruled by reason—not internally by their own rational parts (only the philosopher-kings manage that) but externally by the reason of their philosopher rulers:

Why do you think that the condition of the manual worker is despised? Is it for any other reason than this: when one has by nature a feeble portion of the best part of the psyche [reason] one cannot rule the brood of beasts within one [appetites], but can only serve them and learn to flatter them? . . . Therefore, in order that such a man may be ruled in like manner to the best man [the philosopher-king], we say that he ought to be the slave of that best man who has a divine ruler within himself. It is not to harm the slave that we say he must be ruled, as Thrasymachus thought subjects should be, but because it is better for everyone to be ruled by divine reason, preferably within himself and his own, otherwise imposed from without, so that as far as possible all will be alike and friends, governed by the same thing. (590c2-d6)[3]

Then, instead of having a desire structure that is pathologically self-frustrating, each psychological type will fully achieve its own primary ends, its own happiness (586d4-e2).

2.4 EDUCATION AND DESIRE

The ascent in psychological type from money-lovers to honour-lovers to wisdom-lovers, or philosophers, is not in any obvious way an ascent in intelligence.[4] Intelligence (*phronēsis* or *nous*) may be the same in each of them.[5]

"The power to learn and the organ with which to do so is present in everyone's psyche" (518c4-6). But it is fixed or focused on different things by the different desires which rule in different types of psyche. A money-lover's ruling desires keep his intelligence focused on achieving appetitive ends:

Reason and aspiration he makes to sit upon the ground beneath the king [appetite], one on either side, reducing them to slaves, the first he will not allow to reason about or examine anything else than how a little money can be made into much, while he does not allow the other part to honour or admire anything else but wealth and wealthy men, or to have any other ambition than the acquisition of wealth or of anything which may contribute to this. (553d1-7)

An honour-lover's ruling desires keep his intelligence focused on how to get as many victories and as much prestige as possible: "And I think you see that honour-lovers, if they cannot be generals, are captains; if they cannot be honoured by men of importance and dignity, they are content to be honoured by insignificant and inferior men, for they have a passion for honour at any price" (475a9-b2; 549c2-550b7). A wisdom-lover's ruling desires keep his intelligence focused on the pursuit of truth: "It is obvious to anyone that the part with which we learn is always straining to know where the truth lies and that of the three it cares least for money and reputation" (581b5-7).

Within its own domain, however, the intelligence of any one of these types may be as great as that of any of the others:

49

Have you never noticed in men who are said to be wicked but clever, how sharply their little psyche looks into the things to which it turns its attention? Its power of sight is not inferior, but it is compelled to serve evil ends, so that the more sharply it looks the more evil it works. . . . Yet if a psyche of this kind had been hammered at from childhood and these excrescences had been knocked off it which belong to the world of becoming and have been fastened upon it by feasting, gluttony, and similar pleasures, and which like leaden weights draw the psyche to look downward—if, being rid of these, it turned to look at things that are true, then the same psyche of the same man would see these just as sharply as it now sees the things to which it is directed. (519a1-b5)[6]

A money-lover may be just as intelligent in pursuing appetitive goals as a philosopher is in pursuing rational ones (3.10).

Because intelligence may be the same in people of different psychological types, but is focused on achieving different goals by the different sorts of desires which rule in their psyches, Platonic education is aimed primarily not at the transmission of information or at the inculcation of intellectual skills, but rather at the removal or moderation of as many of a person's unnecessary desires as his nature permits.

Education then, I said, is the art of doing this very thing, this turning around, concerned with the way in which this power [intelligence] can be most easily and efficiently turned around [from the world of becoming until it can endure to look at being and at the brightest of the beings, the good itself (518c8-d1)], not an art of producing sight [intelligence] in it. It takes as given that sight is there, but not rightly turned or looking at what it ought to look at, and accomplishes this end. (518d3-7)

As unnecessary desires are moderated through appropriate training and education, intelligence is turned like the shadow on a sundial from furthering appetitive ends to furthering rational ones.

2.5 THE CAVE

So far we have been concerned primarily with the different kinds of desires Plato recognizes, and with the different goals they set for intelligence in the people in whom they rule. We turn now to the question of the different cognitive resources available to intelligence in determining how best to achieve those goals. To answer it, we must examine those brilliant but difficult analogies, the Sun, Line, and Cave, which lie at the core of

Plato's metaphysical, epistemological, and ethical vision. The fit between cognitive resources and goals will be explained in 2.12.

Because the Line and Cave are introduced to explain the Sun, and because the Cave "illustrates the effects of education on us" (514a1-2), and is therefore most immediately connected to the foregoing discussion, I shall reverse the textual order of presentation, beginning with the Cave and ending with the Sun. With luck, the journey will then be one of increasing illumination.

The prisoners bound in the Cave, with access only to shadows or images cast upon a screen in front of them (514a1-515c3), are tethered by bonds of unnecessary appetite, for they have not received any of the kind of education or training Plato advocates.[7] I shall refer to people who cannot escape even these bonds as *bound cave-dwellers*.

When, through training in a craft (4.6), or through training in music and gymnastics (4.5), a prisoner is purged of his unnecessary appetites, he is freed from his bonds and "turned around" (515c7; cf. 518d3-4) to look at the puppet-like objects (514b4-6) which are the originals of the shadows and images he had previously been seeing—"all kinds of artifacts, statues of men, reproductions of other animals in stone or wood fashioned in all sorts of ways" (514c1-515a1). Some will stay fixed at this level, unable to make it up "the rough, steep path" (515e6) which leads out of the Cave into daylight. These *unbound cave-dwellers* are tethered by necessary appetites.

Others are able to escape the Cave. Through systematic training in music, gymnastics, and the mathematical sciences (522c1-531e3; 2.9, 4.5, 4.8) the bonds of necessary appetite are broken, and these men are released into sunlight. There, having grown accustomed to their new realm, they see the originals of the things of which they previously saw only models: "They first see shadows most easily, then the reflections of men and other things in water, then the things themselves [*auta*]" (516a6-8). The *bound daylight-dwellers* who remain fixed at this level are tethered by bonds of aspiration or spirited desire.

A person who, through education in dialectic and practical polis management (532a1-540c2; 2.11, 4.7), can escape even the bonds of aspiration, seeking honour only insofar as it is necessary to sustain life and not as a genuine benefit (581e2-4), at last sees the cause of all these shadows, models, and originals:

> [He] would be able to see the sun, not images of it in water or some alien place, but the sun itself in itself [*auton kath' hauton*] in its own place, and be able to contemplate it. . . . And after that he would be able to reason that it is the sun which provides the seasons and the

years, which governs everything in the visible world, and is also in some way the cause of all the other things he used to see. (516b4–c2)

He has gone as far as anyone can go, at least in this life (3.9), being tethered—if we can still call it that—only by rational desires. Such people are *unbound daylight-dwellers*.

We shall meet all of these characters again in 2.7.

2.6 PROLOGUE TO THE LINE

In the Line analogy, which is "linked necessarily in its entirety" with the Cave (517a8–b1), we find out more about the nature of the objects seen by the *dramatis personae* of the Cave, and discover what the specific psychological power exercised by each of them is. This intricate analogy will occupy us for four sections, to which the present one is prologue.

It is widely known that Plato holds that there are forms, and that forms are universals or properties of some sort that are unique (507b2–7), that "remain always the same in all respects" (479a2–3), and that "are objects of thought, not of sight" (507b9–10). It is less well known, but nonetheless true, as we shall see, that forms are not the only unusual type of property he countenances.

In Book 3, in a nonmetaphysical section discussing the education of the guardians, we find the following passage:

> And if there are images of letters in water, we shall not know them until we know the letters themselves, but the knowledge of both is part of the same craft or training. . . . I mean, by the gods, that neither we nor the guardians we are raising will be educated in music until we know the different forms of moderation [*ta tēs sōphrosunēs eidē*], and those of courage, and those of generosity, and those of high-mindedness, and all their kindred, and their opposites too, moving around everywhere, and see them in the things in which they are [*enonta en hois enestin aisthanōmetha*], both themselves and their images [*kai auta kai eikonas autōn*], and do not neglect them in small things or great, but believe that the knowledge of both is part of the same craft or training. (402b5–c8)[8]

The forms of moderation (and the rest) referred to, being many, being in motion, and being visible, cannot be the unique, unchanging, nonvisible, Platonic form of it. Yet, since they are in particular things, and are called *eidē*, a word Plato also uses to refer to Platonic forms (596a5–b4), they seem to be properties of some sort. I shall call them *modes*. In addition to modes, the passage also recognizes images of them, which are also visible in particular moving and changing things. Since an image cannot be of itself, and a form cannot be visible or moving, these images must be distinct from both modes and forms. I shall call these images *qualities*.

This complex ontology, which in 2.7 will become even more complex with the addition of *figures*, holds the key to a consistent interpretation of the Sun, Line, and Cave, and, indeed, of the *Republic* as a whole. That interpretation, in turn, and not the present passage alone, is the ultimate basis for discerning the rich ontology—textual interpretation, like all theory-construction, is a holistic business. But the passage is there all the same, not a sheet anchor, perhaps, but a reassuring kedge anchor securing that interpretation to a definite text.

But what are qualities, modes, and figures? What, for that matter, are forms? At this stage, we must be content not to know. Nor must we try to guess their natures from the names I have given them, which are no more than tags for easy reference. All that is certain, at this stage, is that the *Republic* seems to countenance at least three distinct kinds of properties—forms, modes, and qualities.

2.7 THE LINE

The formula for the Line is as follows:

> Understand then that there are two of them [the good itself and the sun] and that the one rules over the intelligible kind and realm and the other over the visible. . . . So, then, do you understand these two forms [*eidē*], visible and intelligible? . . . Then as it were take a line divided into unequal sections, and subdivide each of them, that is the section of the visible kind and the section of the intelligible kind, in a similar proportion; and the subsections will be related to one another with respect to clarity and obscurity—in the visible, the one subsection being images, and by images I mean first shadows, then reflections in water and close-grained polished surfaces, and everything of that kind. . . . In the other subsection of the visible, then, put that of which the other is the image—the creatures around us and all the products of nature, and the whole category of manufactured things. . . . And would you also be willing, I said, to say that it [the visible section] has been divided into parts as far as truth and falsity are concerned, with the image standing to the original in the same ratio as what is believed [*to doxaston*] stands to what is known [*to gnōston*]? . . . Consider now how the section of the intelligible is to be divided. . . . In the one subsection the psyche, using as images the objects that were imitated in the visible section, is compelled to conduct its investigations from hypotheses, travelling not to a first

principle, but to a conclusion; in the other subsection of the intelligible—the one which proceeds to an unhypothetical first principle—the psyche conducts its investigations without the likenesses which were in the other subsection, making its way by forms alone. (509d1-510b9)

The result of following this formula appears, with some additional material, in the Frontispiece.

Given our discussion of 402b5-c8 in 2.6, it is a reasonable conjecture that the visible subsections of the Line, that is, AD and DC, have qualities and modes, or instantiations of them, as their respective contents. For the items referred to as (visible) images in that passage were qualities, and the visible things of which they were the images were modes. (We shall see why the contents of AD instantiate qualities and those of DC instantiate modes in 2.11.)

This brings us to the intelligible section. The second subsection of the intelligible (EB) is described as follows:

Understand also that by the other subsection of the intelligible I mean that which reason itself [*autos ho logos*] grasps by the power of dialectic. It considers the hypotheses [of the mathematical sciences] to be not first principles, but to be hypotheses properly so-called, steps and sallies toward what is unhypothetical, namely, the first principle of everything; having reached this, it reverses itself, and comes down to a conclusion, without making use of anything visible [qualities or modes] at all, but only forms themselves, moving on from forms to forms, and ending in forms. (511b2-c2)

Hence there is no doubt that its contents are forms.

In the first subsection of the intelligible (CE), the psyche uses modes as images of other things that it investigates by means of hypotheses:

You know that they [geometers] use visible modes [*horōmenois eidesi*] and talk about them, but they are thinking not of them, but of the models of which they are likenesses; they are making their points about the square itself [*tou tetragōnou autou*] and the diagonal itself [*diametrou autēs*], not about the ones they draw, and similarly with the others. These things which they fashion and draw, of which shadows and reflections in water are images, they now in turn use as images, seeking to understand those things which one cannot see except by means of intellect. (510d5-511a1)

That the things in question are neither qualities nor modes is manifest—qualities and modes are visible, the contents of CE are intelligible. But neither can they be forms. One reason for this is that each of the subsections of the Line has a distinct psychological power set over its contents (511d6-e4; quoted below), and powers are distinct just in case they are both set over different things and do different work (477c9-d5; 2.8). Another reason is that the powers set over the contents of CE and EB differ in clarity (533d4-534a2; 2.9), and powers which differ in clarity do so because the objects over which they are set have a different share in truth (511e2-4). A third reason, less inferential than the two just mentioned, is that Plato indicates, in no uncertain terms, that the contents of CE and EB differ:

> I understand, he [Glaucon] said, but not completely—for in my opinion you seem to be speaking of an enormous task—that you want to distinguish that part of what is which is intelligible and is contemplated by dialectical knowledge [*to hupo tēs tou dialegesthai epistēmēs tou ontos te kai noētou theōroumenon*] as being clearer than the part contemplated by the so-called sciences. The starting points of the sciences are hypotheses, and although those who contemplate the objects of the sciences are compelled to do so by scientific-thought [*dianoiai*] rather than sense perception, still, because these men do not go back to a first principle, but proceed from hypotheses, you do not think that they have dialectical-thought [*noun*] about these objects, even though, given such a principle, they are intelligible [*noētōn*]; and you seem to me to call the state of mind of geometers, and the like, scientific-thought [*dianoian*] rather than dialectical-thought [*noun*], in order to indicate that scientific-thought [*dianoian*] is something between [*metaxu*] opinion [*doxēs*] and dialectical-thought [*nou*].—You have grasped this very satisfactorily, I said. (511c3-d5)

There is little room for doubt, then, that CE must contain a fourth kind of thing over and above qualities, modes, and forms. These are the *figures* referred to in 2.6.[9]

It remains to discuss the division of the Line into the visible section (AC) and the intelligible section (CB). On the present showing, it seems to be a division within the class of properties. In fact, as we shall see in 2.8-9, it divides the properties into sensible properties, which we would ordinarily speak of seeing or sensing, and abstract properties, which can be grasped only through complex mathematical theories (*Statesman* 285d9-286a7). So, very roughly speaking, the distinction between visible properties and intelligible ones is akin to the distinction, familiar from the philosophy of science, between observational properties and theoretical properties, or between properties accessible to minimally theory-laden observation and those accessible only to maximally theory-laden thought.

The contents of the subsections of the Line are then as follows. In the first subsection of the visible (AD), we have qualities; in the second (DC), modes. In the first subsection of the intelligible (CE), we have figures; in the second (EB), forms.

Now, as we have seen, each of these four types of properties has a different psychological power set over it, which makes use of it to do its own distinctive kind of work:

> There are four conditions [pathēmata] in the psyche corresponding to the four subsections of the Line: dialectical-thought [noēsin] for the highest; scientific-thought [dianoian] for the second; folk-wisdom [pistin] for the third; and perceptual-thought [eikasian] for the fourth. Put these in the due terms of a proportion, and consider that each has as much clarity as the contents of its particular section have a share in truth. (511d6-e4)

We shall soon have some idea what these powers actually are, and why I give them unfamiliar names.

Although dialectical-thought, scientific-thought, folk-wisdom, and perceptual-thought are distinct powers, they are closely similar both in internal structure and in psychological rôle. First, the things they are set over are all systematically connected to a single thing, the good itself. Second, each of them is a complex power which consists of a cognitive component, intelligence (2.4), and a conative component, which is either an appetitive, a spirited, or a rational desire (2.2). The latter component focuses the former on the distinctive type of property the complex power itself is set over (2.12). Finally, each power is the complete psychological power, both cognitive and conative, of one of the psychological types we met in 2.2. The powers are not the component faculties of a single psyche, but the complete "mind frames" of psyches of different types. The support for these radical claims emerges forcefully when we juxtapose the Line and the Cave, as in the Frontispiece.

The psychological powers of the inhabitants of the Cave appear on the visible section of the Line (AC). The bound cave-dwellers, who have received no appropriate Platonic education or training at all, have their intelligence focused by their ruling unnecessary appetites exclusively on images cast onto a screen. They are lovers of food, drink, and sex (2.12, 3.3-7), who exercise perceptual-thought. The entities they see are qualities.

The unbound cave-dwellers, whose unnecessary appetites have been curbed by training in a craft, have their intelligence focused by their ruling necessary appetites on models of men, animals, plants, and artifacts, which are the originals of the images seen by their tethered colleagues. They are money-lovers, who exercise folk-wisdom. The entities they see are modes.

Outside the Cave are those whose psychological powers appear on the intelligible section of the Line. The bound daylight-dwellers, whose unnecessary appetites have been curbed by training in music and gymnastics, and whose unnecessary spirited desires have been curbed by systematic training in the mathematical sciences (4.8), have their intelligence focused by their ruling spirited desires on the men, animals, plants, and artifacts of which the unbound cave-dwellers see only models. They are honour-lovers, who exercise scientific-thought. The entities to which they have intellectual access are figures.

Finally, the unbound daylight-dwellers, having had even their spirited desires curbed by training in dialectic and polis management, have their intelligence focused by their ruling rational desires on the sun. They are wisdom-lovers, or philosophers, who exercise dialectical-thought. The entities to which they have intellectual access are forms.

Since the sun is "in some way the cause of all the other things" (516c1-2) mentioned in the Cave analogy, and since these are either men (and so forth), or models of men (and so forth), or images of models of men (and so forth), the objects arrayed on the Line must be related as follows: qualities are images of models of figures; modes are models of figures; and figures—and hence their models and images as well—are caused by the good itself, which is a rational structure of forms (2.11). Thus the objects over which the complete powers are set are all systematically related to the good itself.

Since one who sees only an image of a model of a figure sees more darkly than one who sees the model itself, and since he in turn sees more darkly than one who sees the figure itself face to face, the metaphor of mirroring (either in two or in three dimensions) which is crucial to the Cave analogy should help explain why perceptual-thought, folk-wisdom, and scientific-thought have each as much clarity as the contents of their sections of the Line have a share in truth (511e2-4). In 2.9 we shall see why the relationship between figures and forms, and consequently that between scientific-thought and dialectical-thought, cannot be accommodated in the same mirroring terms.

As we move up out of the Cave progressively releasing the psyche from the bonds first of unnecessary appetites, then of necessary appetites, then of spirited desires, but without necessarily increasing its intelligence (2.4), it first exercises perceptual-thought and is the psyche of a lover of food, drink, and sex, then exercises folk-wisdom and is the psyche of a money-lover, then exercises scientific-thought and is the psyche of an honour-lover, then exercises dialectical-thought and is the psyche of a philosopher. Thus each of these powers just is intelligence appropriately focused by these different ruling desires, and each is the complete power of a different type of psyche.

It should now be clear why I have not followed the common practice of translating *noēsis* as 'understanding', *dianoia* as 'reasoning', *pistis* as 'belief', and *eikasia* as 'imagination'. For these translations inevitably suggest that the powers in question are the component faculties of a single psyche. And this, as we have just seen, is not so. The coined terms I have employed instead—'dialectical-thought', 'scientific-thought', 'folk-wisdom', and 'perceptual-thought'—are intended to avoid this suggestion and to dispel the illusion of understanding that familiar terms carry with them. But like the terms 'quality', 'mode', 'figure', and 'form', they are not intended to be taken as independent guides to the natures of the powers they name. What these powers actually are is a matter for a developed psychological theory, not for semantics.

2.8 KNOWLEDGE AND OPINION

Where on the Line is knowledge to be located? Which of the four complete psychological powers is capable of acquiring it? One part of the answer to these questions is provided by the complex argument at the end of Book 5 (475c11–480a13), in which Plato undertakes to prove that without forms knowledge is impossible. Since this is the only argument in the *Republic* that gives a clear reason to countenance forms, its importance to Plato's enterprise is difficult to exaggerate. If it fails, a vital cornerstone of the metaphysical and epistemological foundations of his defense of justice crumbles. But if it succeeds, forms are provided with impressive philosophical *bona fides*, and our question about the location of knowledge on the Line is answered—although the answer will not be complete or fully intelligible until the end of 2.9. For if forms are necessary for knowledge, knowledge must be located together with forms and dialectical-thought in the second subsection of the intelligible (EB).

Before taking up the argument itself, I want to excerpt five topics for preliminary discussion. The first of these is the principle of identity Plato proposes for powers, of which we have already made use in 2.7. The second is the nature of the audience to whom the argument is directed, and the effect on them that it is intended to achieve. The third is the claim that "what is completely is completely knowable, and what is in no way is completely unknowable" (477a2–4). The fourth is a view about the nature of knowledge which emerges in the course of discussing that claim. The fifth is a key concession which Plato thinks his audience must make.

Once these are explored, the argument itself will prove much more tractable.

Powers (*dunameis*), which are properties that enable things to do work of some sort (477c1-4), are distinct just in case they are both set over different things and do different work: "What is set over [*epi*] the same things and does the same work, I call the same power; what is set over something different and does different work, I call a different power" (477d2-5). But it is by no means obvious why this must be so. Why cannot powers which do the same work differ by being set over different things? Why cannot powers set over the same things differ in the work they do?[10] These are difficult questions, to which I shall not attempt a general answer. Instead, I shall focus exclusively on the powers crucially involved in Plato's argument, namely, the four complete psychological powers discussed in 2.7, and the three cognitive powers knowledge (*epistēmē*), opinion (*doxa*), and error (*agnoia*).[11] For if Plato is right about these powers, as I am persuaded he is, then it will not much matter whether he is also right about other powers as well.

Because the complete psychological powers are complete mind frames, which enable a psyche to do all the work that psyches typically do (2.7), and because knowledge, opinion, and error are precisely cognitive powers, both types of powers must enable the psyche to form beliefs about things. Since in one of their simpler, if not their simplest, forms such beliefs involve predicating a property F of something, each power must enable a psyche to do two distinct kinds of work. First, it must enable the psyche to identify F, that is, to produce an account, however inchoate, which says what F is. Second, it must enable the psyche to determine when a particular property in something fits that account, or is an occurrence of F—when, more simply, the particular thing is itself an instance or occurrence of F (2.14). Needless to say, if the first task is inadequately performed, the second will inherit its inadequacies.

Of these two tasks it is the first that preoccupies Plato. For he holds that knowledge of what F is must precede all other knowledge about F, including knowledge of what things are F (354c1-3, 402b5-c8). Because of this, it seems reasonable to suppose that the clarity or cognitive reliability of the complete psychological powers is a matter of how well they carry out the task of saying what F is, and that the different types of properties over which they are set—the quality of F, the mode of F, the figure of F, and the form of F—are somehow the results of their different attempts to carry it out.

Since qualities are images of modes, which are models of figures, which are caused by a form (the good itself), a natural way to elaborate this supposition, given what we already know about these properties, is as follows. Perceptual-thought, even when it is performing optimally and making no mistakes, produces an account of F that does not distinguish visible properties that are to some degree like F from F itself. Consequently, some properties that fit its account will not be F; some properties that are F will not fit its account. Hence its account of F is unreliable. Those who exercise perceptual-thought will sometimes form false beliefs, sometimes true ones. But despite the fact that perceptual-thought's account fails to capture F, there is some property it does capture. This is the quality of F.

In the same way, folk-wisdom, even when it is performing optimally, produces an account of F that does not distinguish visible properties that are to some greater degree like F from F itself. As a result, folk-wisdom's beliefs, too, will be sometimes true, sometimes false. But because something has to be more like F than the quality of F in order to fit its account, folk-wisdom is clearer or more cognitively reliable than perceptual-thought. The property its account captures is the mode of F.

Finally, at least for present purposes, scientific-thought and dialectical-thought, when they are performing optimally, produce accounts of F that result in only true beliefs about visible properties. These powers differ, as we shall see in 2.9, not regarding the visible, but regarding the intelligible. The properties their accounts pick out are figures and forms respectively.

On the strength of this speculative reconstruction, the evidence for which will emerge below and in 2.9-12, it seems that we should understand a power to be *set over* a type of property just in case the accounts it produces specify properties of that type. This means that a power will use the properties it is set over in making its own judgements. When dialectical-thought makes judgements of its own it employs forms, but it has cognitive access to qualities, modes, and figures, and knows what each of them is (520c1-6; 2.11). Consequently, we must not confuse having cognitive access to a property with being set over it. A power is set over a type of property just in case the latter is the most cognitively reliable type of property to which it has cognitive access.

We are now in a position to see why Plato is right about the identity conditions of the complete and cognitive powers under scrutiny. For we know from 2.7 that each of the complete powers is set over a distinct type of property, and it follows at once that each must produce different work consisting (at least in part) of accounts of properties which possess different degrees of cognitive reliability. Similarly, we know that each of the three cognitive powers produces a different sort of work: knowledge produces beliefs that are always true; opinion produces beliefs that are sometimes true, sometimes false (477e6-7); and error produces beliefs that are always false. Since these beliefs clearly possess different degrees of cognitive reliability, it seems reasonable to conclude that the powers that produce them must be set over different types of properties. So at least as far as the powers involved in his argument are concerned, Plato's principle of identity for powers seems to be a plausible one.

I turn now to the second of the topics I distinguished, the nature of the audience to which Plato's argument is directed, and the effect it is intended to have on them.

The audience for the argument consists of "sightseers" and "craft-lovers." And the first important clue to their identity is that they have no cognitive access to forms:

> I set apart and distinguish those of whom you were just speaking, the sightseers [philotheamonas] and the craft-lovers [philotechnous] and practical men, and those whom we are now discussing, and whom alone one would call philosophers. . . . The lovers of sounds and the sightseers delight in fine tones and colours and shapes, and in everything fashioned out of them, but their thought is incapable of apprehending the nature of the fine itself and of enjoying it. (476a9-b8)

Because of this, we know that the complete psychological power they exercise must be either perceptual-thought or (at best) folk-wisdom. For with the exception of scientific-thought, which is not introduced until Books 6 and 7, only these complete powers fail to give access to forms. Since the very name given to the sightseers suggests that they exercise minimally theory-laden sense perception, and since training in a craft leads to the exercise of folk-wisdom (4.6), it is an attractive conjecture that the sightseers exercise perceptual-thought, while the craft-lovers exercise folk-wisdom.

Although these two groups are united in their lack of access to forms, including the form of the fine, they both believe in such things as *ta polla kala* (476c2-3, 478e7-479a5). Now this phrase is ambiguous. It can mean *the many fine things*, in which case it is most naturally understood to refer to the many particular things that happen to be fine, or it can mean *the many fines* (or *types of fineness*), in which case it is most naturally understood to refer, not to particular things, but to properties or property instantiations. Controversy has raged over which of these interpretations best captures Plato's intentions.[12] But given our discussion in 2.6-7, it is clear that only the latter fits in with the larger movement of his thought. For that discussion has prepared us to encounter people who believe in the many qualities or modes of fineness visible in things as opposed to people who believe in the unique, unchanging, intelligible, invisible form of the fine, but it has done nothing to prepare us to meet people who believe that there are many fine things as opposed to people who believe in some sort of property of fineness. Hence there is good reason to understand *ta polla kala* as referring (indiscriminately) to either the many qualities or the many modes of the fine. The translations given below reflect this.

The audience for Plato's argument, then, consists of people who believe in the many qualities or modes of F, but not in the unique form of F. The effect the argument is intended to achieve is to convince them that the complete psychological powers they exercise enable them to opine but not to know:

> He, then, who believes in qualities or modes of the fine [*kala pragmata*], but neither believes in the fine itself [*auto kallos*] nor is able to follow when someone tries to lead him to the knowledge of it, do you think that his life is like dreaming or waking? Look at it this way: Is this not dreaming, namely, whether asleep or awake, to believe that a likeness is not a likeness, but rather the thing itself which it is like?—I, at least, he [Glaucon] said, would say that a man who does that dreams.—Well, then, what about the opposite case, the man who believes in the fine itself [*auto kalon*] and is able to see both it and the participants [*ta metechonta*] in it [qualities and modes], and doesn't believe that the participants are it, or that it itself is the participants—is he, in your opinion, living in a dream or is he awake?— He is very much awake, he replied.—Wouldn't we be right in saying that this man's thought is knowledge because he knows, while the other's is opinion because he opines?—Most certainly.—What if the man we say opines but does not know gets angry with us and disputes the truth of what we say? Will we have some way to soothe and gently persuade him, while hiding from him that he is not in his right mind?—We must have. (476c2-e2)

Because of this, Plato's argument must be constructed within the intellectual universe of the sightseers and craft-lovers, using materials they are prepared to countenance. It cannot use forms, or truths about them, without begging the question.

This brings us to my third topic, the claim that only "what is completely is completely knowable."

As a first step towards discovering what the different things are that knowledge, opinion, and error are set over, Plato introduces the following claim:

In however many ways we examine the question, we can hold this to be certain: what is completely [*to pantelōs on*] is completely knowable [*pantelōs gnōston*], and what is in no way is completely unknowable [*mē on medamēi pantēi agnōston*]. (477a2-4)

Since the sightseers and craft-lovers, in the person of Glaucon (476e7-9), accept this claim without hesitation, it cannot be about forms or anything else out of the ordinary. It is intended to be obvious and irresistible, not contentious or hair-raising. The problem is to find an interpretation of it which meets this requirement and also makes philosophical sense of Plato's argument.[13] To this problem the foregoing discussion provides the essential clue.

We know that the sightseers and craft-lovers believe in the many qualities or modes of F, but not in the unique form of F, while the philosophers believe in the form. We know that the mistake the former make, which results in their being said to live in the dream world of opinion, is that they "believe that a likeness is not a likeness, but rather the thing itself which it is like" (476c6-7), while the philosopher is said to live in the real world of knowledge because he can distinguish the thing itself from its likenesses (476d1-3). Since qualities and modes are images or likenesses (2.6), and since the powers exercised by the sightseers and craft-lovers are set over them, while those of the philosopher are set over forms, it seems certain that the likenesses under discussion are qualities and modes, and that the things themselves are forms.

On this showing, Plato's idea, and it is an idea which we shall interrogate in a moment, seems to be this. The sightseers and craft-lovers would judge that some property is F when in fact it is not F, but only like F to some degree. Therefore, when they judge that a property is F, they merely opine that it is F. The philosophers, on the other hand, judge a property to be F only if it is F itself. Therefore, when they judge that a property is F, they know that it is F.

This view about knowledge makes it overwhelmingly likely that part of what is meant by the troublesome claim we are trying to decipher is this: what is F can be known to be F, and what is not F cannot be known to be F. For it is difficult to see how Plato could hold both that philosophers have knowledge because they judge something to be F only if it is F, and that to be knowable something has to meet some condition other than that of being F. If I am right about this, then part of the claim is as obvious and uncontentious as Plato suggests. For not even sightseers and craft-lovers are likely to deny that only what is F can be known to be F, and that what is not F cannot be known to be F.[14]

But there is more to it than that. For the principle speaks not simply of what is knowable and what is unknowable, of what is and what is not, but of what is "*completely* knowable" and what is "*completely* unknowable," of what "is *completely*" and of what "is *in no way*." We must now try to explain the contribution these modifiers make to Plato's thought.

As we move up the Line from the quality of F to the form of F, the properties we encounter resemble F itself to different degrees. The quality of F minimally resembles F, the mode of F resembles F to a somewhat higher degree, and the form of F completely resembles F itself. Since these degrees of resemblance express degrees of cognitive reliability, and since error is the most unreliable of the cognitive powers, the property it is set over—the *antiform* of F, as I shall call it—ought to resemble F in no way at all. Consequently, we can think of the different types of property these powers are set over as follows. Forms are complete resemblers; modes are moderate resemblers; qualities are minimal resemblers; antiforms are complete nonresemblers. Hence, if x has a property G that completely resembles F, x instantiates the form of F. For properties or universals that completely resemble one another are identical (*Cratylus* 432b1-c6 seems to extend this doctrine to particulars as well).[15] If, on the other hand, x has a property G that moderately or minimally resembles F, then x instantiates, in one case, a mode of F, in the other, a quality of F. If, *per impossibile*, x instantiated a property G that in no way resembled F, then x would instantiate the antiform of F.

Now if antiforms are complete nonresemblers, the antiform of F does not resemble F in any way. But a property of this sort cannot be (predicatively) anything at all. It is an *Unding*—a nothing.[16] And a power set over it will, in consequence, be set over nothing. That is why the following argument is not as shocking as it would otherwise be:

> Does one then opine what is not [*to mē on*]? Or is it impossible even to opine what is not? Consider. Does not the person who opines set his opinion over something [*epi ti pherei tēn doxan*]? Or shall we reverse ourselves and say that it is possible to opine, yet to opine nothing [*mēden*]?—That is impossible.—Then he who opines opines some one [*hen*] thing?—Yes.—But surely that which is not is not one thing [*ouch hen*], but rather nothing [*mēden*]?—Yes.—But we had to assign error to what is not, and knowledge to what is?—That's right, he said.—So one opines neither what is nor what is not?—Apparently not. (478b6-c7)

Opinion is set over a kind of property, a minimal resembler or a moderate resembler. But error is set over a complete nonresembler, a nothing. Since the cognitive capacity of a power is a function of the type of property it is set over, how else could error *always* be wrong about everything?

It is reasonably clear, then, that "what is completely" should be understood as "what completely resembles F" and "what is in no way" should be understood as "what in no way resembles F." By parity of reasoning, it seems that "what is completely knowable" should be understood as "what completely resembles what is knowable" and that "what is completely unknowable" should be understood as "what completely resembles what is unknowable." After all, being knowable and being unknowable are properties—Fs.

In my view, then, Plato's principle, when fully unpacked, comes down to this: if something completely resembles F, it has a property that completely resembles being knowable to be F; if it in no way resembles F, it has a property that completely resembles being unknowable to be F.

If this is Plato's principle, then his confidence that the sightseers and craft-lovers—who may well be as intelligent as he is (2.4)—will find it irresistible seems reasonably well placed. For surely all it adds to the uncontentious message we extracted from it above—that only what is F can be known to be F and that what is not F cannot be known to be F—is a relatively transparent account in terms of resemblance of the conditions under which a particular property is the property F.

Now for the fourth topic. Plato holds, if I am right, that the reason the sightseers and craft-lovers cannot know that anything is F is that they would judge something to be F that is not F (and vice versa). The question is whether he is on intelligible philosophical ground in holding it. A brief example of a type that has played an important rôle in recent work in epistemology will point us in a promising direction.

A is driving through farming country with his family. As he passes the various buildings, pieces of machinery, and animals, he identifies them for his young son to whom they are novel. "That's a barn," he says, "That's a tractor," "That's a sheep." A has no doubts about his identifications. In particular, he has no doubt that the last-mentioned object x is a sheep, which in fact it is. He grew up on a farm. His eyesight is excellent. Each object is clearly visible, and each has features characteristic of its type.

Given this much information, most people not in the grip of some form of skepticism would say that A *knows* that x is a sheep. After all, he is justified in believing it, and it is in fact true. Suppose, now, that we are given some additional information. We are told that, unknown to A, he has just entered an area full of a newly developed breed of goats that look very like ordinary domestic sheep, and that if x had been replaced with one of them, A would have mistaken it for a sheep. Given this new information, most would agree that A does not know that x is a sheep.

What the added information tells us is that A's power to discriminate sheep is not reliable, that it would sometimes result in false beliefs. Thus in order to count as knowing that x is F it is not enough that a person have a justified true belief that x is F; in addition his belief-forming power must be reliable, there must be no relevant situation in which he would judge that x is F when x is not F.[17]

The bearing of this on Plato's argument is clear. The sightseers would judge a quality of F to be F even if it is not F; the craft-lovers would judge a mode of F to be F, even if it is not F. It follows that the belief-forming powers they exercise—perceptual-thought and folk-wisdom—are unreliable. As a result, even when the beliefs of the sightseers and craft-lovers are both true and justified, they never amount to knowledge.

The philosophers, by contrast, would judge a property to be F only if it actually is F. Hence their belief-forming power is reliable. The question is, are their beliefs also justified? For justification also seems to be crucial for knowledge.[18] In 2.9, we shall see that they are: it is their mastery of a dialectically defensible, empirically adequate, universal theory that alone gives the philosophers access to forms. It follows—and follows simply from their cognitive access to forms—that the philosophers have knowledge, not mere opinion.

The fifth, and final, preliminary topic is this. Plato believes that the sightseers and craft-lovers must concede that each of the many qualities or modes of F is plainly also not F:

> These things premised, I shall say I want a word with, and an answer from, the good fellow who does not believe in the fine itself or in any form of the fine itself, which remains always the same in all respects, but who believes in the many qualities or modes of the fine [polla ta kala], that sightseer who cannot bear to hear anyone say that the fine or the just or any of the others is one. We shall say to him: "My dear sir, of all the many qualities or modes of the fine, is there one which isn't plainly also base? And is there one of those qualities or modes of the just which isn't plainly also unjust? Or one of those qualities or modes of the holy which isn't plainly also unholy?"— No, it is necessary, he [Glaucon] said, that they plainly be both fine in a way and base, and so with all the other things you asked about.—And again, are the many qualities or modes of the double [ta polla diplasia] plainly any the less halves than doubles?—Not one.—And likewise with qualities or modes of the big and the small, the light and the heavy, will any of them be more one of these things than it is its opposite?—No, he said, each of them will always partake of both. (478e7-479b8)[19]

The question is, why is this so? What is it about the qualities and modes of F that makes it true that they are no more F than not F? What is it that guarantees that the sightseers and craft-lovers must concede that they are no more F than not F?

Aristotle tells us that Plato introduced the forms because he was "persuaded by the Heraclitean argument that sensibles are always flowing" (*Metaphysics* Mu 1078b12-32). And he explains that a sensible is flowing or in Heraclitean flux just in case it is both F and not F simultaneously (*Metaphysics* Gamma 1005b24-25, 1012a24).[20] It seems reasonable to suppose, then, that the features of the modes and qualities of F which led Plato to conclude that they are no more F than not F must be those in which they differ from forms. Hence the qualities and modes of F should be no more F than not F because they are many rather than unique, visible (or sensible) rather than intelligible, and changing rather than immutable (2.6).

The qualities and modes of F are many, not because they have many instances—forms can possess that feature (2.11)—but because perceptual-thought and folk-wisdom produce many nonequivalent accounts of F (or identify F with a number of nonidentical properties). This is borne out by 479d3-5, which refers to "the multitude's many conventional accounts [*ta polla nomima*] of the fine."[21] In this respect, the sightseers and craft-lovers are like those interlocutors of Socrates who, when asked what F is, reply with a list of different accounts instead of with a formula or account that picks out a unique property (*Euthyphro* 5d7-6e2; *Laches* 190e7-192b8; *Meno* 71e1-77b1; *Theaetetus* 146d3-148d7). It follows immediately that a property can satisfy one of these accounts but not another. It will then be F, according to those accounts, but also plainly not F.

In addition to producing many accounts of what it is to be F rather than just one, perceptual-thought and folk-wisdom are restricted to qualities and modes in constructing those accounts. Since qualities and modes are visible properties (2.6-7), this means that the accounts perceptual-thought and folk-wisdom produce will be insensitive to differences that are not visible but intelligible. Hence in those cases—and for Plato it is all cases (2.9)—in which F differs from not-F in ways not reliably accessible to insufficiently theory-laden sense perception, their accounts will not discriminate between F and not-F, but will confuse them with one another (523e3-524c13, 602d6-9). And, again, F will emerge as plainly also not F.

Since the *Republic* contains no clear illustrations of the epistemological consequences of the mutability of qualities and modes or the immutability of forms, it is necessary to resort to conjecture. The accounts of properties produced by perceptual-thought and folk-wisdom are couched exclusively in terms of visible properties. And it follows from this, I think, that they will sometimes make reference to visible, material standards or paradigms.[22] They will, for example, say such things as that something is a foot long if its end points coincide with the end points of a foot rule. But then their accounts will be no more reliable than their visible, material standards are stable and unchanging. Since all sublunary things undergo change and decay (546a1-3), this means that something that fits the account of F at one time may not fit it at another, not because the thing itself has changed, but because the standard to which the account makes essential reference has altered. Again, F will plainly be not F on these accounts, and vice versa.

But why must the sightseers and craft-lovers concede that each of the qualities or modes of F is no more F than not F? We are not told explicitly, but I do not think that there is any great mystery about what Plato has in mind.

Given the kinds of accounts they produce of what F is, each of the sightseers and craft-lovers will have an inconsistent (or potentially inconsistent) set of beliefs. As a result, each is a prime candidate for the Socratic elenchus. For, whatever else it may be, the elenchus is certainly a device for forcing people to concede that their accounts of what F is lead to contradictions. The elenchus will bring the offending accounts into the open, and force the sightseers and craft-lovers to acknowledge that they entail that each of the qualities or modes of F is no more F than it is not F.

With so much as prologue, let us try to decipher the argument itself. It is convenient to distinguish three stages. In the first, Plato uses the principle of identity for powers we discussed earlier to distinguish knowledge, opinion, and error from one another, and to identify the kind of property over which each is set. In the second, he uses these findings to show that the power exercised by the sightseers and craft-lovers is opinion, not knowledge. Finally, in the third, he argues that in order to have knowledge one must have access to forms.

Knowledge, opinion, and error are distinct powers because each enables a psyche to do different kinds of work: knowledge insures that it always forms true beliefs; opinion insures that it sometimes forms true beliefs, sometimes false ones (477e6-7); error insures that it always forms false beliefs. It follows that they must be set over different things (477e8-478b2).

Because knowledge always involves true beliefs, it must be set over complete resemblers or forms: "Knowledge is set over what is [F], to know it as it is [hōs echei]" (478a6). Because error always involves false beliefs, it must be set over complete nonresemblers, or antiforms. It follows that opinion must be set over something other than what completely resembles F or what in no way resembles F: "One opines neither what is [F] nor what is not [F]" (478c6). For opinion is distinct both from knowledge and from error.

Now if something resembles F either minimally or moderately but not completely, it falls in between what completely resembles F and what in no way resembles F: "If a thing is such as to be [F] and not to be [F], wouldn't it lie between what is unmixedly [F] and what is in no way [F]?" (477a6-7). Hence a power falling between knowledge and error in cognitive reliability or clarity must be set over it: "Then, since knowledge is set over what is [F], while error is of necessity set over what is not [F], we must find something between knowledge and error to be set over that which lies between these things, if there is such a thing" (477a9-b1). But opinion occupies this position. For, unlike knowledge, it is sometimes wrong, and, unlike error, it is sometimes right: "Isn't it apparent to you, I asked, that opinion is darker than knowledge but clearer than error?" (478c13-14). Therefore, it must be set over what partakes of "both being [F] and not being [F]" (478d5-9). "It seems that it is now left for us to find that which partakes of both being [F] and not being [F], and cannot be called unmixedly one or the other, so that if we find it, we can rightly call it the opinable, and in this way assign extremes to extremes and intermediate to intermediate" (478e1-5). This is the task of the second stage of the argument.

The sightseers and craft-lovers, still in the person of Glaucon (476e7-9), concede that each of the many qualities and modes of F is also plainly not F (479a5-b10): qualities are minimal resemblers, modes are moderate resemblers. Since this means that the qualities and modes of F satisfy the accounts perceptual-thought and folk-wisdom produce of the opposite of F fully as well as those they produce of F itself, each of them is just as much not F as it is F (479b9-10). But F and not-F are opposites, so that nothing can be both F and not F (436b8-9; 3.2). Hence the qualities and modes of F are neither F nor not F, nor both F and not F:

> They are like the ambiguous jokes at feasts, he [Glaucon] said, or like the children's riddle about the eunuch who threw something at a bat; they riddle about what he threw at it and what it was sitting on. For the many qualities or modes [of F] are also ambiguous and one cannot think of them as being fixedly [F] or not being [F], or as being both or neither. (479b11-c5)

Since things of this sort have opinion set over them (478d5-9), opinion must be set over the many modes and qualities of F.

But we know that perceptual-thought, which is exercised by sightseers, is set over qualities, and that folk-wisdom, which is exercised by craft-lovers, is set over modes. Hence given Plato's principle of identity for powers, it follows that both sightseers and craft-lovers exercise opinion, not knowledge:

> We shall affirm, then, that those who gaze on the many qualities or modes of the fine [*polla kala*] but do not see the fine itself [*auto to kalon*], and who are incapable of following another who leads them to it, and who see the many qualities or modes of the just [*polla dikaia*] but not the just itself [*auto to dikaion*], and so on with all the rest—such people, we shall say, opine everything, but know nothing of the things they opine about. (479e1-5)

Qualities and modes are adequate for doxastic purposes, but not for epistemic ones.

This brings us to the third stage of the argument (479e7-480a13). The qualities and modes of F are inadequate in this way because they are less than complete resemblers, no more F than not F. And they are less than complete resemblers because they have the defining features of qualities and modes—they are many, visible, and mutable. But forms do not suffer from this defect, they are complete resemblers—unique, intelligible, and immutable. Therefore, forms are necessary for knowledge.

Stripped to its bare bones, then, and represented simply as an inference, Plato's argument is as follows:

(1) A knows that x is F if and only if x is F, A believes, and is justified in believing, that x is F, and A's cognitive, belief-forming power is reliable.

If A is a sightseer or craft-lover, then

(2) A exercises a cognitive power that is set not over forms, but over qualities or modes.

As a result,

(3) A accepts accounts of what F is that can be satisfied both by F itself and by things that are not F, but only like F to some degree.

Therefore,

(4) There are relevant situations in which A would judge that x is F when x is not F.

Therefore,

(5) A's cognitive power is unreliable.

Therefore,

(6) A cannot know, but can only opine, that *x* is F.

If, on the other hand, A is a philosopher, then

(7) A exercises a cognitive power set over forms.

As a result,

(8) His beliefs are true, they are justified by the best universal theory of everything, and the power by which he forms them is reliable.

Therefore,

(9) A has knowledge, not opinion.

Therefore,

(10) Sightseers and craft-lovers have opinion, not knowledge; philosophers have knowledge.

If this reconstruction is on the right track, the argument with the sightseers and craft-lovers is an ingenious and philosophically penetrating attempt to show that only reliable belief-forming powers, with access to unique, intelligible, immutable properties, which satisfy the law of non-contradiction, can produce knowledge.[23] If it is possible to know what F is, or to know that *x* is F, there must be such a thing as the form of F. For forms, unlike qualities and modes, are properties of precisely the sort required.[24] The argument is not, as many have claimed, a failed attempt to prove that particulars have contradictory properties and are too unstable to be known, or that forms are the only things that can be known. Indeed, if it did prove either of these things, it would reduce the entire enterprise of the *Republic* to absurdity. For if the philosopher-kings could not have knowledge of the polis they rule, and the people in it, they would be deprived of a credential that, on Plato's view, is required to make their rule legitimate, namely, that they alone know how best to rule (4.7).[25]

2.9 SCIENCE AND DIALECTIC

It is a persistent doctrine of Platonic epistemology that knowledge differs from true belief, even from justified true belief, in being dialectically defensible. In the Socratic dialogues, Socrates always presupposes that those who cannot defend their answers to his "what is it?" question against the elenchus do not know the answer to it. In the *Meno*, the crucial difference between true beliefs and knowledge is said to be that the former "run away from a person's mind" while the latter, being tethered by "calculation of the reason," is stable and immovable (97e2-98b5). In the *Theaete-tus*, knowledge is said to be "neither perception, nor true belief, nor true belief together with an account" (201c8-210b3). In the *Timaeus*, we are told that in addition to the fact that knowledge (*nous*) "can always give a true account," while true belief cannot, "the former is immovable by persuasion, but the other can be persuaded away" (51e2-6). And, of course, the doctrine is in the *Republic*, too. Those who possess only true belief are compared to "blind people who chance to follow the right road" (506c6-9), and those "who cannot distinguish in an account the good itself" and cannot "survive all refutation" are said not to know what it, or any other good, is (534b8-c5). But although it is at the centre of Plato's views about knowledge from early to late, this doctrine seems profoundly mysterious. Why should knowledge have to be dialectically defensible? In this section, we shall see why.

Because he has not yet introduced scientific-thought when he constructs the argument with the sightseers and craft-lovers, Plato works simply with opinion, on the one hand, and knowledge, on the other. Consequently, the cognitive status of scientific-thought remains undecided. In Book 7, however, it is decisively settled:

> We have often called these things "sciences" [*epistēmas*] through force of habit, but they need another name, clearer than opinion, less clear than knowledge—we described them as scientific-thought [*dianoian*] before. But busy men shouldn't spend their time disputing about names. . . . It will therefore be sufficient to call the first subsection knowledge, the second scientific-thought, the third folk-wisdom, the fourth perceptual-thought. The last two together we call opinion [*doxan*], the first two intellect [*noēsin*]. (533d4-534a2)

Scientific-thought is neither knowledge nor opinion, then, but something between the two.

To understand why Plato thinks this, and what exactly he means by it, we must explore his views about the mathematical sciences (as I shall continue to call them), and about the differences that exist between them and dialectic, the science employed by dialectical-thought.

The first step towards knowledge involves replacing the inadequate accounts of properties produced by perceptual-thought and folk-wisdom, which confuse properties with their opposites in the way explained in 2.8, with accounts produced by intellect, which clearly distinguish genuine opposites from one another:

> Now, what about this? Does sight perceive the bigness and smallness of them [fingers] adequately, and does it make no difference to it

whether the finger is in the middle or at the end? And similarly with touch as regards the thick and the thin, the hard and the soft? And do the other senses reveal such things without inadequacy? Or doesn't each of them rather do the following: first, the sense set over the hard is of necessity also set over the soft, and it reports to the psyche that the same thing is both hard and soft when it perceives it to be so? . . . And isn't it necessary, I said, that in such cases the psyche in turn is puzzled as to what this sense means by the hard, if it says that the same thing is also soft, and what it means by the light and the heavy, if it says that the heavy is light and the light heavy? . . . It is likely then, I said, that in such cases the psyche, summoning calculation and intellect, first tries to determine whether each of the things mentioned to it [the big and the small, the thick and the thin, the hard and the soft, the light and the heavy] is one or two. . . . If it is plainly two, each [of the big and the small, etc.] is plainly distinct and one. . . . Then if each is one, and both two, the psyche will think that the two are separate. For it would think the inseparable to be not two, but one. . . . Sight, however, perceived the big and small, not as separate, but as mixed up together. Isn't that so? . . . And in order to clear all this up, intellect [noēsis] was compelled to perceive the big and the small too, not mixed up together, but separate, the opposite way from sight. . . . And it is from such circumstances that it first occurs to us to ask what the big is and what the small is. . . . And so we called the one the intelligible and the other the visible. (523e3–524c13)

The accounts produced by intellect will be couched in quantitative, structural, mathematical terms, rather than the qualitative terms favoured by opinion: "And haven't measuring, counting, and weighing proved to be most gracious helpers in such cases? As a result of them we are not ruled by a thing's looking bigger or smaller or more or heavier; rather we are ruled by that which has calculated, measured, or even weighed" (602d6–9). Hence the first step towards knowledge is a step away from visible qualities and modes, and towards intelligible, structural, mathematized properties, or figures.

But, of course, there would be little point in carrying out this conversion if it resulted in complete falsehood, or in the same kind of unreliability that plagued qualities and modes themselves. The mathematical sciences must be capable of reliably reaching some kind of truth if their accounts of properties are to be worthwhile. And in Plato's view they are capable of this. At their best, the mathematical sciences succeed in producing accounts of F that reliably result in true beliefs about the visible.

That is why the bound daylight-dwellers, who exercise scientific-thought (2.7), are said to reach "the final goal of the visible" (532b1-2), and to see "the things themselves" (516a6-8; cf. *Euthydemus* 290c3), and why aspiration, which rules in their psyches, is "by nature the helper of reason, if it has not been corrupted by bad upbringing" (441a1-3). That is why dialectic is a "coping-stone"[*thrigkos*] for the sciences, not a substitute for them (534e2-535a1).

This process of replacing qualitative accounts with empirically reliable quantitative ones is carried out across the board until all properties, including such evaluative ones as the fine and the good (531b2-c7), have been appropriately mathematized by the combined sciences of arithmetic, plane and solid geometry, dynamics, astronomy, and, above all, harmonics, so that they become released from their indeterminacy-inducing dependence on our sensory apparatus (529a9-531d6). It is this process that is meant, I think, when the young scientists are described as having to acquire "a synoptic view" of the relationship of the mathematical sciences to each other and "to the nature of being [*tēs tou ontos phuseōs*]" (537c1-3).

When the mathematical sciences have accomplished this Herculean task (511c3-4), dialectic is ready to wing its interpretative flight.

Although the accounts produced by the sciences are empirically reliable and hence epistemically more adequate than those produced by folk-wisdom, they suffer from a characteristic defect:

> No one with even a little experience of geometry will dispute that the science itself directly contradicts the accounts produced by its practitioners. . . . They give ridiculous accounts, though they cannot help it, for they speak like practical men and all their words point to doing things. They talk of "squaring," and "applying," and "adding," and the like, whereas the whole of their study aims at knowledge. . . . And must we not agree on a further point? . . . That it is knowledge of what always is [*tou aei ontos gnōseōs*], not of what comes into being and passes away. (527a6-b6)

The accounts produced by the sciences embody inconsistent beliefs about the forms themselves. For example, they speak of doing things to forms, or moving or changing them, when forms must "remain always the same in all respects" (479a2-3) if they are to be adequate for epistemic purposes (2.8). That is why the properties that fit their accounts are figures, not forms. Figures are, by implication if not intent, changeable; forms are unchangeable.

In addition, figures seem to suffer from a second kind of defect, namely, that, like qualities and modes, they are *many* instead of unique. This is suggested by the following rather difficult passage:

It [mathematics] forcibly leads the psyche upwards and compels it to talk about the numbers themselves [*peri autōn tōn arithmōn*]. It won't at all permit anyone to propose for discussion numbers that are attached to visible or tangible bodies. You know what men who are clever in these matters are like. If, in the course of the argument, someone tries to divide the one itself [*auto to hen*], they laugh and won't permit it. If you divide it, they multiply it, taking care that the one should never be plainly not one but many parts. . . . Then what do you think would happen if someone were to ask them, "You wonderful fellows, what kind of numbers are you talking about, in which the one is as your axiom claims it to be, each one equal to every other one, without the smallest difference, and containing no parts?"—I [Glaucon] think they would answer that they are talking about those numbers that can be grasped only by scientific-thought [*dianoēthēnai*] and that cannot be grasped in any other way.—Do you see then, my friend, I said, that it is likely that this study is really necessary for us, since it is plain that it compels the psyche to use dialectical-thought itself [*autēi tēi noēsei*] on the truth itself? (525d5-526b3)

The thought here seems to be this. Mathematicians make fun of those who identify the one with some visible or tangible unit, since any such unit, having many parts, will be many as well as one. But at the same time, their own account of the one allows for the existence of many ones, each without parts, and each identical to all the others. And that view is just as beset by aporiai as the view they disparage.[26] So mathematics leads us in the right direction by forcing us to countenance theoretical entities or intelligibilia, but it does not take us all the way to our destination, because the accounts it gives of intelligibilia are defective, and do not allow us to see them clearly.

A third defect in the sciences is more straightforward. Dialectic aims to give an account of everything: "No one will dispute with us that there is any other inquiry [than dialectic] that attempts to establish systematically with regard to all things [*peri pantos*] what each of them is in itself [*peri ho estin hekaston*]" (533b1-3). The mathematical sciences, on the other hand, take some things for granted:

I think you know that the students of geometry, calculation, and the like hypothesize the existence of the odd and the even, and the various figures, the three forms [*eidē*] of angles, and other things akin to these, in each of their studies, and regard them as given, and treating them as absolute starting points, do not deign to give any account of them, either to themselves or to others, taking for granted that they are obvious to everyone. These are their first principles, and going consistently from them they reach an agreed conclusion on what they started out to investigate. (510c1-d3)

Thus dialectic is at once more general than science and more probing and demanding.

However, it is not enough that the dialectician be able to defend each of the accounts he produces in isolation from the others; he must also be able to defend them as a unified whole. Otherwise a shrewd practitioner of the elenchus might be able to uncover conflicts between them. Thus in producing each account the dialectician must have an eye to all the others, not resting content until he can fit them all together in a coherent unified theory of everything. It is for this reason that he is described in the following ways:

> You must look to this when you are about to decide which is a philosophic nature and which is not. . . . You must look to see if it has any share of small-mindedness. For nothing is more opposed to the quality of a psyche that is always seeking to grasp everything—both divine and human—as a whole, than such narrowness of grasp. . . . Nor will a psyche that is lofty enough to theorize about all time and all substance [*ousias*] believe that the life of man is a big thing. (486a1-6)

> It is also, I said, the real test of the dialectical nature: the person who sees things as a whole [*sunoptikos*] is a dialectician; the one who can't, isn't. (537c6-7)

The scientist's views are partial; those of the dialectician are at once unified and universal. This is the fourth difference between dialectic and the sciences.

It is possession of this dialectically defensible, unified theory that grants the dialectician access to the first principle of everything (511b3-c2). This first principle is the "greatest object of study [*megiston mathēma*]"—the good itself (505a2):

> When someone attempts by means of dialectic to discover without any of the senses through an account [*dia tou logou*] what each thing is in itself [*ho estin hekaston*] and does not desist until he grasps what the good itself is [*auto ho estin agathon*] with reason itself [*autēi noēsei*], he reaches the final goal of the intelligible just as the prisoner escaping from the Cave reached the final goal of the visible. (532a5-b2)

This principle is the exclusive preserve of the dialectician: "Nothing less than the power of dialectic could reveal it [the good itself], and that only to one experienced in the sciences we have described [the mathematical sciences]—there is no other way to get at it" (533a8-10; cf., 2.13). Hence the fifth major difference between dialectic and the mathematical sciences is that they are hypothetical while it is not. We shall see shortly what this difference amounts to.

The upward path of dialectic (511b3-7) consists, it seems certain, in developing the dialectically defensible unified theory of everything from the true theories of the visible world produced by the mathematical sciences. For until one has developed such a theory one cannot have reached the good itself which is the terminus of that path:

And you call a dialectician the person who can give an account of the substance [*tēs ousias*] of each thing? And if he cannot give an account to himself and others, so far as he cannot, you will deny him knowledge [*noun*] on the matter?—How could I say he had it?—And the same applies to the good itself. The person who cannot distinguish in an account the good itself from everything else, who does not, as in a battle, survive all refutation, striving to judge things according to their substance [*kat' ousian*] and not according to opinion [*kata doxan*], holding on through all this without tripping in his reasoning—such a person you will say does not know the good itself or any other kind of good. (534b3-c5)

It also seems certain—although here the direct evidence is sparser—that it is by producing accounts which survive dialectical scrutiny that dialectic "destroys the hypotheses [*tas hupotheseis anairousa*]" (533c8) employed by the mathematical sciences. For in Book 4 Plato seems to imply that the alternative to adopting a proposition as a hypothesis is to refute all the dialectical objections that can be raised against it:

All the same, I said, in order that we may not be obliged to waste time examining all such objections and making sure that they are not true, let us proceed on the hypothesis [*hupothemenoi*] that this is so, with the understanding that if the matter should ever be plainly otherwise, everything that results from the assumption shall be invalidated. (437a4-9)

It would seem, then, that dialectic "destroys the hypotheses" of the mathematical sciences, not by throwing them out, but by reformulating them in an extensionally equivalent, but conceptually more adequate, way.[27] On this showing, dialectic is unhypothetical, not because its empirically adequate first principle can be incorrigibly intuited (dialectic grants access to the good, not the other way around), but because it can be defended against all dialectical objection. How else, indeed, could a genuine *first* principle be defended?[28]

On the upward path, dialectic, like the mathematical sciences, makes use of accounts that seem "obvious to everyone" (510c7-d1). Consequently, it still has one foot in the visible world of qualities and modes, it still uses them, as mathematicians do, to try to make points about forms (510d5-511a1). This is the path taken in the *Republic* (435c9-d5; 1.13). Because of this, dialectic initially suffers from the same inadequacies that plague all such "obvious" accounts (2.8). But unlike the sciences, which treat these accounts as needing no further support beyond that provided by common sense and so end up with figures instead of forms, dialectic treats them as hypotheses "properly so-called" (511b5), propositions which, even if empirically adequate, must be incorporated into a dialectically defensible, fully mathematized, unified theory of everything before they can be considered as established. Once this incorporation is completed, the accounts dialectic provides are freed from their dependence on qualities and modes. At this point, dialectic has completed the great project of synthesis and unification with which it began, and has gained access to the good itself. Armed now with this formidable theory, dialectic "reverses itself," and "comes down to a conclusion" about what the things in the world are, "without making use of anything visible at all, but only forms themselves, moving on from forms to forms, and ending in forms" (511b7-c2).

> It is then our task as founders, I said, to compel the best natures to reach the study which we have said to be the greatest, to see the good itself, to scale that upward path. When they have completed their journey and seen it sufficiently, we must not allow them to do what is now permitted . . . to stay there and to refuse to go down again among those prisoners [in the Cave] or share their labours and honours, whether these be of little or of greater worth. (519c8-d7)

This journey back down into the Cave, back down to rule the Kallipolis in the light of knowledge of the good itself, is the downward path. It is the path travelled by those whose knowledge is founded, not on opinion or tradition, but on the nature of things—a path described, but not travelled, in the *Republic* (504b1-7; 1.13), for not even Socrates has actually seen the good itself (2.11).

I think we can now understand both the cognitive status of scientific-thought and why the mirroring metaphor encountered in 2.7 cannot accommodate the relative difference in clarity, or cognitive reliability, of scientific-thought and dialectical-thought. Perceptual-thought, folk-wisdom, and scientific-thought produce increasingly more reliable, or more nearly true, theories of the visible world. That is why scientific-thought is "clearer than opinion." Its beliefs about the visible are true. But dialectical-thought does not differ from scientific-thought in this way. Rather it produces a more reliable account of the intelligible world than scientific-thought. That is why scientific-thought is "less clear than knowledge" (cf. 2.10).

But it is also true, I think, that having seen how dialectic differs from the mathematical sciences, we can understand why Plato thinks dialectical defensibility is required for knowledge. For even a quick glance at the five differences discussed above reveals that they all boil down to dialectical defensibility. Put the other way around, dialectical defensibility simply boils up to those differences. To hold that knowledge must be dialectically defensible is simply to embrace a full-blooded *epistemological holism*. It is to think that only a unified theory of everything, visible *and* intelligible, which takes nothing for granted, which appeals to no hypothetical principles, is adequate for epistemic purposes.

Whether Plato is right about this, whether only such a theory can provide the kind of reliability and justification required for knowing, is another question, of course—one whose final answer awaits the outcome of further work in epistemology. But it is also a question whose answer waits on further work on the *Republic*. For we have not yet come to the end of our exploration of Plato's epistemology. The Sun analogy remains, and it will cast dialectical-thought in a new and clearer light.

2.10 MATHEMATICAL ASPECTS OF THE LINE

The formula for the Line (quoted in full in 2.7) begins as follows: "Take a line divided into unequal sections, and subdivide each of them . . . in a similar proportion." If we begin with a line nine units in length, and incorporate into it the results established in 2.6-9, we get the figure which appears as the Frontispiece. Notice that in any line divided according to these specifications, DC and CE must be of equal length.

Immediately following the formula for the Line, we are told that "it [the visible section] has been divided into parts as far as truth and falsity are concerned, with the image standing to the original in the same ratio as what is believed [*to doxaston*] stands to what is known [*to gnōston*]" (510a8-10). Clearly, this is a doctrine about the properties the different powers are set over, not about the powers themselves. More precisely, it is about the degrees of truth—or better about the degrees of relative closeness to truth—of the accounts of properties that the powers produce. On the assumption that Plato is still including the mathematical sciences as branches of knowledge (533d4-6), so that the section of the Line referred to as *to gnōston* is CB—and, indeed, no other hypothesis is consistent with the text—his claim is that

$$AC : CB :: AD : DC.$$

The ratio of the degree of closeness to truth of the account of F produced by opinion (at its best) to that of the account of F produced by scientific-thought or dialectical-thought is the same as the ratio of the degree of closeness to truth of the account of F produced by perceptual-thought to that of the account produced by folk-wisdom. Given the mirroring metaphor, discussed briefly in 2.7, we can see, at least in a provisional way, what Plato has in mind. When a person exercises perceptual-thought his account of F will do no more than pick out an image of a model of a figure of F. When a person exercises folk-wisdom, on the other hand, his account of F will pick out a model of a figure of F. And that puts him one step closer to figures than his predecessor. But figures are empirically adequate properties; scientific-thought reaches the truth about the visible world (2.9). Thus the ratio of perceptual-thought's degree of closeness to truth to that of folk-wisdom is 1 : 2. By the same token, the ratio of opinion's degree of closeness to truth to that of intellect is also 1 : 2. Since the relative lengths of the relevant sections and subsections of the Line express these ratios, it follows at once that

$$AC (3) : CB (6) :: AD (1) : DC (2)$$

Two Stephanus pages after he gives the formula for the Line, the relative clarity (or cognitive reliability) of the powers on it is connected with the degree of closeness to truth of their accounts: "Put these [the complete psychological powers] in the due terms of a proportion, and consider that each has as much clarity as the contents of its particular section have a share in truth" (511e2-4). But it is not until Book 7 that we discover the precise nature of the relations he has in mind:

> We have often called these things "sciences" through force of habit, but they need another name, clearer than opinion, less clear than knowledge. . . . Call the first sub-section [EB] knowledge, the second [CE] scientific-thought, the third [DC] folk-wisdom, and the fourth [AD] perceptual-thought. The last two together [AC] we call opinion, the first two [CB] intellect. Opinion is concerned with becoming [*peri genesin*], intellect with substance [*peri ousian*]; and as substance is to becoming, so intellect is to opinion, knowledge is to folk-wisdom, and scientific-thought is to perceptual-thought. We pass over the proportions between the objects over which they [the powers in the subsections] are set, and the division of either section,

the opinable and the intelligible, into two, Glaucon, lest it embroil us in a great many more arguments than those that went before. (533d4-534a8)

The proportions mentioned are these:

substance : becoming :: intellect : opinion
CB (6) : AC (3) :: CB (6) : AC (3)

intellect : opinion :: knowledge : folk-wisdom
CB (6) : AC (3) :: EB (4) : DC (2)

knowledge : folk-wisdom :: scientific-thought : perceptual-thought
EB (4) : DC (2) :: CE (2) : AD (1)

Hence beyond the assertion that scientific-thought is clearer than opinion in general, nothing is said about the relative clarity of scientific-thought and either dialectical-thought or folk-wisdom, and no claims are made about the relative closeness to truth of the accounts produced in the subsections of the visible or those produced in the subsections of the intelligible.

It seems clear, therefore, that Plato never intended the proportions of the Line to symbolize the relative closeness to truth of all the objects on it, or the relative clarity of all the complete powers. If he had, we would be able to simply read off the very results that "require a great many more arguments to establish."

The proportions of the Line, therefore, symbolize only the things explicitly mentioned, and none of those characterized as requiring further argument. Consequently, we cannot infer anything from these proportions about the relative clarity of scientific-thought and folk-wisdom, or about the relative closeness to truth of their accounts. More especially, we cannot infer that they are equally clear, or that their accounts are equally close to the truth, from the fact that the sections of the Line to which they are assigned, DC and CE, must be of equal length. This equality is simply not a functioning part of the simile, as the green of the shamrock was not a functioning part of Saint Patrick's use of it as a simile for the Trinity.[29]

2.11 THE SUN

Socrates disclaims knowledge of the exact nature of the good itself, but offers to describe it by analogy with the sun, which is "the offspring of the good itself and most like it" (506e2-5): "What the good itself is in the intelligible world in relation to dialectical-thought and intelligible things, the sun is in the visible world in relation to sight and visible things"

(508b12-c2). First, just as the sun is neither the power to see nor a colour (507d11-e2), but a visible thing (508a11-b10), which causes us to see colours and colours themselves to be visible (508a3-6), so the good itself is neither the power to know (that is, dialectical-thought) nor truth (508e6-509a5), but a knowable thing, which causes us to know and true things to be known (508e1-4). And, second, just as "the sun not only gives visible things the power to be seen, but also provides for their generation, growth, and nurture, though it is not itself the process of generation" (509b2-4), so "not only do knowable things receive from the good their power to be known, but their very being and substance [*to einai te kai tēn ousian*] derives from it, though the good itself is not substance, but beyond substance [*ousias*] in dignity and power" (509b6-10). The key to this evocative and resonant analogy is provided, as Plato intends, by the Line and the Cave (509c1-511e5, 517a8-c5).

From our discussion of the latter analogies (2.7), it is clear that dialectical-thought is not simply a faculty of theoretical or propositional knowledge, but a complete psychological power. Indeed, it is, as we shall see, the most inclusive practical power, which aims to construct a maximally stable or unified (462a2-b2), maximally self-sufficient (369b5-c4), maximally happy (420b3-8) human community or polis. And forms, which are its stock in trade, are not simply the properties that the best overall theory needs in order to explain and describe the world as a whole, but the properties that the complete practical power needs in order to determine how to change the world so that people will really flourish in it.

Dramatic support for this heterodox view of dialectical-thought emerges when we follow out the implications of the discussion of users, makers, and imitators in Book 10.

> In the case of each kind of thing there are three crafts: one which uses it, one which makes it, one which imitates it. . . . And the virtues and fine points and appropriateness of each manufactured thing, each animal, and each course of action have to do solely with the use for which it is made or adapted by nature. . . . It necessarily follows that the user of anything is the one who knows most about it, and that he is the one to tell the maker what its good or bad points in actual use are. . . . As, for example, the flute-player tells the flute-maker which flutes respond well in playing, and which kind to make, while the maker follows his instructions. . . . The man who possesses knowledge gives instructions about good and bad flutes, and the other, trusting him, makes them. . . . Then with regard to one and the same thing, the maker, through association with, and being compelled to listen to, the one who knows, will have true belief [*pis-*

tin orthēn] about its good qualities and defects, while the user has knowledge [*epistēmēn*] about them. (601d1-602a1)

This passage strongly suggests that only users of a kind of thing have knowledge of it. But we know already that only those who exercise dia-lectical-thought have such knowledge (2.8-9). Hence it follows that those who exercise dialectical-thought must be users.[30] They must be people who tell makers how something is to be made. How what is to be made? To find out we need only track down what dialecticians have experienced in actual use.

Now the only people who exercise dialectical-thought at full power, so to speak, are philosopher-kings, for they alone have completed the entire fifty-year education programme that results in knowledge of the good itself (496d9-497a5). So if we can find what they have experienced in ac-tual use, we will have solved our problem. But the only thing of which they have exclusive and extensive practical experience is polis manage-ment, for they spend fifteen years engaged in it before they can have knowledge of the good (539e2-540c2). What they have knowledge of in actual use, then, is a polis.[31]

If this is correct, then the aim of dialectical-thought is to discover the model or blueprint of the Kallipolis (472d9-e1). Of course, this is what we find Socrates, who exercises dialectical-thought by divine dispensa-tion (496a11-e2), engaged in after his transformation in Book 2. But, in addition, it is one of the activities explicitly ascribed to the philosopher-kings:

> As he looks upon and contemplates things that are ordered and eter-nally the same, that neither do nor suffer injustice, but are all in an intelligible order, he imitates them and tries to become as like them as he can. Or do you think it is possible to consort with something one admires without trying to imitate it oneself? . . . So the philos-opher, who consorts with what is ordered and divine, tries to be-come as ordered and divine himself as a person can. . . . And if it becomes necessary for him to stamp into the malleable mores of peo-ple—whether public or private—the patterns that he sees there, do you think that he will be a poor craftsman of moderation, justice, and all the rest of demotic virtue? . . . They [the philosopher-kings] would take the polis and human mores as a drafting board, but first of all they would clean it—no easy task. . . . Then, I think that as they work they would glance frequently in either direction, now at the form of justice [*to phusei dikaion*], the form of the fine, the form of moderation, and the like, now at the ones they are trying to im-plant in men, rubbing out one and putting in another way of life [in

the model of the polis] until they produce that flesh-tint, so to speak, which Homer too called the godlike in men. (500c2–501b7; cf. 540a8–b1)

Thus the dialectician emerges, not simply as the person who knits the wool provided by the mathematical sciences into a dialectically defensible unified theory of everything, but as a master craftsman who knows how to use that theory to design, and in the person of the philosopher-king to actually construct, the best possible kind of polis (*Timaeus* 68e6–69a5).

The best possible kind of polis, the kind that is "completely good" (427e7), is the one in which everyone is maximally happy: "In founding our polis, we are looking not to the exceptional happiness of any one group, but, as far as possible, to that of the whole polis" (420b5–8). Hence the dialectician is the craftsman of the happiest or most flourishing kind of human community (500e1–4).

Another important consequence of the discussion of users and makers is that the good itself must be (or at least include) what the blueprint of the Kallipolis picks out, the complex structure that only the best possible polis possesses or instantiates (473a5–b2, 540a8–b1).[32] For the philosopher-king knows the good and bad features of only those things he has experienced in actual use. Consequently, the good he comes to know through his fifteen years' experience of polis management (540a4–b1) must be (or include) political good—what Aristotle calls "the highest of all goods achievable by action" (*Nicomachean Ethics* 1095a16–17).

It is a mistake, then, to accuse Plato of giving the philosopher-kings the wrong credentials for ruling well.[33] He would be guilty of this if dialectical-thought were merely a theorizing power. However, this is not his view. The philosopher-kings do indeed have "knowledge of each being [*hekaston to on*]," but they are also "not inferior to others in experience [*empeiriai*] or in any other part of virtue" (484d5–7; cf. 485a1–9, 539e2–540a4). It is true that they are master theoreticians. But they are, in addition, master craftsmen who know how to use their knowledge to make, or to commission others to make, a better world. They not only understand the world; they change it.

If the good itself is (or includes) the structure possessed by the Kallipolis, what are forms and how are they related to the good? The short answer is that forms are constituents of the good, that the good is a rational or intelligible structure of forms (500c2–5). This answer is too short, but it is on the right track.

The reason it is too short is that the existence of "bad" forms, such as the form of the base, the form of injustice, and the form of the bad is explicitly acknowledged (475e9–476a4, 402b5–c8, 596a6–b4). If they were constituents of the good itself, things that instantiated them—bad things—could also instantiate the good itself. And Plato is clear that this is impossible: nothing can instantiate both members of a pair of opposite forms (2.8).[34]

Still, the short answer is on the right track. The philosopher-king aims to design and make a polis that instantiates the good itself. To do this he needs to know both how things are and how they could be changed in order to promote maximal human happiness. Forms are simply the properties needed in the theory that provides him with this knowledge. Since the polis that instantiates the good itself will instantiate many such properties, it is reasonable to think that the good itself is an ordered structure of forms. But there is no reason to think that all forms are components of that structure. Some, like the form of injustice or the form of the bad, are determinately excluded from it. Their inclusion in the good itself would lead to contradiction. Consequently, the general relation between forms and the good itself is this: either a form is a component of the good itself or it is prevented from being such a component by the principle of noncontradiction. Thus some pairs of opposite forms will be components of the good—for example, the forms of the big and the small or the light and the heavy (523e3-524c13)—but not all such pairs will be.

On this interpretation, and ignoring forms that are excluded from the good itself, the form of F might usefully be thought of as a complex product of what Fs can be, and what they should be in order to maximally contribute to human happiness. Put another way: the form of F is what Fs would instantiate in the best of all possible human worlds. The "can" in the first of these formulations must be taken seriously—witness the reiterated demand that the Kallipolis be a real possibility, not mere pie in the sky (375e6-7, 456b12-c2, 472d9-473b2, 499c2-5). As befits the stock in trade of a practical power, forms must be real possibilities, ways that actual things could be (2.14).[35]

It is an easy inference from the account of the relation of forms to the good itself that the philosopher-king alone knows, not only how to make the best kind of polis, but also how to make every good thing that can be made. To know how to make even something as apparently humble as a good bed, one must know the good itself and what kind of bed is a component of it (504c4-505b3, 517c3-5, 534b8-c5). At the beginning of Book 10, this conclusion is embraced with enthusiasm.

For every 'many' that share a common name, a unique form is assumed to exist:

> Shall we, then, begin by adopting our usual method? For we are, as
> you know, in the habit of assuming a form, always one form, in

connection with each of the many [*peri hekasta ta polla*; sc. qualities or modes] to which we apply the same name. . . . Let us then take any of the manys that you wish. For example, there are many [qualities or modes of] beds and tables. . . . But there are only two forms of these, one of the bed and one of the table. (596a5-b4)[36]

And while the unique form is not made by any craftsman (596b9-10)—forms are eternal and immutable (479a2-3; 2.8)—a craftsman "looks towards the form [*pros tēn idean*]" of the bed in making the kind of beds that we use (596b6-8). Now, we know that no ordinary craftsman can have access to the form of the bed *in propria persona*; only philosopher-kings have autonomous access to forms of any kind (2.8-12). Hence the craftsman's access to the form of the bed must be mediated. And that is precisely what we are told. The craftsman is a maker, someone who exercises folk-wisdom. He has "true belief" about what kind of beds he should make, not autonomously like someone who exercises scientific-thought, but only because he is "compelled to listen" to the user who "has knowledge about them" (601e7-602a1). And the user who has knowledge—about beds, or about any of the other kinds of things "to which we apply the same name"—is, of course, the philosopher-king.[37]

It is possible to reach this conclusion by a more treacherous and tortuous route. I follow it now because it winds through some independently interesting territory. I take the conclusion itself to be already secured.

The story begins with the carpenter discussed a moment ago. He, we saw, "does not make the form [of the bed], which we say a bed is in itself [*ho dē phamen einai ho esti klinē*],[38] but he does make some kind of bed [*klinēn tina*]" (597a1-2). The bed that is in itself a bed is the *first bed*. The carpenter's bed, which is made by looking towards the form, is the *second bed*. By imitating the latter, the painter makes the *third bed*: "You will say that what he makes are not true [beds]; yet in a way the painter also makes a kind of bed, does he not?" (596e9-10). Hence

> we get then these three kinds of beds: one which is in nature [*hē en tēi phusei*][39] which I take it we would say a god makes [*theon ergasasthai*], or who else? . . . one which is the work of the carpenter. . . . And one which the painter makes . . . Painter, carpenter, god, corresponding to three kinds [*eidesi*] of beds. (597b5-14)

Now, it is easy to get the impression that, whatever the first bed is, the second and third beds are particulars. But this cannot be the case. What is under discussion here must be the familiar qualities, modes, figures, and forms. For, first, the passage speaks of images and originals, and that means qualities, modes, or figures, on the one hand, and forms, on the other (2.8-9). Second, these beds are referred to as *kinds* of beds (597b14). Finally, the form of the bed is introduced in the usual way by contrasting it with *ta polla*, and that phrase, as we know (2.8), refers to the many modes and qualities, not to the many particulars.

However, if the passage concerns these four familiar kinds of properties, why are there only three kinds of beds, not four? Perhaps the answer lies in the point of the story of the three beds, and in the odd status of figures. The point of the story is to determine the degree of distance from truth of the beds the painter makes. The carpenter's bed, being a product of training in a craft and folk-wisdom, instantiates a mode of a bed. And modes are models of figures. But figures capture the truth about the visible realm (2.9). Therefore, the carpenter's bed is no further from the truth about that realm for being a model of a figure than it would be if it were a model of a form. It is at two removes from the truth, not three, in either case. It follows that the painter's bed, which is an image of the carpenter's bed, instantiates a quality, and is at three removes from the truth, not four. (Qualities are at three removes from the truth, and modes two, because the Greeks counted the first member of a series as well as the last: the day after tomorrow was the third, not the second, day.) So it is unnecessary to introduce both figures and forms in order to determine the degree of distance from truth of the painter's products. And that, I surmise, is why reference to figures is omitted. In this respect, the argument here is like the argument with the sightseers and craft-lovers (2.8).

If I am right about this, the first bed is the form of a bed, the second bed is a mode of a bed, and the third bed is a quality of a bed. But of course one cannot make a form, mode, quality, or kind directly—they are properties, not particulars. Making them is always a matter of making a particular instance of them. Consequently, when we are told that a god makes the first bed, a carpenter the second, and an artist the third, this does not mean that anyone makes a form, figure, mode, quality, or kind. Forms are not made—as Plato has reminded us a bare two Stephanus pages earlier (596b9-10), and elsewhere always maintains—nor are modes, qualities, or kinds. Particular instances of them are made.

From beds I turn to bedmakers. In the first part of Book 10 (595a1-608b3), poet-imitators, who make third-grade copies of beds, are contrasted with a god who can make things that really are beds (597b5-7)—and, since beds are only an example, all the other kinds of things to which we apply the same name as well. Within a few pages, poet-imitators are contrasted in precisely the same terms with users (601a9-602b10). And within a few more pages we are reminded of the ancient dispute between poetry and philosophy (607b1-d1). Hence there are potentially three triadic contrasts here: god, maker, imitator; user, maker, imitator; philosopher-king, maker, imitator. But we already know that the second and third triads are identical, for users have to be philosopher-kings. I suggest that the first and third are identical too: the god in question is the philosopher-king.

In Book 6, we are told that the philosopher-kings are really divine: "If it [the philosophic nature] were to find the best political constitution, as it is itself the best, then it would be apparent that it is really divine [*tōi onti theion ēn*] and all others human in their institutions and natures" (497b7-c3). In Book 10, we are told that the god, the really divine being, who makes the first bed, is a king:

> Very well, I said, you call the imitator [e.g., the painter] one whose product is at three removes from what is by nature [*apo tēs phuseōs*]. . . . This will then be true of the tragedian, if indeed [*eiper*] he is an imitator; he is naturally third from *a king* [*apo basileōs*] and the truth, and so are all other imitators. (597e3-8)

Since philosopher-kings are really divine, and the really divine maker of the first bed is a king, it is difficult to avoid the conclusion—no other divine kings being anywhere in evidence in the *Republic*—that the maker of the first bed is a philosopher-king.[40]

It follows, as we might have expected on general systematic grounds, that there are not three contrasts in operation in Book 10, but only the familiar contrast between those with cognitive access to forms, those with access to modes, and those with access to qualities. What is new is the claim that poets belong in the latter class (4.13).

Having introduced the ordinary craftsman who makes the second bed, Socrates describes an extraordinary one:

> Well now, see what you call this craftsman.—Which one?—The one who makes all the things that all other craftsmen severally produce.—That's a clever and wonderful [*thaumaston*] man you're talking about.—Wait a moment and you will have better reason to say so. For this same craftsman is able to make not only all kinds of furniture but all plants that grow from the earth, all animals including himself, and the earth and the heavens and the gods, all things in the heavens and all things in Hades below the earth.—He is, indeed, a wonderful, clever fellow [*sophistēn*]. (596b12-d1)

But this description is ambiguous. It fits both the poet-imitator and the philosopher-king.

That the description fits poet-imitators is clear—anyone with a mirror can make images of everything (598d7-602c11). But how could it possibly fit the philosopher-king? How could even a Platonic polymath make the gods, the heavens, the animals, and himself? The answer is contained in the preceding pages of the *Republic*.

The philosopher-king does not make anything *ex nihilo* any more than the Demiurge in the *Timaeus* does. The philosopher-king is a craftsman, not a miracle-worker. What he does is take the raw materials that lie to hand and make them really useful and good. Included among these are the traditional stories about the gods, and "about things in the sky and beneath the earth," which are our only source of information about such things (382c10-d3, 427b2-c4; *Timaeus* 40d6-e4). When these stories have been appropriately redrafted, along the lines suggested in Book 2 (377e1-392a1), they dispose their hearers to virtue, become really beneficial and useful (386b10-c1), and represent the gods as they really are (379b1-383c7). In this way, the philosopher-king "makes" the gods of tradition real gods, or what gods really are, namely, always good and beneficial to humans (379b1-c7). He makes the plants and animals (including human beings) by using techniques of selective breeding to produce those strains or breeds that are best capable of insuring human happiness (459a1-b12)—that is why animals are included among things that have a use at 601d4-6. He makes himself, not by being *causa sui*, but by using his knowledge of how the world as a whole works to reshape himself through training and education, so that he can flourish to the greatest degree possible (500c2-e4, 576e6-588a11; 3.6-7, 4.7, 4.9).

If these activities can legitimately be called making—and Plato is willing to include much less full-blooded ones under that expansive rubric (597a1-2)—then we must concede that the description of the extraordinary craftsman fits the philosopher-king like a glove: the extraordinary craftsman who really knows how to make beds, gods, animals, himself, and every other kind of thing as well is the philosopher-king. Thus we have reached by a second route the conclusion that philosopher-kings know how to make every kind of thing.

Now I do not think that it is simply chance that the description that introduces the discussion of poets and philosophers fits both poet-imitators and philosopher-kings. Indeed, both of Glaucon's initial responses to it (596c3, d1) underline its ambiguity—a *thaumastos* can be either a wonder-worker or a poet; a *sophistēs* can be either a genuinely wise man or a pseudo wise man, a sophist. What Plato is doing, I think, is dramatizing the threat poet-imitators pose, even to good men like Glaucon and Adeimantus, by showing just how difficult it is to distinguish them from philosophers. Poets are widely thought to know what virtue is, and how to teach it (598d7-e5, 606e1-5), but in fact they are only imitators, producers of third-grade images of true things, who do not have even so much as true belief about them (602a8-9). Philosophers, by contrast, really know about virtue, and what kind of life is best. Philosophers, as one might put it, instantiate the form of the teacher of virtue, poets instantiate only the quality.

But to those in the Cave qualities are difficult to distinguish from forms, poets are difficult to distinguish from philosophers. That is why poets pose such a threat to our well-being; choosing the wrong master in these matters can ruin one's entire life. It is also why

> it should be our chief concern that each of us neglect all other studies and search for and study this: whether in any way he may be able to learn of and discover the person who will give him the power and the knowledge to distinguish the good life from the bad, and everywhere to make the best choice that the conditions allow. (618c1-6)

So, "when anyone reports to us about someone he has met that he is a man who knows all the crafts, and everything else that men severally know, and that there is nothing that he does not know more precisely than anyone else" (598c7-9), we had better not be precipitate in replying to him that "he is a simple fellow and that, as it seems, he has encountered some magician and imitator and been deceived by him into believing him to be all-wise because he himself does not know what knowledge, lack of knowledge, and imitation are" (598d2-5). For if we are precipitate, we may expose, not his inability to distinguish forms from qualities, real beds from third-grade imitations, philosophers from poet-imitators, but our own. As a result, we may miss the chance of finding the one person who could teach us to live well—the philosopher.

We are now ready to decipher the Sun analogy.

It is clear that the good itself is neither dialectical-thought nor truth (508e6-509a5) but a knowable thing—a rational or intelligible structure of forms. It is no doubt less clear how such a thing could cause us to know or truths to be known (509b6-10). But we shall see that there is nothing occult about it.

The goal pursued by every psyche is what is really good:

> Is it not obvious that in the case of just things and fine things many are content with what is reputedly such [ta dokounta], even if it isn't really such, and are content to act, acquire possessions, and form opinions on this basis? But when it comes to good things no one is satisfied with what is only reputedly such, but all seek what is really such [ta onta], and disdain mere opinion. (505d5-9)

But it is through their connection with the good itself—the form of the good—that things become really good: "The form [idea] of the good is the greatest object of study, and . . . it is by relation to it that just things and all the rest [*kai talla*] become useful and beneficial" (505a2-4; cf. 379b11-13). It follows that

> the person who cannot distinguish in an account the good itself from everything else, who does not, as in a battle, survive all refutation, striving to judge things according to their substance and not according to opinion, holding on through all this without tripping in his reasoning—such a person you will say does not know the good itself or any other kind of good. (534b8-c5)

But only dialectical-thought gives us this knowledge: "Nothing less than the power of dialectic could reveal it [the good itself], and that only to one experienced in the sciences we have described [the mathematical sciences]—there is no other way to get at it" (533a8-10; cf. 505a6-b1, 517c3-5). Hence the desire for what is really good cannot be satisfied by any psyche until it exercises dialectical-thought and knows the good itself.

The good itself causes us to know and knowable things to be known, then, not by goading us from behind to know them (the desire for what is really good does that), but by luring us from in front. It is because we want what only knowledge of the good itself can give us—stable long-term happiness—that those who are able climb the rough, steep path that leads out of the Cave, up the Line, and into the light of the Sun.

This brings us to the second and more difficult part of the analogy: knowable things derive their "very being and substance" from the good itself, which is "beyond substance in dignity and power" (509b6-10). To decipher it, we must confront four separate issues. First, how extensive is the class of knowable things—just which things owe their being and substance to the good? Second, is the being of something the same as its substance or are they distinct? Do knowable things owe a double debt to the good or only a single one? Third, why are knowable things indebted to the good in this way? Fourth, what does it mean to say of the good that it is "beyond substance in dignity and power"? Many readers will recognize these as among the most disputed questions in the interpretation of Plato.

Knowledge cannot exist without forms. We cannot find out "the truth about the equal, or the double, or any other ratio" or property by observing sensible objects or properties alone (529a9-530a2). But despite the near uniformity of interpretative opinion to the contrary, knowledge is not only about forms (2.8-9). The dialectician tries to "establish systematically with regard to all things [*peri pantos*] what each of them is in itself" (533b1-3), and to "give an account of the substance of each thing" (534b3-4). His psyche is "lofty enough to theorize about all time [*pantos chronou*] and all substance [*pasēs ousias*]" (486a8-9), and seeks "the perception of anything that it does not know [*ho mē oiden*], whether it is something that has been, or is, or is going to be" (572a2-3). His vision is totally inclusive (537c6-7). He knows the very same things about which others have only opinion (402b5-c8, 601e7-602a1). He knows what qualities, modes, and figures are as surely as he knows the good itself, and all the other forms:

> Therefore, you [philosopher-kings] must each in turn go down [into the Cave] and live there with the others and grow accustomed to seeing in the dark. When you are used to it, you will see countless times better than those there: you will know each image [quality or mode] for what it is [*gnōsesthe hekasta ta eidōla hatta esti*], because you have seen the truth about the fine, and the just, and the good. (520c1-6)

The theory of which the dialectician is a master is a unified theory of everything (2.9). Hence it is that the good itself is the cause of "all the things [*pantōn*]" that the dialectician sees in the course of his journey toward the sun (516c1-2). For the class of knowable things is the universal class: all things owe their being and substance to the good.

We must now determine whether this constitutes a single debt or two distinct debts. When Plato talks about being (*to on*), or complete being (*to pantelōs on*), or about the being (*to einai*) of something, he is referring to what we call *predicative* being, not to *existential* being, or existence. This emerged quite clearly in our analysis of his argument with the sightseers and craft-lovers (2.8). Hence the being of something is expressed by the property that tells us what it really is or what it is *in itself*. And such a property is a form: "We postulate a unique form of each [of the many qualities and modes], believing that there is but one, and call it what each of them is in itself [*'ho estin' hekaston*]" (507b5-7). But forms, in contrast to qualities and modes, are precisely the properties that express the substance (*ousia*) of something. Hence the philosopher-king is said to judge things "according to their substance [*kat' ousian*]" rather than "according to opinion [*kata doxan*]" because he alone has access to forms (534b8-c5).

It seems clear, then, that being and substance are the same. Things owe a single debt to the good itself, not two distinct debts.[41] It remains to explain the precise nature of what they owe.

In the case of forms and their instances this is easily done. The being or substance of a thing is what it is in itself. And what a form is in itself, I have argued, is either a component of the good itself or something excluded from being such a component by the principle of noncontradiction. Hence forms owe their being and substance to the good in that their very identity as forms depends on it: the inclusion-exclusion relation they bear to the good determines what they are. To be a form is precisely to be either a component of the good itself or the opposite of such a component.

But a form is something that expresses the being or substance of its instances. Consequently, the latter are what they are because of their relation to it. On the plausible assumption that such debts are transitive, it follows that they owe their being and substance to the good as well. To be an instance of a form is to instantiate something that is either a component of the good or the opposite of such a component.

The kind of bed the philosopher-king makes instantiates a form. For it is "in itself a bed" (597c3), and a form, as we have seen, is what each of some many is in itself (507b6-7). However, no other kind of bed instantiates that form (597a1-e4). A similar conclusion is reached with considerably more fanfare in Book 5:

> Then were we not, as we say, trying to make a model in words of a good polis? . . . [But] is it possible to realize anything in practice exactly as it is described in words? . . . Then do not compel me to show that the things we have described in theory can exist exactly as we have described them. If we are able to discover how a polis that most nearly answers to our description might be constituted, shall we say that we have shown that those things are possible that you told us to prove so [sc. that the Kallipolis could come into being]? (472d9-473b1)

Hence when a polis exists that comes as close to fitting the blueprint of the Kallipolis as actual things can come to fitting a theory, it will be the Kallipolis and instantiate the good itself (4.2). But this will not come about unless "philosophers become kings in our poleis or those now called kings and rulers genuinely and adequately philosophize" (473c11-d2). It seems to follow that forms, whether of beds or of poleis, normally come to be instantiated only through the activities of philosopher-kings.

It follows that few things currently instantiate forms. For there never have been any philosopher-kings. This conclusion is hardly news, but it does raise an important question. If things do not for the most part instantiate forms, what do they instantiate?

To find out, we need only turn back to the Line. There the contents of DC, the subsection which contains modes, are catalogued as follows: "the creatures around us and all the products of nature, and the whole category of manufactured things" (510a5-6). Hence many of the things around us instantiate modes. But others are "images [of modes], and by images I mean first shadows, then reflections in water and close-grained polished surfaces, and everything of that kind" (509e1-510a3). These instantiate qualities, the contents of AD. Included in this group are pictorial images (597d11-e4), representations of human beings and their actions in plays and poetry (597e6-8), and, indeed, all things that are the products of an understanding of the world based on, or determinately influenced by, such representations (598d7-608b10).

How does the being or substance of these things, the current inhabitants of the world and their actual properties, depend on the good itself?

The world around us and its contents, viewed from the undistorting perspective of dialectical-thought, are our attempts to make a really good world (505a5-9), a world that instantiates the good itself, and whose contents instantiate forms. Like all attempts, they are defined in terms of their goals. A failed soufflé is what it is, and not a successful omelette, because the goal was a soufflé. In the same way, the actual world and its contents are what they are, not because, or not completely because, of their intrinsic characteristics, but because of their relation to the goal they are attempts to reach. They are all differentially failed attempts to realize the good itself and its constituent forms. That is their true being and substance.

Now in my view this dependence that attempts have on goals is the key to the mirroring metaphor we encountered in 2.7 and 2.10. The philosopher has a formula, based on an empirically adequate, dialectically defensible, unified, universal theory, for producing the kind of cows (say) that will maximally contribute to human happiness. Hence his cows instantiate the form of the cow. The scientist too wants to produce cows of this sort. But because he lacks such a theory, and has true belief, not knowledge, his cows instantiate only a figure of a cow. None of the cows in the fields around us are the product even of a complete science of cows. But some are products of the traditional techniques of selective breeding and fragmentary science I have been calling folk-wisdom. Based on less adequate understanding, folk-wisdom's cows are less successful than those of the scientist. They instantiate a mode of a cow.[42] Finally, there are the cows that are products of the kind of understanding that results from looking at plays, or reading poems, or unaided perception. These are the least successful attempts to produce really good cows. They instantiate some of the qualities of a cow. Hence a quality is, so to speak, a failed mode, a mode is a failed figure, and a figure is a failed form. Thus the chain of dependence from qualities, through modes and figures, to forms is complete. All things depend for their being and substance on the good itself.

It is precisely because of this asymmetrical dependence of all other things on the good that the latter is described as being "not substance, but beyond substance in dignity and power" (509b8-10). They are substances; it is the substance of substances.

2.12 Powers and Goods

With the Cave, Line, and Sun behind us, it is time to try to further de-mythologize Plato's views about the complete psychological powers—perceptual-thought, folk-wisdom, scientific-thought, and dialectical-thought—and the distinctive type of properties over which each is set.

Dialectical-thought is the complete psychological power of the philosopher-king who designs and rules over the Kallipolis—the polis in which everyone is as happy as possible. It is also the complete power of the philosophic man whose life is devoted to acquisition of the pleasure of knowing the truth (2.2), a power which consists of intelligence focused by rational desires on that rationally ordered structure of forms, the good itself.

Now it would be unintelligible that dialectical-thought should play both these rôles if, for example, the philosopher-kings ruled the Kallipolis out of general benevolence, or because they wanted to increase the amount of rational order in the world,[43] or simply because they enjoyed ruling for its own sake. For what are any of these things to a person single-mindedly pursuing the pleasure of knowing the truth? And, in fact, the philosopher-kings have none of these motives. They do not enjoy ruling for its own sake; if they did, they would be unfit to rule (517c7-d2, 519e1-521a8). And while it is true that they love the Kallipolis, they do so only because they believe that its well-being is connected biconditionally to their own (412c12-d7). They rule, in other words, because doing so is the best means to their own happiness, that is, to the stable acquisition of as much of the pleasure of learning and knowing the truth as possible throughout life (3.7, 4.9). That is why a single power, set over a single type of property, and doing a single kind of work (2.8), enables the philosopher to know the truth and the king to rule.

Because the same power does both these things, the blueprint for the Kallipolis must also be the blueprint for the polis in which the conative component of the philosopher's complete power—his ruling desire—is best satisfied. This plainly suggests, I think, that dialectical-thought has a familiar Humean structure: it consists of a desire, which determines the end or goal to be pursued, and intelligence, which works out the best means of satisfying that desire. However, Plato adds an important wrinkle to this Humean picture. The desire in question also determines how far intelligence will pursue its studies, how much it will learn about the world (2.4, 3.10). The desire for the pleasure of knowing the truth not only determines the philosopher's end, it also determines what intellectual resources—what sorts of theories, what level of technical skill—he will be able to muster in its pursuit. It is a bit difficult to see both kinds of determination in the case of dialectical-thought, but we shall see them quite clearly when we turn to the other complete powers. This double determination of ends and intellectual resources is what I have been calling *focusing*.

In addition to the good itself, to which only those who exercise dialectical-thought have access, there is the good the honour-lover sees. In the Cave analogy, this is represented by the moon which is the doppelgänger of the sun available to bound daylight-dwellers: "They first see shadows most easily, then the reflections of men and other things in water, then the things themselves. And among these, they would see the things in the sky more easily at night, the light of the stars and the moon more easily than the sun and the light of the sun" (516a6-b2). Only if they were released from the bonds of spirited desires would they take the next step and actually see "the sun itself in itself in its own place" (516b5-6). But the bound daylight-dwellers cannot take this step because their spirited desires for the pleasure of being honoured are too strong. Hence they have access only to an image of the good itself. Because bound daylight-dwellers have access to figures, I shall call this image a *figure of the good*.

Like the good itself, which is a complex of forms, a figure of the good is a complex of figures. But unlike the theory that gives access to the good itself, the theory developed by scientific-thought, which gives access to a figure of the good, is, even when it is performing optimally, an adequate theory of the visible world only. It cannot give an accurate picture of the good itself or any of the other inhabitants of the intelligible world (2.9-10). If the above account of the structure of the complete powers is correct, we ought to be able to explain this fact by reference to scientific-thought's component spirited desires.

Our question is this: Why should someone whose ruling desire is for the pleasure of being honoured develop the intellectual resources necessary to yield true beliefs about the visible world, but not those necessary to yield true beliefs about the intelligible world?

In most cultures, and certainly in classical Athens, honour is conferred primarily on military heroes who are successful in defending their country in times of danger, or who add to its wealth and prestige by making new conquests on its behalf. But for success of this kind, and even for success in science, medicine, and technology, all that is necessary by way of intellectual resources is true belief about the visible world. As long as a person's logistics prove successful (526d1-6), as long as he sticks to his post when it is good to do so (429b8-c3), he will be honoured as wise in counsel and courageous in battle (430c2-3). As long as his scientific theories are empirically adequate he will, so to speak, be a candidate for a Nobel Prize. His inability to defend his views about wisdom, courage, numbers, or other intelligibilia against dialectical attack is neither here nor there. So if someone develops only those intellectual resources necessary to acquire the pleasure of being honoured in a reliable way, there is good reason to think that he will rest content with true belief about the visible world, and will omit the five-year course in dialectic and the fifteen years of practical politics that would show him how to chart the pathways of the intelligible.

An honour-lover, then, will want to develop his intellectual resources to at least the level at which they reliably provide the kind of true belief about the visible world required for social success. But why is this the highest level possible for him? If he is as intelligent as a philosopher (519a1-b5; 2.4), and lives in a society in which dialectical proficiency is the highroad to honour, why could he not develop exactly the same intellectual resources as the philosopher?

Plato's ingenious solution to these pressing problems—most clearly suggested by the description of the oligarchic man at 553d1-7, and by the account at 581c8-e4 of how the three primary psychological types view their lives—is this. Because an honour-lover's ruling desires are for the pleasure of being honoured, he will study dialectic only for the sake of the honour it yields. For him dialectical study is no more than a C-good, harsh in itself, but bringing pleasant G-consequences (1.9, 1.11). As a result, he never experiences the pleasure of knowing the truth, which is intrinsic to dialectical-thought. If he did, he would prefer it to his own distinctive pleasure and be a philosopher, not an honour-lover. For the pleasure of knowing the truth is the most pleasant of all (3.6). And because he misses the pleasure of knowing the truth, he will miss the good itself. For he will try to design a world in which everything, even knowing the truth, is pursued only to the extent that it brings honour. He will take the structure of that world to be the structure of the happiest world (3.7). He will mistake a figure of the good for the good itself. Therefore, even an honour-lover trained in dialectic is forever condemned by his ruling desires to misperceive the intelligible world. True belief about the visible is the most he can achieve.

One other good remains for discussion. In the Cave analogy it is represented by the fire that the newly unbound cave-dwellers see when, released from the bonds of unnecessary appetites, but still in thrall to necessary ones, they turn away from the shadow show to gaze on something more substantial (514b2-3, 515c8). The fire they see is a *mode of the good*. It is a structure of modes that mirrors at two removes the good itself. The theory which gives cognitive access to it is the *Weltbild* of the money-lover, whose ruling passion is for the pleasure of making money (2.2).

The intellectual resources of a money-lover amount to no more than opinion, a power which, even when it is performing optimally, sometimes yields true beliefs about the visible world, sometimes false ones (2.8). We must now try to explain why this is so.

The primary ways of making money, and the only ones available in the Kallipolis, where ruling and guarding bring no cash benefits (416d3-417b8), are the crafts and professions that provide the goods and services others want or need. Hence a money-lover will want to develop at least the intellectual resources necessary to practice one of them successfully—that is why money-lovers are also craft-lovers (476a10). But to succeed in making money as a shoemaker (say), it is enough that one be able to make shoes that satisfy the visible standards of desirability in shoes employed by the majority of people (493e2-494a2), whether these reliably yield true beliefs about the visible or not. For one's financial success as a shoemaker is determined by what others think desirable and worth buying, not by what is in fact desirable.

A money-lover, then, will want at least the intellectual resources necessary to go that far. But could he go further? Could he, for example, match the intellectual resources of the honour-lover and come to exercise a power which would yield only true beliefs about the visible? The account of the money-loving oligarchic man shows that he cannot. The oligarch will not allow reason "to reason about or examine anything else than how a little money can be made into much," nor aspiration to "admire anything else but wealth or wealthy men, or to have any other ambition than the acquisition of wealth" (553d1-7). It follows that even a money-lover who is smart enough to share the honour-lover's intellectual training will do so only as an extrinsic means to achieving his own ruling pleasure. Consequently, he will not experience the superior pleasure of being honoured (3.7), and will continue to evaluate the world and its contents in terms of their potential for producing his own distinctive pleasure. He will always mistake a mode of the good for the good itself. As a result, his beliefs about the visible will sometimes be false no matter how much science he learns.

Alone among the complete powers, perceptual-thought does not grant access to any kind of good at all. That is why nothing the bound cave-dwellers see is an analogue of the sun. One reason for this is that the component unnecessary appetites of perceptual-thought cannot be satisfied by a single unitary pleasure. And having a single pleasure or primary goal is, on Plato's view, a necessary condition of having a good (519c1-3;

3.5-8). This important difference aside, perceptual-thought has the same structure as the other complete powers.

Someone who exercises perceptual-thought wants the pleasures of food, drink, and sex above all others. Therefore, he will want to exercise minimally theory-laden sense perception at the very least. For without it he cannot experience even those pleasures. But this level of cognition is also the most he can aspire to. For although such a person may learn a craft or science as an extrinsic means to his appetitive goals, although (like the democratic man) he may "at times occupy himself with what he imagines to be philosophy" (561d2), he will never find new sources of pleasure in these. To him they will always be C-goods—intrinsically unpleasant means to the sensual indulgences he really enjoys. Hence his standards of evaluation will remain unimproved by whatever training he gets for himself. He will always judge things in terms of their capacity to give him sensual pleasure. He will remain tethered in the Cave forever.

From powers I turn to the properties over which they are set.

Earlier we saw that dialectical-thought is set over forms, scientific-thought over figures, folk-wisdom over modes, and perceptual-thought over qualities (2.7). Now an equivalent description is available. Dialectical-thought is set over the good itself, scientific-thought over a figure of the good, folk-wisdom over a mode of the good, and perceptual-thought over qualities. Unlike its predecessor, this description shows clearly that, with the explicable exception of perceptual-thought, the different complete powers are set over different goods or different images or conceptions of the good. By pursuing the identity of these goods we will reach a better understanding of forms, figures, modes, and qualities.

We know that the good itself is the structure of the polis in which the philosopher-king believes he will best satisfy his ruling desire for the pleasure of knowing the truth, and that its substructural components are forms (2.11). Since the moon, which is an analogue of a figure of the good, is a sort of reflection of the sun, which is an analogue of the form of the good, and since a mode of the good is a model of a figure of the good, the figures and modes of the good must also be polis-structures. It seems a reasonable conjecture, then, that a figure of the good is the structure of a polis in which the honour-lover believes his ruling desire for the pleasure of being honoured is best satisfied, that a mode of the good is the structure of a polis in which the money-lover believes his desire for the pleasure of making money is best satisfied, and that their respective substructural components are figures and modes.

Each of these three distinctive pleasures, then, provides a standard or yardstick of goodness in poleis and their components. The money-lover judges things—whether they are political constitutions, men, animals, or beds—in terms of their capacity to enrich him. The honour-lover judges them by their capacity to bring him honour. The philosopher judges them by their capacity to enable him to learn the truth. It is these standards which are embodied in forms, figures, and modes.

On this account, Plato's goods are the structures of pleasure-worlds, and forms, figures, and modes, the components of those structures, are the structures of pleasure-world constituents.

Qualities disturb this picture only slightly. First, they embody not a single standard but several competing standards, each corresponding to one of the appetitive person's distinct competing pleasures. Second, qualities are not components of a single pleasure-world, because multiple competing pleasures do not give rise to a single such world. But otherwise qualities are similar in structure to modes and forms.

Now one might be inclined to conclude that if pleasures are the standards of goodness in worlds and world constituents, there is no way to assess those standards objectively. The money-lover has his pleasure, the honour-lover his, the philosopher his, and that's the end of the matter. But this is not Plato's view. The philosopher's pleasures are objectively more pleasant than the honour-lover's, and his, in turn, are objectively more pleasant than the money-lover's (2.14, 3.6). The philosopher's pleasure has knowing the truth as an essential component, so that to get what he most wants the philosopher has to try to see the world as it really is, undistorted by fantasies or illusions. The honour-lover and the money-lover by contrast have pleasures which sustain, and are sustained by, false beliefs (3.10). In the case of the honour-lover who is performing optimally, these are false beliefs about the intelligible world; in the case of the money-lover who is performing optimally, they are false beliefs about the visible world. Therefore, even when their complete powers are performing optimally, these people cannot build the world in which their ruling desires are best satisfied. Moreover, and it is important to keep this vividly in mind, folk-wisdom and scientific-thought can be relied upon to perform optimally only in the Kallipolis. For unless they are held in place by elenchus-resistant tethers provided by the philosopher-kings, beliefs—even true beliefs—are unstable and prone to wander away (413a9-c3, 506c6-9; 2.8-9). That is why money-lovers and honour-lovers need to be ruled by philosopher-kings in order to achieve their goals in a reliable way (586d4-e2, 590c2-d6). Consequently, whether we look at the ends pursued or at the intellectual resources necessary to achieve them reliably, we find objectivity at work. The authority of values is the authority of truth, that is, of reality.

2.13 THE DEVELOPMENT OF THE THEORY OF FORMS

If the interpretation proposed in the foregoing sections is cogent, then the Cave, Line, and Sun not only fit together perfectly, something they are traditionally thought not to do,[44] they also embody a theory of forms very different from the one traditionally found in them. In this section, we shall examine the place of the traditional theory in the development of Plato's thought about forms and see how and why he modified the theory in the *Republic*.[45]

Because he believed that we cannot be happy or lead the good life unless we are virtuous (352d2-354a9), and that we cannot acquire the virtues, or discover anything else about them, until we know what each of them is (*Laches* 190b5-7; *Meno* 71b3-7), Socrates searched by means of the elenchus for accounts of the traditionally recognized virtues—courage, temperance, piety, friendship, justice, and wisdom. But while it is easy to see how the elenchus can expose conflicts in people's beliefs about virtues, it is not easy to see how it could possibly yield knowledge of what a virtue is, unless it is assumed at the outset that some beliefs about virtues are recognizably true. False beliefs, even if they are consistent and defensible against elenctic attack, cannot amount to knowledge. So unless people have access to true beliefs about the virtues, the elenchus cannot yield knowledge of what the virtues are.

But what could possibly guarantee that this is so, that everyone has some true beliefs about the virtues? This is the problem Plato confronts in the *Meno*. Having shown that Meno does not know what virtue is, and having claimed to be in the same situation himself (71b1-80d3), Socrates proposes that they search together for the knowledge they lack: "All the same I am willing to go along with you to investigate and inquire into what it is" (80d3-4). But instead of agreeing to this procedure in the manner of earlier interlocutors (*Charmides* 166c7-e7; *Protagoras* 348c5-349d8), Meno raises a problem about the very possibility of doing what Socrates suggests. This is his famous paradox of inquiry:

> But in what way will you inquire [*zēteseis*] into something when you don't in any way know what it is? What sort of thing, among those things you do not know, will you set up beforehand as the object of inquiry? Or to put it another way, even if you come right upon it, how will you know that *it* is the thing that you didn't know? (80d5-8)

We cannot examine the class of just things (say) to find out what is common to them because unless we know what justice is, we cannot assemble the right class. And if by chance we did assemble it, through happening fortuitously upon justice, we could not know that it was the right one.

Socrates' response to this "contentious argument" (80e2) is as follows. He uses the elenctic examination of the slave boy (82a7-85b7) to establish that it is possible to have true belief about something without having knowledge of it (85c6-7). This shows that Meno's argument does not work in every case. For if it is possible to have true belief about something without knowing it, it is possible to identify the object of inquiry without having knowledge of it. But, of course, a single counterexample is not sufficient by itself to defuse the paradox. Meno could argue, as many have done, that ethics is very different from geometry. To counter this line of response Socrates offers an explanation of the slave boy's true belief that is quite general:

> The psyche, since it is immortal and has been born many times and has seen all things [*panta chrēmata*] both here and in Hades, is not unlearned; so we need not be surprised that it is possible for it to recall the knowledge of virtue or anything else [*peri allōn*], which things, as we see, it knew before. All nature is akin, and the psyche has learned all things [*hapanta*], so that when someone has recalled one thing—"learned it," as we say—there is no reason why he should not find out all of the rest, if he keeps a stout heart and does not grow weary of the search, for inquiry and learning are nothing but recollection [*anamnēsis*]. (81c5-d5)

If this explanation is correct, then inquiry into anything is possible, for each of us has true beliefs about all things (85d13-e5).[46]

It only takes a moment, however, to see that recollection pure and simple is no solution to Meno's paradox. For if someone wants to inquire into justice, he must recollect some true beliefs about *it*. But how can he be sure that the beliefs he recollects are really about justice and not about temperance or piety or something else altogether? This paradox of recollection seems to be every bit as troublesome as the paradox of inquiry. Indeed, they are one and the same paradox.[47]

Plato faces up to this problem, or so it seems to me, in the *Phaedo*.[48] There a distinction is drawn between two kinds of recollection:

> Well, now you know what happens to lovers whenever they see a lyre or cloak or anything else their loves are accustomed to use: they recognize the lyre, don't they, and they get in their mind the idea of the boy whose lyre it is? And that is recollection? . . . Again now, is it possible on seeing a horse or lyre depicted to be reminded of a man, and on seeing Simmias depicted to be reminded of Cebes? . . .

And also on seeing Simmias depicted to be reminded of Simmias himself? . . . In all these cases, then, doesn't it turn out that there is recollection from similar things and also from dissimilar things? (73d5-74a3)

But the motive for drawing this distinction has remained a mystery.[49] Once we set the passage in the context of the paradox of recollection, however, a natural explanation suggests itself. For recollection from similar things is precisely the kind that will resolve that paradox: if we know that we are engaging in it, and not in recollection from dissimilars, we can be confident that we are recollecting the right thing. What we need, then, is some test by which we can distinguish these kinds of recollection. And this is just what Plato goes on to provide. Taken together with the lack of an alternative account of what he is up to, this gives a measure of plausibility to the idea that he has our paradox in mind.

The test proposed is the following: "Whenever one is reminded of something from similar things mustn't one experience something further: mustn't one think about whether the thing is lacking at all in its similarity to the thing one is reminded of?" (74a5-7). So, for example, if someone sees a fine thing, he may be reminded of the fineness which he seeks to know, but equally well he may be reminded of goodness, with which he associates fineness. However, he can tell that he has been reminded of the right thing if he can significantly wonder whether it is exactly similar to the fineness which reminds him of it.

Throughout the remainder of the *Phaedo* recollecting forms always means recollecting them *from similars* (74d4-75d5).[50] This, together with the introduction of forms as the objects of recollection, is the important modification or addition that the *Phaedo* makes to the account of how recollection operates.

Now this stratagem will not work unless forms are indeed similar to the visible things that remind us of them. But what does similarity amount to? One natural thought is that it is to be spelled out in terms of sharing a property (*Parmenides* 132d9-e1), that a visibly fine thing is similar in the right sort of way to the nonvisible form of the fine just in case the latter itself possesses the property of being fine. On this view, the forms required by the doctrine of recollection would have to possess the properties of which they are the forms, they would have to be self-instantiating. So self-instantiation, a feature that many believe to be essential to canonical Platonic forms, has an intelligible basis in that doctrine. It is another question, of course, whether Plato himself ever thought that forms had to possess this feature. But one controversial passage in the *Phaedo* appears to assert that they do: "It seems to me that if anything else is fine besides the fine itself, it is fine for no other reason than that it participates in that fine; and the same goes for all of them" (100c3-6; cf. *Symposium* 210e6-211b5). If this is indeed what Plato has in mind, and that is a hotly debated issue, then the forms required by the doctrine of recollection are not only intelligibly self-instantiating, they are explicitly so.[51]

Nor is it a surprise to find Plato arguing that forms and the sensible properties that remind us of them must be *nonidentical*. For if they were identical, then instead of sensible properties simply reminding us of forms, they would actually be presenting us with them, and recollection would be excess epistemological baggage. The argument in question runs as follows:[52]

> We say, don't we, that there is something equal—I don't mean a stick to a stick, or a stone to a stone, or anything else of that sort, but some further thing different from all of those, the equal itself . . . Or isn't it plainly different to you? . . . Look at it this way: aren't equal sticks and stones, the very same ones, plainly equal to one but not to another [*tōi men isa phainetai tōi d'ou*]? . . . But now, are the equals themselves [*auta ta isa*] ever plainly unequal, or [is] equality [ever plainly] inequality [*hē isotēs anisotēs*]? . . . Then those equals are not the same as the equal itself. (74a8-c5)

If, once again, we set this argument in the context of Plato's ongoing attempt to explain how in the face of the paradox of inquiry the Socratic elenchus can yield knowledge, and bear in mind the argument with the sightseers and craft-lovers, whose predecessor it almost certainly is (*Phaedo* 83c5-8; 2.8), we can see what he has in mind.

If recollected forms are to enable us to escape the circle of mere opinion and arrive at a solid foundation of knowledge and truth, our access to them must be "direct" or uncontaminated by already existing beliefs or theories: "Philosophy . . . persuades the psyche to trust nothing else but itself alone, when it thinks in itself of the beings in themselves" (83a1-b2). This fact, together with the close resemblance that must hold between the self-instantiating forms and the sensible properties or particulars that remind us of them, makes it attractive to model that access on sense perception. And, indeed, forms are said to be objects of *psychic vision* (83b4).

We know, however, that sensible properties (for example, the qualities and modes familiar from the *Republic*) are cognitively unreliable. The very sensible property (for example, being a case of paying a debt) which makes one act just, can make another unjust (100e8-101b2). The question arises, then, whether forms might not suffer from a similar defect. Could we not see equal sticks and be reminded in the right sort of way of the equals themselves, and then find that we had got hold of a property that could be instantiated by things which also instantiate inequality? Plato's answer is that we cannot: the equals themselves, and the equality they instantiate, can never be plainly unequal. This, I suggest, is why Plato concludes that forms cannot be identical to sensible properties. The former are *cognitively reliable*; the latter are not. Hence by Leibniz' Law, they must be distinct.

In addition to being self-instantiating, nonidentical to sensibles, directly cognizable, and cognitively reliable, a recollected form is *simple*. It is *incomposite (asuntheton)* (78c1-8); it has no parts. And it is *uniform (monoeides)* (78d5-7); it instantiates no properties except the one of which it is the form, and those categorial properties, such as simplicity and cognitive reliability, which all forms instantiate. If this were not so, if the fine itself or one of its parts could instantiate some property other than fineness, then recollecting the form would not guarantee finding the right property; in search of what fineness is, one might recollect the fine itself, only to focus on one of its parts, or on its goodness, thereby missing the very property one wanted to know. Hence simplicity, too, finds a natural home in the doctrine of recollection.

This brings us to the most famous feature of traditional Platonic forms, *separation (chōrismos)*.

According to Aristotle, Plato believed that forms are separate from sensible particulars (*Metaphysics* 987a29-b10, 1078b12-1079a4, 1086a31-b13). This, he argued, was the major problem with Platonic forms, the major difference between them and the immanent universals he favoured himself. But what exactly he means by separation is far from obvious, and must be tracked down.

In the *Categories* (1b25-2a10), Aristotle divides the beings into ten very general classes (*katēgorēmata*). There are *substances*, such as a particular man or horse, each of which is a "this such [*tode ti*]" (*Metaphysics* 1029a28); *quantities*, such as four feet or five feet; *qualities*, such as white or knowing grammar; *relations*, such as double, half, larger; *wheres* or *places*, such as in the Lyceum or in the marketplace; *whens* or *times*, such as yesterday or last year; *positions*, such as lying or sitting; *havings*, such as having shoes on or having armour on; *doings*, such as burning or cutting; and *undergoings*, such as being cut or being burned. Very roughly speaking, the division is between the particular things (substances) which have properties, on the one hand, and the various kinds of properties they can have, on the other.

In *Metaphysics* Zeta 1 (1028a31-b2), Aristotle claims that substance (*ousia*) is prior to the other categories in nature, in definition, and in knowledge. And he explains the natural priority of substance by saying that "of the other categories of things, none is separate [*chōriston*], but only it." In *Metaphysics* Delta 11 (1019a1-4), he explains that "something is prior in nature and substance when it is possible for it to be [*einai*] without other things, but not them without it." Hence it seems that separation is necessary, but not sufficient, for natural priority; that X is separate from Y just in case X can be without Y, and that X is naturally prior to Y if, in addition, Y cannot be without X.

We now have a formula which seems to encapsulate Aristotle's conception of separation. But how is that formula, which contains the multiply ambiguous verb 'to be', best understood? There are many putative answers.[53] But the most plausible interpretation, in my view, is that X is separate from Y just in case X can *exist* without Y. On this interpretation, separation amounts to *existential independence*, and Platonic forms are separate from sensibles just in case they are existentially independent of them.[54]

The next question we face is why, in the absence of express Platonic avowal of the existential independence of forms from sensibles,[55] Aristotle believed that Plato was nonetheless committed to it. The answer is to be found in his account of the argument which, in his view, led Plato to separate the forms.

That account begins in *Metaphysics* Mu 7:

> The belief in forms came about in those who spoke about them, because, in regard to truth, they were persuaded by the Heraclitean argument that all sensibles are always flowing, so that if knowledge and thought are to be of anything, there must, in their view, be some different natures, other than sensibles, which remain unchanged; for there is no knowledge of flowing things. . . . And they called beings of this sort forms. (1078b12-32)

That is to say:

(1) Plato believed that sensible particulars and properties were all flowing or changing.

(2) He also believed that knowledge and definition required unchangeable properties or universals, namely, the forms.

And, as a consequence of (1) and (2),

(3) Plato believed that forms were not identical to sensible particulars or properties.

This is a more or less accurate recapitulation of the argument with the sightseers and craft-lovers (2.8).

Later, in Mu 10, Aristotle summarizes the earlier passage and then continues as follows:

> But since they took it to be necessary that were there to be any substances besides the ones that are flowing and sensible they would have to be separate [*chōristas*] from them, and since they had no others available, they set apart the substances spoken of universally [the forms], so that it followed that universals and particulars were almost the same sort of thing. (1086b7-11; cf. 1086a32-b2)

This passage is regrettably murky, but the natural way to take it seems to me to be this:

(4) Because Plato believed that the forms were universals, he believed that they had to be instantiated by some kind of particular substance which, by (3), had to be nonsensible.

(5) Having nothing available to fill this rôle except the forms themselves, he made the forms into nonsensible, particular substances.

(6) In this way, the forms came to be universals, on the one hand, and both separate and particulars, on the other.

Aristotle seems to be claiming, then, that it is by making the forms into their own nonsensible particular instances, thereby making them both particular and universal, that Plato separated them from sensibles.

Let us reflect for a moment on what this means. Aristotle is not accusing Plato of thinking that forms can exist without being instantiated by particulars. He represents Plato as rejecting that idea just as firmly as he does himself. Hence separation is not the doctrine that forms exist whether any particular instantiates them. Rather it is the doctrine that they exist whether any *sensible* particular instantiates them because each of them is always instantiated by a nonsensible particular, namely, itself. Thus separation is firmly grounded in self-instantiation, and is as much a Platonic commitment as the latter.

In summary, the doctrine of recollection is introduced to solve the paradox of inquiry, and the archetypally Platonic forms of tradition—self-instantiating, nonidentical, directly cognizable, cognitively reliable, simple, and separate—are integral parts of that doctrine.

In Book 1 of the *Republic*, Thrasymachus argues that our ethical beliefs are determined by the interests of our rulers rather than by the facts. If he is right, no amount of elenctic examination of those beliefs will result in ethical knowledge. To work, the elenchus needs to draw on beliefs guaranteed to be free of this kind of influence. And recollected beliefs are, of course, tailor-made to fill this bill, for they are formed outside the rulers' sphere of influence.

But there is no mention of recollection in the *Republic*. The psyche lives through a cycle of deaths and rebirths, and each rebirth is preceded by an amnesia-inducing drink of the waters of Oblivion. But it does not acquire knowledge of forms while disembodied, nor recollect it when on earth. The virtuous are rewarded in heaven, not educated. And what they forget are their experiences, not the answers to Socrates' questions (614b1-621b6; 5.5).

Nor is the nexus of doctrines about forms that I have argued goes hand in hand with recollection present in the *Republic*. Forms in the *Republic* share two of the features of their traditional predecessors. They are cognitively reliable, and, because of that, they are not identical to sensible qualities or modes (2.8). But there the similarities end.

For, first, forms are never described as self-instantiating. There is nothing in the *Republic* remotely parallel to *Phaedo* 100c3-6 or *Symposium* 210e6-211b5. It is not the form of the bed that is really or in itself a bed, but the bed the philosopher-king makes by looking to the form (2.11). It is not the form of justice that is just, but either a polis or a psyche in which the structure which is justice inheres (368e1-2, 434d2-435b2; 5.2-4).

Second, because forms are no longer self-instantiating, they no longer possess the feature on which their separation from sensibles is based. Forms in the *Republic* are not logically unhygienic confusions of universality and particularity. They are real possibilities, ways actual things might be, "paradigms fixed in the nature of things" (*Parmenides* 132d1-2; 2.11).

Third, forms are no longer simple. The good itself, being (or including) the structure of the Kallipolis, is a rational or intelligible structure of forms of great complexity (500c2-501b7; 2.11). The form of justice is the complex property something has just in case each of its three component parts does its own work (441d8-e2).

Fourth, and most crucially for present purposes, forms are no longer objects of direct, non-theory-laden cognition. No one can know a form unless he knows the good itself. And no one can know the good itself unless he has mastered the mathematical sciences and dialectic and has had fifteen years' experience in practical politics (533a8-10; 2.11). The crowning moment of that arduous education may well involve something akin to illumination (*Seventh Letter* 344b3-c1), but the fact remains that forms are reached only through complex mathematical theories, not theories through recollection of theory-independent cognition of forms.

One final matter. Book 7 expresses moral qualms about using the elenchus on young people—it turns them into moral skeptics and sensualists

(1.3). But its employment is not simply restricted to the mature. It is restricted more narrowly to those thoroughly versed in mathematical science (537c9-539e2). Since Socrates used the elenchus both on acknowledged experts, such as Protagoras or Thrasymachus, and on people with no specialized training whatsoever, such as Polemarchus, this is another major Platonic recession from Socrates.

Plato raises a problem, then, about the Socratic elenchus to which recollection would provide a solution of sorts. The *Republic*, however, does not mention recollection, develops a new theory of forms, which unlike the traditional theory makes forms inappropriate objects of recollected direct cognition, and restricts the use of the elenchus to those who have received a specialized training in science.

In light of our discussion in 2.4-9, the explanation for these four facts is readily apparent. We never begin an inquiry in a doxastic vacuum; we are never entirely devoid of beliefs. Even the bound cave-dwellers who have received no appropriate education have some opinions about the objects they deal with and observe. And these opinions, however inadequate they may turn out to be, can be sufficient to put them in touch with a particular object of inquiry. At this point science takes over, pursuing its researches until it develops an empirically adequate theory of the object in question. It is this theory that is the source of the true beliefs the dialectician needs to free himself from the circle of opinion, tradition, and folklore. The honest toil of science has accomplished what recollection tried unsuccessfully to provide through thievery. But whereas recollection provides each person with an uncontaminated source of true belief, making each a suitable candidate for elenctic examination, science is not so democratic—only those who have studied it have access to the truths it uncovers. That is why when Plato discovered that science could provide the true beliefs he needed to solve the Meno paradox, he simultaneously abandoned recollection, the traditional theory of forms required by it, and the democratically employed Socratic elenchus (cf. 5.2).[56]

Plato, then, once held the traditional theory of forms. But in the *Republic* he abandoned it, and replaced it with a new and far superior theory. And it is this theory, in my view, that he continued to hold until the end of his career. He modified it in the *Sophist*, *Philebus*, and *Timaeus* and considered dialectical objections to it in the *Parmenides* and *Theaetetus*, but he never abandoned it. If I am right about this, and that is something that only extended investigation of the later dialogues can determine, then the *Republic* is the key to understanding Plato's thought as a whole. For, on the one hand, it explains why he gave up both the Socratic ethical theory of his early dialogues and the recollection-based theory of his middle dialogues, and, on the other hand, it contains his most detailed exposition of the theory he continued to hold, with modifications, in his late dialogues. It thus illuminates and unites all of his dialogues, early, middle, and late.

2.14 THE LIMITS OF PHILOSOPHY

We turn now from Plato's views about properties to his views about particulars, their relations to forms, and the type of access we have to them.

I have spoken of forms as real possibilities, and of particular things as instantiating forms. And while, as we shall see, this sort of talk needs no apology, there is more complexity here than it suggests. For although Plato does believe that forms are real possibilities, which can be instantiated by particular things, he does not think all forms can be completely or perfectly instantiated by such things. The Kallipolis, for example, is a real possibility; an actual polis can instantiate it. But it seems that no actual polis can completely or perfectly instantiate it (473a1-b2; cf. 4.2). The question is, why does Plato think this? Part of the answer is metaphysical. It emerges most clearly in the discussion of pleasure in Book 9. The other part is epistemological. It emerges most clearly in the discussion of the decay of the Kallipolis in Book 8.

In the course of an argument that the philosopher enjoys a truer and more substantial pleasure than the money-lover (3.6), a doctrine about *relational* forms emerges:

> Which partakes more of substance [*ousias*], being filled with bread, drink, relishes, and food generally, or being filled with true belief, knowledge, wisdom [*nou*], and, in sum, all of virtue? Judge it this way: that which holds to what is always the same [*aei homoiou*] and immortal [*athanatou*] and true [*alētheias*], is itself of that kind, and comes to be in something of that kind is more [*mallon einai*], don't you think, than that which holds to what is never the same [*mēdepote homoiou*] and mortal, is itself of that kind, and comes to be in something of that kind? (585b12-c5)

Now we know from 2.8 that "is completely" means "is completely F," for some form F, and that being completely F is a matter of completely resembling the form of F. Hence when we are told that one F "is more [*mallon einai*]" than another, this must mean that it more completely resembles the form of F than the other. This suggests that the present doctrine should be understood as follows. If there is a single relational form R (being filled), and two differently qualified instances of it (3.2), R_1 (being filled with knowledge) and R_2 (being filled with food), and x is related by R_1 to y, and z is related by R_2 to w, then R_1 more completely resembles R than does R_2 if (i) x and y are always the same, immortal, and true, while (ii) z and w are never the same, and mortal.

Consequently, what Plato seems to be offering us are the conditions under which one pair of things more completely or perfectly instantiates a relational form than another pair. But the conditions themselves need to be deciphered in order to be understood.

In the course of an argument for the immortality of the psyche (608c1-611a9; 3.8), disease is said to destroy the body by causing it "to be a body no longer [to mēde sōma einai]" (609c7). Then, at 610e10-611a2, immortality of the psyche is inferred from the fact that it "is always being [aei on einai]." And this is inferred, in turn from the fact that nothing destroys the psyche. It is difficult to resist the conclusion that for an F to be always being is just for it to be always being F, and that for it to be immortal is simply for it to be always and unalterably F.

The key to the proper understanding of truth is provided by the following passage: "And does the substance [ousia] of what is always the same [aei homoiou] partake any more of substance than of knowledge? . . . Any more than of truth? . . . And if less in truth, less in substance also?" (585c7-12). To partake fully in substance is to be an F that fully resembles the form of F (2.11). And to resemble a form F completely is to resemble completely the form of being knowable (2.8). Finally, to resemble completely the form of being knowable is to resemble completely being true. For what can be known must be true. Thus degree of resemblance to substance is tied to degree of resemblance to a form, which is tied to degree of resemblance to being knowable, which is tied to degree of resemblance to being true.

That both immortality and truth are to be understood in terms of completely resembling a form, and that being always the same is explicitly connected with substance, knowledge, and truth (585c7-12), makes it overwhelmingly likely that for an F to be always the same is for it always to resemble the form of F completely, and that for an F to be never the same is for it never to resemble that form completely.

We shall see in 3.6 that this interpretation fits in well with the remainder of Plato's argument. But one mark in its favour is already clear. If being always the same means being changeless, as some interpreters hold, then it is impossible to understand how something always the same could come to be filled with something else that is always the same, as Plato's argument requires.[57] But on the present proposal this idea presents no difficulties. For it means no more than that something that always resembles a form completely (a psyche) comes to be filled with something else that always resembles a form completely (knowledge).

Plato's doctrine about relational forms amounts to the following, then.

If there is a single relational form R, and two differently qualified instances of it, R_1 and R_2, and x is related by R_1 to y, and z is related by R_2 to w, then R_1 more completely resembles R than does R_2 if (i) x and y always and unalterably resemble their respective forms completely, while (ii) z and w never unalterably resemble their respective forms completely.

Consequently, the claim that the psyche and knowledge are always the same and immortal and true (585d1-6) means that the psyche always and unalterably resembles the form of a psyche completely, and that knowledge always and unalterably resembles the form of knowledge completely. The claim that the body and food are never the same and mortal (585d1-6) means that the body never unalterably resembles the form of a body completely, and that food never unalterably resembles the form of food completely. And understood in this way, these claims are intelligible products of Plato's theory. The psyche is always and unalterably a psyche (3.8), knowledge is always and unalterably knowledge. But a body is never unalterably a body; food is never unalterably food. Bodies decay and die. Food is digested or spoils. Hence while there is no obstacle to a psyche or knowledge completely resembling a form that is itself immortally and unalterably what it is (2.6, 2.8), neither a body nor food—nor, indeed, anything that is not immortally and unalterably what it is—can do this. Between the mortal and alterable, on the one hand, and forms, on the other, an insurmountable barrier to *complete* resemblance is set.

Since being always and unalterably F is a condition of completely resembling the form of F, which is a condition of completely or perfectly instantiating that form, we can now see why Plato thinks that while some forms can be perfectly instantiated, others cannot.

Although this doctrine does not surface until rather late in the argument, I think that its roots lie deep in Plato's views about forms and their relation to the good itself. A good F must instantiate the form of F. But, other things being equal, one thing is better than another if it is more resistant to change and decay. "The best things," as we are told in Book 2, "are least liable to change or alteration" (380e3). Hence a completely good F will be always and unalterably F. It will always maximally contribute to human happiness. And an F that is otherwise no better than a G will be a better F than the other is a G if it is always and unalterably F while the other is neither always nor unalterably G. That is why being filled with knowledge is better than being filled with food.

The psyche, then, completely or perfectly instantiates the form of a psyche. Knowledge completely or perfectly instantiates the form of knowledge. But neither the body nor food completely or perfectly instantiates the relevant form, although the philosopher-kings insure that each comes as close to doing so as a mortal and mutable thing can.

And therein lies a problem, which will lead us from metaphysics into epistemology. For can we not imagine the powers of the philosopher-kings to counteract death and decay growing without limit, growing to such an extent, in fact, that they can insure that things which instantiate forms instantiate them always and immortally, always perfectly? Plato's answer is that we cannot. The seeds of the ultimate decay of even the works of the philosopher-kings lie within the philosopher-kings themselves, and cannot be entirely removed.

In Book 8, Plato raises the question of how and why the Kallipolis will decay, putting his answer into the mouths of the Muses, who speak "in high tragic tones, as if they were speaking seriously, playing and jesting with us, as if with children" (545d7-e3). Perhaps for this reason Plato's views on this topic have proved difficult to understand.[58] But when the words of the Muses are deciphered, they reveal the limits of the philosopher-kings, the limits of philosophy itself.

According to the Muses, all living creatures have periods in which they produce good offspring and periods in which they produce bad ones (546a4-7), these cyclical periods being determined by arcane geometrical numbers:

> For a human birth there is a period determined by the first number in which root and square increases, comprehending three dimensions and four limits, of elements that make things like and unlike and wax and wane, and which make all things rationally correspond to one another. Of these elements, the lowest in the ratio of four to three, married to five, give two harmonies when cubed: the one, a square, so many times a hundred; the other, of equal length one way but an oblong, one side a hundred numbers obtained from the rational diameters of five, each reduced by one, or from the irrational diameters each reduced by two, the other side a hundred cubes of three. This whole geometrical number controls this kind of thing—better and worse [human] births. (546b4-d1)[59]

It is in part because of these cyclical periods that "everything that is born is liable to decay" (546a2).

But this is not the whole story where human beings are concerned. The Muses make this clear on two occasions. Immediately following their description of the geometrical number, they tell us that "this whole geometrical number controls this kind of thing—better and worse births [*geneseōn*]—and when your rulers, in ignorance of them [*has*; sc. the births],[60] join brides to grooms inopportunely, the children will have neither good natures nor good fortunes" (546c6-d3). Immediately preceding the description of the geometrical number they say the same thing with a small—but as we shall see, significant—addition:

> Even though the leaders of the polis you educated are clever, none-theless they will not succeed in obtaining good offspring or no off-spring by calculation together with sense perception [*logismōi met' aisthēseōs*], but it will escape them, and the day will come when they will beget children when they ought not. (546a7-b3)

So the other element in the Muses' explanation of the decay of the Kalli-polis is that, for all their prodigious knowledge, the philosopher-kings cannot know how to reliably bring couples together who, because they are at the right places in their cycles, will produce the best kind of off-spring.

The question is, why can they not know this? It is possible, certainly, that there is simply no answer to this question, that we here confront a brute fact. But I find that hard to believe. In my view, the Muses' answer is contained in the phrase "calculation together with sense perception." The philosopher-kings know what each quality, mode, figure, and form is. They know the answer to every Socratic "what is it?" question. They are able to calculate the Muses' geometrical number—certainly nothing in the story suggests that they cannot. But to know where in his cycle each guardian or ruler is, it is not enough to know what each property F is; one must also know whether this particular thing is F. And judgements of that sort involve sense perception, not just calculation or theory. But sense perception always involves an ineliminable margin of error. That is another reason why it is "natural for practice to attain less truth than theory," another reason it is impossible "to realize anything in practice exactly as it has been described in words" (473a1-4; 529a9-530b5).

It is these errors, initially inconsequential, but ramifying over time, that bring down the Kallipolis. For when, in the absence of better-equipped candidates, the children of improperly matched parents become guardians, they pay insufficient attention to music and gymnastics (546d5-8). And when the best of them actually become rulers, they are unable to manage the eugenics programme correctly (546d8-547a1), so that "lack of likeness and inharmonious irregularity arise in the polis, breeding war and hostility" (547a2-5). The Kallipolis then declines from an aristocracy to a timocracy.

According to the Muses, therefore, the philosopher-kings are subject to two limitations, one biological and somewhat arcane, the other cognitive and readily intelligible. The biological limitation is that the quality of the philosopher-kings is determined by where in a natural cycle their parents are when they are conceived. The cognitive limitation is that they must employ sense perception in order to realize their theories in practice.

On this reading, the Muses serve to remind us—as the gods so often do in Greek tragedies—that however much we come to know, we will never have absolute mastery of our fates. Not even philosophy can take all the chance out of marriage.

2.15 AGENTS AND SPECTATORS

The separation of facts and values, which our culture has now more or less institutionalized, so that to call something a value judgement is tantamount to dismissing it as a subjective prejudice, may be expressed in three distinct but related doctrines. The first is epistemological. No amount of knowledge of the way the world is (fact) tells us how it ought to be, or what we ought to do (value). The second is psychological. The power or capacity to acquire knowledge is independent of moral character. There is nothing a good person can know, or come to know, that a bad person cannot know, or come to know. The third is metaphysical. No fact is a value; no factual proposition entails an evaluative one. All three doctrines are rejected in the *Republic*. And this, to a large extent, determines its shape and preoccupations.

Since philosophy took "the epistemological turn" with Descartes, the enemy of knowledge has been skepticism—an abstract, intellectual enemy to be combated abstractly and intellectually. Plato does not much discuss epistemological skepticism. For him, as for Freud, the real enemy is desire-induced fantasy. We do not know how the world really is, not because, for all we know, we might be on Mars in jars, but because desire distorts our vision so that we see what we want to see, rather than what is in fact there. This is a concrete enemy, a real causal nexus in the world, which must be combated concretely. Hence for Plato, the solution to the problem of how to acquire knowledge, and escape the cave of fantasy, is not so much abstract and methodological as educational, political, and concrete. Intelligence is the slave of desire; desire is the slave of character and habit; character and habit are the joint products of a malleable nature, on the one hand, and training, education, and socialization, on the other; these things, in turn, are, in large part, under the control of the polis, its rulers, laws, and constitution. Epistemology has to start from there.

These facts explain why Thrasymachus is partly right. The powerful rulers can determine how their weaker subjects perceive and evaluate the social world, including themselves, precisely because the access that intelligence has to the facts is controlled by desire, which is shaped by the laws and constitution of the rulers. But they also explain, as we shall see more fully in subsequent chapters, why Thrasymachus is wrong. He is wrong, first of all, in thinking that the strong can exploit the weak for their own advantage. The desire to exploit in the name of pleonectic satisfaction is itself the chief kind of desire which locks the psyche in the bonds of fantasy and ultimate frustration. The tyrant, like the master in Hegel's *Phenomenology of Spirit*, is more thoroughly enslaved and exploited than any he exploitatively rules. Second, Thrasymachus is wrong in thinking that in his account of the polis he has reached a place in thought at which the spade is turned. Intelligence is the slave of fantasy-inducing desires. But the situation is remediable. For nature and the social and political institutions that shape desires can themselves be shaped by intelligence. Conditioning is never complete, the veil of fantasy is never totally opaque, as Thrasymachus' own theory demonstrates. We can discover which desires distort our vision, and how to diminish or counteract their influence through political change.

Here—and, again, I am looking ahead—the virtues enter the picture. For it is by inculcating temperance, courage, wisdom, and justice, through training, habituation, and education, that the Kallipolis can free the intelligence of some people from the grip of fantasy and superstition, enabling them to discover, through science and dialectic, what the world is really like. Hence it is that knowledge is available only to the virtuous, and virtue only (or only reliably) in the Kallipolis.

In common with all people, those freed in this way want what is really good for themselves: stable, long-term, maximal happiness. The difference between them and others is that, released from the bonds of fantasy, they know how to get it. The assumption here is that the true overall theory of the world as a whole, including the psychopolitical parts of it, enables them to discover what is really good for people and how to reliably achieve it. The values are the facts. Knowledge of values is factual scientific knowledge.

Forms are the correlates of this knowledge, the properties that things would have in the happiest of really possible worlds. Qualities, modes, and figures are the correlates of the various, and variously inadequate, world views that fall short of providing knowledge, the properties that things have in this world (qualities, modes) or in a world transformed by science (figures).

For this reason, forms are neither what we think of as real properties nor what we think of as mental or intentional properties. And the same goes for qualities, modes, and figures. The latter are certainly the products of desire-induced fantasy. But they are not, any more than forms, simply in people's heads. They are embodied in worlds that have been transformed by thought to accord with its own fantasy conception of the good. Hence the world around us, though we can kick it Dr. Johnson—fashion, is itself a fantasy, albeit one of stone and steel. It is not the real world. The world that embodies the forms, should it ever come into being, is the real world, the world in which our desires are really satisfied.

What goes for reality goes for truth as well. So, while we think of truth as an accurate representation of the way things actually are, Plato relates both truth and reality to the forms. A true theory of the world is one that captures the form of the good; the real world is the one that instantiates that form. For us truth is theoretical truth. For Plato it is practical truth. If the real world is the world in which our desires are really satisfied, the true theory is the one that tells us how to realize that world.

Plato's metaphysics and epistemology are, then, quite different from our own. Ours are for spectators, who, because their principal aim is to make a true, explanatory representation of the actual world, have the option of remaining aloof from ethics and politics. Plato's are for agents, who, because their principal aim is to change the world in order to realize the good, are involved in ethics and politics from the beginning.

Not long ago, it was possible to dismiss a whole philosophy because it did not respect the allegedly unbridgeable gap between facts and values. Happily, this is no longer so. The fact/value distinction, the "spectator theory of knowledge," the metaphysics of representing or mirroring, are all under attack.[61] This not only enables us to command a clearer view of theories that avoid these doctrines, it gives us an incentive to explore them—an incentive which is all the greater when the theories are as deep and imaginative as Plato's and elaborated in a work that is as great a contribution to art and literature as it is to philosophy.

THREE

PSYCHOLOGY

Indeed it is the possession of a body that is the great danger to the psyche, to our human and thinking life, which it is surely less accurate to describe as a miraculous entelechy of animal and physical life than as an imperfect essay— as rudimentary in this sphere as the communal existence of protozoa attached to their polyparies or as the body of a whale—in the organization of the spiritual life.   —PROUST

3.1 INTRODUCTION

Chapter 2 began more or less in the middle of Plato's theory of the psyche. As a result, there is much about the latter that we do not know. We do not know why the psyche has parts at all, or why it has reason, aspiration, and appetite as its parts. We do not know what precisely a psychic part is, or what it is for a part to "rule" a psyche. We do not know whether psyches are mortal or immortal, complex or simple. We know neither the ontology nor the laws of Platonic psychology. In this chapter, I shall try to fill these gaps in our knowledge by exploring Platonic psychology from the ground up. This will involve some repetition, but I think the gain in clarity and depth of understanding will more than compensate for it.

I shall begin with the notorious argument in Book 4 that the psyche has three distinct parts.[1]

3.2 THE TRIPARTITE PSYCHE

At the outset of the argument for the tripartition of the psyche, the following principle is introduced: "It is obvious that the same thing won't be willing to do or suffer opposites [*tanantia*] in the same part of itself in relation to the same thing at the same time" (436b8-9; cf. 436e8-437a2). Let us call this the *principle of opposites* (PO) and pursue its meaning.

The examples given of opposites—good and evil, just and unjust, fine and shameful, pleasure and pain (361c3-4, 475e9, 583c3)—make it clear that opposites are incompatible properties. PO does not seem to be about all such properties, however, but only about relational ones, or those that a thing can do, suffer, or be (436e9), in some respect or part of itself, in relation to something. And it cannot be about all relational properties, but only about relational forms. For of the four kinds of properties that Plato recognizes—qualities, modes, figures, and forms—only incompatible forms cannot be coinstantiated (2.8-9). That is why the argument for the tripartition of the psyche fairly bristles with the special linguistic devices Plato uses when forms are in view. On this showing, PO is simply the principle of noncontradiction, formulated in terms of properties rather than propositions, and restricted to properties that are relational forms.[2]

Although seen in this light PO is about as incontrovertible as a principle can be, there seem to be counterexamples to it, albeit of a distinctly Megarian stamp: "A man is standing still but moving his hands and head . . . therefore, he is moving and standing still at the same time. . . . Whole spinning tops move and stand still at the same time, for, while remaining in the same spot, they turn around their axes" (436c9-d8). Socrates does not dismiss these examples out of hand—the man and the top can be described as moving or as not moving. Instead, he diagnoses them as involving synecdoche, or the figurative transference of a property possessed by a part of a thing to the thing as a whole. Synecdochically speaking, the man and the top are both moving and standing still. Literally speaking, it is one part of the man or the top that is moving, and another part that is standing still. The moral to be drawn—and we shall see it drawn in the case of the psyche—is that all apparent violations of PO are synecdochical.

Another principle about relational forms that has a crucial part to play in the argument for psychic complexity is the *principle of qualification* (PQ): "Of all things that are such as to be related to something, those that are somehow qualified are related to a thing that is somehow qualified, as it seems to me, while those that are severally just themselves are related to a thing that is just itself" (438a7-b2; cf. 438d11-13). But unlike PO, PQ does not wear its interpretation on, or near, its face, so we must scrutinize the illustrations of it to discover what it means.

One set of these illustrations, and the set most relevant to the argument at hand, involves the forms of psychological relations:

Shall we say that there is a form [*eidos*] of desires of which what we call thirst and hunger are the clearest examples? . . . Isn't the one for drink and the other for food? . . . Insofar as it is thirst [*kath' hoson dipsa esti*], would it be for more than that of which we say that it is the desire? For example, is thirst thirst for hot drink or cold, or much or little, or, in a word, for drink somehow qualified? Or isn't it rather that where heat is present as well as thirst it would cause the desire to be also for something cold as well, and where cold for something hot, and where the thirst is much because of the presence of muchness, it will cause the desire to be for much, and where little for little? But thirst itself [*auto to dipsēn*] will never be for anything other than what it is in its nature [*pephuken*] to be for, drink itself [*autou pōmatos*], and hunger for food.—That's the way it is, he [Glaucon] said, each desire itself [*autē hē epithumia*] is only for that thing itself which it is in its nature to be for, while the desire for something somehow qualified depends on additions. . . .—And what about the various sorts of knowledge? . . . Isn't it the same way? Knowledge itself [*epistēmē autē*] is knowledge of what can be learned itself [*mathēmatos autou*], or whatever it is that knowledge should be of, while a somehow qualified knowledge [*epistēmē tis*] is of a somehow qualified thing. I mean something like this: when knowledge of building houses came to be, didn't it differ from the other kinds of knowledge and so was called building-knowledge? . . . And was that not because it was somehow qualified as different from all the other kinds? . . . And was it not because it was of something somehow qualified that it itself became a somehow qualified knowledge, and isn't this true of all crafts and kinds of knowledge? (437d2-438d9)

But other examples are not psychological at all.

Don't you understand, I said, that the greater is such as to be greater than something? . . . Than the less? . . . And the much greater than the much less, and the going-to-be-greater than the going-to-be-less? . . . And, further, the more in relation to the fewer, the double to the half, and everything of that sort; and, again, heavier to lighter, faster to slower; and, further, the hot to the cold and everything like them—doesn't the same hold? (438b4-c4)

This establishes beyond doubt that PQ concerns all relational forms and not just the forms of psychological relations. Like PO, PQ is a logical principle, not a psychological one.

It seems that the doctrine embodied in these illustrations, the doctrine on which PQ relies, is that relations have what later writers have called *formal* objects, and that it is these that Plato has in mind when he speaks of the *natural* object of a relation, or the thing to which it is in its nature related.[3] If this is correct, the natural object of a relation R is the property F that y must have if it is to be possible for x to stand in relation R to y. Thus drink is the natural object of thirst, for only what is drink can be thirsted after. Food is the natural object of hunger, for only food can be hungered for. What can be learned is the natural object of knowing, for only what can be learned can be known. The smaller is the natural object of the relation of being bigger than, for x cannot be bigger than y unless y has the property of being smaller than x. Clearly the list can be continued: the natural object of cleaning is what is dirty; of killing, what is alive;

of divorcing, one's spouse; of burning, what is combustible; of stealing, what belongs to another. Indeed, it is always possible to produce the natural object of a relation simply by modalizing the relation itself—the natural object of a relation R is always, trivially, the R-able. Hence the doctrine that relations have natural objects is more harmless than it might initially appear.[4]

Let us now test this hypothesis about what natural objects are against PQ itself. PQ says that if a relation is qualified, its natural object must be qualified too, although not necessarily in the same way, and that if the natural object is qualified, the relation must also be qualified:

> I do not mean that the qualification has to be the same for them both—for example, knowledge of health or disease is not healthy or diseased, and the knowledge of good and evil does not itself become good or evil—but that when knowledge became, not knowledge of the thing itself that knowledge is of, but knowledge of something somehow qualified, the result was that it itself became a somehow qualified knowledge, and this caused it to be no longer called knowledge without qualification [epistēmēn haplōs], but, with the addition of that particular qualification, medical knowledge. (438e1-8)

Now if the natural object of a relation were just its *material* object, or the item that happened to be its second term on a particular occasion, PQ would be transparently false. The material object of A's present thirst is x, that glass of wine in front of him. But it does not follow from the fact that A is thirsty for x that his thirst is a vinous one. He may simply be thirsty, and x the only available drink. Nor can we infer from the fact that A has an unqualified thirst for x that x is unqualified drink. There is no such thing as unqualified drink. But if, as I have suggested, it is formal objects which are under discussion, PQ becomes not only intelligible, but, perhaps, true. For if we qualify a relation, we must it seems qualify the property any object of that relation must have. And if we qualify the property in question, the relation, too, must be qualified. This is particularly clear when the natural object is just the relation itself modalized. Consequently, there is good reason to accept the hypothesis that natural objects are formal objects.

The argument for the division of the psyche into three parts follows directly upon the discussion of PQ.

> Then as for thirst, I said, wouldn't you include it among things that are related to something? Surely thirst is related to . . . drink. Therefore a somehow qualified thirst is for a somehow qualified drink, but thirst itself [dipsos auto] is neither for much nor for little, for good

nor for bad, nor, in a word, for drink somehow qualified, but thirst itself is in its nature only for drink itself [*autou pōmatos monon auto dipsos pephuken*]. . . . Hence the psyche of the thirsty, in so far as he is thirsty [*kath' hoson dipsēi*], does not want anything else but to drink [*piein*], and longs for this and is impelled towards it. . . . Therefore, if ever something draws it back when it's thirsting, wouldn't that be something different in it than that which thirsts and drives it like a beast to drink? For it cannot be, we say, that the same thing, with the same part of itself, in relation to the same, at the same time, does opposite things. . . . Now would we assert that sometimes there are thirsty people who are not willing to drink [*ouk ethelein piein*]? . . . What, then, should one say about them? Isn't it that there is something in their psyche that bids them to drink and something forbidding them to do so, something different that overrules that which bids? . . . Doesn't that which forbids such things come into being, when it comes into being at all, as a result of calculation, while what drives and drags is a result of affections and diseases? . . . Hence it is not unreasonable for us to claim that they are two, and different from one another, naming the part of the psyche with which it calculates, reason [*to logistikon*], and the part with which it lusts, hungers, thirsts, and gets excited by other appetites, irrational appetite [*epithumētikon*], companion of certain indulgences and pleasures . . . Therefore, I said, let these two forms [*eidē*] in the psyche be distinguished. (439a1–e3)

The inferential structure of the argument is clear enough:

(1) Thirst is a relational property.

Since the natural object of thirst is drink, it follows from PQ that

(2) The natural object of thirst itself is drink itself.

Therefore,

(3) The psyche of a thirsty person, insofar as he is thirsty, wants only to drink.

But

(4) Some thirsty people are not willing to drink (439c2–3), that is, they do not want to drink.

Therefore,

(5) Some people simultaneously want to drink and do not want to drink.

But

(6) Wanting to drink and not wanting to drink are opposites.

It follows from PO that

(7) They must be located in different parts of the psyche.
(8) Not wanting to drink is a result of calculation.
(9) Wanting to drink is the result of affections and diseases.

Therefore,

(10) The part of the psyche which wants to drink is irrational appetite; the part which does not want to drink is reason.

What is not clear is whether the inference goes through.

Many critics focus on (6). They point out, quite rightly, that a person can want something under one description, and not want it under another, without thereby violating PO. Oedipus wanted to marry Jocasta, he did not want to marry his mother; he wanted to exile the murderer of Laius, he did not want to exile himself. The result was a tragedy, not a violation of a logical principle.

This criticism, however, which appeals to the so-called opacity of psychological relations, does not cut very deep. For it seems clear that the psychological relations Plato has in mind are, like the nonpsychological ones treated together with them, referential or transparent, not attributive or opaque. And transparent psychological relations relate a psyche to something in the world regardless of how it is described or characterized. The person in Socrates' example wants to drink this stuff here in front of him; he also wants not to drink that same stuff. The conflict in his desires is real, not Oedipal.

Still, it might be objected that this does no more than get Plato out of the fire into the frying pan. For it might be claimed that what is impossible in the example is not that the person should have both of the desires in question, but that he should satisfy both of them with the drink in front of him.[5]

This is a telling objection, of course, but not yet a conclusive one. In a psychological theory of the sort advocated by Hobbes, for example, a desire for x is an "endeavour" or small motion of the psyche toward x; and an aversion to x is a motion of the psyche "fromward" x (as Hobbes puts it).[6] And in such a theory it is impossible for a single psyche (or psychic part) to desire x and be averse to x simultaneously. For nothing can be moving toward x and moving away from it simultaneously. Similarly, if desires are dispositions to move or act—as many philosophers believe—it is equally difficult to see how a single psyche (or psychic part) could both desire x and be averse to x. For it seems that nothing could be simultaneously determinately disposed to try to get x and determinately disposed to avoid getting x. Hence the objection is at best inconclusive—plausible theories of desire provide a safe refuge from it.

But did Plato actually hold such a theory? I think he did. First, he is quite prepared to countenance psychic motions. At 583e9-10, "pleasure and pain coming to be in the psyche" are described as "a sort of motion [*kinēsis tis*]." Throughout the argument for psychic division, desires are described as "drawing back," "driving," and "dragging" the psyche (439b3-6, 439c9-d2), language which strongly suggests a dynamical psychology. Second, all of the candidate nonpsychological counterexamples to PO involve motion. This suggests that the psychological ones also involve motion (439b3-11). Finally, in other dialogues Plato's commitment to psychic motions and a dynamical model of the psyche is clear. In the *Phaedrus*, which in my view is earlier than the *Republic* (2.13), the psyche is described as being "ever in motion [*aeikinēton*]" (245c5). And in the *Laws*, Plato's last dialogue, "wish, reflection, forethought, counsel, true and false opinion, joy, grief, confidence, fear, hate and love" are said to be "akin to motions [*kinēseis*]" (897a1-4). Whether or not Plato accepted such a view when he wrote the *Republic*, the point remains that he is on intelligible psychological ground in holding that a psyche (or psychic part) cannot simultaneously have a determinate desire for x and a determinate aversion to x. Which is not to say that it cannot dither ambivalently between the two.

The last two objections we shall consider are much more serious. Each confronts the basic mechanism of the argument for psychic division, one claiming that the mechanism generates more psychic parts than Plato wants, the other claiming that it does not conclusively generate any psychic parts at all.

The first of these objections is as follows. If conflicting desires must, for the reasons just canvassed, be lodged in distinct parts of the psyche, it seems that, instead of having just three parts, the psyche will actually be indefinitely divisible. Consider, for example, how appetite might be divided by conflict. A wants a hot drink and does not want a sweet one. He believes of x, the drink in front of him, that it is both hot and sweet. It seems to follow that he will have opposite desires in relation to x. So is not appetite itself complex? Has not the psyche as many parts as it has desires that can conflict?[7]

The second objection is this. The argument for psychic division implies that if A is related by R to x, and is simultaneously related by the opposite of R to x, then A must have at least two parts, one related by R to x and the other related by the opposite of R to x. But why is it A that is divided in this situation rather than x? Surely we could equally well claim that x has two parts, and that A is related to one of them by R and to the other by the opposite of R.

Let us return to A, and fill in some of the details of his predicament. A wants a hot drink. He believes that x is such a drink. So he wants x. Then he discovers that x is sweet. Being averse to sweet drinks, he wants not to have it. Finally, he discovers that x is the only hot drink available. At this point, he forms a new "compromise" attitude to x in which both of his original desires are, as it were, "represented." If his desire for hot drink is much stronger than his aversion to sweet, this compromise attitude might be a proportionately weaker desire for x. If his aversion is stronger, the compromise attitude might be a proportionately weaker aversion to x. If the desires are of comparable strength, the compromise attitude might be ambivalence or indifference.[8] But even if for some reason no compromise attitude is formed, one surely *can* be formed.

Because A's desires can form a compromise, there is little incentive to think that they divide the psyche. Like two forces that form a resultant force, they pull the psyche not in opposite directions, but in a new direction determined by both of them working together. Consequently, if we take the dynamical model of the psyche seriously, we need not see every conflict of desires as giving rise to psychic division. In particular, we need not see A's appetitive x-related desires as doing so. Only desires that conflict without being able to form a compromise will be of the right sort to give rise to a divided psyche.

But are there any such desires? I think there are. And I think that PQ, and the theory of natural objects, are Plato's attempts to characterize them, and to explain why they cannot form a compromise.

When attitudes form a compromise they are modified. And because they are modified, their natural objects must be appropriately modified too; modified relations must have modified natural objects. If no appropriate natural object is available for a compromise attitude, compromise is blocked; no modified natural object, no modified relation. In the example we were considering there is such a natural object. The natural object of A's desire for x is *hot drink*. The natural object of his aversion to x is *sweet drink*. The natural object of his compromise attitude to x is, surely, *hot sweet drink*. It is towards *this* that he is ambivalent, or has an appropriately weaker desire or aversion. And it is the possibility of forming such an object that explains why compromise formation is possible. But if no such object is available, A's desires will irremediably conflict, and his psyche will be divided by it.

Perhaps all this sounds a bit arcane. But the strange terminology and unfamiliar doctrine should not blind us to the underlying fact that, however we are to explain it, A's conflicting x-related appetites can compromise.

If this is Plato's line of thought, we would expect *his* examples of division-generating conflict to involve attitudes whose natural objects cannot combine, in the way that A's do, to form a compromise natural object. And that is precisely what we find.

Two of these examples are concerned with conflict between appetite and reason. The first (439a1-e3, quoted above) is a conflict between desires; the second (602c1-603a2) is a conflict between beliefs. The third example (439e3-441c3) is a two-way conflict between appetite and aspiration, on the one hand, and aspiration and reason, on the other. I shall discuss them in that order.

A, we are to suppose, has an appetitive desire—namely, thirst—to drink the stuff x in front of him. At the same time, he has a rational desire not to drink it. The latter has come into being as a result of calculation, and is strong enough to hold him back from drinking. The natural object of his thirst is *drink*. But what is the natural object of his rational aversion to drinking? Plato's answer must be pieced together.

Reason, the part of the psyche in which this aversion is located, is described as "exercising forethought on behalf of the whole psyche [*hapasēs tēs psuchēs*]" (441e4-5), or of "the whole psyche and the body" (442b6-7). It is also said to possess "within itself the knowledge [*epistēmēn*] of what is beneficial for each part, and for the whole composed of the community of these three parts" (442c5-8). Hence it is reasonably clear that what reason calculates about is what is jointly and severally most beneficial for the psychic parts and the body, or, in other words, the overall good of the person or psyche considered as a complex whole. And this more or less entails that a desire that comes into play as a result of such calculation, or which itself causes the calculation to take place, must have as a component of its natural object *what is good for the psyche as a complex whole*.

If this reconstruction is roughly correct, the natural object of A's rational aversion to x must be something like *drink not jointly and severally most beneficial to the psychic parts and the body*, or *drink not good for me*, or, most succinctly of all, *not-good drink* (438a1-5).

In this example, then, we have two conflicting desires in relation to the same x: an appetitive desire the natural object of which is *drink*, and a rational aversion the natural object of which is *not-good drink*. If these are to form a compromise attitude, it must be possible to combine their natural objects to form a new, appropriately qualified natural object for that attitude. But this is not possible. For the result of combining them is, after simplification, just *not-good drink* again. And this is not a new natural object, but the natural object of the original rational aversion. Consequently, these desires conflict irremediably and pull the psyche in opposite directions. It follows, given PO, that they must be assigned to distinct psychic parts.

Prescinding from theory, we might put the matter like this. A's rational x-related desire is engaged by a belief about what is best for his psyche as a complex whole. And that belief absolutely excludes his drinking x. Clearly, then, no compromise between his rational aversion to drinking x and his appetitive thirst for it is possible. If his thirst is satisfied with x, his rational aversion is frustrated, and A will have succumbed to weakness of will (3.3). If his rational aversion to x is satisfied, his thirst must be frustrated, and A will have exhibited self-control. So whether we accept Plato's way of looking at the matter or not, we have reason to go along with him—A's rational aversion to x and his appetitive thirst for x irremediably conflict.

The second example of conflict between reason and appetite reveals a different way in which the natural objects of psychological relations can prevent them from forming compromises.

By Zeus, I said, this imitating is concerned with something that is third from the truth, isn't it? . . . Now on which of the parts of a man does it have the power that it has? . . . Surely the same magnitude doesn't appear equal to our sight from nearby and from a distance. . . . And the same things appear crooked when we see them in water and straight when we see them out of it, and also [the same things seem to be] both concave and convex, due to sight being misled by the colours, and every confusion of this sort is clearly present in our psyche. And because they exploit this weakness in our nature shadow shows, puppeteering, and many other tricks of that kind fall nothing short of magic. . . . And haven't measuring, counting, and weighing proved to be most gracious helpers in such cases? As a result of them we are not ruled by a thing's looking bigger or smaller, or more or heavier; rather we are ruled by that which has calculated, measured, or even weighed. . . . And this surely must be the work of reason in the psyche. . . . And often to this [toutōi; sc. reason], when it has measured and indicates that some things are larger or smaller than others or that they are equal, the opposites are apparent [phainetai] about the same things at the same time. . . . And did we not say that it is impossible for the same thing to believe opposites about the same things at the same time? . . . The part of the psyche, then, that believes against measurement is not the same as the part that believes in accord with it. (602e1–603a2)[9]

In this case A measures x, and as a result comes to believe that it is not longer than y. But at the same time x continues to look longer than y to him, so that he simultaneously believes that the same x is longer than y. Hence A is related to x both by the relation of believing of it that it is not longer than y and by the relation of believing of it that it is longer than y. For Plato these relations are opposites, which must, therefore, be in distinct parts of the psyche.

Now it might seem that this is wrong. For, after all, the relations in question are not logical contraries. A can believe of x that it is not longer than y and simultaneously believe of it that it is longer than y. We need only suppose that, due to the opacity of belief, A does not realize that he is related to a single x in both these ways. However, just as in the case of conflicting desires, this sort of appeal to the opacity of psychological relations does not seem to have much bearing on the argument for psychic division. What we are to imagine, in the present example, is that on a particular occasion A responds to a single x, which he knows to be a single x, in two ways. On the basis of looking at it, he forms the belief that it is longer than y. On the basis of measuring it, he forms the belief that it is not longer than y. In such circumstances, there is no lurking opacity to prevent A from realizing that his x-related beliefs conflict, that he has, in effect, a single contradictory x-related belief. But if it is reasonable to think that no one can believe an explicit contradiction of this sort,[10] A's beliefs are genuine opposites, and no one psyche can have both of them in the same psychic part. So if a single psyche clearly *seems* to have both of them, we must infer that it has them in different parts of itself.

A good example of this sort of conflict in beliefs occurs when one is trying to perform a task such as trimming one's hair by looking in a mirror. One knows that left and right are reversed. Hence one knows that things are not as they are seen to be. But one's hand continues to react to visual clues as if they were. To explain one's odd behaviour in such circumstances, it is necessary to refer both to a "reasoned" belief about where things seen in mirrors actually are and to an ingrained or instinctual belief that things are where they are seen to be. There is, so to speak, one law in our members and another in our psyche.

However, not all pairs of apparently conflicting beliefs give rise to a divided psyche. Consider the following example. A believes on the basis of touch that x is round. At the same time, he believes on the basis of sight that x is not round but elliptical. Thus appetite, the seat of such beliefs (3.4), seems to stand in opposite relations to the same thing, and to be complex rather than unitary. Once again, the psyche is threatened with indefinite divisibility rather than tripartition. But this argument fails because the beliefs it appeals to are not genuine opposites. Their natural objects, *what feels round* and *what looks not round*, can form a compromise natural object, namely, *what feels round and looks not round*. And this compromise object is the natural object of a perfectly intelligible belief. A single thing can be sensed as round and not round without contradiction. That is precisely the basis of Plato's criticism of the epistemic adequacy of qualities and modes, which are defined in terms of sensible properties (2.8).

In Plato's example of conflicting beliefs, on the other hand, compromise is not possible. For forms are part of the picture. The question facing the psyche is, which of two opposite forms does x instantiate? Is it longer than y or not longer? Sight suggests one answer, reason the opposite. Both cannot be right. *What is both longer than y and not longer than it* is not the natural object of a possible belief—explicit contradictions cannot be believed. Here compromise is blocked by the logical incompatibility of the two natural objects involved. In the first example, it was blocked by the fact that one natural object was already part of the other, so that their conjunction resulted in nothing new. It is between these two poles that compromise is possible.

I turn, now, to the third example, or pair of examples.

> Now is the part that contains spirit and with which we feel anger a third part, or is it of the same nature as either of the other two?— Perhaps, he [Glaucon] said, it is the same as appetite.—But, I said, I once heard something that I believe, that Leontius, the son of Aglaion, was going up from the Piraeus under the outside of the North Wall when he saw some corpses lying beside the public executioner. He felt a desire to look at them, but at the same time he was disgusted and turned away. For a time he struggled with himself and covered his face. But, finally, overpowered by the desire, he pushed his eyes wide open, and rushed towards the corpses, saying, "Look for yourselves, you evil wretches, take your fill of the beautiful sight." . . . It certainly proves, I said, that anger sometimes makes war against the appetites as one thing against another. (439e3-440a6)

Here anger, a spirited desire, is distinguished from a sexual appetite— Leontius was notorious for his love for boys as pale as corpses. A page later, anger is distinguished from rational desires.

> It is not difficult, he said, to show that it is different. For even in small children one can see that they are full of anger right from birth, while as for calculation [*logismou*], some seem never to get a share of

it, and the majority do so quite late.—By Zeus, I said, that is well put. And in beasts too one can see that what you say is so. Besides, our earlier quotation from Homer bears it out, "He struck his breast and reproached his heart with words [sc. Endure, heart; you have endured more shameful things before (390d4-5)]." For here Homer clearly presents the part that has calculated about better and worse as different from the part that is angry without calculation. (441a7-c2)

Odysseus is outraged at the way his maids are behaving with Penelope's suitors, and wants to kill them at once. But this would spoil his plan to kill the suitors. Hence reason wants to postpone killing the maids, because this would be better.

In the Leontius example, appetite desires to look at the corpses, and so finds itself in conflict with aspiration, which desires not to look at them. In the Odysseus example, aspiration desires to kill the maids at once, and so conflicts with reason, which desires to postpone killing them. The question is, what is to prevent these conflicts from resolving themselves in compromise? As before, PQ must provide the answer. Plato must show that anger resists forming compromise objects either with an appetitive desire or with a rational one, that it has a natural object that remains unchanged when combined with the natural object of a conflicting appetitive desire and that does not change the natural object of a conflicting rational desire when combined with it.

We may get a clearer picture of this predicament by lapsing for a moment into formalism. Let O_a, O_s, and O_r be the natural objects of an appetitive, a spirited, and a rational desire respectively. The conditions O_s must satisfy may then be expressed in two simple equations:

$$O_a + O_s = O_s$$

and

$$O_s + O_r = O_r$$

But we already know some sample values for O_a and O_r, namely, *drink* and *drink jointly and severally beneficial to the psychic parts*. Putting these into the equations we get,

$$Drink + O_s = O_s$$

and

$$O_s \; + \; \begin{array}{c} drink\ jointly\ and \\ severally\ beneficial \\ to\ the\ psychic\ parts \end{array} = \begin{array}{c} drink\ jointly\ and \\ severally\ beneficial \\ to\ the\ psychic\ parts \end{array}$$

Hence it is reasonably clear that O_s must be something like *what is jointly and severally beneficial to a proper subset of the psychic parts*.

The question of whether the Leontius and Odysseus examples succeed in factoring out a third psychic component seems, then, to boil down to that of whether anger can be plausibly represented as a desire the natural object of which has this sort of partial good as a component. But a detailed exploration of that question is better left for the less abstract surroundings of 3.4, where I shall argue for an affirmative answer to it. For the moment, I shall simply assume that if anger has a natural object of this sort, then the argument for distinguishing aspiration from appetite and reason is as good as, because formally identical to, the argument for distinguishing them from one another.

With these details before us, we can see that the idea we set out to test against Plato's examples has borne fruit. For all three of those examples involve attitudes the natural objects of which make any compromise between them impossible. It seems reasonable to conclude that Plato intends only such irremediable conflict to divide the psyche. That is why the psyche has just three parts, not indefinitely many.

By the same token we can also see why Plato holds that such conflict divides the psyche rather than the object to which the psyche is related. For there is no general way to divide a drink into a part that is just *drink* and another part that is just *not-good drink*. If drinking anything at all would be bad for the psyche as a complex whole, then any part of a drink that appetite desires will be a part reason desires not to have.

PQ and the theory of natural objects, then, offer solutions to both of the criticisms from which we set out. They at once guarantee, contrary to the second objection, that conflict divides the psyche and, contrary to the first objection, that it does not overdivide it. Both PO and PQ are, therefore, crucial to the proper functioning of this subtle and ingenious argument for the tripartition of the psyche.

Moreover, underneath the pattern that is the finished structure of that argument another now stands exposed. This is the pattern formed by the three kinds of desires—appetitive, spirited, and rational—and the distinctive, and definitively different, relations of their natural objects to the good.

3.3 Origins and Merits of Psychic Division

Ontology, it is fabled, recapitulates philology. But argument seldom recapitulates aetiology. We usually arrive at a philosophical conclusion by one route and argue for it by another. For this reason origins often illuminate what argument conceals, showing us merits in the conclusion which are largely independent of the merits of the argument used to support it. Plato's division of the psyche is a case in point. The abstract argument for it is brilliant, but its conclusion has independent attractions, some of which are most clearly revealed by its intellectual origins. In this section, I shall try to uncover those origins and defend the division of the psyche without appealing to PO, PQ, and the rest.

In the *Protagoras,* and in many other dialogues written prior to the *Republic,* Socrates argues that akrasia (incontinence, weakness of will) is impossible: "No one who either knows or believes [*oute eidōs oute oiomenos*] that something else, which is in his power to do, is better than what he is doing, subsequently does the other, when he can do what is better" (358b7-c1; cf. *Gorgias* 475d4-e2; *Apology* 25d8-26a7).[11] All our experience tells against this conclusion, but it is very hard to resist just the same. For, surely, "no one freely goes for bad things or things he believes to be bad; it's not . . . in human nature to be prepared to go for what you think to be bad in preference to what is good. And when he is forced to choose one of two evils, nobody will choose the greater when he can have the lesser" (358c6-d4). One does not need a complex philosophical argument to be persuaded that akrasia is impossible, for this very principle, which has enormous intuitive plausibility, seems to entail that it is impossible.[12] What we really need is an explanation of how to reconcile the principle with the existence of akrasia.

The most commonly offered explanation of this sort is that belief or knowledge about what is best to do can be "overcome by desire," resulting in a choice of something other than the best:

> The opinion of the many about knowledge [*epistēmēs*] is that it isn't something strong, which can control and rule a person; they don't look at it that way at all, but think that often a person who possesses knowledge is ruled not by it but by something else, in one case desire [*thumon*], in another pleasure, in another pain, sometimes lust, very often fear; they just look at knowledge as a slave that gets dragged around by all the others. (352b3-c2)

But Socrates undertakes to show that this explanation is incoherent.[13] If he is successful, belief in the existence or possibility of akrasia will be hard to justify.

The many hold that

(1) The good is pleasure, and evil pain (353c3-355a5).

They also hold that

(2) Sometimes A knows or believes that x is worse than y, but overcome by desire for the pleasures of x, chooses x (355a5-b3).

But (1) licenses the substitution of "less pleasant" for "worse" in (2). And this yields

(3) Sometimes A knows or believes that x is less pleasant than y, but, overcome by desire for the pleasures of x, chooses x (355d1-356a1).[14]

And (3) is absurd, because

(4) One must choose the more pleasant over the less, the less painful over the more, and of competing pains and pleasures one must choose the pleasure if it outweighs the pain, and avoid the pain if it outweighs the pleasure (356b3-c1).

Hence the explanation of akrasia offered in (2) is unacceptable.

Now (4) presupposes two other principles that prove to be of great importance, namely,

(5) The strength of A's desire for x is always directly proportional to the amount of pleasure he believes x will yield

and

(6) All desire is for pleasure and nothing else.

For without (5) a stronger desire for a smaller pleasure might overpower the desire for a larger one. And without (6) A might fail to choose the larger pleasure out of a stronger desire for something other than pleasure. (5) and (6) do the real work against the many's explanation of akrasia. (4) is only a front for them.

But it is not only advocates of hedonism who have to worry about (5) and (6). This emerges quite vividly when we dissociate (5) and (6) from hedonism by resubstituting 'good' for 'pleasure' in them, resulting in

(7) The strength of A's desire for x is always directly proportional to the amount of the good he believes x will yield (presupposed at 355d1-e4)

and

(8) All desire is for the good and nothing else (*Gorgias* 467c5-468b4; *Lysis* 218c4-219d2).

For these two principles make it impossible to explain akrasia in *any* of the ways mentioned at 352b3-c2 (quoted above). With (7) and (8) in force knowledge or belief about what it is best to do cannot be overcome by desire.[15]

Thus Socrates' argument throws us back full force on the antiakratic principle which attracted us at the outset: "It's not in human nature to go for what you think to be bad in preference to what is good."

It cannot be reasonably doubted, in my view, that Plato developed the tripartite psychology of the *Republic* in response to this argument, and that he docketed (8) as its suspect premise; witness the prefatory remarks to PQ:

> Therefore, let no one catch us unprepared . . . and cause a disturbance, alleging that no one desires drink but rather good drink, nor food but good food, on the grounds that everyone after all desires good things, and that if thirst is a desire, it will be a desire for good, be it drink or anything else of which it is a desire, and similarly with the others. (438a1-5)[16]

(8) is illegitimate because appetitive desires are not for the good, however it is conceived, and spirited desires are not for the overall good. Since one of these desires can be stronger than the other, and either of them can be stronger than a conflicting desire for the overall good, akrasia of various sorts is possible after all, and for much the sort of reason that we were inclined to think. Leontius' spirited desire to avoid looking at the sexually attractive corpses is overcome by his appetitive desire to look at them. The philosopher-kings, who alone possess knowledge of the good, are least likely to act contrary to that knowledge (442c4-443b2). But there is no suggestion that it is impossible that they should.

The beauty of this account of akrasia is that it preserves all of our initial intuitions intact. Akrasia can occur, and it is caused by desire overpowering belief or knowledge about what it is best to do. But it is also true that no one voluntarily goes for what he thinks bad over what he knows or believes to be good. This is so because the desires that cause incontinent action do not aim specifically at the bad, which is not their natural object, but at food, drink, sex, or honour, which may, in some circumstances, happen to be bad. However, because they do not aim specifically at the overall good, which is not their natural object either, they can, if they are strong enough, give rise to voluntary actions other than those we know or believe to be best.

These desirable features of Plato's account of akrasia give us a strong philosophical motive to look sympathetically on his division of desires. But once we accept that division, his doctrine of the tripartite psyche is difficult to resist. For, as we are about to discover, that doctrine is to a large extent just the doctrine that there are different sources of motivation in the psyche, each with its distinctive goal, which can come into conflict with one another without being able to settle their differences.

On this reconstruction of its origins, the theory of the divided psyche was developed in response to Socrates' paradoxical views on akrasia, and completely undermines them. If I am right, Plato not only abandons the craft analogy and the Socratic elenchus, he also abandons that most Socratic of all doctrines, that akrasia is impossible (1.2).

3.4 THE CORE CONCEPTION OF THE PSYCHIC PARTS

At the heart of the argument for the division of the psyche, we find an extremely abstract core conception of the psychic parts. Appetite is the locus of good-independent desires, the natural objects of which do not have the good of the psyche or any of its parts as components. Aspiration is the locus of part-good-dependent desires, the natural objects of which have the good of only part of the psyche as a component. Reason is the locus of whole-good-dependent desires, the natural objects of which have the good of the whole psyche and its parts as a component. In this section, I want to bring this abstract characterization down to earth by showing that the desires, or conative attitudes, assigned to each of the parts fit the core conception of them. This will give that conception the concrete psychological content it currently lacks. In addition, it will give us a clear sense of the unity or integrity of the psychic parts themselves.

Appetite is introduced as the seat in the psyche of "lust, hunger, and, thirst" (439d6-9), desires elsewhere characterized as the "clearest [*enargestatas*]" examples of its contents (437d3) and (collectively) "the biggest and strongest thing" in it (580e1-2). This is more than sufficient sanction, I think, to take them as representative appetitive desires.

Now if A thirsts for x, x must be drink. That is why drink, or the property of being drink, is the natural object of thirst (3.2). But it does not follow from the fact that A thirsts for x that x must be good for A, or even that A must believe that it is good for him: x may be positively harmful for A even though he thirsts for it; A may be too far down the phylogenetic scale to be capable of reflexive beliefs about his own good— even flies can be thirsty. Consequently, the good of the psyche or of its parts, cannot be a component of the natural object of thirst. Thirst is good-independent. Parallel considerations show that the other representative appetites are also good-independent.

One wrinkle in this tidy account, which will be important in 3.6-7, merits discussion here. Appetitive desires fall into two major subspecies, necessary appetites and unnecessary ones (2.2). Are both good-independent, or are only unnecessary desires good-independent? There is substantial evidence in favour of the latter alternative. First, unnecessary appetites "lead to no good or indeed to the opposite" (559a3-6); necessary appetites are appetites "whose satisfaction benefits us" (558d11–e3). This ties necessary appetites to the beneficial, and thereby to the good (379b11), and severs unnecessary appetites from the good. Second, bound cave-dwellers, who are ruled by unnecessary appetites (2.5), are denied all access to the sun (the visible analogue of the good), since nothing projected onto their shadow screen corresponds to it (514a2–515c3; 2.12). Unbound cave-dwellers, however, who are ruled by necessary appetites, have access to the fire, which is a doppelgänger of the good (514b2–3, 515c8; 2.12). Again, unnecessary appetites are severed from the good while necessary ones are tied to it. Finally, the oligarchic man is described in terms that leave little room to doubt that necessary appetites are good-dependent. The oligarch "enslaves his other desires" (554a5–8), including his desires for food, drink, and sex, the better to satisfy his psyche's "insatiable desire to attain what [he] has put before [himself] as the good, namely, the necessity of becoming as rich as possible" (555b9–10, 562b3–4).[17]

However, if only unnecessary appetites are completely good-independent, what are the natural objects of necessary appetites and spirited desires? The most plausible candidates are these. Unnecessary appetites have natural objects that do not involve the good of the psyche or its parts; they are good-independent. Necessary appetites have the good of appetite as their natural object; they are appetitive-part-good-dependent. Spirited desires have the good of aspiration as their natural object; they are spirited-part-good-dependent. We shall see that the natural candidates are also Plato's, and that spirited-part-good-dependent desires are also appetitive-part-good-dependent (3.6, 3.9).

I turn now to aspiration, the dark horse of the psychic parts.[18] It is introduced as "the part with which we feel anger" (439e2–4). Under anger is included the rage of infants (441a7–9) and of beasts (441b1–2), Odysseus' outrage at Penelope's maids for their sexual misconduct with her suitors (441b3–c2), and Leontius' disgust with himself for his incontinent corpse-gazing (439e6–440a3). Hence our first task must be to discover what unites these seemingly diverse psychological phenomena. Only then will we understand why spirited desires are part-good-dependent.

Anger is an emotion which, like many other emotions, involves both a belief and a desire. If A is angry with B, then (typically) he must believe that B has purposely done something bad to him and desire to retaliate as a result.[19] Now the embedded belief here appears to be both reflexive and good-relative. If A believes that B has done something *bad* to him, some conception of his own good, and what conduces to it or detracts from it, must bear on his belief. This conception, however, and the level of self-conscious reflection it involves, need not be very sophisticated or explicit. An infant cries to be fed. If it is not fed soon enough, its cries turn to cries of rage. It is crying, not only because it is hungry, but out of awareness that its desire for food is being frustrated. When it is finally offered its mother's breast, it strikes at it in retaliation, trying, as it were, to restore the fit between the way things are, the real, and the way it thinks they should be, the ideal. What explains this pattern of behaviour, and is exemplified in it, is prototypical anger. Plato is on good psychological ground, then, in allowing that children "are full of anger [thumou] right from birth" (441a7-9), and that beasts too exhibit it.

Although the conception of his good involved in someone's anger need not be very sophisticated or complete, it may, of course, be very sophisticated indeed. Odysseus' anger at Penelope's maids involves an elaborate conception of his own honour and social standing and of the sort of behaviour due to him, and his household, because of it.[20] Leontius' anger at himself for gazing at the corpses involves a sophisticated conception of what sort of sexual interests it is proper for a man like himself to have. Hence anger stretches from infantile rage to sophisticated self-disgust.

Because anger essentially involves a belief about the good, and a desire which engages with it to produce appropriate restorative action, anger is good-dependent. But since the conception of the good need not be either sophisticated or complete, there is no reason to think that anger is whole-good dependent. Anger falls "between" good-independence and dependence on the whole good.[21] This makes it intelligible, if not yet fully intelligible, that it should be classed as part-good-dependent.

By contrast with the core conceptions of appetite and aspiration, the core conception of reason's constituent desires is clear-cut. For no one is likely to deny that we sometimes calculate about what it would be in our overall best interests to do, and act on the calculation. If we are to explain such actions in the usual way, by reference to our beliefs and desires, some of our desires must have our overall good as their natural object. In Plato's tripartite psychology such desires will be whole-good-dependent.

All things considered, then, the core conception of the conative constituents of the psychic parts is possessed of a reassuringly high degree of extratheoretic, folk-psychological cogency. At the same time, the psychic parts themselves have begun to take on a measure of unity. For we can now see them as congregations of conative attitudes united by the degree of their good-dependence. It is a vision that merits elaboration.

If all rational desires are whole-good-dependent, they all have a common aim or goal. But this means that they form a single unified source of motivation in the psyche, pushing it in a single direction. Reason is a dynamical unity in the psyche, then, not just a collection of desires that share a common characterization. It remains to be seen whether the same can be said of aspiration and appetite. For in their case things do not look nearly so straightforward.

Anger is Plato's canonical spirited desire. But many other emotions—fear, jealousy, shame, pride—also seem to fit the core conception of spirited desires. For each of them involves a conception—an enrichable and expansible conception—of the good, and a desire to keep us in line with that conception when our own behaviour, or that of others, disturbs the match between reality and our ideals.[22] Now there is no *a priori* reason to believe that a single conception of the good will always be involved in all of these emotions. But neither is there any *a priori* reason to believe that it is impossible that this should be so. Conceptions of the good are acquired through training, education, and socialization. As things stand these shaping forces are not designed to promote maximum integration in our emotions. But if they were so designed, as they are in the Kallipolis, then anger, fear, jealousy, shame, and pride could all involve the same conception of the good. And in this condition, at least, these spirited desires too would form a single source of motivation, urging the psyche in a single direction.

Finally, we come to appetite. The natural objects of the desires for food, drink, and sex, being good-independent, have no common content out of which a common goal can be fashioned. That is why appetite is characterized as "multiform," and as lacking a single name: "as for the third part, because of its multiform nature, we had no one name to give it" (580d11-e1; 590a7). There is, however, one thing that is the best means of satisfying it, namely, money: "we have called it the money-loving part because such appetites [lust, hunger, and thirst] are best satisfied by means of money" (580e5-581a1). Hence appetite can also become at least a pseudo-unity in the psyche if all of its constituent desires are so moderated by training in a craft (4.6) that they promote the acquisition of money. That is why money, or the pleasure of making it (581c8-e4; 3.6), is represented as the good of appetite, and the natural object of necessary appetite (555b9-10, 562b3). Making money is not intrinsically pleasant—it is a C-good (357c5-d2; 1.9). But because money is a means to the pleasures of food, drink, and sex, making it takes on an aura of derivative pleasantness, which may in the end make it seem intrinsically pleasant.[23] When the pleasure of making money is said to be a distinct pleasure, I think something like this is meant. So although unnecessary appetites are not a single unified motivating force with a single aim or goal, necessary appetites are (2.12). They, like rational and spirited desires, push the psyche in a single direction.

On this showing, necessary appetitive desires, spirited desires, and rational desires have a belief that something is the good as one component, and a desire to realize that good as another. Consequently, they are somewhat like emotions as these are usually understood. And the psychic parts these desires constitute—appetite, aspiration, and reason—are, among other things, unified sources of motivation, each urging the psyche towards its own peculiar good (3.5).

In addition to containing desires or conative attitudes, appetite, aspiration, and reason also contain cognitive ones: "And did we not say that it is impossible for the same thing to believe opposites about the same things at the same time? . . . The part of the psyche [appetite], then, that believes against measurement is not the same as the part [reason] that believes in accord with it" (602e1-603a2; 3.2). Consequently, we must try to determine how cognitive attitudes are distributed among the psychic parts, and how their presence affects our conception of those parts as unified centres of motivation.

Here the theory explored in Chapter 2 comes to our aid. All beliefs involve properties (2.8). And these properties will be either qualities, modes, figures, or forms (2.6-7). If the psyche that has the beliefs in question is ruled by unnecessary appetites, its beliefs will involve a quality; if it is ruled by necessary appetites, its beliefs will involve a mode; if it is ruled by aspiration, its beliefs will involve a figure; if it is ruled by rational desires, its beliefs will involve a form. I suggest, therefore, that a belief belongs to a psychic part just in case the property it involves is of the most cognitively reliable kind to which a psyche ruled by that part has cognitive access. Thus beliefs involving qualities are assigned to appetite (603a7), and beliefs involving forms to reason (603a4-5).

But this suggestion does not as yet explain anything. We want to know why beliefs that contain qualities are assigned to appetite.

I suspect that Plato's line of thought is this. The parts of the psyche are akin to primitive psyches. Each is equipped with the appropriate desires, and with intelligence. And just as a psyche ruled by the desires in a part has its cognitive resources determined by those desires, so a psychic part has its cognitive resources determined by its constituent desires. Thus appetite continues to exercise perceptual-thought even when it is part of a reason-ruled or aspiration-ruled psyche, which, as a whole, exercises dialectical-thought, or scientific-thought. Even in such circumstances appetite's beliefs remain those of a complete psyche with access to qualities. That is why there can be the kinds of conflicts in beliefs that Plato cites. In a reason-ruled or aspiration-ruled psyche, however, appetite's beliefs are not the causally effective ones, as they are in a psyche in which appetite itself rules. There, if conflict occurs, it is reason's or aspiration's beliefs that win out.

If this conjecture about the cognitive contents of the psychic parts is correct, it becomes attractive to think of these parts as simply instantiations of the complete powers themselves, which realize the powers to different degrees depending on how the psyche of which they are a part is ruled. Dialectical-thought is fully realized, and gains access to forms, only in a psyche ruled by reason. In other psyches it fails to develop its full potential because its cognitive development is limited by the nonrational desires in the ruling part (2.12). Scientific-thought is fully realized, and gains access to figures, only in a psyche ruled either by reason or by aspiration. Folk-wisdom is fully realized, and gains access to modes, only in a psyche ruled either by (necessary) appetite or by aspiration or by reason.

Appetite, aspiration, and reason now emerge, as they did in 2.12, not simply as unified sources of motivation, each pushing the psyche towards its own peculiar good, but as psychic unities, each with its own characteristic vision of reality, its own peculiar *Weltanschauung*, to impose on the psyche it rules.

3.5 PSYCHIC RULE

The work of a psychic part, its psychological rôle or function, is either to rule the psyche or to be ruled in it: "Every part . . . does its own work be it ruling or being ruled" (443b1-2). Hence to develop the core conception of the psychic parts further we must investigate the notion of psychic rule.

Psychic rule is introduced in Book 4 by analogy with political rule (441d5-442b3; quoted below). But the most illuminating discussion of it in strictly psychological terms occurs in Book 9. "As there are three parts, there are also, it seems to me, three pleasures, one peculiar to each part, and so with desires and rules [*archai*]" (580d7-8). Appetite's "pleasure and love are concentrated on profit" (581a3-4); aspiration's are concentrated on being honoured and gaining victories (581a9-b2); reason's are concentrated on gaining wisdom and learning the truth (581b5-9). Because of this (581c3), and because different psyches are ruled by different psychic parts (581b12-c1), "we say that there are three primary types of people: philosophic, victory-loving, and money-loving" (581c3-4). Moreover, these people find most pleasant a life devoted to the peculiar pleasure of the part that rules in them:

> If you chose to ask these three kinds of people in turn which of these lives is the most pleasant [*hēdistos*], each would give the highest praise to his own. The money-lover will say that compared to making a profit, the pleasures of being honoured or of learning are worth nothing except insofar as they produce money. . . . And what about

the honour-lover . . . doesn't he believe that the pleasure of making money is vulgar and, on the other hand, that learning—whatever learning doesn't bring honour—is smoke and nonsense? . . . And what are we to think the philosopher considers the other pleasures are worth compared with that of knowing the truth as it is, and always enjoying it while he learns? Won't he hold them to be far behind? In fact, he calls these pleasures really necessary because he would not want them if they were not necessary for life. (581c8-e4)

It seems clear, then, that a part rules a psyche just in case the whole psyche (or the person whose psyche it is) aims at the peculiar pleasure of that part, believing it to be more pleasant than any other. Hence rule has both a conative aspect and a cognitive aspect, corresponding to the two aspects of the psychic parts themselves.

One particularly clear piece of testimony in favour of this account of rule is provided by the vivid portrait of the oligarch in Book 8. The oligarch is ruled by necessary appetite (559d1-2; 2.3). Consequently, if the above account of rule is correct, he ought to believe that wealth is better than anything else, and pursue it in preference to honour or learning. And this is precisely how he is characterized. The oligarch "prizes wealth above everything" (554a1-2), and sets it before himself as the good (562b3-4, 562b9-10). He reduces reason and aspiration to slaves, forcing them to aid in the acquisition of wealth rather than allowing them to go after their own peculiar pleasures: "The first he will not allow to reason about or examine anything else than how a little money can be made into much, while he does not allow the other part to honour or admire anything else but wealth and wealthy men, or to have any other ambition than the acquisition of wealth, or of anything which may contribute to this" (553d2-7). Hence his only good is to become as rich as possible (555b10). Nothing else matters, except insofar as it contributes to that end.

Although rule always amounts to the same double determination of belief and desire, it has two crucially different sub-species:

I think we shall say that a person is just in the same way that a polis is just. . . . We have surely not forgotten that this polis was just because each of the three classes in it was doing its own work [to heautou . . . prattein]. . . . Then we must remember that for each of us, too, the one in whom each part does its own work will himself be just and do his own work. . . . Isn't it proper, then, for reason to rule, since it is wise and exercises forethought on behalf of the whole psyche, and for aspiration to obey and be its ally? . . . These two parts, then, thus nurtured [in music and gymnastics], and having truly

learned their own work, will exercise authority over appetite . . .
and they'll keep watch over it lest it be filled with the so-called pleasures of the body and become big and strong and no longer do its
own work, but attempt to enslave and rule over what is not properly
ruled by its kind, subverting everyone's entire life. (441d5-442b3)

When reason rules it is doing its own work. This is *proper rule*. When
appetite or aspiration rules it is not doing its own work. This is *improper
rule*.

Proper rule differs from improper rule in two distinct, but intrinsically
related, ways. The first is a matter of ends or goals, and the capacity to
achieve them. Only reason's constituent desires have "the good of the
whole psyche and of the body" (442b6-7) as their natural object. Only
reason "has within itself the knowledge of what is beneficial for each part,
and for the whole composed of the community of these three parts"
(442c5-8). Consequently, when the whole psyche aims at reason's peculiar good, it is aiming at the peculiar goods of the other parts as well. That
is why reason is "doing its own work" (441d12-e4) in ruling. For "what
is best for each thing is also most properly its own" (586e2; 3.6). And
what is best for reason, and for the other parts as well, is that reason rule
(586d4-e2, 590c8-d6; 2.11-12, 3.7).

The second difference between proper and improper rule is more a
matter of means than of ends. Reason does not force appetite and aspiration into pursuing its peculiar good (which is also their own). It is not an
enlightened despot governing through *force majeure*. Instead, reason "persuades" them to consent to its rule through a process of training and education begun in childhood and designed by the philosopher-kings, who
are themselves ruled by reason, to have this very effect. As Socrates puts
it, "The rulers and the ruled share a common belief [*homodoxōsi*] that reason should rule" (442c11-d1). Appetite and aspiration, on the other hand,
"enslave" the psyches in which they rule (442b1, 553d2, 554a7, 569c3-4,
575a1-2). Each uses its superior strength (442a8) to force the other parts
into pursuing its peculiar good, instead of persuading them through education and training (548b7-c2, 554d1-2). A properly ruled psyche exhibits the harmony consent brings (441e8-442a2, 442c10-d1, 443d3-e2),
while an improperly ruled psyche exhibits the discord which is the result
of coercion (554d9-e5).

The question we now face is, how does reason bring it about that appetite and aspiration agree with it that it should rule? What precisely does
such agreement or consent consist in?

Through training and education, all necessary appetites can come to
have the same good, the good of appetite, as a component of their natural

objects. The same is true, *mutatis mutandis*, of spirited desires. Surely, then, further training and education might bring it about that the good of appetite, the good of aspiration, and the good of reason (that is, the good of the whole psyche) are consonant. Appetite might pursue, and be satisfied by, just the amount of money, and aspiration might pursue, and be satisfied by, just the amount of honour, that reason judges best overall. In this event, the goods of the psychic parts will be parts of the good of the whole (3.7). And just as the parts are unified by having a single good to aim at, the psyche itself will be unified in the same way. Thus the man whose psyche is properly ruled

> orders the things that are really his own business [*tōi onti ta oikeia*] and rules himself, he puts himself in order, becomes his own friend, harmonizes the three parts, exactly like the three notes in a harmonic scale, lowest, highest, middle, and any other parts there may be in between as well, binds them all together, and so becomes entirely one from many [*pantapasin hena genomenon ek pollōn*], moderate and harmonious. (443d3-e2; cf. 462a9-d5)

So harmony, or consonance among the desires in the different psychic parts about what to pursue, seems to make good psychological sense.

But, as we saw in the previous section, the psychic parts have cognitive components as well as conative ones. They have distinctive *Weltanschauungen* as well as distinctive goals. Indeed, they have distinctive *Weltanschauungen* because they have distinctive goals (2.12). That is why harmony in their conative components brings about harmony in their cognitive components as well. If appetite is satisfied by precisely the amount of money reason judges to be best, it will identify the good with a structure of a polis in which it reliably gets just that much money throughout life (that is, with a mode of the good). In the same way, if aspiration is satisfied by precisely the amount of honour reason judges best, then it will identify the good with a structure of a polis in which it reliably gets just that much honour throughout life (that is, with a figure of the good). The result is that appetite, aspiration, and reason will each believe that the structure of the Kallipolis is the good. Since the Kallipolis is ruled by the philosopher-kings, who are themselves ruled by reason, to believe that its structure is the good is to believe that it is good that reason rule. But to believe that it is good that reason rule is just to believe that reason should rule.

All things considered, then, we need not be skeptical about proper psychic rule, or the equivalent notions of psychic harmony and psychic unity. Certainly the notion of psychic rule is introduced by analogy with political rule. But it is not an irreducibly political concept forever tainting

Platonic psychology with ineliminable and unexplanatory metaphoricity. Instead, it is a fully intelligible psychological concept, which is interestingly analogous to the more familiar political concept used to introduce it.

3.6 PLEASURES

To put the finishing touches to the core conception of the psychic parts we must interrogate Plato's rather complex account of the peculiar goods of those parts. In this section, we shall examine his account of what is, in effect, the content of those goods. In 3.7, we shall look at his account of their form. What is meant by form and content will become clear as the discussion proceeds.

The account of content to which I refer is contained in the second and third of the triad of "proofs" (580c9-d1, 583b1-2) in Book 9 that the philosopher-king is "the best, the most just, and the most happy," while the tyrant is "the worst, the most unjust, and the most wretched" (580b9-c3). Instead of dismembering those proofs by trying to extract that account from them, however, I shall first present them *in toto*, and only then abstract the pertinent material. We shall then have three candidate peculiar goods. It will remain to show that they do indeed fit the core conception of the goods of the psychic parts, for it will be far from obvious that this is so.

Because the psyche has three parts, "there are also . . . three pleasures, one peculiar to each part" (580d7-8). Appetite's "pleasure and love are concentrated on profit," aspiration's are concentrated on victories and honour, reason's are concentrated on learning and knowing the truth (581a3-b7). These pleasures are the contents of the candidate goods of the psychic parts (562b3-4, 581a3-4; 3.7). They are also the major determinants of the relative happiness of the lives of the different types of people in whose psyches those parts rule (3.7).

The chief obstacle to discovering which life is in fact most pleasant, which life most happy, is that each of the three types of people awards the palm of victory to his own life and pleasure (581c8-e4).

> Since, then, there is conflict between the several forms of pleasure [*tou eidous hai hēdonai*], and between the lives themselves, not about which is the finer and which the more base, which the worse, which the better, but about which is itself the more pleasant and free from pain, how can we determine which of them speaks more truly? (581e6-582a2)

The second of the proofs of the superiority of the philosophic life (580c9-583b2)—the first explicitly about pleasure—turns on a proposal about how disputes of this sort are to be resolved: "By what must things that are going to be well-judged be judged? Isn't it by experience [*empeiriai*], dialectical-thought [*phronēsei*], and argument [*logōi*]? Or could anyone use better standards than these?" (582a3-6). But if these are the proper standards, then we must favour the philosopher's estimation of the relative pleasantness of the three types of lives over those of the honour-lover and money-lover. For, first, he has experienced the pleasures available in the others' lives since his youth (582a8-b2), whereas "the pleasure to be gained from contemplating being cannot be had by anyone except the philosopher" (582c7-9). Second, he alone has "gained his experience in the company of dialectical-thought [*phronēseōs*]" (582d4-5). Third, he alone is a master of argument (582d7-e5).

Since the philosopher awards first prize to his own life and pleasure, second prize to the life and pleasure of the honour-lover, and third prize to the life and pleasure of the money-lover, this is the authoritative and reliable ranking of these lives and pleasures in terms of pleasantness and happiness (583a1-b2).

Two common objections to this argument merit discussion. The first is that it fails to get off the ground because it falsely presupposes that judgements of relative pleasantness are liable to error and to assessment by objective standards when in fact they are subjective and incorrigible.[24] But not only is this objection not decisive, it is not even clearly relevant. It is not decisive because it simply assumes that first-person avowals of relative pleasantness are incorrigible when, in fact, their status is controversial. It is not clearly relevant because the pleasures in question are not private or subjective experiences on the order of tingles, tickles, and thrills, to which the individual might, with some vestige of philosophical plausibility, be argued to have "privileged access." No such feelings could produce money (581c10-d3) or honour (581d5-8), or be necessary to sustain life (581e3-4). The pleasures in question are activities, such as eating, having sex, making money, gaining honour, or learning the truth. And to determine their relative pleasantness is not to rank the relative intensities of the private pleasurable sensations they may produce, but to rank the activities themselves considered as pleasures, or as essential components of pleasures (1.11). It is to ask, for example, whether they are absorbing, whether they are completely satisfying, whether they become boring in the long run, whether they can be engaged in throughout life, whether they can be engaged in continuously or only from time to time, whether they necessarily involve pains or frustrations of any sort, and so on. Consequently, we are on intelligible ground in favouring the judgement of the philosopher. For experience, sound practical wisdom, and dialectical skill are precisely the things that enable us to answer questions of this sort well.

The second objection is this. Only someone who devotes himself exclusively and wholeheartedly to sensual indulgence, or the winning of honours, knows what these lives, and the pleasures they afford, are really like. The philosopher simply has not sufficiently tasted them for his assessment to have any real authority. He no more knows the pleasure that seduction brings to Don Giovanni, or that triumph in battle brings to Ajax, than the child labouring over her scales does the pleasure that *Die Walküre* or *Parsifal* affords the perfect Wagnerite.[25]

There is no denying that this objection is initially appealing. But reflection exposes its weakness. To determine the bearing of experience on the authoritativeness of testimony, we need to know what the effects of the experience are. Acid freaks claim that only the experienced tripper knows the pleasures that LSD has to offer. But we know too much about the effects of LSD on the general capacity to make sound judgements and accurate discriminations to take their claim at face value. In the same way, Socrates himself argues that

> it is not possible for a psyche to have been brought up from youth among wicked psyches, to have associated with them, and itself to have indulged in every kind of injustice, and to be able to judge other people's unjust deeds from its own case as it might diseases in the body. Instead, it must itself have been inexperienced and uncontaminated by wicked habits when it was young, if it is to be fine and good and make healthy judgements about just things. . . . Therefore, the good judge must not be young, but old, one who has learned late what injustice is, not from observing it in his own psyche, but from having studied it in other people as something alien to himself, recognizing after a long time that it is naturally bad, not by having experienced it [*ouk empeiriai*], but through knowledge [*epistēmēi*]. (409a1–c1)

To decide whether experience of a particular sort brings authority, rather than the special, and suspect, insights of faith, addiction, or delusion, we need a general theory of how the psyche works. Our procedure here must be modelled on *The Future of an Illusion*, rather than on opinion polls. Without such a theory to back it up, as Plato's theory underwrites the authority of the philosopher, the present objection cannot be more than inconclusive. Don Giovanni and Ajax might be like the perfect Wagnerite, or they might be like the acid freak.

In the third proof of the superiority of the philosophic life (583b2–588a11), which is described as "the greatest and most decisive overthrow" (583b6–7), the account of pleasure is set out in greater detail, and a psychological explanation of how it is possible for the money-lover and honour-lover to overestimate the pleasantness of their favourite pleasures is provided.

Between pleasure (*hēdonē*) and its opposite, pain (*lupē*) (583c3),[26] there is such a thing as being neither pleased nor pained (583c5), this being a kind of psychic calm (*hēsuchia*) (583c7-8). But when this state follows upon one of pain it is pleasant: "And there are many other circumstances in which you find that people, while in pain, praise freedom from pain, and relief from that, as the most pleasant, and not enjoyment [*to chairein*] itself" (583d6-9). Conversely, "whenever a person's enjoyment of something ceases, then this cessation of pleasure is painful" (583e1-2). It follows that the same state "will at times be pain and at times pleasure" (583e4-5). But this is impossible. For it is not "possible for that which is neither [pleasure nor pain] to become both" (583e7).

The same conclusion can be reached by considering the nature of pain and pleasure: "Surely, both pleasure and pain coming to be in the psyche are a sort of motion aren't they? . . . And didn't we see just now that to feel neither pain nor pleasure is a kind of calm of the psyche and an intermediate state between the two?" (583e9-584a2). So, once again, "it cannot be right to think that the absence of pain is pleasure, or the absence of enjoyment pain" (584a4-5).

Finally, there are pleasures which "are not preceded by pain, but they suddenly become extraordinarily great, and when they cease they leave no pain behind" (584b6-8). The pleasures of smell are of this sort, in Plato's view. We are pleased by the smell of night-flowering jasmine on the offshore breeze, but our pleasure is neither preceded nor followed by pain.

Therefore, even though the calm state between pleasure and pain is pleasant when it follows pain, and painful when it follows pleasure, "there is nothing sound about these appearances so far as the truth about pleasure is concerned [*pros hēdonēs alētheian*], but they are a kind of illusion" (584a9-10).[27] In other words, we cannot infer from them that "pure pleasure is escape from pain, or pain escape from pleasure" (584c1-2). We have strong intuitive reasons, then, backed by an attractive fragment of theory, not to accept as our account of what pleasure is that it is just the absence of pain.

Now if pure pleasure is not escape from pain, then most of the pleasures "which reach the psyche through the body" (584c4-5) will not be pure, because they are "some kind of escape from pain" (584c6-7). Among these are the characteristic pleasures of the money-lover, those of satisfying his appetites for food, drink, and sex. For all these are preceded by pain, agitation, or discomfort. Not all body-based pleasures, however, are impure. Those of smell, being neither preceded nor followed by pain,

are pure. Nor are all impure pleasures body-based. Some are wholly psychological in origin—for example, "the pleasures of anticipation which
arise from the expectation of future pleasure or pain" (584c9-11). Included in the latter class are the characteristic pleasures of the honour-
lover. The pleasure of being honoured is mixed with the pains of envy,
that of victory is mixed with the pains associated with violence, that of
spiritedness with the pains of bad temper (586c7-d2).[28] Therefore, the
characteristic activities of both of the philosopher's rivals are impure
pleasures mixed with painful conditions.

But for all that has been shown so far the philosopher's pleasures might
be no more pleasant than those of making money or being honoured. For
the latter, though impure, might yet contain enough pure pleasure to
make them more pleasant overall than learning the truth, even when the
pure pain they contain is taken into consideration.[29] The remainder of the
argument, and by far the most complex part of it, is intended to show
that this is not so (585a8-587b9). The philosopher's pleasure is not only
pure but *true*. And because it is both pure and true it is more pleasant than
those of either the money-lover or the honour-lover.

The initial stage of the argument begins with an account of desire and
a correlative account of pleasure. And though neither of these is uncontroversial, I think that each has sufficient folk-psychological plausibility
for Plato's explanatory purposes (1.12).

A desire on this account is a kind of emptiness or inanition: "Are not
hunger and thirst and such things kinds of states of emptiness of the
body? . . . And ignorance and lack of good sense, in turn, kinds of states
of emptiness of the psyche?" (585a8-b4). And pleasure, not surprisingly,
is having that emptiness appropriately filled: "Being filled with things
appropriate to our nature is pleasure" (585d11). When one is hungry, eating or filling oneself with food, which is the natural object of hunger, is
pleasant, and so is actually being full or being satisfied. The journey is
pleasant, and so is being at the destination.

From this account of pleasure is derived an account of *true* pleasure.
That is why we find Socrates asking: "Which is the truer being filled, that
which is less or that which is more [*plērōsis de alēthestera tou hētton hē tou
mallon ontos*; sc. being filled]?" (585b9-10). That is why the remainder of
the argument is devoted to showing that being filled with what the philosopher most wants is being more truly or substantially filled (585c7-13)
than is being filled with what the money-lover or honour-lover most
wants.

Since this part of the argument has already been discussed in 2.14, I
shall give only its bare outlines here.

There is a single relation R (being filled), and two differently qualified instances of it, R_1 (being filled with knowledge) and R_2 (being filled with food). The natural object of R_1 is the form of F (knowledge). The natural object of R_2 is the form of G (food). And x and y come closer to completely or perfectly instantiating the form of R by being related by R_1 than z and w do by being related by R_2 if (i) x always and unalterably instantiates the appropriate form, and y always and unalterably instantiates the form of F, while (ii) z does not always and unalterably instantiate the appropriate form, and w does not always and unalterably instantiate the form of G (585b12-c5).

Now, a body is never unalterably a body; food is never unalterably food. But a psyche is always and unalterably a psyche (3.8). Knowledge is always and unalterably knowledge. It follows that something filled with knowledge comes closer to realizing the form of being filled completely or perfectly than does something filled with food (585d7-9).

This gives us the conclusion sought:

If being filled [*plērousthai*] with what is appropriate to our nature is pleasure, that which is more filled with things that are more [what they are] more really and truly enjoys a more true pleasure, while that which partakes of things that are less [what they are] is less truly and surely filled and partakes of a less trustworthy and less true pleasure. (585d11-e4)

The philosopher's pleasure is more true and more substantial than that of the money-lover.[30]

This brings us to the last leg of the argument. Truth in pleasure is a matter of having the inanition that is a particular desire filled with what always and unalterably instantiates the form that is the natural object of that desire. But only reason knows what will truly satisfy appetite and aspiration, and how to reliably achieve it (2.11-12, 3.2-5, 3.7). It follows that

those desires of even the money-loving and honour-loving parts which follow knowledge and argument, and pursue with their help those pleasures which reason [*to phronimon*] approves, will attain the truest pleasures possible for them because they follow truth, and the ones that are most their own, if indeed what is best for each thing is also most properly its own. . . . Therefore, when all of the psyche follows the wisdom-loving part and there is no inner strife, the result for each part is that in other things it does its own work as well and is just, and in particular it enjoys its own pleasures, the best pleasures and, so far as possible, the truest pleasures. (586d4-587a1)

Hence the further a psyche is from being ruled by reason, the further it is from true pleasure.

This is the lot of the tyrant. For, being ruled by lawless unnecessary appetites (2.3, 3.8), he is as far from rational rule as it is possible to be: "Is not that which is most remote from argument also remote from law and order? . . . And didn't the erotic and tyrannical appetites come to light as most distant? . . . And the kingly and well-ordered ones least distant?" (587a10-b3). It follows that "the tyrant will lead the least pleasant life, and the king the most pleasant" (587b8-9).

Since this is the conclusion Socrates set out to establish, he could simply stop at this point. Instead, he proceeds to calculate "how far the king is superior to the tyrant in the truth of his pleasure" (587d12-e1). It is tempting to dismiss this calculation as a joke. And there is no doubt that it has its comic side. However, it would hardly be a worthwhile joke unless it had some basis in the serious theory that leads up to it.

The oligarch takes for true pleasure what is in fact an image at three removes from the king and the truth (587c9-10). For between him and the philosopher-king falls the timocrat (2.3). This makes three removes, not two, because, as we saw in 2.11, the Greeks counted the first member of a series as well as the last.

The tyrant, in turn, takes for true pleasure an image of pleasure at three removes from that of the oligarch. For between the two falls the democrat. Socrates concludes that the tyrant is "thrice three times removed from true pleasure" (587d3-4).

But the tyrant's image of pleasure is, like all images, two-dimensional (587d6-7), whereas the true pleasure of the philosopher-king, being a substantial reality, is, presumably, three-dimensional. Hence, if a one-unit square represents the degree of closeness to true pleasure of an image nine times removed from it, true pleasure should be represented by a nine-unit cube. It follows that "the king lives 729 times more pleasantly than the tyrant, and that the tyrant is the same number of times more miserable" (587e1-4). This "amazing calculation" (587e5) brings the third bout between the tyrant and the philosopher-king to a characteristically quantitative and dramatic close.

Unfortunately, even if we treat removes *à la grecque*, it is exactly 5.832 times too dramatic. In order to reach the number 729, which seems to have had arcane Pythagorean significance (there were, allegedly, 729 days and nights in the year and 729 months in the "great year" recognized by the Pythagorean philosopher Philolaus),[31] and so make a rather "in" joke, Socrates has made two fast moves. First, he has illegitimately capitalized on the Greek manner of counting series to count the oligarch twice, once as the last term in his first series (philosopher, timocrat, oligarch), and again as the first term in his second series (oligarch, democrat, tyrant). Second, he has multiplied the number of times the tyrant is removed from the oligarch by the number of times the oligarch is removed from the philosopher-king when he should have added them. This allows him to claim that the tyrant is nine times removed from true pleasure when, in fact, he is only five times removed from it. The true series is philosopher (1), timocrat (2), oligarch (3), democrat (4), tyrant (5). Hence a five-unit cube, not a nine-unit one, represents true pleasure. The philosopher-king lives only 125 times more pleasantly than the tyrant.

With the details of these two arguments before us, it is possible to set out the conception of pleasure they presuppose and, to some degree, articulate.

The first argument shows that for Plato, unlike Bentham, pleasure is not a single kind of experience or mental state logically distinct from the activities that give rise to it: the pleasure of learning the truth is no mere G-consequence of learning it; rather learning the truth is an essential component of that pleasure (1.11). In the same way, eating, drinking, and having sex are essential components of the appetitive person's pleasures, and being honoured is an essential component of the honour-lover's pleasure. That is why there are three primary pleasures (580d7-8), not one pleasure and three ways to get it. Rediscovered in recent times, this type of view has become a commonplace of many philosophical discussions of pleasure.[32]

Although Plato recognizes irreducibly distinct pleasures, the second argument shows that he thinks they are commensurable. Again, this is not because there is a single experience the extent or intensity of which provides a common measure of their pleasantness, but because assessing things as pleasures involves judging them by a single set of standards. Included in this set, on Plato's view, are *purity* and *truth*. An activity which involves the appropriate satisfaction of a desire is a pure pleasure just in case it has no components or concomitants that are pains. It is a true pleasure just in case it always and unalterably satisfies. And the truer and purer—or more nearly true and pure—a pleasure is, the more pleasant it is. All of this is no doubt controversial, but it has the distinct merit of suggesting objective standards for the assessment of the relative pleasantness of activities which make a fair amount of sense. In discussions of pleasure, a topic on which our own philosophical grip is far from secure, this is by no means an achievement to be despised.

Armed with this elaborate theory of pleasure, we are ready to return to our initial topic.

Plato's candidates for the contents of the peculiar goods of the psychic parts are the irreducibly distinct, yet comparable, pleasures that most truly satisfy or fill the desires or inanitions in those parts. In the case of appetite, this is the pleasure of making money; in the case of aspiration, it is the pleasure of being honoured; in the case of reason, it is the pleasure of knowing the truth. It remains to show that these candidates are actually qualified to hold office, that they can satisfy the appropriate desires as these are characterized in the core conception of the psychic parts (3.4).

If we glance at the core conception of reason, we see at once that there is nothing *pro forma* about this task. On that conception, reason is the locus of whole-good-dependent desires. But what grounds do we have to think that desires of that kind can be satisfied by the pleasure of knowing the truth? Nor do things look any easier when we turn to aspiration and appetite. Why should we think that spirited-part-good-dependent desires can be satisfied by the pleasure of being honoured, or that appetitive-part-good-dependent desires can be satisfied by the pleasure of making money?

The pleasure of making money does not directly satisfy appetite's desires for the pleasures of food, drink, and sex, so it cannot be the content of the good of appetite in any straightforward way. But neither did Plato think it could. Money is simply the closest thing to a good that appetite has, the best means to satisfying its desires. If unnecessary appetites are to contribute maximally to the acquisition of money, however, they must be moderated through education and training in a craft until they become necessary (4.6). In this condition, they have making money as the equivalent of their natural object. For if they are satisfied, money will be optimally acquired, and if money is optimally acquired, they will be best satisfied. Consequently, the pleasure of making money, which has making it as an essential component, can (indirectly) satisfy appetitive-part-good-dependent desires. It can be the content of the good of appetite.

Just as the pleasure of making money does not directly satisfy appetites, the pleasure of being honoured does not naturally satisfy all spirited desires. But, again, this is no objection to Plato. The point at issue is whether that pleasure can satisfy those desires, not whether it naturally satisfies them. Now, as we have seen, spirited desires are like emotions. They embody a conception of the good, and a desire to keep us in line with that conception. But the conception of the good they embody is not unalterable; it can be, and typically is, shaped by education and training. Because of this it can coincide with a culture's conception of what is honourable. And if the two conceptions coincide, then what satisfies spirited desires will attract honour, and what attracts honour will satisfy spirited desires. Hence the pleasure of being honoured can be the content of the good of aspiration.

This brings us to rational, or whole-good-dependent, desires. On Plato's view, only someone who exercises dialectical-thought can know the truth about everything, and only someone whose psyche is ruled by reason can exercise dialectical-thought (2.2-12). By the same token, someone's rational desire for the whole good is satisfied just in case his psyche is ruled by reason (3.5, 3.7). A psyche knows the truth, then, if and only if its whole-good-dependent desires are satisfied. It follows that the natural object of rational desires can be specified either as the whole good or as knowing the truth. Consequently, rational desires as characterized in the core conception are satisfied by the pleasure of knowing the truth.

Since these three pleasures can satisfy the appropriate component desires of the psyche as these are characterized in the core conception, each possesses the feature it needs to be the content of the good peculiar to its respective part.

The psychic parts themselves have now taken on a somewhat clearer profile. Each is a unified source of motivation urging the psyche towards a distinctive kind of pleasure, and representing that pleasure as the content of the good.

3.7 HAPPINESS

Every psyche pursues what is really good, and "all its actions are done for its sake" (505d11-e1). And what is really good is life in the Kallipolis, the polis which comes as close as a mutable thing can to realizing the good itself completely or perfectly (2.11-12, 2.14). But what about that life makes it really good? Plato's answer is that it alone is as happy as sublunary human life can be. Happiness is the ultimate, indeed the only, criterion of choiceworthiness in lives (*Symposium* 205a2-3; 1.10, 4.9). But what is happiness? When we have answered this question, we shall have a better picture, not only of the peculiar goods of the psychic parts, but of the good itself.

It is useful to treat happiness under the two heads distinguished at the beginning of 3.6. First, what is the content of the happiest life, what are its substantial goals? Second, what is its form or structure, what are its formal goals?

We already have the outlines of an answer to the question of content. For the two proofs we examined in 3.6 are not simply about pleasure and relative pleasantness, they are also about happiness and relative happiness. Indeed, each is explicitly presented as a separate proof that the life of the philosopher-king is "the best, the most just, and the most happy," and that the life of the tyrant is "the worst, the most unjust, and the most wretched" (580b8-c4; 580c9-d1, 583b2-6).[33] This seems to establish beyond reasonable doubt that the content of the best and happiest life is the pleasure of knowing the truth, which is the most pleasant, or purest and truest, pleasure, and that the contents of the other decreasingly good and happy primary types of lives are the decreasingly pleasant pleasures of being honoured and making money (583a1-11).

It is important to be clear, however, that neither knowledge nor pleasure is the good:

> Furthermore, you certainly know that the many believe that pleasure is the good, while the more sophisticated believe it is knowledge . . . and that those who believe this cannot tell us what the knowledge in question is, but in the end they are compelled to say that it is knowledge about the good. . . . They blame us for not knowing the good, and then talk to us as if we did know the good. For they say that it is knowledge of the good, as if we knew what they mean by good. . . . And what about those who say that pleasure is the good? Are they any less confused than the others? Or aren't they too compelled to agree that there are bad pleasures? . . . So I think they have to conclude that the same things are good and bad. (505b5-c11)

Hedonism is false, even blasphemous (509a6-10). And the Socratic doctrine that wisdom is the good is false as well. But those who think that the good is pleasure or that it is knowledge have not entirely missed the boat. For the good is the structure of the world within which the pleasure of knowing the truth is reliably made available to those who find it most pleasant (cf. *Philebus* 60a7-67b10). Thus Plato's account of the good, which preserves the insights of both "the many and the wise," while resolving the aporiai they generate, is of the sort that Aristotle, who has some rather ungracious things to say about the good itself, commends (*Nicomachean Ethics* 1145b2-7).

Although appeals to content (pleasure) yield "the greatest and most decisive overthrow" (583b6-7) of the tyrant by the philosopher-king, Plato thinks that it is possible to establish that the latter is happiest, the former most wretched, simply by appealing to the form or structure of their psyches and lives (580b8-c4).

Now there are really two questions here. First, how should someone's psyche, his inner life, be structured in order to contribute optimally to the satisfaction of his ruling desires? Second, how should his polis, his outer life, be structured so that it too will optimally contribute to this end? For psychic structure is the product, through education and upbringing, of political structure, and depends on it for its success—if the world is not obliging, even the best desire structure will not guarantee happiness. That is one reason why it is only in the Kallipolis that private happiness is possible (473e4-5; 4.9).

The elaborate account of the relation of desire structure to happiness is spread throughout the discussion of the philosopher-kings in Books 4, 6, and 7 and the discussion of the timocrat, oligarch, democrat, and tyrant in Books 8 and 9. Much of it is already familiar, but its salient points bear brief recapitulation.

The content of our desire for food typically comes to be embedded in it, not through a process of rational reflection, but through the eating habits developed in our early prereflective lives. We want "Syracusan cuisine," "Sicilian-type dishes," and "Attic pastries" (404d1-10), not because we have determined that this is a sensible diet to follow, but because we developed a taste for them at our mother's knee. And the same is true of many of our other desires and emotions. Their contents, too, are deposited in them simply by the accidents of our affective lives.[34] Only younger women attract us because they alone resemble the girl who took us for our first childhood walks. The price we pay for this is often very high, as Proust reminds us. With increasing self-awareness, understanding, and rationality we find that many of our desires and emotions have the wrong contents, given our overall goals, so that we do not want them to be satisfied in action. But contents once embedded are often impossible to uproot or modify. Our only option may be forcible repression; we must become the gaolers of our desires in order to avoid becoming their prisoners. This involves frustration, and, with it, an increased risk that when our guard is down, and "the reasonable, gentle, and ruling part slumbers" (571c3-5), we will act against our better judgement. By strict control of the circumstances under which we form our desires and emotions, Platonic education tries to reduce these risks by insuring that, as far as our natures allow, our appetites and spirited desires have only the contents we would choose for them if we were fully rational, and aware of all the relevant facts (4.4-8). The different psychological types Plato recognizes—philosopher, timocrat, oligarch, democrat, tyrant—represent the different natural limits education encounters in trying to achieve this outcome.

The philosopher's psyche, like all embodied psyches (3.8), has three parts, each of which seeks, and is satisfied by, its own peculiar pleasure. Hence the potential for psyche-dividing conflict exists in him just as it does in money-lovers or honour-lovers. Platonic education, however, has reduced that potential to a minimum, and with it the likelihood of having to pay the price associated with such conflict, whether it be frustration of his ruling desires through akrasia (605c6-606d7; 3.3) or frustration of his other desires through self-control or improper rule (554a2-e5; 3.5). For in his psyche appetitive and spirited desires are neither starved, as they would be if he were self-controlled, nor overindulged, as they would be if he were weak-willed (571e1-2). Instead, they have been so moderated by training and education "that neither their pleasures nor their pains will disturb the best part, but will allow it in itself and alone to search for and reach out for the perception of anything that it does not know, whether it is something that has been, or is, or is going to be" (571e2-572a3). As a result, his psychic parts have the "common feelings of pleasure and pain" that are the cause of psychic unity (462a9-d5; 4.10). His appetite desires the amount of money (or of food, drink, and sex) that his aspiration honours, and his reason determines to be best. The three parts of his psyche are satisfied or frustrated in unison.

I think we would all agree that, whatever our goals in life, we would welcome a psyche with a desire structure of this harmonious kind, and that, *ceteris paribus*, we would want to have been brought up in a way that maximized our chance of having such a psyche.

The timocrat, who is ruled by aspiration, has moderated his appetites through training in gymnastics and, to a lesser extent, in music (548c1-2, 403c9-404e1), and is one step away from having the best kind of desire structure. For he has neglected "the true Muse, that of dialectic and philosophy" (548b8-c1). As a result, his rational desires, which cannot be satisfied without dialectical training (537c9-540c2), are frustrated. And because he lacks dialectical training and adequate training in music, which are "the best of guardians" (549b3-4), he is more likely to suffer from incontinence, abandoning honour for money (549a9-550b7). Still, at his best his desires are almost as harmonious as the philosopher's. For at least his appetite and aspiration are in agreement.

One step down from the timocrat is the oligarch (553a1-555b1), who is ruled by necessary appetites (2.3). He ignores music and gymnastics altogether (554b4-6). He holds his unnecessary appetites in check, "not by persuading them that they had better not, nor by training them by reason, but by necessity and fear" (554d2-3). He enslaves reason and aspiration, forcing them to contribute to the support of his ruling pleasure, rather than satisfying them with their own (553d1-7). Thus two parts of his psyche are frustrated, and a third, which contains his unnecessary appetites, is forcibly repressed. As a result, his risk of incontinence is higher than the timocrat's (559d4-561a5). But "even though the true virtue of a single-minded and harmonious psyche by far escapes him," he is still "more respectable than many," because "for the most part his better appetites control his worse ones" (554d10-e5).

Yet another step away from psychic harmony is the democrat (561a6-562a2). He is unique among the pathological types in not being ruled by a single psychic part. Instead, "he establishes his pleasures on an equal footing and so spends his life always surrendering the rule of himself to whichever of them happens along, as though it were chosen by lot, until it is satisfied, and then to another, dishonouring none, but fostering them all equally" (561b2-5). The only desires he excludes—*pace* 561b7-c4, which suggests that he keeps a completely open house—are lawless unnecessary ones (572b10-573b4; 2.2-3).

Because the democrat identifies the good with freedom to do whatever he wants (562b9-12), we might be inclined to believe that his psyche is ruled in just the way it should be to best achieve that good (561e5-6). But in fact "there is no plan or necessity to his life" (561d5-6); one desire interferes with another and none is ever really satisfied (561c6-d5). It is not freedom that he achieves, but anarchy, which he mistakes for freedom (560e5; 4.14).

We have now reached the bottom of the heap, and the first of the three proofs about the relative happiness of the philosopher-king and the tyrant (576e6-580c8). We encountered its successors in 3.6.

The tyrannical person's psyche is ruled by lawless unnecessary appetites (575a1-2), which are "free of all control by shame or reason" (571c8-9). Consequently, he has a minimal chance of satisfying his desires. For, first of all, even if he did develop a plan for his life, his appetites, being free of rational control, would almost certainly derail it: "The tyrannically ruled psyche will always be least likely to do what it chooses—speaking of the psyche as a whole; for being always forcibly driven by a gadfly it will be full of disorder and regret" (577e1-3). Second, even if his appetites did not upset his life plan, they would still, since they are insatiable and without law or limit (2.2), insure his perpetual frustration: "The tyrannical psyche must always be poor and unsatisfied" (578a1-2), and "cannot in any way satisfy its appetites" (579e1-2). So, simply because of its desire structure, simply because of the way it is ruled, the tyrannical psyche is condemned to frustration, incontinence, and unhappiness.

But the person ruled by lawless unnecessary appetites is not the most wretched. That lot falls to "the tyrannical person who does not lead a private life, but is forced by some misfortune to become a tyrant" (578c1-3). For being outnumbered by the subjects he enslaves, he will be forced to flatter and reward some of them in order not to be overthrown. A slave to his own lawless unnecessary appetites to begin with, he has put upon himself "the harshest and most bitter slavery to slaves" (569c3-4). In his case, both inner life and outer life conspire to yield the worst possible outcome.

Thus just as the philosopher is happier ruling in the Kallipolis, where both inner and outer life optimally contribute to the satisfaction of his rational desires, than being a private citizen under someone else's rule (496d9-502b9), the tyrannical person is more wretched as a tyrant than as a private citizen. Philosopher-king and tyrant are, therefore, the extremes of happiness and unhappiness (360e1-3), and, if Plato is right, of justice and injustice as well.

We can now understand why Plato so resolutely rejects the popular Thrasymachean view that happiness just is pleonectic satisfaction, or having more and more, without limit, of the pleasures we most want (359c3-5, 591d6-9). If we are to satisfy all of our desires reliably, we must impose on them limits of the sort that the philosopher-king imposes on his. We must have desires that are satisfied by just the amount of the pleasures of making money (of eating, drinking, and sex) and of being honoured, and of knowing the truth that are vouchsafed the philosopher-king in the Kallipolis. For his life is the happiest life available (4.9).

Although the philosopher achieves a measure of happiness far beyond that of the money-lovers and honour-lovers after his fifty-year Platonic education, he is by no means capable of achieving such happiness on his own. Unless, like Socrates, he receives supernatural aid (496c3-5), he must be properly trained from birth if he is to realize his capacity for happiness to the full. And he will not receive this training except in the Kallipolis. This leads to our second question: How should someone's polis be structured or ruled so that it will further his overall life plan as far as possible?

Because we are not self-sufficient, and cannot satisfy all of our own needs and desires, we must live in a polis with others, exchanging goods and services with them. Given our hedonistic aims, and the fact that we are at the mercy of our surroundings when we first come into the world, we would want this to be the polis in which we are given the early education and training necessary to guarantee us access to the truest and purest pleasure of which we are naturally capable, and in which we are assigned a social rôle that brings us as much of that pleasure as possible throughout life. In Plato's view this is the Kallipolis in which philosophers are kings, honour-lovers are soldier-police, and money-lovers are producers (cf. Chapter 4).

Whether we look to content, to psychic structure, or to political structure, then, the philosopher-king ought to be our model if we want to be as happy as possible—the more like him we are, the happier we will be (472c4-d2).

Goodness, happiness, and pleasure are thus related in the following way. The good itself is the structure of the Kallipolis in which everyone lives the happiest life possible given his nature. And the happiest life is the one which is so structured that it is as truly and purely pleasant throughout as it can be.

It is an easy inference from this that the peculiar good of a psychic part is the structure of the polis within which as much as possible of the pleasure characteristic of that part is reliably made available throughout life. Thus a psychic part is a cognitional and motivational unity within the psyche which presents the structure of a polis within which its own peculiar pleasure is maximized as being the good and which urges the psyche towards the realization of that structure.

3.8 IMMORTALITY AND SIMPLICITY

Although we are not told until the eleventh hour (611a10–612a7), the psychological theory we have been exploring correctly characterizes the psyche for no more than a brief phase (608c9–d1) in its history, and is far from being an accurate guide to its "true nature" (612a3–4). This section marks a transition from the lengthy account of the psyche as it is when "maimed by its association with the body" (611c1–2) to the page-long account of it as it is in itself. Since what effects this transition is an argument for the immortality of the psyche, we shall begin with it.

To understand this argument we must first come to grips with the notion of a *proper bad thing* (609a3–4). This notion is not defined, but the examples given suggest that Plato has the following in mind. Something is bad for an F if it "destroys and corrupts it" (608e3). Something is properly bad for an F if Fs are naturally prone to be destroyed or corrupted by it. Hence "ophthalmia [is properly bad] for the eyes, illness for the whole body, mildew for grain, rot for wood, rust for iron or bronze" (608e6–609a2).[35]

Next, we are given a principle about proper bad things, and a claim about what things are properly bad for the psyche. The principle is this: "The bad or evil thing proper to each thing destroys it, or if this does not [totally] destroy it, nothing else does" (609a9–b1). If rust does not destroy iron, or rot wood, nothing will destroy them. The claim is that the only things properly bad for the psyche are the moral and intellectual vices, "injustice, licentiousness, cowardice, and ignorance or lack of learning" (609b11–c1).

Once both of these are granted, the argument moves swiftly. For, as Glaucon readily admits, the vices do not seem to totally destroy the psyche—the unjust destroy others, not themselves (609d5–e4). And this, together with principle and claim, entails that nothing destroys the psyche.

It "is always being [a psyche], and if it is always [a psyche], it is immortal" (611a1-2; 2.14).

The weakest link in this inference is the claim that only the vices are properly bad for the psyche. A mind-brain identity theorist would argue against it. He would say that since the psyche and the body (or brain) are identical, anything properly bad for the one is properly bad for the other, and vice versa. Now, the things that are properly bad for the body destroy it (609c5-d2). On the identity theorist's view, they will *ipso facto* destroy the psyche as well. This criticism is not decisive, of course; its own presuppositions are too controversial for that. But it serves to show that the claim to be able to identify all of the things properly bad for the psyche is itself unacceptably controversial.

Adherents of the less controversial and more attractive view that the psyche, even if it is not identical to the body (or brain), at least depends for its existence on the latter will also reject this argument. They would say that even if things that are properly bad for the body are not properly bad for the psyche, they can destroy it by destroying the body (or brain) on which its existence depends. On this view, if the claim that the vices are alone properly bad for the psyche is true, the principle that only the things properly bad for something destroy it is false. For the psyche will not be destroyed by the vices, but it will be destroyed by the other things which destroy the body. If, on the other hand, the principle is true, the claim is false. For then the things which destroy the body will be properly bad for the psyche.

No doubt there are ways to defend the argument against these criticisms, neither of which entirely divests it of its charm. But the criticisms are sufficiently stubborn to justify our having serious reservations about any part of the defense of justice that appeals to the immortality of the psyche (5.4).

"It isn't easy . . . for something to be immortal that is composed of many things [*suntheton ek pollōn*], and isn't put together in the finest way" (611b5-8). Therefore, the psyche must be simple (611a10-b3). This conclusion seems to conflict with the earlier view that the psyche is tripartite. But the conflict is no more than apparent. For "what we have said about the psyche before is true of it as it plainly is at present [*en tōi paronti phainetai*]" (611c6-7). But at present it is "maimed by its association with the body and other bad things" (611c1-2). If we observed it in its unmaimed state, we would see that "in its true nature" it is simple or "uniform [*monoeidēs*]," not complex or "multiform [*polueidēs*]" (612a3-5).

Socrates' instructions on how to achieve this perspective on the psyche are as follows:

This is where we must look Glaucon . . . to the psyche's love of wisdom, and to realize what the things are that it apprehends, what associations it longs for because it is akin to the divine, the immortal, and what is always being [tōi aei onti; sc. what it is], and what it would become like if it were to give itself entirely to this longing and were brought by it out of the depths of this sea in which it is now sunk, and were cleansed, and the rocks and barnacles which, because it feasts on earth, have grown around it in a wild, earthen, and rocky profusion, as a result of those so-called happy feasts, were knocked off it. (611d8-612a3; 518d9-519b5)

Expressed in less figurative terms, the idea is surely this. The philosopher does not want appetitive and spirited pleasures for their own sake (581e2-4; 2.2), but he has to pursue them to some small degree in order to prevent his frustrated appetites and spirited desires from disrupting his pursuit of the pleasure of knowing the truth (571d6-572b1; 3.7). If he could rid himself of his appetitive and spirited desires entirely, he would. One way to do this is to become disembodied. For appetitive and spirited desires are the result of embodiment—the "maiming" referred to at 611c1-2. A disembodied psyche would not need food, drink, sex, money, or the approval of others. Hence, all things being equal, the philosopher would want to become disembodied if he could. So, if the philosopher's desire for the pleasures of knowing the truth were fully effective, it would, so to speak, pull his psyche free of his body altogether, free of the desires that are the result of embodiment. His psyche would then be identical to its rational part. For multiplicity of parts is a consequence of irremediable conflict among desires, and such conflict cannot occur among rational desires alone (3.2). Thus if we follow Socrates' instructions, we indeed end up with a vision of the psyche that coincides with the account of its true nature.

On this way of looking at it, the claim that the psyche is truly simple does not force Plato to retract anything in his earlier theory of it. Rather, it drives him to extend that theory in a natural, but by no means inevitable, direction. For the psyche becomes simple through loss of some of its motives or desires, and, in a less dramatic fashion, this happens all the time. What is mysterious is the way the psyche brings about this change in its desires, namely, by becoming disembodied.

Plato's thought moves from immortality to simplicity, then, and employs the possibility of disembodiment—which is never in doubt (609d6-7)—to explain both how psychic simplicity can be compatible with psychic complexity and how it can be achieved. But even if we resist this movement, and reject both immortality and disembodiment, it remains the case that the psyche's temporary complexity is compatible with its essential simplicity. Indeed, the view that the psyche is really simple is an intelligible extension of the theory that it is temporarily complex. Thus viewed in secular psychological terms, Plato's brief portrait of the psyche's true nature is not such a radical departure from his vastly richer portrait of it as it is in this life.

3.9 AN OUTLINE OF PLATONIC PSYCHOLOGY

Initial readings of the *Republic* leave one with the impression that the ontology of Plato's psychological theory is a baroque, even byzantine, affair comprised of psyches, psychic parts, psychic powers or faculties, desires, pleasures, and psychological types. In fact, as we shall see, it is closer to the Bauhaus than to the baroque. For all the psychological entities Plato recognizes, and, indeed, all the fundamental concepts of his psychology, can be constructed out of, or characterized in terms of, *desires*, which are inanitions that cause the psyche to try to fill them as completely and permanently as possible (3.6), and *intelligence*, which is a power to develop formulas for the satisfaction of desire, formulas which have theories (beliefs) about the world as constituents (2.8-11).

Desires fall into six classes, each of which can be defined in terms of good-dependence. For the division of desires is in many ways simply a register of the different degrees to which satisfaction of a given ruling desire involves the satisfaction of the psyche as a whole. And satisfaction of the psyche as a whole is a measure of success in achieving the good (3.2, 3.7).

A psyche ruled by *lawless unnecessary appetites* is as far from the harmony required to achieve satisfaction of its desires as possible. All of its desires, appetitive, spirited, and rational, remain unsatisfied. That is why such appetites are as non-good-dependent as possible.

A psyche ruled by *nonlawless unnecessary appetites* is still very far from being harmonious, but since no lawless unnecessary appetites are present in it, it is closer to harmony and satisfaction than its predecessor. Since its desires are at least subject to the constraints of external laws, it sometimes partly satisfies some of its appetites. Hence nonlawless unnecessary appetites, though still non-good dependent, are less so than lawless ones.

A psyche ruled by *necessary appetites* has achieved a small measure of psychic harmony because its appetites have all been moderated and organized so that they will promote the acquisition of a single thing, money, which will—albeit indirectly—best satisfy them with the pleasures of food, drink, and sex. Its spirited and rational desires, however, remain unsatisfied. Hence necessary appetites are only appetitive-part-good-dependent.

A psyche of the type we shall meet in 4.8, which is ruled by *unnecessary spirited desires*, has further moderated its necessary appetites, so that they will be satisfied with the amount of food, drink, and sex that will enable it partially to satisfy its ruling desires with the pleasure of being honoured. Its spirited desires, however, since they remain unmoderated, will be less than optimally satisfied, and its rational desires will remain unsatisfied. Nonetheless, a psyche of this sort is more harmonious and satisfies more of its desires than one ruled by necessary appetites. Therefore, unnecessary spirited desires are to some degree spirited-part-good-dependent, and being such, they are appetitive-part-good-dependent too. For they cannot be satisfied unless necessary appetites are also satisfied.

A psyche ruled by *necessary spirited desires* has moderated both its appetites and its spirited desires so that the former will be satisfied with the amount of food, drink, and sex that will enable it to satisfy its ruling desires with the pleasure of being honoured. Of its desires only the rational ones remain unsatisfied. Therefore, necessary spirited desires are spirited-part-good-dependent, and, since their satisfaction involves the satisfaction of necessary appetites, they are also appetitive-part-good-dependent.

A psyche ruled by *rational desires* has moderated both its appetites and its spirited desires so that the former will be satisfied with the amount of food, drink, and sex, and the latter with the amount of honour, that will enable it to satisfy its ruling desires with the pleasure of knowing the truth. Since all of its constituent desires are satisfied, it enjoys the maximum of psychic harmony, the maximum of satisfaction. Therefore, rational desires are whole-good-dependent.

Once the division of desires is in place the definition of the five psychological types that comprise Plato's psychopathology is straightforward (2.3, 3.7). The *tyrant* is ruled by lawless unnecessary appetites. The *democrat* is ruled by nonlawless unnecessary appetites (among other things). The *oligarch* is ruled by necessary appetites. The *timocrat* is ruled by (unnecessary) spirited desires. The *philosopher* is ruled by rational desires.

When desires differently related to the good conflict, they do so irremediably, and must therefore be located in different parts of the psyche (3.2). Since desires of this sort fall into three primary types, this gives rise to the tripartite psyche. *Appetite* is the locus of appetitive desires. *Aspiration* is the locus of spirited desires. *Reason* is the locus of rational desires. The psyche itself is identical to reason. But when it is embodied it acquires appetitive and spirited desires in addition to rational ones. The result is that it becomes tripartite instead of simple (3.8).

These psychic parts are more than repositories of desire. Each is a motivational unity within the psyche urging the psyche towards the satisfaction of its desires in preference to others. Each is equipped with its own characteristic beliefs about the good, its own characteristic *Weltanschauung*. These are the products of the complete psychological powers, *perceptual-thought*, *folk-wisdom*, *scientific-thought*, and *dialectical-thought*. And each of these powers, in turn, is simply the result of the double enslavement of intelligence to the type of desire that rules in the psyche whose complete power it is. A psyche ruled by necessary appetites identifies the good with a structure of a polis in which it believes the maximal amount of the pleasure of making money is reliably made available throughout life. It will use its intelligence only to calculate the best means to the pleasure of making money, and will develop its cognitive resources only to the extent that doing so leads to that pleasure. Hence, it will have cognitive access only to *modes*, and will exercise folk-wisdom. Similarly, a psyche ruled by necessary spirited desires identifies the good with a structure of a polis in which it believes a maximal amount of the pleasure of being honoured is reliably made available throughout life, has cognitive access to *figures*, and exercises scientific- thought. And a psyche ruled by rational desires identifies the good with the structure of a polis in which it believes a maximal amount of the pleasure of knowing the truth is reliably made available throughout life, has cognitive access to *forms*, and exercises dialectical-thought (2.12).

This brings us to two other key notions in Plato's psychological theory, namely, *pleasure* and *happiness*. Pleasure is having a desire satisfied with something which instantiates the form that is the natural object of that desire. *True* pleasure is having one's desires satisfied with something which always and unalterably instantiates such a form. *Pure* pleasure is pleasure that does not involve pains or frustrations of any sort. The truer and purer (or more nearly true and pure) a pleasure is, the more pleasant it is.

But the pleasure of knowing the truth is the truest and purest of the pleasures. For if the pleasure of making money is one's end, both one's spirited and one's rational desires will be frustrated. And if the pleasure of being honoured is one's end, one's rational desires will be frustrated. But if the pleasure of knowing the truth is one's end, all one's desires will be satisfied. Hence only the philosopher will be really satisfied by achieving his ends. It follows that only he can achieve complete happiness. For happiness consists in the acquisition of as much pleasure as possible throughout life. And complete happiness consists in the acquisition of as much of the truest and purest pleasure throughout life as possible, coupled with the minimum amount of pain or frustration (3.7).

Psychic rule, psychic harmony, and *psychic unity* remain. A psyche is ruled by a particular psychic part when its complete psychological power, and so its conception of the good, is determined by the desires in that part, and when the whole psyche aims at the satisfaction of those desires in preference to any others. It is *properly ruled* when all three parts share a belief that the ruling part should rule, something they will do just in case their desires are satisfied when that part rules. Only rational rule meets this criterion. For only a rationally ruled psyche succeeds in satisfying all of its desires. A psyche is harmonious just in case all of its desires are satisfied or frustrated in unison, and it is unified just in case its parts share their pleasures and pains. Since these conditions, too, obtain only in a psyche ruled by reason, proper rule, psychic harmony, and psychic unity all come to much the same thing.

From the ontology of Plato's theory of the psyche we turn to its laws. Many of these are explicitly mentioned in the *Republic*, but the most basic ones, like the basic psychological entities they govern, for the most part lie concealed beneath its surface. Moreover, just as in ontology, parsimony, not extravagance, is the rule. All the laws of Platonic psychology can be derived from a few basic ones.

The first basic law (L1), which governs the overall operation of the psyche, states that *every psyche pursues the good* (505d11-e2; 3.7). Alternatively expressed, L1 states that *everyone wants to live in a polis whose structure guarantees him as much as possible of the purest and truest pleasure of which he is capable throughout life, coupled with the minimal amount of pain or frustration.* It is this law that explains why someone with the natural capacity to be a philosopher will become a philosopher-king if he can, and will spend as much time learning the truth as is compatible with satisfying his other (moderated) desires through ruling in the Kallipolis (4.9). I suspect that L1 lies behind the canalization law which states that *when someone's desires are strongly directed to one thing, they are weakened towards other things* "like a river that has been canalized" (485d6-8). When a psyche tastes the purer and truer pleasure of knowing the truth, it no longer wants the less pure and less true pleasures of being honoured or of making money (485d10-e1; 3.6). Here, perhaps, is the beginning of an account of the way desires can be moderated.

The second basic law (L2) governs desires. It says that (ceteris paribus) *the stronger desire is the one that will be satisfied in action.*[36] It is this law that explains why people are by nature of different psychological types. If a person's appetites are too strong to be appropriately moderated, he is a money-lover. If his appetites can be moderated, but not his spirited desires, he is an honour-lover. If both his appetites and his spirited desires can be appropriately modified, he is a philosopher (2.2). We see L2 exemplified in the behaviour of Leontius, whose appetitive desire, being stronger than his spirited desire, causes him to act incontinently. L1 explains why everyone strives for the purest and truest pleasure possible; L2 explains why only some succeed in getting it.

The third basic law (L3) governs the interaction between desire and intelligence. It says (i) *desire determines a person's ends and causes intelligence to calculate the means to them*, and (ii) *desire determines the cognitive resources available to intelligence in performing that task*. It explains why people ruled by different desires have different cognitive resources, and exercise different complete psychological powers (2.7-9, 2.11-12).

L1, L2, and, L3 are fairly clearly basic. But are they the only basic laws? To answer this question it is necessary to catalogue the other laws mentioned in the *Republic*, and to determine whether they can be derived from these three.

A fourth law (L4) of Platonic psychology states that *by imitating someone, by acting like him, one comes to have a character like his*. That is why the future guardians must imitate only the sort of people they are to become (392c1-398b8), and why we become just, or as nearly just as possible, by doing just acts, and unjust by doing unjust ones (444c10-d1). Without L4, Plato's entire educational programme, especially the restrictions imposed on music, would lack a rationale.

Now L4 may be basic. But we can at least sketch out something like a derivation of it from L1, L2, and L3. What we have to imagine is this. In an educational setting, a child acts like a person of a certain type. This performance draws approval and praise from his peers and, perhaps, from his teachers as well. As a result, some of his spirited desires are satisfied and he experiences the pleasure of being honoured. His desire for that pleasure will now cause him to want to act in the approved way. If this desire is effective, what began as imitation of another will become his own way of acting. Similarly, in a social setting just actions tend to elicit approval and praise (612d3-9), which satisfy spirited desires. Desire for pleasure of being honoured tends to produce the desire to continue to act in that way. Again actions give rise to the disposition to perform them.

A fifth psychological law (L5) is a close relative of L4. It states that *if a person admires something, he imitates it* (500c6-7). On the assumption that one admires only what one believes to instantiate the good, L5 is a consequence of L1. For if one wants to instantiate the good oneself, one must want to imitate, or be like, something one believes to instantiate the good.

A sixth psychological law (L6) states that *one loves something most when one believes that its doing well is biconditionally tied to one's own* (412d4-7). To determine its status, we must first find out what love is. The *Lysis* connects love and desire: we love something just in case it is useful or profitable to us, just in case it satisfies some desire of ours (210c5-d4, 215b1-3). On the assumption that this continues to be Plato's view in the *Republic*, which does not itself contain any explicit account of love, L6 can be rendered intelligible on the basis of L1. If F is the natural object of a desire, the things that come closest to satisfying that desire with the purest and truest pleasure possible are those which come closest to completely or perfectly instantiating the form of F (3.6). And the closer something comes to completely or perfectly instantiating a form of this kind, one which is a component of the good itself, the closer it comes to being a good F (2.11). And the closer it comes to being a good F, the closer it comes to doing well the work that only Fs do, or that Fs do best (352d2-354a9; 5.2). If the F in question is a psyche, the closer it comes to being a good psyche, the closer it comes to being a psyche that lives well or happily. For the work proper to psyches is living. Suppose, now, that A loves *x*, and that *x* is an F. It follows—omitting reference to beliefs—that *x* must satisfy some of A's desires. Presumably, then, the better *x* satisfies those desires, and the purer and truer the pleasure it provides, the more A will love it. But the closer *x* comes to this condition, the closer it comes to being a good F, one that is itself doing well what Fs do. And the closer A comes to being satisfied in this way, the closer he comes to doing well. Hence we have arrived at L6. One loves something most if its doing well is biconditionally tied to one's own (5.5).

Finally, there is the law (L7) that states that *a person does best at a craft just in case it is the one craft for which he has the highest natural aptitude and he practices it exclusively throughout life.* No law is more often repeated in the *Republic*, and none seems more central to Plato's thought, whether about the psyche or about the polis. If Plato held it, it must be counted as a basic law of his psychology, for it cannot be derived from the others. However, I do not think that he did hold it. As I shall argue in 4.3, L7 is no more than an image of the law he does hold. And the latter, unlike its image, is firmly rooted in L1, L2, and L3.

On the assumption that this claim about L7 can be made good, we may say that L1, L2, and L3 are the only laws, desire and intelligence the only entities, that Platonic psychology really needs.

3.10 REASON AND RATIONALITY

It is clear from the preceding outline that Plato's psychological theory is closely similar in structure to the familiar belief/desire psychology that we associate with David Hume, and that, rightly or wrongly, we think of as being folk psychology. Because of this, Hume's theory is a useful foil to Plato's. For there are differences as well as similarities between them.

It might seem, at least at first glance, that the most glaring difference between the two theories is that Plato attributes motivating power to reason, while Hume makes reason the impotent "slave of the passions." But it should now be clear that this is a misapprehension. Plato does indeed attribute autonomous motivating force to reason (*to logistikon*). But the latter is not the Platonic counterpart of Humean reason. Humean reason is a cognitive and ratiocinative mental faculty, the psychological rôle of which is restricted to calculating the means to ends set by desire. *To logistikon*, by contrast, is a unified source of motivation, which contains both conative and cognitive elements. The real counterpart here is intelligence (*phronēsis*), which is entirely cognitive and ratiocinative. And it is, if anything, more enslaved to desire than Humean reason is to the passions (2.12). Hence what initially appears to be a deep difference or incommensurability between Plato's theory and Hume's turns out to be a deep, if not the deepest, similarity between them. The real deep differences lie elsewhere.

For the most part Hume accepts the *instrumental theory* of rationality, according to which we are not subject to a charge of irrationality provided that we reliably do what best satisfies our desires whatever they happen to be. On this theory, desires themselves cannot be irrational. Hence Hume's notorious remark that it is "not contrary to reason to prefer the destruction of the whole world to the scratching of my finger."

Hume sometimes suggests, however, that desires are subject to at least one kind of rational criticism. He remarks that "a passion can never, in any sense, be call'd unreasonable, but when founded on a false supposition, or when chuses means insufficient for the design'd end."[37] When this suggestion is developed, as it is not by Hume, it yields the *deliberative theory* of rationality, according to which we are not subject to a charge of irrationality provided that we reliably do what best satisfies, not our actual desires, but those that we would have if we had engaged in a process of "ideal deliberation," that is, if we had been aware of the relevant facts, thinking clearly, and free from distorting influences. On this view desires are irrational if they are sustained by irrational beliefs.[38]

A third theory of rationality is the *critical theory*. It is best approached by contrast with the deliberative theory. According to the latter, someone's desires are rational if, having engaged in a process of ideal deliberation, he would keep them. According to the critical theory, this is not the case. For someone's desires may themselves prevent him from seeing things as they are. If he has them, ideal deliberation will lead him to want to keep them. A money-lover will want to continue to be ruled by his necessary appetites no matter how long he deliberates. But if he were ruled not by them but instead by rational desires, and had complete access to the truth, ideal deliberation would lead him to want to avoid being ruled by them. According to the critical theory, desires are irrational if they block our access to the truth in this way, and we are irrational if we act to satisfy such desires.[39]

Unlike Hume, who for the most part holds the instrumental theory of rationality, Plato holds the critical theory (1.12, 2.7-12, 3.6-7). So there is a deep difference between Plato and Hume as regards the nature of reason, but it lies in their theories of rationality or reasonableness, not in their views about the rôle of the faculty of reason or intelligence in the psyche.[40] And the differences do not end there.

A second important difference between Plato and Hume also emerges quite forcefully from 3.9. Unlike Hume's theory, but very much like another great modern theory of the psyche, Sigmund Freud's, Plato's is a psychogenetic, or developmental, theory. And, again like Freud's, it identifies the desire for pleasure of different sorts as the force that both produces that development and, in other circumstances, stifles it. First we experience appetitive pleasures. Then, if we are lucky in the natural lottery, and in our family and surrounding culture or polis, we experience the more pleasant pleasures of approval (being honoured). Then, if our luck holds, we experience the still more pleasant pleasures of knowing the truth and being autonomous adults in our own right (590e2-591a3; 4.14). The child first wants to please itself, then it wants to please its parent, then it wants to be its parent. This ascent of desire is the path, subject to *fortuna*, and rarely negotiated with complete success, of increasing autonomy, freedom, pleasure, and realism. If we are unlucky, our desires block us from finding pleasure at higher levels, confining us to lower levels where we achieve at least some satisfaction. This is the path, also subject to *fortuna*, and often followed, of dependence, servitude, frustration, and illusion. It is because Plato holds this theory of psychic development that he holds the critical theory of rationality.

Far from being an ancient curiosity, then, Plato's theory of the psyche, largely coherent, supported by subtle argument, and possessed of considerable folk-psychological plausibility, is among the greatest philosophies of mind, and one from which we can still learn.

FOUR

POLITICS

The individual can go far, far in his seventy years, indeed in his thirty years if that is all he has—it is amazing even to the gods! But . . . when one sees how well he knows how to gain but how ill to preserve, that he gives no thought to the fact, indeed, that through procreation he could prepare the way for an even more victorious life; then . . . one grows impatient and says to oneself, "Nothing can come of mankind in the long run, its individuals are squandered, chance in marriage makes a grand rational progress of mankind impossible."   —NIETZSCHE

Political-ethical life [*Sittlichkeit*] is the Idea of Freedom because it is the good become alive.   —HEGEL

4.1 INTRODUCTION

Nothing in the *Republic* has aroused more hostility in its readers than its political theory. That is one reason my account of Plato's response to Glaucon and Thrasymachus did not begin with it. My strategy has been to discuss metaphysics, epistemology, and psychology first, in the hope that my unorthodox views on these somewhat less emotionally charged topics, meeting with less resistance, would pave the way for my equally unorthodox views on Plato's politics. For the latter, it will emerge, is firmly based in his metaphysics, epistemology, and psychology.

4.2 THE STRUCTURE OF THE ACCOUNT OF THE KALLIPOLIS

The account of the Kallipolis, of the good or maximally happy human community, which is the centerpiece of Plato's political theory, occurs in three stages, each of which describes a distinct model or paradigm polis (472d9-e1)—the *First Polis* (369a5-372d3), the *Second Polis* (372e3-471c3), and the *Third Polis* (473b4-544b3), as I shall call them.

In Book 5, Socrates undertakes to show that the Second Polis is not simply an ideal, but a realizable ideal, a real possibility (473a1-b2; cf. 2.14). What he actually does, however, is show that the Third Polis is a real possibility (473b4-544b3). And the Third Polis is not the same as the Second. First of all, they have different—albeit related—constitutions:

Not one of our present constitutions is worthy of the philosophic nature. . . . If it [the aforesaid nature] were to find the best political constitution, as it is itself the best, then it would be apparent that it is really divine and all others human in their institutions and natures.

Obviously you are going to ask next what constitution that is.—You are wrong there, he said. I was not going to ask that, but whether it was the constitution we described when we were founding our polis [the Second Polis] or not.—In other respects it is that one, I said, but we said [*errēthē*][1] even then that there must always be something present in the polis possessing the same understanding of its constitution as guided you, the lawgivers, when you made the laws. (497b1-d2)

Second, the two poleis are explicitly characterized as being distinct:

That is easy, he [Glaucon] said, for then [at 449a5], as now, talking as if you had completed your discussion of the polis, you said that you assumed that the polis you had described [the Second Polis] was good, and the good man was the one who resembled it, although it seems that you had still a finer polis [the Third Polis] and man to tell us about. . . .—Your recollection, I said, is most correct. (543c7-544b4; cf. 2.14)

The question is, why does Plato proceed in this way?

A natural line of thought is this. The Second Polis is not, *by itself*, a real possibility. That is why no attempt is made to show that it is. But when modified in some respects it is a part, or submodel, of a distinct model polis which is a real possibility, namely, the Third Polis. Hence if Plato can show that the latter is a real possibility, he will have shown that the Second Polis is a real possibility as well.

If the Second Polis stands in this relation to the Third, the thought suggests itself that the three poleis might constitute an ordered series of good poleis each of which, when modified, is a component of its successor, only the third and final member of the series being by itself a real possibility. And this suggestion, in turn, suggests another—namely, that the account of the Kallipolis incorporates such an ordered series of poleis as a way of explaining why the Kallipolis must have the elaborate structure it does, replete with philosopher-kings, guardians, and producers, if it is to be a real possibility.

These suggestions will be substantiated and developed in subsequent sections. What we shall discover is this. The First Polis is the Kallipolis for money-lovers. But it is not a real possibility because it includes nothing to counteract the destabilizing effects of unnecessary appetites and the pleonexia to which they give rise. For this guardians are required. When these are added, the result is the Second Polis, which contains the political institutions necessary to produce such guardians. The Second Polis is the Kallipolis for honour-lovers and money-lovers. But it is not a real possibility either because it includes nothing to counteract the destabilizing effects of false belief. For this philosopher-kings are required. When these are added, the result is the Third Polis, which contains the political institutions necessary to produce philosopher-kings. The Third Polis, which is a real possibility, is the Kallipolis for money-lovers, honour-lovers, and philosophers. The First Polis is, to use a convenient Hegelianism, "overcome but preserved" in the Second, and the Second is overcome but preserved in the Third.

On this view, Plato is at work on the Kallipolis from the moment he begins the account of the First Polis at 369b5. His method is more nearly one of slowly drawing back the veil to uncover more and more of what he has in mind than of introducing and discarding first one model polis, then another. Failure to notice this is one of the major reasons Plato's political theory has been so poorly understood and so reviled.

4.3 SPECIALIZATION

We must now examine a principle that plays a somewhat complex part in the account of the Kallipolis.

We may begin with a doctrine and a principle based on it. The doctrine is the *unique aptitude doctrine* (UAD), according to which each person is born with a natural aptitude for a unique craft or type of work, whether it is carpentry, pottery, medicine, guardianship, or ruling. The principle is that each member of the Kallipolis must practice exclusively throughout life the unique craft for which he has a natural aptitude. I shall call this the *prescriptive principle of specialization* (PS).

Now even a careful reader of Books 2 through 5 might be forgiven for sympathetically entertaining the view that Plato accepts both doctrine and principle. After all, we are told explicitly that "a physician has a different nature than a carpenter" (454d1-5), that "one woman is a physician by nature, another not, one is by nature musical, another nonmusical" (455e6-7), and that people must stick to one craft for which they have a natural aptitude throughout their lives (370a7-b2, 374a6-c2, 394e3-6, 423c6-d6, 433a4-6, 443b7-c7, 453b2-6). But despite all this apparent evidence, I am convinced that Plato accepts neither UAD nor PS. He uses them, and gives the impression that he accepts them—we shall have to try to understand why. But in the end they are no more than shadows of his actual thought (443b7-c7).

The first point to make against UAD is that Plato holds views that conflict with it. For example, we are told that the rulers are to be selected from the class of guardians on the basis of how well they perform in guardian training (536e6-537d8; 4.7-8), and that having a natural aptitude for a craft is simply a matter of how easily and quickly one learns it:

> Was this the basis of your distinction between someone with a natural aptitude for something and someone without it—that the one learned it easily, the other with difficulty; that the one, after only a brief period of instruction, could discover much for himself in the matter studied, while the other, after much instruction and drill, could not even remember what he had been taught; that the one's body adequately served his mind, while the other's hindered his? Are there any other ways by which you distinguished those with a natural aptitude from those without it?—No one, he said, will be able to name any others. (455b4-c3)

It follows immediately that philosophers have a natural aptitude for two distinct crafts, guardianship and ruling.

But it is not only these views about guardian education and the selection of rulers that make it unlikely that Plato held UAD; the whole tenor of his thought about the psyche, and about crafts for that matter, does as well. In Book 2, for example, crafts are assigned to the class of C-goods on the grounds that they "are painful and difficult, but beneficial, and for their own sake we would not want them, but only for the rewards and other benefits that result from them" (357c5-d2; 1.9). Nobody—whether producer, guardian, or philosopher-king—actually enjoys his craft. All crafts are mere extrinsic means to something else that is wanted. Hence there is really no room in Plato's theory for someone who is naturally suited for a craft because it alone intrinsically satisfies some desires of his. But if people are not apt for a particular craft because of their desires, how is their supposed aptitude to be explained? The natural thought is that it must be a matter of cognitive power. In Plato's psychological theory, however, differences in cognitive power are not fine-grained enough to explain how one person could have a natural aptitude for carpentry and another for pottery. For, according to that theory, all "craft-lovers" exercise the same complete psychological power of folk-wisdom (2.8). Rulers (wisdom-lovers), guardians (honour-lovers), and producers (money-lovers) differ in cognitive powers, but individual money-lovers all have the same power. It is for this reason, I believe, that while we hear of the children of producers being taken off to be trained as guardians because of their natural aptitudes (415b3-c6), and of guardians being demoted to the ranks of producers for failing to live up to expectations (468a5-7), we never hear of a carpenter's child being removed to a potter's house for upbringing because he has no aptitude for his father's craft. Indeed, Plato seems simply to assume that the normal thing is for a child to follow in the craft of his parents (4.6). So, although Plato is committed to thinking that people are born with a natural aptitude to rise to a certain cognitive height (so to speak), there is no place in his theory for the view that they are born with a natural aptitude for a unique craft, even if the crafts in question are as broadly characterized as producing, guardianship, and ruling.

We may conclude that Plato does not hold UAD. He does not think that people have a natural aptitude for exactly one craft. And if he does not hold this view, he cannot hold PS either. For the latter transparently presupposes the former.

But if Plato rejects UAD and PS, why does he court misunderstanding by so clearly seeming to embrace them? Perhaps the answer lies in the doctrine and principle he does accept, and in the overall strategy of his argument.

Plato rejects unique aptitudes, but he clearly accepts the *unique upper-bound doctrine* (UBD), according to which a person's ruling desires set a unique upper limit to his cognitive development. Indeed, this doctrine is the cornerstone of his psychological theory (3.1-10). Because he accepts UBD, Plato also accepts the *principle of quasi specialization* (PQS), which states that each person in the Kallipolis must practice exclusively throughout life the one craft, whether producing, guardianship, or ruling, that demands of him the highest level of cognitive development of which he is capable: money-lovers must be producers of some kind; honour-lovers must be guardians; philosophers must be kings (434a3-b7).

Now it is clear that UAD and PS are close relatives of UBD and PQS. However, there is also an important difference between them. The latter presuppose Plato's triadic division of the Kallipolis into producers, guardians, and rulers (not to say his entire psychological theory), the former do not. Consequently, Plato can use the former, but not the latter, to construct an argument for that division which relies on plausible, pre-theoretical premises of the sort that Glaucon and Adeimantus are willing to concede (1.12-13). But because the work he needs them to do could be done by the doctrine and principle he does accept, he will still be free, when the appropriate time arrives, to reject unique aptitudes and specialization as excess baggage—although this will not deter him from using them again when it is convenient to do so (453b2-456c2).

By the middle of Book 4, the Kallipolis has been shown to need producers, guardians, and rulers (4.5-6), and the first rough sketch of its structure, constitution, legal system, and religion has been completed (419a1-427d1). The time is ripe to make the substitution referred to:

> If a carpenter attempts to do the work of a cobbler, or a cobbler that of a carpenter, and they exchange their tools and their honours, or

the same man tries to do both, and all other similar exchanges [between producers] are made, do you think that this does any great harm to the polis?—Clearly not, he [Glaucon] said. (434a3-8)

This entails that the Kallipolis will not enforce PS. Why forbid something if it does no great harm? The Kallipolis will, however, enforce PQS:

> But if one who is by nature a workman or some other sort of moneymaker is tempted by wealth, or by the mob, or by his own strength, or some other such thing, and attempts to enter the class of guardians, or one of the guardians tries to enter the class of rulers, for which he is not fitted, and these exchange their tools and honours, or when the same man tries to do all these things, then I think you will agree that these exchanges, and this sort of meddling, are the ruin of the polis. (434a9-b7)

PS is abandoned; PQS is put in its place. Indeed, it emerges a few pages later in Book 4 that PS was never anything more than a useful image or shadow of justice: "It was a sort of image of justice [*eidōlon ti tēs dikaiosunēs*], this principle that it is right for one who is by nature a cobbler to cobble exclusively, and for the carpenter to practice carpentry exclusively, and so with the others" (443c4-7). PQS, on the other hand, is its substance: "But in truth, as it seems, justice was something like this. It consists in someone doing his own work not externally, but internally, and in the true sense his own. It means that someone must not allow the parts of his psyche to do each other's work, or meddle with one another" (443c9-d3). A psyche is just if its three constituent parts obey PQS; a polis is just if its three parts obey that same principle (434c7-10). If this is correct, then, not only does PS have no place in Plato's psychological theory, it has no place in his theory of justice either.

Despite all of this argument and evidence, it is hard to shake the view that Plato really did hold UAD and PS. Maybe he did not need them. Maybe he had no business holding them. Maybe his larger theories positively conflict with them. Still, on the most straightforward reading, the text of the *Republic* shows him reveling in them. In the face of this fact, we have two options. We can rest content with seeing that these extreme doctrines do not play any essential rôle in Plato's defense of justice, whatever he himself may have thought. Even if we go no further than this, we will have removed a major obstacle to taking that defense seriously; for there is no doubt that UAD and PS are serious obstacles both to plausibility and to sympathy. Or we can go further and accept the account of Plato's intentions given above. This requires us to depart somewhat from straightforward interpretative strategies, but it leaves Plato with a cogent and consistent position rather than a muddled and inconsistent one. The text may not compel us to take that further step, but it certainly invites us to take it. Nothing in the following sections presupposes that step. I have made free with UAD and PS just as Plato does, while remaining nonetheless committed to their eliminability.

4.4 PRODUCERS

The First Polis (369a5-372d3) is a notorious stumbling block to interpretation. Some believe that it is actually a false start, perhaps left unexcised from an earlier version of the *Republic*. Most believe that at the very least it has no clear place in Plato's argument.[2] I am unpersuaded by these claims. In my view, the First Polis is that part of the Kallipolis in which money-lovers, and only money-lovers, are made as happy as it is possible for them to be. But the argument in support of this view will not be complete until we confront the vexed question of the education and training of the producers in 4.6, and that of the lies of the rulers in 4.11.

The first thing to notice about the characterization of the First Polis is that no desires are attributed to its inhabitants except appetitive desires. These people work, feast, and have sex, but they neither fight nor philosophize:

> First then let us investigate the kind of life that our people will lead when they have been thus provided for. Will they not make bread and wine and clothes and shoes? They will build houses for themselves. In summer they will work without clothes or shoes, but in winter they will be adequately clothed and shod. For food they will make flour from wheat and meal from barley, and kneading and cooking these, they will serve fine cakes and loaves on reeds or clean leaves. Then, reclining on rustic beds of bryony and myrtle, they will feast together with their children, drinking of their wine. Crowned with wreaths they will hymn the gods and enjoy each other, bearing no more children than their means allow, cautious to avoid both poverty and war. (372a5-c1)

Nor are they motivated by every kind of appetitive desire. Needs are mentioned (369c9-d4), as are appetites that are beneficial, but not essential for survival, such as the desire for relishes (372c3-d3, 559a11-b5; 2.2). But when the "luxurious polis" (372e3-471c3) is described, it is made clear that no one in the First Polis has any unnecessary appetites. For the former is differentiated from the latter precisely on the ground that its members, unlike the members of the First Polis, "abandon themselves to the unlimited acquisition of wealth, disregarding the limit set by our necessary desires [*tōn anagkaiōn*]" (373d9-10), and so pursue "a multitude of things that exceed the requirements of necessity [*tou anagkaiou*]" (373b3-4). It is reasonable to conclude that the inhabitants of the First Polis are ruled by their necessary appetites. But people who are ruled by necessary appetites are money-lovers. It follows that the inhabitants of the First Polis are all money-lovers; no philosophers and honour-lovers live there.

Associated with each desire is a craft that caters to its satisfaction (342a1-d1). Following Plato, I shall call these "crafts concerned with the polis," or simply *polis crafts* (421a1-2, 433a4-6, 455a1-3, 455d6-e2). Two distinct lines of thought in the *Republic* have bearing on these. The first is that some people are by nature better equipped for one polis craft, some for another (370a7-b2). The second is that a person does better at a polis craft, producing better results more efficiently and easily, if he practices it exclusively throughout life instead of dividing his energies between two or more such crafts (370b3-4, 374a6, 374b6-c2, 394e2-6, 397d10-e8). Woven together, these ideas result in the unique aptitude doctrine (UAD): A person does best at a polis craft, producing the highest-quality results, just in case his natural aptitude for it is higher than his aptitude for any other, and he practices it exclusively throughout life.

Now UAD is a descriptive empirical principle, not a prescriptive one. Yet within four Stephanus pages of its introduction at 370c3-5 we find that it has acquired prescriptive force:

> We prevented the cobbler from trying to be at the same time a farmer or a weaver or a builder instead of just a cobbler, in order that the work of the cobbler be finely done; so with the others, each was to have one trade for which he had a natural aptitude, stick to it for life, and keep away from other crafts, so as not to miss the opportunities to practice his own craft well. (374b6-c2)

How did UAD acquire this new status? What justification did Plato have for thinking that the First Polis would enforce this prescriptive principle of specialization (PS) on its members? The answer suggested in the passage just quoted, and by far the most plausible answer, is that the First Polis has been designed to insure the optimal, long-term, stable satisfaction of the necessary appetites of its money-loving inhabitants, and that PS has been incorporated into its constitution because UAD suggests that doing so will alone guarantee that outcome. Thus the First Polis is intended to be one in which necessary appetites are optimally satisfied throughout life (372d1-3).

One step remains. We saw in 3.7 that a money-lover is maximally happy on Plato's view if he is successful in making the profit necessary to satisfy his necessary appetites optimally throughout life. We may conclude that Plato intended the First Polis to be one in which money-lovers are maximally happy.

It should be obvious, however, that the First Polis is no more self-sufficient than its members. For, first of all, it lacks the means of defending itself against such consequences of unnecessary appetites as war and civil strife (373e4-7). Thus it is stable only in a fantasy world in which people never pursue pleonectic satisfaction (359c3-5), never lose control of themselves or succumb to akrasia. Second, it lacks philosopher-kings with access to the good itself. And without them no polis can insure its own happiness (473c11-e5).

But neither is it intended to be self-sufficient. Plato offers it to us, not as an autonomous polis, but as a constituent, or as the forerunner of a real possibility that is a constituent, of a larger whole that is being slowly revealed. It is a polis whose acropolis is obscured from view. In it we see money-lovers living in harmony and happiness with one another. What we do not see, but will shortly be shown, is the acropolis with its guardians and rulers who underwrite that harmony and happiness, and without whom it would not be possible (473e4-5, 500e1-4). In that larger polis the First Polis is—to resort once more to that convenient Hegelianism—overcome but preserved.

4.5 Guardians

When unnecessary appetites are included in the motivational apparatus of the members of the First Polis, it becomes a "luxurious polis" (372e2). When this polis is "cleansed" (399e5-6) of unnecessary appetites, it emerges as the Second Polis. This is the part of the Kallipolis in which honour-lovers are made as happy as possible.

Among the new motivational factors introduced, the most important in terms of its political consequences is the unlimited desire for wealth to which the other unnecessary appetites naturally give rise (580d10-581a1). For this desire leads inevitably to geographical expansion, which in turn brings the luxurious polis into conflict with other poleis, whose members have likewise abandoned themselves "to the unlimited acquisition of wealth, disregarding the limit set by our necessary desires" (373d9-10). The result is war, "and many other bad things for the polis, both public and private" (373e4-7). To wage war as well as possible the polis will need an army. And UAD being granted, and PS enforced, this will have to be an army of professional full-time soldier-police. These are the *guardians*.

It is important to recognize that the guardians are introduced to defend the polis, not simply against other hostile poleis, but also against the unnecessary appetites, which are the root cause of such conflict. Since these desires exist inside the polis as well as outside it, the guardians have a policing function from the outset. That is why it is said that they will insure that "the enemies without shall not have the power, nor the friends within the desire, to harm the polis" (414b1-6; cf. 415d9-e3). It is because people are naturally prone to unnecessary appetites, which are destructive of social and political unity, that guardians are required. Hence the apparent detour through the luxurious polis in fact exposes the justification for introducing the guardians into the Kallipolis.

Now that the need for people to discharge this particular function within the Kallipolis has been established, the question immediately arises, especially given UAD and PS, of what natural endowments someone must have in order best to discharge it (374e4-376c5).

To be guardian material a person must be naturally quick to see things, naturally fast and strong, and naturally brave and high-spirited (374d4-375b8). He must, in other words, have all the natural aptitudes of a good soldier.[3] But, in addition to these aptitudes, which will enable him to be appropriately harsh to enemies, he must possess those which will make him gentle to his friends. Otherwise, the guardians "will not wait for others to destroy the polis but will destroy it themselves first" (375c2-4). In a slightly strange passage, which looks back to the discussion of friendship with Polemarchus (334c1-335a2) and forward to the characterization of the philosopher-kings (499a11-540c7), Socrates argues that a person will have this mixed potential if, like "a pedigree guard dog" (375e1-2), he is by nature "a lover of wisdom and a lover of learning" (376c1-2). For a dog of this kind "distinguishes the demeanour of a friend from that of an enemy by nothing other than that he has learned the one and is ignorant of the other" (376b3-4). And anyone "whose criterion of the friendly and the alien is knowledge and ignorance," must be a lover of learning and wisdom (376b4-6). I doubt that any more is intended here than the natural idea that if guardians are to be harsh to enemies and gentle to friends, it must be possible to train them to distinguish the one from the other in a reliable fashion. Otherwise they might be harsh or gentle to the wrong people.

The next topic is the education and training of the natural guardians (376c7-412b7). Here two questions arise. First, what acquirable skills, dispositions, and traits of character must be inculcated in the guardians? Second, how must the polis inculcate them?

In addition to having all the military skills and capacities requisite in a good soldier-policeman, the guardians must be steadfast and unchanging of character (380e3-381e6, 429e7-430b2). They must be brave (386a6-388e4), loyal to their fellows (386a3-4) without being overattached to them (387d1-388e3), and given neither to extremes of lamentation nor of mirth (388e5-389b1). They must be truth-loving (389b2-d6), moderate (389d7-390d6), and neither avaricious nor bribable (390d7-8). Finally, they must "attain to the greatest degree of gentleness towards each other, and those whom they are protecting" (416b9-c3).

This brings us to the second question. To develop the acquirable characteristics requisite in a good guardian, potential guardians must undergo a lengthy training in music and gymnastics (376e2-4). Some parts of this begin in infancy:

> Then it seems to follow that we must begin by controlling the storytellers. Whatever fine stories they compose we shall select, but those that are not fine we shall reject. Then we shall persuade nurses and mothers to tell their children only the ones we have selected, and in this way shape their psyches far more than they shape their bodies through their handling of them. (377b11-c5)

But the crucial parts of guardian training do not seem to begin until age ten. For the first generation of philosopher-kings, faced with the task of founding the Kallipolis, are willing to work with anyone under that age (540e5-541a1). This training continues until the seventeenth or eighteenth year, and is then followed by two or three years of intensive physical training (537b2-6).

In addition to training in music and gymnastics, young guardians learn their craft by imitating and assisting those who are already masters of it:

> Men and women will march out to war together, and, what is more, will take their children with them, when these are sturdy enough, in order that, like the children of other craftsmen, they may observe the activities of which they must be masters when they are fully grown. And as well as observing these, they must assist and help in all the business of war and serve their fathers and mothers. Or have you never noticed how it is in crafts, how for example the children of potters look on as helpers before they actually put their hands to the clay? (466e4-467a5)

Nor does the young guardians' early education end there. For in the discussion of the Third Polis it is made clear that, simultaneously with their apprenticeship, young guardians receive unsystematic training (537b8-c3) in the mathematical sciences:

> Now all this study of calculation and geometry and all the preliminary studies that are the necessary preliminaries to dialectic must be offered to them in childhood, but our method of teaching must not

be compulsion . . . but rather play. That will better enable you to observe what each of them is fitted for by nature. (536d5-537a2)

Consequently, there is more to the early education of the guardians (*primary education* as I shall call it) than the moulding of the relatively more affective and less cognitive aspects of their characters—although not, perhaps, a lot more (4.8).

The account of primary education completed, the question arises of who among its recipients should rule in the Second Polis: "All right, I said. What must we determine next? Isn't it who among these will rule and who be ruled?"(412b8-9). Given Plato's psychopolitical theory it is inevitable that the question should arise, and in just this form. In each polis, the stronger rules (2.15). In the Second Polis, the guardians are stronger than the producers (419a1-420a1). Consequently, the group that will rule that polis will consist of guardians. The only live issue is what properties a guardian must have to be a member of the ruling group. And that is precisely the issue Plato pursues.

Because ruling is a craft, which people learn by being apprenticed to those who are already masters of it, the rulers must be "the most skilled at guarding the polis" (412c9-10) and must be the older guardians, and the ruled the younger ones (412c2-4). Hence they "must be the best guardians of their belief that they must always do whatever they believe to be best for the polis" (413c5-7). The argument for this rather unexpected requirement is this:

> Now as the rulers must be the best among the guardians, mustn't they be the most skilled at guarding the polis? . . . And for this mustn't they be intelligent and capable and care for the polis? . . . Now someone cares most for that which he happens to love? . . . And he loves something most when he believes that the same things are advantageous to himself and to it, and that when it is doing well he himself is doing well along with it, and if not, then the opposite? . . . Then we must select from the other guardians such men as seem to us plainly inclined through the whole course of their lives to be eager to do what they believe to be advantageous to the polis, and who would be least likely to agree to do the opposite. (412c9-e3)

This leaves no doubt that the best rulers are those who securely believe that their own advantage and happiness and that of the polis are biconditionally tied. Unless we are to suppose that the rulers are deceived on this matter, a possibility excluded by the fact that their belief must be true (412e10-413d3), we must conclude that the rulers are being selected with an eye both to what is advantageous to the polis and to what is advantageous to themselves.

It is the group possessed of these features—older, most skilled in ruling, and secure in the true belief that what is advantageous to the polis is also advantageous to themselves and vice versa—that must rule the others: "Aren't these the people it is truly most correct to call complete guardians, so that the enemies without shall not have the power, nor the friends within the desire, to harm the polis? The young people, whom we were calling guardians up to now, we shall call auxiliaries and helpers of the rulers' convictions" (414b1-6). The rulers of the Second Polis are the complete guardians, as opposed to the auxiliaries.

Now it is easy to slip into the assumption that the complete guardians are the very people who will later emerge as philosopher-kings. And, of course, if this is correct, then the Second Polis contains philosopher-kings, and its guardian class contains wisdom-lovers as well as honour-lovers. But I do not think that it is correct.

First, the complete guardians receive only primary education, and this gives no access to forms. Second, they have true opinion, and a settled disposition to cling to it, but they are never said to have knowledge. Third, it is "political courage" (430c3-4) that enables them to cling to their true beliefs in the face of "pleasure or fear" (413a4-d3). This is made explicit in Book 4:

> I mean, I said, that courage is a kind of preserving . . . the preserving of the belief inculcated by the law through one's education about what things and what kind of things are to be feared. And by preserving that belief under all conditions I mean preserving it in the face of pains and pleasures and desires and fears. (429c5-d1; cf. *Laches* 191c8-e2)

But political courage is the virtue characteristic of the guardians, not of the philosopher-kings (429a8-430c7; 5.2). Fourth, the complete guardians are older men selected late in life for their devotion to the well-being of the polis, but future philosopher-kings are picked out early in life because they have both that quality and a natural aptitude for systematic mathematical science, dialectic, and practical polis management. This is made clear in Book 7, where the two methods of selection are explicitly contrasted:

> In most respects the same natures must be chosen. . . . But in addition we must now require that they not only be noble and tough, but also have the natural gifts required for this type of education. . . . In our earlier selection we chose older people, but in this one that will

not do . . . all large and frequent labours belong to the young. (536c7-d3)

Finally, the complete guardians are told a "noble lie" (4.10)—the Myth of the Metals: "Could we, I said, contrive one of those lies that are sometimes necessary, of which we were just now speaking [at 382a4-d3], one noble lie to persuade, in the optimum case, the rulers themselves, but if not them, the rest of the polis?" (414b8-c2). But we know that such lies are the sole prerogative of the true rulers: "So it is proper for the rulers, if for anyone at all, to lie for the advantage of the polis in cases involving enemies or citizens, but everyone else must keep away from this sort of thing" (389b7-9). Since the complete guardians are being lied to, it follows that they cannot be the true rulers.

Thus the complete guardians are not philosopher-kings, and the distinction between guardians and auxiliaries, though it may prefigure the distinction between wisdom-loving philosopher-kings and honour-loving guardians, is not itself that distinction.

If this is correct, the Second Polis contains only honour-lovers, or, since the First Polis is included as an appropriately transformed constituent of the Second (397d10-e8, 462a2-464b4), honour-lovers and money-lovers.

In Books 3 and 4, the effects of primary education are described as threefold: First, it enables its recipients to recognize the different modes and qualities of moderation, courage, generosity, high-mindedness, and the other virtues and vices for what they are, namely, models of figures, or images of models of figures (402c1-6; 2.6). Second, it brings aspiration into harmony with reason, so that both these psychic parts "exercise authority over appetite" (442a4-5). Third, it gives its recipients political courage, "the power to preserve through everything the true and lawful belief about what is to be feared and what not" (430b2-4). In other words, primary education gives a person true beliefs about the visible manifestations of the virtues and vices (notice that only virtues and their opposites are mentioned at 402c1-6), and hence cognitive access to their figures; for access to figures is required for reliably true belief about the visible world (2.8-10). But it does not give him access to figures generally, or to forms (4.8). It brings a person's emotional responses into accord with reason—whether his own or someone else's (590c8-d6). As a result, neither fear nor temptation will cause him to do anything other than what reason judges to be best.

Because primary education has these effects, it guarantees, as far as training and education can, that the guardians will be successful in battle against the enemies of the polis (provided, of course, that reason gives them the right instructions). And this, as we shall see, is the key to their stable, long-term happiness. But before we take up that topic, we must explore another aspect of the guardians' life, namely, their living arrangements. For these, too, make an important contribution to guardian happiness.

At the end of Book 3, and again in Book 5, it is made clear that the guardians have a very different way of life than the producers, and that they are brought up, educated, and housed in a different part of the polis (415d6-e4, 460c1-d7). Producers seem to have a traditional family-based way of life (4.12). They engage in manufacture and trade, earn money, own their own houses and other items of property, marry, and rear and educate their own children, with the exception of those who turn out to have the potential to be guardians (415c3-5). Guardians, on the other hand, live Spartan-fashion in a military camp (415d8-9, 416e3-4). They do not form traditional family units: "These women [the female guardians] shall all be common to all these men [the male guardians], and none shall live privately with a man, and the children too shall be common, and no parent shall know its own offspring nor any child its parent" (457c10-d3). They do not even choose their own sexual partners—their sexual and reproductive lives are governed by the eugenics policy of the rulers (459d7-460a10). They are forbidden private property (416d4-6): "Whatever moderate and courageous athletes of war require will be provided by taxation on the other citizens as a salary for their guardianship, in such quantity that there will be neither shortages nor surplus over the year" (416d7-e3). No accumulation of goods is permitted.

If we look at this account of the nature, education, and living conditions of the guardians with an eye to the happiness of the nonguardian members of the polis, it is readily intelligible. No nonguardian aiming to maximize his own happiness would choose to live in a polis in which the soldier-police were anything other than brave, honest, moderate, loyal, and reliably gentle to friends and harsh to enemies, or in which the rulers pursued anything other than what was advantageous to the polis. Nor would any nonguardian choose to live in a polis whose guardians—heavily armed, skilled in warfare, and well organized—competed with him for the same social goods. But if we look at the account with an eye to the happiness of the guardians themselves, it seems somewhat less intelligible. Adeimantus' question at the beginning of Book 4 must be ours as well:

What defense would you offer, Socrates, to the charge that you are not making your guardians happy, and that they have only themselves to thank for this—the polis in truth is theirs, but they derive no good from the polis, in the way that others [other rulers][4] do, who own land, build grand and beautiful houses, acquire furnishings to go with them, make their own private sacrifices to the gods, entertain strangers, and, of course, also possess what you were just talking about, gold and silver, and all the things conventionally believed to belong to people who are to be happy or blessed? One might well say that your guardians look exactly like paid mercenaries who sit in the polis and do nothing except watch over it. (419a1-420a1)

Why would powerful, well-armed people, aiming to maximize their own happiness, live in army barracks, deprived of Syracusan cuisine, Attic pastries, and Corinthian girlfriends (404d1-9), when they could live the life of an Agamemnon or a Darius?

Socrates' answer is that the guardians "living in this way [in the Second Polis] are happiest [*eudaimonestatoi*]" (420b4-5). In Book 5, he explains why (465e4-466a6). First of all, they are spared many evils:

Won't lawsuits and mutual accusations vanish from among them, since they own only their bodies, everything else being common property? . . . Nor would cases of assault or insult occur among them. . . . For, as a result of the laws, they will live in peace with each other. . . . I hesitate to mention the petty evils they will also escape: the poor person's flattery of the rich, all the perplexities and pains involved in bringing up children and making the necessary money to maintain the household, contracting debts and denying creditors, and doing all kinds of things to provide enough money to give to their wives or household slaves to dispense; what and how people suffer from these things, my friend, is plain and sordid, and not worth detailed discussion. (464d7-465c7)

Second, much of their lives is spent in the activities most favoured by superbly trained honour-loving warriors like themselves—hunts and chases, dances, gymnastic and horse-riding contests (412b3-6), and, when necessary, war itself. Those who excel, especially in combating the enemies of the polis, are honoured in true Homeric fashion—crowned with wreaths, chosen as bridegrooms more often than the others, honoured with hymns, their graves cared for and worshipped at as those of divinities (468b2-469b3). Finally, this type of life is theirs, not just for a short chance period, but reliably from infancy till death, and beyond (468e4-469b3). For the Second Polis will survive as long as there is no discord among its guardians (465b8-10, 545c9-d3). And everything has been done to insure that that will be a very long time indeed (462a2–464d5; 4.10).

When bolstered by the account of pleasure in Book 9, these reasons go a long way toward justifying the claim that the life provided to the guardians in the Second Polis is happier than that of the victors in the Olympic Games (465d5-e2), and that only "a silly and childish idea of happiness" (466b7-8) could make them think otherwise. But the question of whether this claim is justified aside, I think that it is now certain that the Second Polis is at least intended to be the Kallipolis for its honour-loving inhabitants.

Even though the Second Polis possesses some of the resources necessary to combat pleonexia, however, and is to that extent closer to being a real possibility than the First Polis, it is not in fact a real possibility either. For without philosopher-kings, who alone have access to the good itself and its constituent forms to guide them, the honour-loving guardians, who have at best true belief about the visible (2.9), cannot insure the long-term success and stability of the Second Polis. Indeed, without philosopher-kings no polis, and no individual, can achieve stable happiness (473e4-5).

4.6 Producers Again

The producers are maximally happy in the First Polis. But do they remain happy when that polis is absorbed into the Second Polis? The answer hinges in large part on the vexed question of whether they are intended to receive primary education.[5]

Primary education is specifically introduced as part of a unified package of social arrangements designed to turn into guardians children who already possess the natural assets requisite in good soldier-police (4.5). Since producers are excluded from the eugenics programmes and living arrangements that are the other components of the package, and since they, like guardians, for the most part breed true to type (415a7-8), scarcely any of the children of producers will have the natural assets that are the prerequisites for primary education. Primary education is for future soldiers (398b3-4, 386b10-c1) or guardians (383c3-4, 387c3-5, 401b8-c1, 402c1-2), not for future producers.

Second, it is never explicitly said that future producers are to receive primary education, and although the various tests by which the philosopher-kings are to be separated out from the general class of guardians who have completed their primary education are specified in detail (4.9), no test by which a more general pool of those receiving primary education is to be separated into guardians and producers is ever mentioned. Given the explicitness of the *Republic* on educational matters, especially innovative ones of this sort, this is strong evidence that no such pool is countenanced. The tests are unnecessary because only children of exceptional guardians (460c1-5), and those rare producer offspring with gold or silver in their natures (415c3-5), receive primary education.

Third, each component of primary education is justified by appeal to some trait of character that a good soldier-policeman, motivated by a desire for honour, should have (4.5). But these are not the traits that an efficient producer seeking profit requires. Hence, if primary education is intended for producers, we are not provided with the kind of rationale for doing it that is carefully provided in the case of the guardians themselves (383c3-4, 386b10-c1, 387c3-5, 387e9-388a3, 394e1-395d1, 398e6-7, 401b1-d3).

Fourth, some of the arguments by which the curriculum of primary education is justified show that it is totally unsuitable for future producers. For example, the argument given in favour of restricting the stories that make up primary education to those requiring students to imitate or impersonate only "gentlemen" (*kaloi kagathoi*),[6] not "metalworkers or other craftsmen," is that because PS (4.3-4) applies to imitation as well as actual crafts, a person should imitate only the one type of person he plans to become (394e1-395b4). On this showing, future producers should be taking the parts of cobblers and carpenters in stories about hard-working and obedient producers, not the parts of Achilles, Ajax, or Odysseus in stories about fierce and courageous warriors.

Fifth, in the Myth of the Metals in Book 3, it is very clearly implied that, except in a very few cases, the children of producers receive a completely different education than the children of the rulers and guardians:

> If a child of theirs [of the rulers] should be born with an admixture
> of bronze or iron, by no means are they to take pity on it, but they
> are to honour its nature appropriately, and drive it out into the work
> ers and farmers; and, again, if from these a child should be born who
> has an admixture of gold or silver, they will honour it, and bring it
> up to join the rulers or guardians, for there is an oracle that the polis
> will be ruined if it ever has a bronze or iron guardian. (415b6-c6; cf.
> 423c6-d6)

Clearly there would be no point in sending a child with iron or bronze in his psyche out among the farmers and craftsmen if he were there going to receive the very same education and honours as guardian offspring.[7]

Sixth, the effects of primary education are sometimes explicitly contrasted with the effects of the kind of education provided to producers: "In the polis we were founding [the Second Polis], who do you think will turn out to be better men—the guardians who receive the education we have described [primary education], or the cobblers who are educated in cobblery?" (456d8-10; a similar contrast is suggested at 405a6-b4, 522a2-b7). This would make no sense if producers actually received primary education.

Seventh, no one "will be educated in music" until he knows what the qualities and modes of moderation, courage, and so on are (402b5-c8). But no one can know this until he has access to the figures of which these things are images. Money-lovers, however, have access only to qualities and modes. It follows that money-lovers, and therefore producers (4.4), cannot be educated in music.

Finally, towards the end of the discussion of primary education, we are told that gymnastics is not aimed primarily at the body, as most people think, but that both it and music are aimed at parts of the psyche (410b10-c3):

> It seems then that a god has given these two crafts, music and gym-nastics, to human beings for these two things, not for the psyche and the body, except incidentally, but for aspiration and for reason, in order that these might be in harmony with each other, each being tuned to the proper degree of tension and relaxation. (411e4-412a2; cf. 441e8-442a2)

But if music and gymnastics are aimed at aspiration and reason, not at appetite and the body, then given the strict analogy between psyche and polis (435a5-b2), they should be aimed at the guardians and rulers, not at the producers.

From evidence that suggests that primary education is not intended for producers, let us turn to evidence on the other side.

Many remarks, especially in Books 2 and 3, strongly suggest that at least some parts of primary education are directed at the entire Kallipolis, not simply at the future rulers and guardians. The following are typical. Stories in which the gods are represented as mistreating their parents "should not be told in our polis" (378b1-6). If the polis "is to be well governed," we shall not allow anyone to say in it that the god is the source of evil, "nor must anyone either young or old hear it said, either in verse or prose" (380b6-c3). Nor must "our mothers, believing bad stories, ter-rify our children with them" (381e1-6). All craftsmen are forbidden "to represent whether in pictures or in buildings or in any other works, char-acter that is vicious, mean, unconstrained, or graceless" (401b3-5).

But these remarks, and the others like them, must be handled judi-ciously. For each of the censorship measures they mention is justified by appeal to specific features requisite in *good guardians*, not to features requisite in good citizens generally. Thus, for example, craftsmen are prohibited from representing what is vicious, not because such representations tend to corrupt all young members of the polis, but solely in order that "our guardians may not, bred among images of evil, as it were in an evil meadow, every day cropping and grazing from many places, collect little by little in their psyches a big evil" (401b8-c3). And this makes it clear, I think, that we cannot infer that the censorship measures in question are enforced on producers, as they are on guardians, in order to shape *their* psyches. It is the psyches of the guardians that are in focus, not those of producers. Since the aim of Platonic education is always to reshape, or "turn around," the psyche of its recipient (2.4), it follows that even if some parts of primary education are directed at the future producers as well as at the future rulers and guardians, they are not directed at the former, as they are at the latter, in order to *educate* them. And that seems to be just another way of saying that primary *education* is not intended for producers.[8]

If primary education is not intended for future producers, what sort of education does Plato think they should receive? In my view, PS more or less exhausts his innovative thought on this topic (4.3-4). Future producers are educated and trained in the Kallipolis through a traditional apprenticeship in a craft. However, and this is the innovative requirement, the craft in question must be the polis craft for which their natural aptitude is highest, and they must practice it exclusively.

The formal discussion of the guardians and their education and training is part of the account of the Second Polis, which is the Kallipolis for guardians (4.5). Similarly, the formal discussion of the rulers and their training and education is part of the account of the Third Polis, which is the Kallipolis for philosopher-kings (4.9). Since the formal discussion of the producers is part of the account of the First Polis, which is the Kallipolis for producers, there is a general structural or compositional reason to think that if the training and education of the producers are discussed anywhere, it will be there.

And that is precisely what we find. In order that the "polis adequately provide" for the satisfaction of the needs that have brought it into being, "one must be a farmer, another a builder, another a weaver," and so on (369c9-d10). Consequently, the training programs for such crafts must exist in the First Polis. But since these will simply be traditional apprenticeship programs they are not discussed—the obvious does not need to be spelled out (412b2-6). Instead, discussion focuses on what is distinctive about these educational proposals, namely, PS.

This account of producer education is further supported by various chance remarks which occur later in the *Republic*. In a passage already quoted, Socrates asks, "Who do you think will turn out to be better men—the guardians who receive [primary education], or the cobblers who are educated in cobblery?" (456d8-10). This suggests that training in a craft is to a producer what primary education is to a guardian. And this suggestion is further supported by the following passage: "And as well as observing these, they [the neophyte guardians] must assist and help in all the business of war and serve their fathers and mothers. Or have you never noticed how it is in crafts, how for example the children of potters look on as helpers before they actually put their hands to the clay?" (467a1-5). Future producers are apprenticed to their parents as future guardians are to theirs.

Thus—on the negative side—there is compelling reason to think that Plato intends primary education to be for future rulers and guardians only, and that any parts of it that are directed to producers are intended not to educate them but to protect future guardians from corrupting influences. And—on the positive side—there is reason to think that Plato intends future producers to receive a traditional apprenticeship training in the single polis craft for which they have as high a natural aptitude as for any other. Hence it is training in a craft that releases an appetitive psyche from the rule of unnecessary appetites, gives it access to modes, and causes it to abandon the pleasures of food, drink, and sex for the more pleasant pleasure of making money.

It is a virtue of this account of producer education that it fits in with the overall argument, at least as I have been expounding it. For it is perfectly intelligible that a self-interested money-lover, largely persuaded by Plato, would want to be trained exclusively in the polis craft for which his natural aptitude is highest—in the Kallipolis, the practice of such a craft is the most efficient means to the pleasure of making money. But it is not at all clear why a self-interested money-lover would want to receive any primary education, except, perhaps, as a means to insuring that the rulers and guardians remain as virtuous as possible. For in the Kallipolis primary education is a means to the pleasure of being honoured, not to the pleasure of making money.

The situation of the producers in the Second Polis seems, then, to be as follows. They are ruled by people who have a settled disposition to do what is best for the polis. They are policed and protected by people who are brave, honest, moderate, loyal, and reliably gentle to friends and harsh to enemies. And neither of these groups competes with them for the money they most want; guardians are honour-lovers, not money-lovers. In addition, the producers receive only the training and education that is required, first, to moderate their unnecessary appetites so that these will not threaten the stability of the Kallipolis, and with it their own long-term happiness; second, to insure the optimal satisfaction of their necessary appetites; and third, to insure that nothing in their way of life will corrupt the guardians.

On this reading, the absorption of the First Polis into the Second does nothing to alter the happiness of producers. If the First Polis is the Kallipolis for producers, so is the Second.

4.7 PHILOSOPHER-KINGS

Having completed his account of the Second Polis in Book 5, Plato turns to the question of how to bring it into being (472c4-473e5). His answer encapsulates the central paradox of the *Republic*: if the Kallipolis is ever to be realized in practice, philosophers must become kings or kings philosophers.

> Unless, I said, philosophers become kings in our poleis or those now called kings and rulers genuinely and adequately philosophize, so that these two things, political power and philosophy, are coinstantiated, while the many natures of those who at present pursue either apart from the other are necessarily excluded, there can be no rest from troubles for our poleis, my dear Glaucon, nor I think for human beings in general. Nor, until this happens, will this constitution which we have been expounding in theory ever, so far as it is possible, come forth in nature and see the sunlight. It is because I saw how very paradoxical this statement is that I have for some time hesitated to make it. For it is hard to realize that there can be no happiness, public or private, in any other polis. (473c11-e5)

The elaboration and defense of this answer leads to the construction of the Third Polis. But before that defense can begin, the philosopher must be properly identified.

The key to his identity lies in his name—wisdom-lover (475b8-9). Because he is a lover, he loves all of what he loves: "Is it necessary to remind you, or do you remember that when we say that someone loves something, if it is rightly said of him, then he mustn't love one part of it and not another, but must love all of it?" (474c8-11).[9] Because it is wisdom he loves, he must love everything that one can learn or come to know: "The one who is willing to taste every kind of learning with gusto, and who turns to learning with enthusiasm, and cannot get enough of it, he is the one we shall rightly call a philosopher" (475c6-8). But this formula is too liberal. For, as Glaucon points out, it includes both sightseers and craft-lovers, "who are what they are because they delight in learning" (475d1-e1).

Hence the next step in identifying the philosopher is to distinguish him from the sightseers and craft-lovers. Once it is taken, philosophers emerge as lovers of true wisdom (or knowledge), as opposed to lovers of opinion (480a11-12), and the forms have decisively entered the picture (2.8). The defense proper can now begin.

Although the argument that only philosophers have access to forms almost settles the question of who should rule the Third Polis (484d8-10), it does not conclusively lay it to rest. For it could be that though the philosophers are superior to the others in cognitive capacity, they are inferior to them in "experience or in [some] other part of virtue" (484d6-7). And the latter defect might outweigh their superior knowledge. But if people naturally qualified both in knowledge and in virtue can exist, they should clearly rule (484d5-485a2). So the defense hinges on whether virtue and knowledge are indeed naturally compatible (485a4-8).

Because the philosophic nature loves all learning, it must also love the truth, for wisdom and truth are so related that no one can love the one but not the other (485a9-e5). Because its desire is focused solely on wisdom and truth, it is not interested in the pleasures of the body or those of making money (485d10-e5). For "when someone's desires are strongly directed to one object, we know that they are thereby weakened towards others, like a river that has been canalized in another direction" (485d6-8; 3.9). Again, because the philosophic nature is not small-minded, but "lofty enough to theorize about all time and all substance," it does not "believe that the life of man is a big thing" (486a8-10). Hence it is brave, for it does not fear death (486b1-5). And being "neither money-loving nor small-minded, nor given to false pretension or cowardice," it must also be just and fair (486b6-13). Finally, since no lover of anything could find it difficult to learn or easy to forget what he loved, the philosophic nature is easily "guided to the forms of each of the beings [*epi tēn tou ontos idean hekastou*]" and does not forget what it has once learned (486c3-d11). It follows not only that all the cognitive and ethical properties requisite in a ruler are naturally compatible, but that all must be coinstantiated by a psyche "which is going to have an adequate and complete grasp of being" (486e1-3). Thus when those who possess a philosophic nature "are completed by education and maturity," leadership of the polis should be turned over to them alone (487a7-8).

The defense of philosopher-kings, however, does not rest on this argument alone. For Plato sees clearly the limits of philosophical arguments that reach conclusions radically at odds with common beliefs. It is not the beliefs that get written off, but the arguments:

Adeimantus said: No one would be able to contradict what you've said, Socrates. But this is how those who hear what you now say are affected on each occasion. They think that because of their inexperience in the game of question and answer, they are at every question led astray a litle bit by the argument, and that when these little bits are added together at the end of the discussion, a big false step appears which is the opposite of what they said at the outset . . . yet [their view about] what is the truth of the matter is not affected by this outcome. I say this with a view to the present case, for someone might well say now that he is unable, as you ask each of your questions, to contradict you, yet he sees that in fact of all those who take up philosophy—not those who merely dabble in it while still young in order to complete their upbringing, but those who linger in it for a longer time—the greatest number become cranks, not to say altogether vicious, while those who seem the best of them are rendered useless to the polis by the studies you recommend. (487b1-d5)

The next fifteen pages (487b1-502c8), filled with passion and rhetorical brilliance, try to undermine this objection by diagnosing its sources.

Just as most sailors do not understand that "a true pilot must of necessity pay attention to the seasons, the heavens, the stars, the winds, and everything proper to the craft if he is really to rule a ship," most people do not understand what ruling actually consists in. Hence they write off as idle stargazers the very people who know how to rule the polis, and put in their place those who promise to satisfy their desires in the short term (487e7-489c10). So one reason philosophers are dismissed as politically useless is that people have a false idea of what ruling is, which derives its authority only from the irrational political practices of their own poleis.

"But by far the greatest slander is brought on philosophy by those who claim to practice it" (489d1-2). These fall into three groups. The largest consists of people who lack the natural capacity for philosophy. They are the ones people have in mind when they say that philosophers are cranks or corrupt. But they are properly termed sophists, not philosophers (495b8-496a10). The second largest group is much smaller than the first. It consists of people possessed of a genuine philosophical nature who fall away from philosophy through being perverted early in life by the force of public opinion (490e2-495b7). Alcibiades—never mentioned by name but recognizable in the discussion (494a11-495b6)—is a case in point. "There remains but a very small group of those who deservedly consort with philosophy," and who persist in their study of it "because the corrupting influences are absent." Though they avoid corruption, however, they do not receive the best nurture. Consequently, they do not develop their full powers, but are "perverted and altered" into people who avoid politics, and are satisfied if they can live a "life free from injustice and impiety, and depart from it with a beautiful hope, blameless and content" (496a11-497c3). Here the presiding genius is surely Socrates himself (496c3-4; 1.2, 1.7).

Therefore, a second reason that people have such a poor view of philosophers is that their stereotypes are defective because based on the wrong originals. For "they have never seen, either in one case or in many, a man made as completely as possible like to and harmonious with virtue, both in practice and in theory, ruling in a polis of like quality" (498e3-499a2).

So people's beliefs about ruling and philosophers have no bearing on genuine ruling or philosophers, and do not threaten the view that only philosophers are fit to rule (503b4-5).

Now that the combination of traits required in a philosopher-king has been shown to be a natural possibility, the next topic is the training and education of the people who possess it (502c10-541b5). A little was said about this in the discussion of the Second Polis, but "it must now be taken up again from the beginning" (502e1-2). For "in our earlier selection we chose older people, but in this one that will not do . . . all large and frequent labours belong to the young" (536c7-d3). The earlier account, provisional and inexplicit (503a7-b1; 4.5), is thus completely superseded by the one we are about to be given.

The new account begins at the end. What the philosopher must finally be brought to is a knowledge of something more important even than the virtues—the form of the good (504d4-505b3).

> For you have often heard that the form of the good is the greatest object of study, and that it is by relation to it that just things and all the rest become useful and beneficial. . . . If we do not know it, even the fullest possible knowledge of other things would be of no benefit to us, any more than if we were to acquire any possession without getting the good of it. (505a2-b1)

Through the analogies of the Sun, Line, and Cave, the nature of the good is progressively explored and characterized (2.4-11), until, seventeen pages later, we are returned to the question of the education of the philosophers (521c1). But that question has now been transformed by knowledge of the destination to be reached.

After primary education to the age of eighteen and two years of intense physical training (537b2-6), those who have performed especially well receive ten years of systematic education in the mathematical sciences

(537b8-c3). For the forms must be defined in mathematical terms if they are to be adequate for epistemic purposes. Those who are again successful go on to five years of training in dialectic (537d3-539e2). For only dialectically defensible theories yield knowledge (2.9). Those who prove successful in dialectic, and in the fifteen-year apprenticeship training in practical polis management which follows it, finally gain access to the good itself and its constituent forms.

> And when they are fifty years old, those who have lasted the whole course and are in every way best at everything, both in practice [*ergois*] and in theory [*epistēmais*], must at last be led to the final goal, and must be compelled to lift up the eyes of their psyches towards that which provides light for everything, the good itself. And taking it as their model, they must put in good order both the polis and themselves for the remainder of their lives, taking turns with the others. (540a4-b1)

For one cannot have knowledge of the good and bad qualities of something unless one has experienced it in actual use (2.11).

Those who have reached that goal are philosopher-kings at last. The polis over which they rule, and which contains the elaborate educational apparatus necessary to reliably produce them, is the Third Polis.

4.8 Guardians Again

It is uncontroversial, I think, that every guardian receives primary education. But as we discover in the account of the Third Polis, some receive considerably more formal education than that. Consequently, not all guardians have the same cognitive resources, nor are all of them of the same psychological type.

Only guardians who successfully complete primary education and education or training in mathematical science, dialectic, and practical polis management actually become philosopher-kings. Since failure is possible in each of these studies, there are potentially three different subclasses of guardians: (1) those who make it through primary education, but not systematic science (acknowledged at 537a9-c3); (2) those who make it through systematic science, but not dialectic (acknowledged at 537c9-d8); and (3) those who make it through dialectic, but not polis management (acknowledged at 540a4-6).

Not all of these sub-classes, however, correspond to real differences in cognitive resources or psychological type. For unless a person actually succeeds in becoming a philosopher-king, he will never develop the true, unified, dialectically defensible theory of everything, which alone grants access to the good itself. Therefore, he will have no knowledge (2.8), and will never experience the pleasure of knowing the truth. Like the man who fails in dialectic, he is an honour-lover, nothing more (2.12, 3.7). Subclasses (2) and (3), then, collapse into the single class that I shall call *officers*.

Officers, however, are very different from the *privates* who constitute (1). This is disguised to some extent by the fact that both are called guardians. But what is actually said about the different effects of primary education, on the one hand, and systematic study of mathematical science, on the other, puts it beyond doubt that guardians of these two classes differ substantially in cognitive resources. And, as we shall see, this difference is the result of a significant difference in psychological type.

The picture of primary education that emerged in 4.5 is aptly epitomized in the description of music Glaucon gives in Book 7: "It educated the guardians through habits; its melodies gave them a certain inner harmony, not knowledge, and its rhythms instilled in them a certain grace" (522a3-6). Primary education inculcates those habits of thought, affective response, and action which are in fact best, together with the skills an effective soldier-policeman would need. But that is all it does (401e1-402a4). The cognitive resources it provides are severely limited both in scope (430b2-4) and in depth (537b8-c5). Consequently, people who receive only primary education might well make good privates, but they would make very poor officers (525b3-6, 527c1-d4).

The major difference between primary education and education in systematic mathematical science is that the latter gives access to figures generally (2.9), not just to the figures of the virtues and vices (4.6). Consequently, officers have access to true beliefs about the entire visible world, whereas privates have reliable access only to its ethical aspects.

I turn now to the psychological differences that underlie these differences in cognitive capacity. We have seen that Plato's theory of psychological types, like so much in the *Republic*, is based on his account of the twofold division of desires into appetitive, spirited, and rational desires, on the one hand, and necessary and unnecessary desires, on the other (2.2-3, 3.1-10). Hence there is room in his theory for at least six different types of psyches: those ruled by lawless unnecessary appetites (tyrants); those ruled by nonlawless unnecessary appetities (democrats); those ruled by necessary appetites (oligarchs); those ruled by unnecessary spirited desires (timocrats); those ruled by necessary spirited desires; and, finally, those ruled by rational desires (philosophers). Somewhere in this elaborate scheme there must be separate slots for privates and officers, but where?

It is quite clear that privates are honour-lovers not appetitive men (4.5).

It is also clear, however, that officers too are honour-lovers, not wisdom-lovers or philosophers. Those who do outstandingly well in primary education are selected for training in the mathematical sciences, and "receive more honours than the others" (537b8-9). Those who are again outstanding receive still "greater honours" (537c9-d8) before going on to dialectic. Hence, if officers are honour-lovers, they have an incentive to pursue a course of studies which ends with dialectic. Philosophers, by contrast, have no such incentive. For the pleasure of knowing the truth is not available until the entire course of studies, including fifteen years of practical polis management, has been completed.

Once privates and officers are both revealed as honour-lovers, it becomes irresistible to conclude, simply on grounds of psychological plausibility, that privates are ruled by unnecessary spirited desires and that officers are ruled by necessary spirited desires. For we can easily imagine someone who wants so badly the immediate approval that comes from being a successful private that he will have no patience for a study that might lead to honour, even greater honour, in ten years, whereas someone else might be able to postpone immediate gratification of his spirited desires, living without much recognition in the present in order to gain greater recognition in the future. The latter is officer material, the former is not.

It would seem, therefore, that Plato's theory of psychological types, itself based on his theory of the divisions of desires, has natural places for both privates and officers, just as his epistemological theory does. Officers are ruled by necessary spirited desires, exercise scientific-thought, and have access to figures generally. Privates are ruled by unnecessary spirited desires, exercise what we might call *musical-thought*, and have access only to ethical figures.

The class of guardians, at first introduced as a single class, later divides into complete guardians and auxiliaries, or officers and privates. Later still it spawns the philosopher-kings. The complexity was always there, just as the full-blown conception of the Kallipolis was implicit in the First Polis, but it is revealed only as its various components find a natural place in the developing argument.

4.9 KALLIPOLIS

Does Plato intend the Third Polis to be the Kallipolis for philosophers, honour-lovers, and money-lovers? Is everyone supposed to be maximally happy there, or only some, or none at all? I shall begin with the philosophers and work down, although part of my discussion of them will be relevant, in an obvious way, to honour-lovers as well.

In Book 2, the terms of the requisite defense of justice are set. We must strip the completely just person of the G-consequences of his justice, and the completely unjust person of the G-consequences of his injustice, "so that our two men may reach the limits, one of justice, the other of injustice, and be judged as to which of the two is happier [*eudaimonesteros*]" (361d1-3). In Book 5, we are reminded that those terms remain in operation:

> It was then to have a model, I said, that we were seeking the nature of justice itself, and the completely just man, if he should come into being, and what kind of man he would be if he did, and likewise in regard to injustice and the most unjust man, so that by looking at how their relationship to happiness [*eudaimonias*] and its opposite seemed to us, we would also be compelled to agree about ourselves as well, that he who was most like them would have a portion [of happiness] most like theirs. (472c4-d1)

In Book 8, these terms are stated again: "Our aim was . . . to examine whether the best man was the happiest [*eudaimonestatos*] and the worst the most wretched [*athliōtatos*], or whether matters stood otherwise" (544a5-8). One page later, the same terms are restated:

> After observing the most unjust of all we may oppose him to the most just; thus we can complete our inquiry into the relation between pure justice and pure injustice with regard to the happiness [*eudaimonias*] and wretchedness [*athliotētos*] of the men who possess them, so that we may be either be persuaded by Thrasymachus and pursue injustice or be persuaded by the argument that is now coming to light and pursue justice. (545a5-b1)

Then, in Book 9, when the comparison of the best and worst men is complete, the results are reported as follows: "The best, the most just, and the most happy [*eudaimonestaton*] is the most kingly who rules like a king over himself, and . . . the worst, the most unjust, and the most wretched [*athliōtaton*] is the most tyrannical who most tyrannizes himself and the polis he rules" (580c1-4). It is difficult to avoid the conclusion, simply on the basis of these so insistent passages alone, that Plato both intended to show that the philosopher-kings ruling the Kallipolis are the happiest of people and thought he had succeeded in showing it.

There are other passages, however, that can give one pause, and make one wonder whether the insistent passages are really to be taken at face value.

When Adeimantus explicitly raises the question about whether or not the guardians are happy in the Second Polis (4.6), Socrates responds:

By following the same path I think we'll discover what to reply. We shall say that it would not be at all surprising if these men, living in this way [the guardians living in the Second Polis], are happiest [eudaimonestatoi]. However, in founding our polis we are looking not to the exceptional happiness [diapherontōs eudaimon] of any one group, but, as far as possible, to that of the whole polis. (420b3-8)

Then, later, when Glaucon asks if it is just to require the philosopher-kings to rule when the life of pure philosophy is so much better, Socrates reminds him of what he has already said to Adeimantus:

My friend, I said, you have forgotten again that it is not the concern of the law to make any one class in the polis do exceptionally well [diapherontōs eu praxei], but to contrive to bring this about for the whole polis, harmonizing the citizens by persuasion and compulsion, and making them share with each other the benefits that each group can confer on the community. And it produces such men in the polis, not in order to allow them to turn in whatever direction each wishes, but in order that it may use them to bind the polis together. (519e1-520a4)

Now there is no doubt that these responses, by contrasting the exceptional happiness of the guardians and philosopher-kings with that of the polis as a whole, suggest that both groups sacrifice some happiness to live in the Second or Third Polis. Nor is there any doubt that the fact that Socrates does not respond simply by asserting outright that the guardians or philosopher-kings are maximally happy in the Second or Third Polis suggests that Plato has a reason not to be so explicit. And what could that reason be other than that he does not intend them to be maximally happy there?

Setting the passages quoted back into their textual contexts will cast them in a very different light, and suggest an answer to that question.

The end of Socrates' answer to Adeimantus runs as follows:

. . . So now too, don't compel us to give our guardians the kind of happiness that would turn them into anything but guardians. . . . For you surely see that guardians of the laws and polis who are not the real thing, but only seem to be such, destroy the polis utterly, just as they alone have the opportunity to govern it well, and make it happy. Hence if we're making true guardians, who are least likely to do bad things to the polis, while our critic is making some farmers into banqueters, happy as they would be at some festival rather than in a polis, then he is not talking about a polis at all. Bearing this in mind, we should examine whether our aim in establishing our guardians should be to give them the most happiness [*pleistē eudai-monia*], or whether that is something we must aim to see develop in the whole polis, and must compel and persuade these guardians and auxiliaries to do the same, so that they'll be the best possible crafts-men in their work, and similarly for all the others, and so as the entire polis develops in a well-governed way, we must leave to each group that share of happiness that is its by nature. (420d5-421c6)

Socrates connects being a good guardian and getting the kind of hap-piness naturally appropriate to a guardian (that is, to an honour-lover) with the unity and stability of the polis. If we try to give the guardians the wrong kind of happiness (that which consists in the pleasure of mak-ing money, for example), we will destroy the polis. The consequences for the guardians will be twofold. First, while the polis yet survives they will get a less pleasant pleasure than the one that is a guardian's by nature (3.7). Second, they will get even that inferior pleasure less reliably and for a shorter term. For the guardians, not being self-sufficient, must live in a polis with others in order to satisfy their needs (369b5-c4). Hence the collapse of the polis spells the end of their satisfactions. That is why it is futile to compare the happiness of people at festivals with the happiness of people in poleis; political life is a practically possible option, perpetual festival life is not. It is also why "if a silly and childish idea of happiness should come into . . . [a guardian's] mind and cause him to use his power to appropriate everything in the polis as his own, he will realize the real wisdom of Hesiod's saying that the half is in some ways greater than the whole" (466b7-c3). The guardian's life in the Second Polis may seem less happy than that of a ruling tyrant, but it really is not. In the Second Polis, the guardians reliably get as much of the most pleasant pleasure available to them as is compatible with their getting it stably throughout life. And it is the only polis in which they can get it: "There can be no happiness, public or private, in any other polis" (473e4-5).

Therefore, the point is not that the guardians must settle for less real happiness in the Second Polis than they could get in some other polis. The point is rather that because individual happiness is reliably available only in a stably happy polis, we must keep our eye on maximizing the happiness of the polis as a whole, and not try to give to individuals the kind of happiness that is inconsistent with political life. Hence there is nothing here to cast doubt on the conclusion reached in 4.6 that honour-loving guardians are intended to be maximally happy in the Second Polis.

Socrates' response to Glaucon, which bears on the happiness of the phi-losopher-kings, recapitulates the general line of thought of his response to

Adeimantus, but adds a new strand to it: a stable polis must be ruled by people who prefer another life to the political one.

> That is how it is, my companion, I said. If you discover a kind of life better than ruling for the prospective rulers, it is possible that your well-governed polis will come into being; for there alone will the really rich rule, those who are rich not in gold but in the kind of wealth which the happy man must have—a good and wise life. But if beggars and those starved for want of goods of their own turn to public life thinking that there they will lay hold of the good for themselves, then it is impossible; for when ruling becomes a prize to be fought for, the resulting war—domestic and civil—destroys these men themselves and the rest of the polis with them. (520e4-521a8)

Only philosophers have a better life available than ruling:

> Then do you have, I said, any other life that despises political rule besides that of true philosophy?—No, by Zeus, he said, I don't.— But men who aren't lovers of ruling are precisely the ones who must do it; for if not, those who do love it will fight over it.—Of course.— Who else then will you compel to become guardians of the polis than those who are most intelligent [phronimōtatoi] about how the polis is to be best governed, and who have other honours and a better life than the political? (521b1-10)

Consequently, only philosophers are equipped to rule in the Third Polis.

At first, this new strand seems to reconfirm the impression from which we set out that Plato does not intend the philosopher-kings to be as happy as possible in the Third Polis. For if there must be a life which they prefer to that of ruling in order for them to qualify as rulers, then it seems that their life in the Third Polis, which requires them to spend some of their time ruling, cannot be the happiest one for them. But if it is not the happiest life, why would self-interested wisdom-lovers, single-mindedly pursuing the pleasures of knowing the truth, settle for it? We are thus reconfronted with Glaucon's question: Is it not doing the rulers "an injustice to compel them to lead a worse life, when they could lead a better one" (519d8-9)?

Since this question presupposes that to require the philosophers to lead anything less than the happiest life possible for them would not be just (352d2-354a9), the answer could either reject the presupposition—which it does not—or simultaneously defend both the justice of the requirement that the philosophers rule and the maximal happiness of their lives. Properly understood this is precisely what it does.

Observe, then, Glaucon, I said, that we shall not be doing an injustice, either, to those who have become philosophers in our polis, and that what we say to them, when we compel them to care for and guard the others, is just. For we shall say that when such men come to be in other poleis they are justified in not sharing in the labours of those poleis, for they grew up spontaneously, against the wishes of the rulers; and a nature that grows of its own accord and doesn't owe its upbringing to anyone has justice on its side when it is not eager to repay the costs of rearing to anyone. But, both for yourselves and for the rest of the polis, we have made you kings and, as it were, leaders of the swarm, in our polis, for you have been better and more completely educated, and are better able to share in both kinds of life [doing philosophy and ruling]. Therefore, you must each in turn go down and live with the others and grow accustomed to seeing in the dark. When you are used to it, you will see countless times better than those there: you will know each image for what it is, because you have seen the truth about the fine, and the just, and the good. And so, for you as well as for us, the polis will be governed by waking minds, and not, as most poleis are now, by dreamers who fight over shadows, and vie with one another to rule, as if ruling were really a great good. For the truth of the matter is surely this: a polis in which the prospective rulers are least eager to rule is of necessity ruled in the way that is best, and freest from civil strife, while the one with the opposite kind of rulers is governed in the opposite way. . . . Do you think that those we have nurtured will disobey us when they hear this, and be unwilling to join in the labours of the polis, each in turn, while living much of the time with one another in the purer region?—They cannot, he said, because we shall be giving just orders to just people. However, each of them will certainly approach ruling as something that it is necessary to do—the opposite of what is done by those who presently rule in our poleis. (520a6–e3)

It is just to require the philosophers to rule, for they have received fifty years of training, education, and upkeep from the Kallipolis. But it is also in their interest to rule—they rule *for themselves* as well as for the others. For if they do not rule, the Third Polis will be torn apart by civil war. And without that polis, even the philosophers cannot be reliably happy throughout life. To quote again 473e4–5: "It is hard to realize that there can be no happiness, public or private, in any other polis."

What, then, of the better life that the philosophers prefer to the life of ruling? Clearly, it is a life devoted entirely to philosophy, and the pleasures of learning and knowing the truth. If such a life were reliably available to them, philosophers would prefer it. That is why they set no intrinsic value on ruling. For them it is a C-good, no more. But a life of pure philosophy is not reliably available outside of paradise. Those allowed to "spend their time continuously in education right to the end" would not willingly rule because they would believe "that they had emigrated while still alive to a colony on the Isles of the Blessed" (519b7-c6). But to satisfy in the real world the needs of his tripartite nature, the ruler has to live in a polis with others, satisfying their needs in return for having his own satisfied. He must, as it were, exchange some ruling for the food and protection he needs in order to spend much of his time doing philosophy (498b6-c4, 520d6-8, 540b2). A life of pure philosophy, like a life spent perpetually as if at a festival, is not a practically possible option for a human being.[10]

Why, then, does Socrates not say outright in response to Glaucon that the rulers are as happy as possible in the Third Polis? In part it is because they would be happier doing philosophy alone. However, that is not a life that even the most complete practical power imaginable—dialectical-thought—can reliably contrive for anyone. But another part of the reason is surely Thrasymachus. For he has argued that the polis is an exploitation machine run by the rulers in their own interest and against the interest of their subjects (1.5). Since Socrates is attacking Thrasymachus' position, it is only to be expected that he would constantly emphasize that the Kallipolis is not a Thrasymachean exploitation machine, that it is designed so that everyone's interest is best served, not just the interest of the rulers: "It is not to harm the slave that we say he must be ruled, as Thrasymachus thought subjects should be, but because it is better for everyone to be ruled by divine reason" (590d1-4).

It seems, then, that we have every reason to take Socrates at his often reiterated word. The philosopher-kings ruling in the Third Polis are "the best, the most just, and the happiest." The Third Polis is intended to be the Kallipolis for philosophers.

What of the producers, privates, and officers? Are they intended to remain maximally happy when the Second Polis is overcome but preserved in the Third? It is difficult to see why not. For all that happens when that *Aufhebung* occurs is that the Second Polis gains the philosopher-kings, and the social institutions necessary to produce them reliably, that it needs in order to become genuinely self-sufficient:

> Let us confidently assert that those desires of even the money-loving and honour-loving parts, which follow knowledge and argument, and pursue with their help those pleasures which reason approves, will attain the truest pleasures possible for them because they follow

truth, and the ones that are most their own, if indeed what is best for each thing is also most properly its own. (586d4-e2)

The Third Polis, which incorporates the Second, which incorporates the First, is intended to be the Kallipolis for everyone—money-lovers, honour-lovers, and philosophers.

4.10 UNITY AND POLITICAL AWARENESS

It is a necessary condition of complete unity or stability in a polis consisting entirely of rationally self-interested agents, who are not subject to coercion and are not the victims of false ideology or any other form of exploitative mystification, that its members should be happier there, and happier in their own terms, than in any other polis. But it is not a sufficient condition. For we can easily imagine such a polis being disunited and unstable because its members, or a significant number of them, are unaware that they are maximally happy. The unity of the Kallipolis requires, not just maximal universal happiness, but universal possession of the intellectual resources necessary to become aware of maximal happiness should doubt arise.

In Book 5, the good the constitution the Kallipolis must try to achieve is characterized as follows: "Is there any greater evil for a polis than that which splits it and makes it many instead of one; or any greater good than that which binds it together and makes it a unity?" (462a9-b2). And we are told that the only way to achieve that good is to insure that the members of the Kallipolis are pleased or pained by the same events:

Does not the having of pleasures and pains in common bind the polis together, when as far as possible all the citizens are pleased or pained by the same things coming into being or passing away? . . . But, on the other hand, the privatization of those feelings, when some suffer greatly while others greatly rejoice when the same things happen to the polis or within it, that dissolves it? (462b4-c1; cf. *Laws* 739b8-e7)

The idea is surely this. The three component classes in the Kallipolis will be unified into a single community just in case whatever satisfies the desires of any class satisfies the desires of the others, and nothing which satisfies the desires of any class frustrates those of another. For pleasure, as we know, is the satisfaction of a desire, pain its frustration (3.6).

Now the basis, or part of the basis, of the claim that the Kallipolis possesses this guarantee of unity is made clear in the following:

It is time now, I said, for us to return to our own polis to see whether it, or some other, possesses the things agreed upon in the argument

to the greatest degree. . . . Besides fellow citizens, what do the people call the rulers in other poleis?—In many they call them despots,
but in democracies they are called just this—rulers.—What of the
people in our polis. Besides fellow citizens what do they call their
rulers?—Guides to safety [sōtēras] and auxiliaries, he said.—And
what do these call the people?—Providers of upkeep and wages.—
What do the rulers call the people in other poleis?—Slaves. (462e4-
463b5)

The implication is that in the Kallipolis, unlike in other poleis, the rulers
and populace believe themselves to be engaged in a mutually beneficial
cooperative enterprise. The guardians believe the populace to be producers who optimally satisfy their need for food and upkeep, not slaves to be
exploited, while the producers believe the rulers to be guardians who optimally satisfy their need for protection and guidance, not exploitative
masters.

And, of course, they do not simply believe this; as we have seen (4.5-
10), their belief is supposed to be true. Each of them is intended to be
happier in the Kallipolis than he would be in any other polis. Indeed, it is
only on the supposition that this is so that we can make any sense of the
claim that the inhabitants of the Kallipolis are all friends (*philoi*) (590c8-
d6). For, on Plato's view, one feels friendship or love (*philia*) for someone
only on the condition that one believes that his happiness is tied biconditionally to one's own (412d2-7).[11]

If the members of all three major classes are to have a belief of this sort,
they must have a sufficiently detailed conception of the Kallipolis, and the
place and function of the three major classes within it, to enable them to
determine that they are indeed best off when the philosophers rule, the
guardians protect, and the producers produce. How else could "the same
opinion exist among the rulers and the ruled as to who must rule" (431d9-
e2)? But where are they to get this conception? The answer lies ready to
hand in 2.12. Platonic education gives the producers cognitive access to a
mode of the good, guardians access to a figure of the good, and philosophers access to the form of the good, each of which is the structure of a
polis. The form of the good is the structure of the polis in which a philosopher-king believes his ruling desire for the pleasure of learning and
knowing the truth would be best satisfied. A figure of the good is the
structure of a polis in which a guardian believes his ruling desire for the
pleasure of being honoured would be best satisfied. A mode of the good
is the structure of a polis in which a producer believes his ruling desire
for the pleasure of making money would be best satisfied. Consequently,
because of the education it receives each class has precisely the cognitive

resources it needs in order to reach and sustain the conclusion that it is better off, and better off in terms of its own characteristic pleasure, in the Kallipolis than elsewhere.

Moreover, Platonic education provides these cognitive resources by modifying desires. As a result, not only do all three classes tend to act on their beliefs, so that akrasia poses a minimum threat to political stability, but there is minimum conflict and maximum harmony between their desires, harmony further guaranteed by the fact that the classes do not compete for the same goods (4.5). It is this harmony that insures the community of pleasures and pains, which is so crucial to political unity. The polis in which the producers' ruling desires are best satisfied is the very same polis as that in which the guardians' ruling desires are best satisfied, and both of these are the same as the polis in which the philosophers' desires are best satisfied—the form of the good is the structure of the Kallipolis, a model of that structure is a figure of the good, and an image of that model is a mode of the good (2.12). For the desires of the producers, guardians, and philosophers—if not, as Rimbaud claims, for ours—there is "a sovereign music."

This is a politically heartening picture of a community based on cooperation, universal maximal happiness, and as full a share of political awareness as nature allows. But is it the full or only story? To be satisfied that it is, we must travel a path which seems to lead in another, politically less attractive direction.

In the Myth of the Metals in Book 3, we are told that the rulers "must regard the other citizens as their brothers, children of the selfsame earth" (414e5-6). But in Book 5, when it seems that this myth is being given some basis in fact, it is really only the guardians who, because of their nonfamilial living arrangements, come close as a class to being *en famille* (463c3-464b7). Moreover, we are told more than once that as long as the guardian class "remains at one with itself," the Kallipolis will remain intact and unchanged (545c8-d3, 465b7-10). Finally, the account of the First Polis in Book 2 creates the impression that if the needs that cause a polis to come into being are to be efficiently satisfied with goods and services of high quality (370c3-5, 374b6-c2), each of the producers must practice exclusively that polis craft for which his natural aptitude is highest. But in Book 4 we discover that even if all producers exchanged their crafts with one another, no great harm would come to the polis (434a3-7; 4.3).

These passages can be read as suggesting that producers are of little account. It does not matter whether the crafts that satisfy appetitive desires—and that includes very many crafts—are efficiently practiced, because it is only producers who set a high value on appetitive pleasures. And it does not matter whether producers' fundamental desires are frustrated, or less than optimally satisfied, because the class of producers is powerless to disturb the stability of the Kallipolis. The family of guardians is so strong that it can keep even a frustrated producer class in order, and prevent them from causing any serious disruption of life.

The picture now is quite different. The life we imagined before is available to the guardians, but the producers do not share in that life. They are simply the slaves of the guardians (590c2-d6).

But this picture is false. Plato requires that the members of the Kallipolis think of themselves as being a large family. But he does this because he believes that family members are typically bound to each other by strong bonds of friendship or love, not because he thinks that family life is intrinsically valuable (465b12-c7). It is the friendship that is vital, not the kinship relations. This being so, it is important to ask what the basis of friendship or love really is for Plato. Fortunately, we are left in no doubt on this matter. One loves someone most when one believes that his happiness is biconditionally related to one's own (412d4-7). So it is not the pseudofamilial relations, which extend only throughout the guardian class, that are the real basis of the Myth of the Metals, but the ties of mutual benefit. And these, of course, extend throughout all three classes in the Kallipolis.

It is true that as long as the guardians remain at one, the Kallipolis will remain stable and unchanged (2.14). But this is a tribute to what the guardians can accomplish through training, education, and watchfulness, not to what they can accomplish through sheer brute force or threats. This is made clear in Book 4:

> Both poverty and wealth make the work of the crafts worse and the craftsmen too. . . . Here, then, is a second group of things that our guardians must guard against and do all in their power to prevent from slipping into the polis without their knowledge. . . . [namely] wealth and poverty: the former makes for luxury, idleness, and political change; the latter for mean-mindedness, bad work, and change as well. (421e4-422a3)

If poverty among the producers, that is to say the frustration of their ruling desire for money, would bring down the Kallipolis, then the guardians cannot preserve the Kallipolis by forcing frustrated producers to practice their polis crafts. What they can do is prevent such poverty from entering the Kallipolis in the first place by insuring, through training and education, that the desires of the producers are moderated, and that moderated, they are satisfied. (Notice that the change among the guardians that precipitates the decline of the Kallipolis affects their ability to preserve music and gymnastics unchanged, not their military power.)

But if there is no question of a frustrated producer class being coerced into obedience by a powerful guardian class, what are we to make of the claim that producers could all exchange their crafts without causing great harm to the Kallipolis? Are we seriously to believe that if a carpenter turns to medicine, he will be just as successful in satisfying his desire for profit as he would be if he stayed with the craft in which he has been trained? If he would not, and if all producers exchanged crafts, what could prevent massive frustration from occurring among the producers? And if the passage just quoted is to be believed, would that frustration not actually destroy the Kallipolis?

What all of these questions ignore is that the influence of the philosopher-kings pervades life in the Kallipolis as reason pervades the life of the philosopher's psyche. Crafts are no exception, as we saw in 2.11. No producer is autonomously a carpenter or a physician. All depend crucially on directives transmitted via the guardians from the philosophers. Producers are more like assembly line workers, interchangeable parts in a vast process controlled by others, than they are like a Hepplewhite or a Chippendale. Consequently, there is little reason to think that if they exchanged crafts with one another, massive frustration of their desire for profit would result.

Thus our second path, when pursued far enough, actually leads back to the politically heartening picture. The members of the Kallipolis are not only happier there than in any other polis; they are aware, or have the cognitive resources necessary to become aware, that this is so.

4.11 THE LIES OF THE RULERS

We are told on a number of occasions that the philosopher-kings will often find it necessary or useful to lie to the guardians and producers. The spectre of false ideology and exploitation is immediately raised.

At the end of Book 2, Socrates introduces a distinction between two types of lie (*pseudos*). The first is "the true lie" or "what is really a lie" (382a4-5, 382c3-4):

> Surely, no one wishes to lie about the governing things [*ta kuriōtata*] to the governing part of himself. Rather he fears having a lie there most of all. . . . I mean that to lie in the psyche about the things that are [*peri ta onta*] and to have been lied to and to be unlearned and to have and hold the lie there is what everyone would least of all accept, and it is in that place that everyone hates a lie most of all. . . . Surely, as I said just now, that would be called the true lie, the error [*agnoia*] in the psyche of the one who has been lied to. (382a7-b9)

The second type of lie is "the verbal lie" or "the lie in words": "The lie in words is a sort of imitation [*mimēma ti*] of the affection [*pathēmatos*] in the psyche, an image of it that comes into being after [*husteron*] it, and not an altogether pure lie [*ou panu akraton pseudos*]" (382b9-c1). Unlike the real lie, which is never useful, the verbal lie is sometimes useful:

> What about the lie in words? When and to whom is it useful, and not deserving of hatred? Isn't it useful against enemies and those of one's so-called friends who, through madness or ignorance, are attempting to do some wrong, in order to turn them away from it? The lie then becomes useful like a drug. And in the case of those stories we mentioned just now, those told because we don't know the truth about these ancient things, making the lie as much like the truth as we can, don't we also make it useful? (382c6-d3)

We have, then, useless and hateful real lies and useful verbal lies, the latter being some kind of imitation of the former.

To be a real lie, or the content of a real lie, a proposition must be about the "governing things" or the things that are, and it must be held or believed by the governing part of the psyche. Now the things that are must be, as we know, the things that are F, for some form F (2.8). Presumably, these are referred to as "governing" because of the connection between forms and the good itself, on the one hand, and the good itself and choice or desire, on the other (2.11, 3.8). And the governing part of the psyche is, of course, *to logistikon*, or reason—the part of the psyche that is concerned about the good of the psyche as a whole (3.2). Hence a real lie is, in essence, one that misleads reason, and so prevents the psyche itself from achieving the good. That is why no one wants to have a real lie in his psyche.

What, then, is a "lie in words"? The formal definition of it as some sort of imitation of a real lie, which comes into being after a real lie, suggests that if A has a real lie in his reason about what is best, and later reproduces it in words to B, A will have uttered a lie in words.[12] But this cannot be what is meant. First, the examples given of verbal lies do not fit this pattern at all. For they are all cases in which the "liar" expresses a proposition which he himself does not believe. Second, the examples all involve deceit. But A is not trying to deceive B.

What, then, is meant by verbal lies? Given what we have discovered about real lies, the following account seems most plausible. B is attempting to do *x*, falsely believing—"through madness or ignorance"—that it is good to do it. A knows that it is not good for B to do *x*. Hence A tells B something he knows to be false in order to prevent B from doing *x*. A has lied to B. But B does not come to have a false belief about the good

209

in the rational part of his psyche as a result. Indeed, he is steered towards the good, not away from it. A real lie misleads "the governing part" of the psyche about the good. A verbal lie may seem to do the same—especially to the person (B in our example) who discovers he has been lied to. For B, of course, believes that doing x is a good thing to do. That is why a verbal lie is "a sort of imitation" of a real lie. But it is not "an altogether pure lie" because it does not in fact mislead reason about the good. The verbal lie comes "after" the real lie, I surmise, because A cannot reliably lie in words until he knows the good itself and is in a position to tell real lies that mislead reason about it. For until he knows the good itself and can, so to speak, reliably *misrepresent* it, he cannot be sure that the lie he tells to B will lead him towards the good rather than away from it. That is why everyone, except the philosopher-kings, must avoid lies altogether (389b2-c6).

I cannot claim that Plato has made all of this as clear as he might have. But no other reading seems to be consistent with the text, and with the subsequent use of the notion of a verbal lie, to which we now turn.

In Book 3, Socrates makes his first reference to the need the rulers will have for lies:

> If what we were just saying [382a1-e7] is right, and a lie is really useless to gods, but useful to men as a kind of drug, clearly we must allow physicians to use it, but not private citizens. . . . So it is proper for the rulers, if for anyone at all, to lie for the advantage of the polis in cases involving enemies or citizens, but everyone else must keep away from this sort of thing. For a private citizen to lie to rulers such as these is as harmful or more harmful than for a sick man to lie to a physician, or an athlete to his trainer about his physical condition, or for a sailor not to tell the truth to the navigator about how things are with the ship, or about how he himself or a fellow sailor is behaving. (389b2-c6)

Clearly, the rulers' lies here are the verbal kind, for only they were earlier allowed to be useful and beneficial. And what is said fits perfectly with our account of such lies. The rulers know the good itself and can reliably steer the polis towards it. Any lies they tell to accomplish this end could not mislead anyone about the good. They could not be real lies. The citizens, by contrast, do not know the good itself. Hence if they lie to the rulers, their lies may be real, leading the rulers and the whole Kallipolis away from the good—just as a patient's lying to his physician may lead the latter to prescribe harmful, rather than beneficial, treatment.

Later in Book 3 (414b8-415d5), Socrates gives an example of the kind of lie the rulers might find it useful to tell. This is the Myth of the Metals.

Since it is referred to as "one of those lies that are sometimes necessary, of which we were just now speaking, one noble lie" (414b8-c1), it is clearly intended to be a verbal lie. Its function is to tie the members of the Kallipolis to each other by bonds of love or friendship (415d3-5). But their friendship is in fact well founded in mutual self-interest. So this lie fits our account. Those who believe it do not come to believe a real lie. For the belief benefits them, and leads them towards the good itself, not away from it.

We last hear about the lies of the rulers in Book 5.

> It is clear that our rulers will have to make considerable use of lies and deceptions for the benefit of the ruled. We said that such things are useful as a kind of drug. . . . It follows from our previous discussion, I said, that the best men must have sex with the best women as frequently as possible, and the opposite is true of the most inferior men and women; the offspring of the former must be reared, but not those of the latter, if our herd is to be of the highest possible quality. Moreover, only the rulers must know of these arrangements, if the guardians are to avoid dissension as far as possible. . . . There will have to be some clever lottery introduced, so that at each of the marriage festivals the inferior people we mentioned will blame chance and not the rulers [when they fail to win partners]. (459c8-460a10)

Here again the lie is intended to be a verbal lie, since it is supposed to benefit the ruled by preserving the quality of the guardian class. And if it really does what it is intended to do, it will fit our account of verbal lies, leading those who believe it towards what is best, not away from it.

One cannot help feeling, however, that Plato's intentions are less than well realized here. For sex is something even honour-loving guardians enjoy—that is why getting to have it often is a reward for them (460b1-5, 468b11-c9). Hence the loss of it, which inferior guardians suffer in the Kallipolis, is a real loss, and one, moreover, for which they are not clearly compensated. They may not be around, after all, when the general decline in the guardian herd finally begins to do some damage to the Kallipolis—although Plato might, perhaps, appeal to his theory of reincarnation here (3.8, 5.4). But if this is a defect in the Kallipolis, it is surely a minor one. Plato has, for contingent historical reasons, simply chosen a less than optimum solution to the problem at hand. For he has no objection to sex *per se*; when guardians are beyond the age of reproduction they are allowed to have sex with anyone they want, provided they avoid incest (461b9-c4). Hence contraception would provide a better solution to the eugenics problem than rigged lotteries.

We may conclude that the lies of the rulers are all intended to be verbal lies, which lead those who believe them towards the good itself, not away from it.

To grasp the philosophical significance of this conclusion we need to draw a few rough-and-ready distinctions. If the subjects in a polis falsely believe that they are happier there than elsewhere, because the world view they have been taught is false, and known to be false by their rulers, they are the victims of *false ideology*. If, on the other hand, the subjects have a true belief that they are happier, but have it because they have been taught to accept a world view that is false (or contains some beliefs that are false), and known to be false by their rulers, their ideology is *falsely sustained*. Finally, if the subjects in a polis believe that they are happier there and their belief is both true and sustained by a true world view, they and their polis are *ideology-free*.

Because the lies of the rulers are verbal lies it is clear that the producers and guardians who believe them are not the victims of false ideology. But because what they believe is false, and known by the philosopher-kings to be false, their ideology is falsely sustained. Hence only the philosopher-kings are ideology-free; the Kallipolis as a whole is not.

However, the world views available to the producers and guardians in the Kallipolis are intended to be as close to the truth as their natural abilities and ruling desires allow. For it is only when guided by the knowledge of the philosopher-kings that the producers' and guardians' (imperfect) access to the world structure that is the form of the good is as reliable as possible (2.12). So although the producers and guardians do not see the world and their place in it with complete clarity, their vision is as undistorted as their natures, fully developed by education, allow.

Now, it is obvious that everyone has a self-interested reason to avoid a polis in which he is the victim of false ideology. But it is not so clear that everyone has a reason to avoid one in which his ideology is falsely sustained, especially if the degree of falsehood involved is minimal. Indeed, it may be rational for him to prefer such a polis to one that is ideology-free. It all depends on what his natural abilities are, and on what he most wants in life. If, for example, he most enjoys a life devoted to the pleasure of knowing the truth, he will be maximally happy only in a polis in which he is ideology-free. But if what he most wants is the pleasure of making money or the pleasure of being honoured, he has every reason to trade some truth in his world view for more of his own favourite pleasure. Indeed, if he lacks the natural ability to escape ideology altogether, he may have no choice in the matter. So the fact that the ideologies of the guardians and producers are falsely sustained, while the philosopher-kings are ideology-free, seems to be a strength in the Kallipolis rather than a weakness. There, and only there, do honour-lovers and money-lovers get the benefits of the freedom from ideology of which they are

themselves incapable. There and only there do philosophers get to see the
world as it is.

4.12 INVALIDS, INFANTS, WOMEN, AND SLAVES

On the basis of the brief remarks in Book 3 (405a1-410b9) about the kind
of medicine available in the Kallipolis, Plato has been taken to advocate
the view that medical treatment should be distributed solely on the basis
of social productivity.[13] If this is what he had in mind, I think we would
all agree that, knowing the thousand natural shocks that flesh is heir to,
few rationally self-interested people would choose to live in the Kallipolis. So it is of some importance to our assessment of how successfully
Plato has carried out his plan to design the maximally happy polis to see
that it is not at all what he intends.

Law and medicine are treated together because each stands in a certain
relation to one's way of life and hence to one's education and upbringing.
If one has been properly trained and educated, one will have little need
for lawyers or for constant medical attention. If one has not been properly
educated, no lawyer or doctor will enable one to live well. It is "shameful
and a great sign of vulgarity to be forced to make use of a justice imposed
by others, who thus become one's masters and judges, because of the lack
of it in oneself" (405b1-4). And it is equally shameful "to need medical
help, not because one has been wounded or because of some of the sea-
sonal diseases, but because of idleness and a way of life such as we described [Syracusan cuisine, Attic pastries, and Corinthian girlfriends]"
(405c8-d2). Medical treatment is to restore people who already possess
good habits to a life worth living. It is not to prolong lives which can be
a benefit neither to those who live them nor to anyone else: "The life of
someone who is constitutionally ill or licentious is profitable neither to
him nor to anyone else; medicine is not intended for him, and he should
not receive treatment, even if he is richer than Midas" (408b2-5). It is this
Asclepius is praised for having seen so clearly; it is this Plato has in view
throughout the discussion.

Asclepius knew the kind of medicine that enables someone suffering
from a fatal disease to cling to a life filled with nothing but medical treatment, but he did not teach it to his sons, "because he knew that everyone
who lives under good laws has a prescribed task in the polis at which he
must work, and that no one has leisure to be ill and to be under treatment
throughout life" (406c3-5). Now in the case of producers Asclepius'
views are uncontroversial:

> When a carpenter is sick, I said, he expects the physician to give him
> an emetic or a purge, or to get rid of his disease by cautery or sur-
> gery. If someone prescribes a lengthy regimen for him, telling him

that he should rest with his head on pillows, and all that goes with this, he would soon say that he has no leisure to be ill, nor is such a life—paying attention to a disease while neglecting the work at hand—of any profit to him. After that, he would bid goodbye to his doctor, return to his usual way of living, and either recover his health, and live doing his own work, or, if his body could not tolerate the illness, die, and escape from his troubles. . . . Because if he could not perform his own work, it would not profit him to go on living. (406d1-407a2)

Notice that there is no question of coercion, or of the carpenter's being denied medical treatment by someone else. If he cannot carry on with his craft, and get the pleasure of making a profit which alone makes his life worth living, then Plato thinks that the craftsman himself would refuse medical treatment.

Nor, as we would expect from the preceding sections, is the point that the interests of the polis must override the individual's interests, or that if people are of no further use to the polis they should be left to die. For Plato thinks that Asclepius' views are equally applicable to rich people who have no assigned polis craft, and who can afford to be ill and under treatment throughout their lives. His reasoning is that giving one's life over to cosseting an illness prevents one from practicing virtue, just as surely as it prevents one from working, and that without virtue life is not worth living even if one has money (407a4-c6). It was because he understood this that Asclepius

taught medicine for those whose bodies are by nature and habit healthy but have some specific disease; he rid them of it by drugs or surgery, and then prescribed their customary regimen, so as not to harm the affairs of the polis. But with bodies diseased through and through he did not attempt to prescribe a regimen, or, by drawing off a little at one time, and adding a bit at another, to lengthen a bad life for a human being, and have them produce offspring in all probability like themselves. He didn't think he should treat those who could not live the regular course of life, on the grounds that they are of no profit either to themselves or to the polis. (407c7-e2)

Whether someone is rich or poor, the goal of medical treatment must be to restore him to a life worth living, not simply to keep him biologically ticking over. If this goal is not achievable, he "will be allowed to die" (410a2-3).

Clearly, nothing in this account entails that those with an illness that prevents them from ever being socially useful, or from returning to their polis craft, will be left without any medical treatment whatever, or that nothing will be done to ease their suffering. They simply will not be kept alive if their lives are not worthwhile to them.

So far Plato has been focusing for the most part on bodily ailments. In the closing sentence, however, he extends the same account to mental illness. Incurable psychopaths, whose unnecessary appetites cannot be moderated through training and education (2.3), will be put to death: "The ones whose psyches are naturally bad and are incurable they will kill" (410a3-4). Again, his thought focuses on the individual as much as on the Kallipolis. For on his view, life is not worth living when our psyche, the "very thing by which we live, is confused and corrupted" (445a9-b1).

No doubt there is plenty of room for debating the merits of this view of medicine, and the question of whether doctors should keep their patients alive at all costs, regardless of the quality of the lives they will lead. Indeed, these are currently among the most controversial topics in medical ethics. But it could hardly be claimed that the view is notably antiphilanthropic or inhumane, or that no rationally prudent person would choose to live in a society that institutionalized it. Indeed, one might well consider positively enlightened its commitment to providing medical care to those who will benefit from it, rather than to those who can simply afford to foot the bill.

From the physically disabled and the criminally insane, we turn to infants.

Deformed guardian infants, infants born to inferior guardians, and infants born to guardians who are beyond the optimum ages for childbearing (fifty in a man, forty in a woman) are to be allowed to die of exposure.

> The children of inferior parents, or any child of the others born deformed, they [the nurses in charge of the rearing pens] will hide, as is appropriate, in a secret and unknown place. . . . However, I think that when women and men have passed the optimum age of having children, we will leave them free to have sex with anyone they wish, with these exceptions: for a man, his daughter or mother, or their direct ancestors or descendants; for a woman, her son or father, and so on. And all this only after exhorting them to see that no child, if any is conceived, shall be brought to light, or if they cannot prevent its birth, to dispose of it on the understanding that no nurture is available for it. (460c3-461c7)

This is a harsh doctrine. But it does not follow from the application of Plato's general theory to infants. No doubt part of what he has in mind is covered by his views on medicine. Sufficiently deformed infants may have minimal prospects of living a worthwhile life. By being allowed to die they may well be benefited. But it is difficult to see how the offspring of inferior or older guardians are benefited by being exposed. For they are likely to be no more inferior than their parents (415a7-8). And that means—since honour-lovers lead a more pleasant life than money-lovers (3.7)—that they will actually be capable of a better life than the producers.

There is no doubt, then, that it can be a misfortune to be an infant in the Kallipolis, and that this is so in large part because Plato refuses to extend the humane protections of his general theory, which are intended to safeguard the happiness of the individual, to infants. The question is, why does he do this? In the absence of direct evidence, the most plausible answer seems to be this. Fourth-century Athenians practiced infant exposure as a method of family planning. Their attitude to it was perhaps akin to the attitude many in our own culture take to abortion or contraception—there was no law against it, for example.[14] So Plato was culturally primed to refuse full ethical standing to infants. Whether he was justified in adopting the views of his fellows on this matter, rather than, as in so many other cases, rejecting them out of hand, remains a controversial question.[15]

Slavery is too obviously bad to be controversial. Few in the ancient world, however, thought that there was anything wrong with it, and Plato was not among them. His works contain no diatribes against slavery. The *Laws* gives what can only be described as ruthless advice about how slaves should be treated (776b5-778a6). But there is a difference between condoning slavery and being positively in favour of it. Did Plato favour slavery? Did he think that the best of all possible poleis had to contain slaves?

In Book 4, Plato includes slaves in a catalogue of the members of the Kallipolis. He writes of PS as being present "in children and in women, in slaves and in freemen, in producers, rulers, and ruled" (433d1-5). In another passage, he writes that while the Kallipolis must never enslave fellow Greeks, it "must behave toward barbarian enemies as the Greeks now do toward each other" (471b6-8). Since Greeks usually enslaved their captives, whether Greek or barbarian, this seems to imply that the Kallipolis will enslave its barbarian captives.[16] But apart from these passages, the *Republic* is silent about slaves.

On the basis of this slim evidence, the most we can infer is that if there are slaves in the Kallipolis, they are as subject to PS as everyone else. For the only provision the constitution of the Kallipolis makes for the acquisition of slaves is the capture of barbarians in war: the guardians fight only in defense against pleonexia and its manifestations (4.5); they do not raid other states for slaves, or engage in the sort of aggressive or expansionist wars that might yield a steady supply of them. Consequently, the presence of slaves in the Kallipolis is by no means a sure thing. If barbarians have been captured in a defensive war, it seems that there will be slaves in the Kallipolis, otherwise not. There is no question, therefore, of the Kallipolis being based on slavery, as Athens was, or of slaves being essential to its functioning.

And even that conditional conclusion is problematic. For if slaves really are subject to PS, it seems that a slave will be legally and constitutionally on a par with every other member of the Kallipolis. The polis craft he practices, the social rôle he occupies, and consequently the degree of happiness he achieves will be determined by his natural talents only, not by his status as a slave. All of which raises the obvious question of just what it could mean to be a slave in the Kallipolis. But it is a question which, in the absence of further textual evidence, I see no profitable way to pursue.

Thus Plato suggests that the Kallipolis might contain slaves; but he also suggests that whatever slaves it contains will be legally, constitutionally, and eudaimonistically on a par with its nonslaves. These remarks leave us in some doubt about whether there are slaves in the Kallipolis or not. But this much does seem certain: Plato did not think that the Kallipolis, the best of all possible poleis, had to contain slaves. Considering the views of his age—including the views of his greatest pupil, Aristotle—that seems to be a step in the right direction.

On the question of infants, Plato seems to have been largely a traditionalist. On the question of slaves, he seems to have taken a small enlightened step away from tradition. On the question of women, he was almost entirely a revolutionary.

With the exception of religious festivals, to many of which she was central, the Athenian woman of the classical period took scarcely any part in public life. As a child she remained in a kind of purdah in her father's house; as an adult she lived in purdah in her husband's house. She took no part in politics, and did not attend symposia, exercise in the palaestra, or engage in the philosophical discussions which were a part of those activities. She may not even have been allowed to attend the theatre. She received little formal education beyond some training in such refined housewifely tasks as "weaving, baking cakes, and cooking vegetables" (455c6-7) and the management of minor household expenses (465c4-6). Athenian culture was her husband's, not hers.

In law, too, she was severely limited and constrained. She was never autonomous, but always under the control of a male *kurios*, or guardian.

Before she married, this was her father. He could expose her as an infant, or bring her up, as he wished.[17] When she was old enough, he arranged her marriage. She did not have to be present at the wedding, and could be removed from the marriage by him at any time without her consent. If he died without a son, she—even if already married—was assigned in marriage to his nearest male kinsman in a fixed order of precedence. Legally speaking, she was the means to the continuity of her husband's family, and if necessary of her father's too, little else.

Just as her person remained at the disposition of her guardian, her property too was totally under his control. Her husband took charge of her dowry upon marriage, although he could not dispose of it. If she survived him, or if the marriage was dissolved, her dowry passed with her to her new guardian, who might be her father or one of his brothers. If she died without children, her dowry returned to her original guardian. But if she had children, she remained with her dowry in the household of their father, and her dowry went to them on her death. The pattern of the disposition of her dowry reveals its purpose. It existed to maintain her as a reproducer of her kind; it went where she bred. If she failed to breed, it returned to her father's family for future investment.

Her erotic and emotional life was expected to centre on her husband and family. His, while it might certainly include his wife, could—and almost certainly would—include erotic or sentimental attachments to a younger man, and perhaps to a concubine or hetaira as well. His wife was legally bound to fidelity, he was not. He could divorce her simply by sending her away—although he had to return her dowry if he did. She could only with great difficulty divorce him without his consent.[18]

The inevitable result of these laws and customs, expressed in terms of class, was that whatever the economic class of her father or husband or guardian, a woman—propertyless, deprived of education or access to culture, and under another's control—actually belonged in a class far below theirs, which their class exploited for its own reproductive purposes.[19]

It is against this background that we can best appreciate just how revolutionary Plato's thought about women is. But it is remarkable against any background.

Upon returning to the topic of the way of life appropriate to the guardians in Book 5, Socrates raises the question of how female guardians should be trained and educated. Should they reduce the amount of work required of the males by sharing their duties, or "be kept indoors on the grounds that because they must bear and rear offspring they are unable to do so" (451d6-8)? Should they be active participants in the traditionally male world of honour, politics, and philosophy or be kept in purdah because of their rôle in reproduction?

It is argued by Socrates' imaginary critic, as it has been by antifeminists throughout the ages, that since males and females have different reproductive rôles, they must have different social rôles, or practice different polis crafts, as well. PS, if nothing else, would seem to require it. But Socrates sees through this pointing out that it is not clear that one's rôle in reproduction has anything to do with one's aptitude for a polis craft:

> Therefore, I said, if the male or female sex is seen to be specially qualified for a particular craft or way of life, we shall say that it ought to be assigned to that one. But if the only difference appears to be that the male begets children while the female bears them, we'll say that no difference between men and women has yet been produced that is relevant to our purpose, and we shall continue to believe that our guardians and their women should follow the same way of life. (454d7-e4)

To make out his objection the opponent must show that men and women have natural aptitudes for totally different polis crafts. And Socrates does not think that he will be able to do this. For though in general men are better than women at most things, natural aptitudes "are scattered in the same way among both sexes" (455d2-e2). Hence the general superiority of men to women provides no basis for assigning women as a sex to one lot of tasks, and men as a sex to another. Individual women are either money-lovers or honour-lovers or philosophers, just like individual men. Hence in the Kallipolis women will not be confined to the home, but will be trained in the polis craft, whether it is producing or guarding or ruling (456a4-5, 540c5-7), for which their natural aptitude is highest—even if this means that people will have to get used to the sight of old women exercising naked in the palaestra alongside the men (452a7-e3). For it is just silly "to look seriously to any other standard of what is fine than the good" (452e1-2).

Because the discussion of women is part of the account of the way of life of the guardians, and because female producers are never explicitly discussed, it is possible to get the impression that these revolutionary proposals apply only to guardian women, and that female producers are intended to lead lives modeled on those of their working-class Athenian counterparts.[20] But stray remarks which have clear application to such women suggest that the life envisaged for them is very different from that. In Book 4, for example, Socrates remarks that the greatest cause of good to the Kallipolis is the presence "in children and *in women*, in slaves and in freemen, in producers, rulers, and ruled" of the principle that "each one should do his own work and not be meddlesome" (433d1-5). The clear implication is that female producers, being just as subject to PS as any other member of the Kallipolis, will be trained in the one polis craft for which they are naturally best suited. Since Socrates implies that there are women with a natural aptitude for carpentry (454d5-9), explicitly mentions female physicians, and claims that natural aptitudes for each polis craft are to be found in both sexes (455d6-e7), it is difficult to avoid the conclusion that female producers are intended to be apprenticed in an appropriate polis craft in precisely the same way as the males.

It is clear, however, that Plato is somewhat vague about the producers, whether male or female, and that he has simply left us in the dark on the important question of who will do the housework, and rear the children, if both parents are employed full-time in polis crafts.

It must be conceded, too, that Plato is not a feminist. He shows no interest in liberating women as such, and implies that they are generally inferior to men (455c4-d5).[21] Moreover, casual remarks reveal a streak of unregenerate sexism and misogyny (431b4-c3, 469d6-8, 557c7-9, 563b7-9). But these are relatively small potatoes, and do not affect the general point that in the Kallipolis all women, producer and guardian alike, receive the kind of education that will free them from the bondage of their unnecessary desires and enable them to experience the most pleasant pleasure possible throughout life; in the Kallipolis, unlike in contemporary Athens (or in our own society for that matter), men and women with the same natural assets receive the same education, have access to the same careers, and have the same chance of maximum personal happiness.[22]

So, vagueness about the producers and occasional sexism aside, the view of women developed in the *Republic* must be considered a triumph of reason over conventional prejudice, and perhaps also over personal taste, of the sort that Plato hoped might one day be the norm in political life, and that he made the foundation of his own ideal polis.

4.13 THE PERILS OF POETRY

Even a cursory reading of the *Republic* leaves one in no doubt that Plato thinks that the most important political institutions in the Kallipolis, or in any other polis, are educational.

> These orders we give them [the guardians], my good Adeimantus, are neither many nor important; they are all secondary if, as the saying goes, they guard the one great thing—though I would call it sufficient rather than great.—What is that?—Their education and upbringing, I said. . . . To put it briefly, the overseers of the polis must cling to this, and see that education is not corrupted without their noticing it, and guard above all else that there should be no change in music and gymnastics. . . . For poetry and music are not changed

anywhere without change in the most important laws of the polis, as Damon affirms, and I believe. (423d8-424c6)

Apprenticeship in a polis craft, primary education, mathematical science, dialectic, practical polis management—these, and not Marx's relations of production, are the base. Everything else, and that includes everything we think of as quintessentially political, is superstructure.

> I think it is pointless to legislate about such things [manners, dress, deportment, and so forth]; they don't come into being, nor are they preserved, by being set down as laws in speech or writing. . . . Rather, Adeimantus, I said, they are likely to follow from the course of one's education. . . . Then, by the gods, what about market business, private contracts people make with each other in the marketplace, and, if you like, contracts with manual workers, actions for libel and assault, the bringing of lawsuits, the impaneling of juries, the payment and assessments of any taxes that may be necessary in markets or harbours, and all the regulations that govern the market, the polis, and the harbour, and all other such things—shall we legislate about those?—It isn't worthwhile, he said, to dictate to gentlemen [andrasi kalois kagathois]. For they will easily find out for themselves whatever needs to be legislated about these things. . . . And if not, he said, they will spend their lives enacting many petty laws and amending them, thinking that that way they will achieve what's best.—You mean, I said, that they will live like those sick people who, because of their licentiousness, aren't willing to abandon their worthless way of life. (425b7-e10)

Given Plato's views about what education can accomplish, themselves the product of his metaphysical, epistemological, and psychological theories, it is hardly surprising that it occupies the key position in his politics.

Nor is surprising that, having completed the account of his own revolutionary educational proposals, and having justified them by showing that they promote both maximal justice and maximal happiness, he should turn in Book 10 to attack his competition, the poets and playwrights who were the purveyors of traditional Greek ethical education. With philosophy adequately characterized in terms of knowledge of the good itself (4.8), Plato is ready to rejoin the "ancient quarrel" between philosophy and poetry (607b1-d1) in full confidence of victory. If education is the political base, this is the gigantomachy.

In the initial discussion in Books 2 and 3, poetry is treated under two heads: content, or subject matter, and style, or diction. The discussion of the former is left unfinished, however, because it is impossible to say what sort of stories should be told about human beings, as opposed to gods and heroes, until the investigation of justice is itself complete:

> The manner in which gods are to be treated has been dealt with, and also divinities and heroes and things in Hades.—It has indeed.—It remains to deal with stories about human beings.—Plainly.—But, my friend, it is not possible to settle this at present.—Why not?— Because I think we'll conclude that what both poets and prosewriters say about human beings is bad; they say that many unjust people are happy and many just ones wretched, that injustice is profitable if it escapes notice, that justice is another's good and one's own loss. I think we'll forbid them to say such things and order them to compose the opposite kind of poetry and tell the opposite kind of tale. Don't you think so?—I know we shall.—Then if you agree that I'm right about this, I shall say that you have agreed about what we've been seeking all along.—You are correct, he said.—Therefore, we shall agree what stories are to be told about men when we have discovered the nature of justice and that it is by nature profitable to the one who has it, whether he seems to be just or not. (392a4-c4)

This naturally leads us to expect that when the investigation of justice is over, we will discover what kind of poetry is to be composed about human beings. And that is surely what happens. The defense of justice ends in Book 9; Book 10 begins with the requisite discussion of poetry about human beings. For while poetry and stories generally are narratives "about past, present, or future events" (392d2-3), the imitative poetry under discussion in Book 10 is about *human beings* and their actions or activities: "We say that imitation imitates human beings performing compulsory or voluntary actions, and as a result of the action, thinking they have done well or badly, and in all of this experiencing pleasure and pain. Was there anything besides this?—Nothing" (603c4-8). So, far from being an unexpected afterthought,[23] the discussion of poetry in Book 10 fills the lacuna in the earlier discussion, and occurs at the logically appropriate point in the overall argument.

At the beginning of that discussion, Socrates reflects back on the now completed account of the Kallipolis, referring with special satisfaction to the exclusion from it of all *imitative* poetry:

> And, indeed, I said, in many other ways too the polis that we founded is exactly right, but I say this particularly when thinking of poetry . . . in not admitting at all such poetry as is imitative [*hose mimetike*]; for now that the parts [*eide*] of the psyche have been sepa-

rated out, it is even clearer to me that such poetry should not be admitted. . . . All such imitations are likely to damage the reason [*dianoias*] of their listeners—or of those, at any rate, who do not have as an antidote the knowledge of what such things really are. (595a1-b7)

But Socrates clearly does not expect his interlocutors to understand what he means by imitative poetry, for he immediately sets about trying to explain what it is (595c7-596a4).

The story of the three kinds of beds, which we analyzed in 2. 11, leads to an account of what an imitator is. By looking to the form, the philosopher-king makes a bed that instantiates the form of the bed and so is in nature a bed. By looking to that bed, the carpenter makes a bed that instantiates a mode of a bed. By looking to the carpenter's bed, the painter makes a bed that instantiates a quality of a bed. Hence the one "whose product is at three removes from what is by nature [F]" is an "imitator [of F]" (597e3-4). In other words, an *imitator* of F, by looking to something that instantiates a mode of F, produces something that instantiates a quality of F. An *imitation* of F instantiates a quality of F and is produced by an imitator of F. It follows that whether one is an imitator, and one's products imitations, in this sense, depends entirely on the type of property one's model and one's product instantiate. If one's model instantiates a mode of F, and one's product instantiates a quality of F, one is an imitator, and one's product an imitation; otherwise not. I shall refer to this kind of imitation as *technical imitation*, or *T-imitation*.

Armed with the concept of T-imitation, Socrates proceeds to argue that tragic poets are T-imitators, and their poetry T-imitative (598d7-608b10).[24] But tragedy is only one of the types of poetry he has in mind. His target is all poetry dealing with human affairs, which are the subject matter of ethics (603c4-8). Tragedy is an example, certainly, but so are epic and comedy (606c2-10). The argument moves on two broad fronts. The first is concerned with the tragic poet, his products, and their degree of closeness to truth. The second is concerned with the effect his products have on the tripartite psyche.

People think that a tragic poet can compose fine poetry only if he knows what he is writing about. But if Homer had really understood human virtue and vice and the other important subjects his poems deal with, he would have tried "to leave behind many fine actions as memorials of himself," and been more "eager to be the subject of a eulogy than the author of one," for nobody gives over his life to making images of something if he can make the thing itself (598d7-599b7). So it seems likely that Homer did not know what virtue and vice are, or how it is best to live, and that his poetry does not contain the truth on such matters.

Nor can tragic poetry be second from the truth. For if it were, Homer would have been "capable of understanding what ways of life make men better in private and in public" (599d4-6), and some poleis would owe their constitutions to him, as the Spartans owe theirs to Lycurgus. Or, failing that, some war would have been won as a result of his advice, or some practical inventions would be credited to him, as they are to Thales, or there would be people living a Homeric way of life, as there are Pythagoreans. But in fact there are none of these things.

Socrates concludes that Homer's productions, being neither the truth nor second from it, must be third from the truth: "Beginning with Homer, all poetic imitators imitate images of virtue and of all the other things they write about, and have no access to the truth" (600e4-6). Like the painter, who T-imitates a carpenter's bed, not as it is, but as it looks from some perspective (597e10-598c5), and is able to deceive those who "judge by colour and shape" (601a2), the tragic poet presents a partial or perspectival word-picture of virtue, and is able to deceive those "who judge by words, and believe that anything said with meter, rhythm, and tune, be it on cobbling, generalship, or anything else whatever, is right" (601a4-b1).[25]

This conclusion is then further supported by the account of users, makers, and T-imitators (2. 11). The user of anything has knowledge of its good or bad points. The maker has true belief about these things because he consorts with the one who knows and is compelled to listen to him (601e7-602a1). But the T-imitator has "neither knowledge nor true belief about the fine points or bad points of the things he imitates" (602a8-9). The writer of tragic poetry does not imitate good or fine people because he does not know what the good and the fine are. Instead, "he imitates whatever seems to be fine to the many who do not know anything" (602b2-4), that is, whatever seems fine to bound cave-dwellers, like ourselves. So, once again, his poems and dramas turn out to be at three removes from the truth, embodiments of qualities, not of modes, figures, or forms.

The arguments about the effects of tragic poetry on the tripartite psyche, of which there are three, begin at this point (602c4-606d8). The first argument, discussed in 3.3, proceeds by analogy with T-imitative painting, and is not intended to be more than likely or plausible (603b9-c2). Painting relies on the fact that our eyes can be deceived: the same object looks smaller at a distance than close up; straight sticks look bent in water; the same things look concave and convex alternately. But measurement and calculation help to undo the deception because their results do not vary with observation conditions or perspective. However, even when we know, through having measured them, that things are not as they appear, they often continue to look the way they did originally, so that we have contrary beliefs about the same thing at the same time. Given the principle of opposites (3.2), these beliefs must be in different parts of the psyche. The belief based on measurement is in reason, so the other must be in "one of the inferior parts within us" (603a7-8). Hence painting "consorts with a part of ourselves far from reasoning, and is its companion and lover for no healthy or true purpose" (603a12-b2). Since this argument can be applied, at least to some extent, to "the imitations we hear" as well as to those we see, it is at least likely that tragic poetry, too, appeals to appetite or aspiration, and is T-imitative.

The second argument abandons the analogy with painting and deals directly with tragic poetry (603b9-605c5). A psyche governed by reason, and aiming to maximize its pleasure or happiness, should not dwell on its misfortunes, but try to make the best of them:

> One should deliberate about what has happened, I said. One must accept the fall of the dice, and settle one's affairs in whatever way the argument determines would be best. One must not behave like children who, when they trip, hold on to the hurt place and spend their time crying; rather one must accustom one's psyche to turn as quickly as possible to healing and setting right the stricken or sick part, replacing lamentation with cure. (604c5-d2)

A stage character modeled on such a person, however, would not be interesting theatre: "The wise and calm character, which always remains more or less selfsame, is neither easily imitated nor, when imitated, easily understood, especially by a festival crowd consisting of all sorts of people gathered together in a theatre; for the imitation is of a type of feeling alien to them" (604e1-6). Hence, and here the principle of qualification (3.2) seems to come into play, "the imitative poet isn't by nature related to the rational part of the psyche, nor is his cleverness of the sort to please it, if he wants to please the many, but rather he is naturally related to the excitable and varied character because it is easier to imitate" (605a2-6). The tragic poet, then, is like the painter. He produces work that is not true, and he appeals to "the irrational part of the psyche, which cannot distinguish the small from the large" (605b8-c2), thereby weakening the control of reason. Hence it is right that he should be excluded from the Kallipolis (605b2-3).

The third argument (605c6-606d8) is Plato's deepest bow to his enemy. Tragic poetry—and comedy also (606c2-10)—is so dangerous that, with few exceptions (595b6-7), it can corrupt good men (605c6-8). For even the best of people, who control their emotions and appetites in their own lives, are moved by poetry, and praise as best the poets who most affect them. This is because the very parts of the psyche repressed in real life are satisfied and pleased by the poets, providing an enjoyable release from repression, so enjoyable, indeed, that few are willing to give it up (606a3-b5). But it is impossible to confine such indulgence to the theatre; it invariably carries over to real life as well. When our appetites and emotions "ought to obey in order that we might become better and happier men," they refuse, and we become "worse and more wretched instead" (606d5-7).

So whether we look to the tragic poet's products and their degree of closeness to truth or to the effects his poetry has on the tripartite psyche, he emerges as a T-imitator and his works as T-imitative.

Leaving aside the merits of these arguments for subsequent discussion, it is clear, and clear not just from explicit statements on the matter (595a5-b1, 605b2-3, 606e1-607b3), that their target is *all* T-imitative poetry. For their strategy is to tar T-imitative poetry with a brush already blackened by T-imitation in general. What is wrong with such poetry is precisely that it is composed by T-imitators, and is T-imitative. T-imitation is the bad thing; epic, tragic, and comic poetry, because of their unique rôle in ethical education, are only the case in point. But if that is so, then *all* T-imitators and *all* T-imitations ought to be excluded from the Kallipolis.

But how can that be? For, despite Socrates' claims to the contrary, not even all T-imitative poetry seems to have been excluded from the Kallipolis. When we look back to Book 3, for example, where the regulations concerning poetry are first introduced, we find that the Kallipolis will admit poetry in "the pure style which imitates only the gentleman" (397d4-5; cf. 392d5-6). Why are poems of this sort not T-imitative? And if they are T-imitative, why is Socrates so confident in Book 10 that all T-imitative poetry has been excluded from the Kallipolis? He cannot simply have forgotten what he said in Book 3, for he repeats a suspiciously similar doctrine in Book 10 itself: "Only so much of poetry as is hymns to gods or celebrations of good men should be admitted into our polis" (607a3-5). Indeed, he repeats it just eight lines before he reminds us that the Kallipolis is free of all T-imitative poetry (607b1-3). So we are thrown back full force on our questions. Why are hymns to the gods and celebrations of good men not T-imitative? And if they are T-imitative, why does Socrates claim that all T-imitative poetry has been excluded from the Kallipolis?[26]

In addition to the concept of T-imitation, Plato also employs a very different nontechnical concept of imitation. Here is a particularly vivid example: "As he looks upon and contemplates things that are ordered and eternally the same, that neither do nor suffer injustice, but are all in an intelligible order, he [the philosopher-king] imitates [*mimeisthai*] them and tries to become as like them as he can" (500c2-5). Imitation in this sense differs from T-imitation in at least three ways. First, it is not restricted to having instances of modes as its models, or instances of qualities as its products. In this case, its models are forms, and its products (if they may be called that) are things that instantiate forms (2.11). Second, the product is the imitator himself appropriately transformed, not a painting or a poem. Imitation, in this sense, is a kind of impersonation, something one does, rather than something one makes (393c5-6). Third, imitation is a matter of style, of acting in the manner or style of someone or something, whereas T-imitation is a matter of content.[27]

It is this nontechnical sense of imitation, and not T-imitation, which he was then in no position to define, that Socrates employs in his discussion of poetry in Books 2 and 3.

Looked at stylistically (392c6-8), rather than from the point of view of subject matter, Homer's poetry is narrative (*diēgēsis*) throughout (392d1-3, 393b7-8). But it is "narrative through imitation [*dia mimēseōs*]" (392d5-6) only where Homer speaks in the person of one of his characters:

> But when he [Homer] makes a speech as if he were someone else, won't we say that he makes his style of speaking as much as possible like that of the person he has told us is about to speak? . . . Now isn't making himself like someone else in voice or looks the same as imitating [*mimeisthai*] the one he makes himself resemble? . . . Then, in this case, it seems he and the other poets employ narrative through imitation. (393c1-9)

There are thus three broad styles in poetry: narration without imitation, as in the dithyramb; narration through imitation alone, as in tragedy and comedy; and a mixture of both kinds of narration, as in epic poetry (394b8-c5). The question is, should either of the latter two be admitted into the Kallipolis, and if so, should any restrictions be imposed on what they imitate (394d1-4)?

The argument which leads to an answer has already been explored (4.6). PS applies to imitation as well as to the crafts (394e1-10). Hence the future guardians must imitate only the kind of people they are to become:

> If, then, we are to preserve our first principle, that our guardians must be kept away from all other crafts, and be most precisely craftsmen of the freedom of the polis, and engage in no activities except those which contribute to this, they must neither do nor imitate any-

thing else. And if they do imitate, they must from childhood imitate what's appropriate to them: men who are courageous, moderate, holy, pious, free, and everything of that sort; and what is slavish, or shameful, or anything else of that sort, they must neither do nor be clever at imitating, so they won't get a taste for the thing itself from imitating it. Or haven't you noticed that imitations practiced from youth onwards become part of one's nature, and settle into habits of gesture, accent, and thought? (395b8-d3)

Hence the only styles of poetry employing narrative through imitation that are allowed in the Kallipolis are those "which imitate only the gentleman" (396b10-397b3, 397d4-5).

Now nothing in either concept of imitation we have been examining excludes the possibility that the same poem should satisfy both of them, or that a poem which does not employ narrative through imitation might nonetheless be T-imitative. Indeed, the Homeric poems and dithyrambs are cases in point. For the former are T-imitations from beginning to end, and also employ narrative through imitation, and the latter involve no narration through imitation, but may well be T-imitative. So the fact that two different concepts of imitation are employed—one in Book 3 and another in Book 10—is not itself sufficient to resolve the apparent conflict we uncovered between the two books. Book 10 excludes all T-imitative poetry. But Book 3 allows dithyrambs and poems in which only good men are impersonated, and either of these may be T-imitative.

To resolve the conflict we must recall that the poems sanctioned for use in primary education have all been bowdlerized by Socrates in his rôle as philosopher-king manqué. Before they pass through his hands, they are T-imitations, third-grade copies of the truth. But after they have been censored, they are not. In this respect they are exactly like, when they are not actually identical to, the traditional tales about the gods. Before these have been censored, they misrepresent the gods; after they have been censored, they represent the gods as they are (377e1-383c7; 2.11). Knowing the forms, as poets do not, the philosopher-kings can transform T-imitations so that they become "as much like the truth as possible," and so make the lies or untruths useful (382d2-3), thereby removing their T-imitative character.

Thus when Plato tells us at the beginning of Book 10 that all T-imitative poetry has been excluded from the Kallipolis, he is referring to the effect that the philosopher's truth-guided, censoring hand has had on all the poetry that has been allowed to remain there, whether it is about gods, divinities, heroes, or men. Some of this poetry does indeed employ narrative through imitation, but none of it is T-imitative. Hence there is no contradiction. T-imitative poets are the enemy targeted for defeat in Book 10; and all of them, and all their autonomously produced works, are excluded from the Kallipolis.

Moreover, it is not only T-imitative poets who suffer this fate. All those ruled by unnecessary appetites, who have cognitive access only to qualities, are excluded. And T-imitators generally are of this psychological type. For the things they make instantiate qualities, nothing more. Therefore, all T-imitators—and that includes painters, musicians, architects, and artists generally—are banished from Plato's happiest polis. Such "artists" as remain compose, paint, write, or design as the producers produce, and the guardians guard—under instruction from the philosopher-kings (377b11, 380c6-9, 401b1-d3). And this transforms both them and their works. In the Kallipolis, philosophy is the sovereign music, the truest tragedy (*Phaedo* 61a3-4; *Laws* 817b1-c1).

Although Plato does banish the artists, the attack in Book 10 is, as we have seen, directed exclusively against the T-imitative poets and playwrights. They are the target because they are the traditional teachers of virtue. The argument in a nutshell is that being a good poet does not qualify one to teach human beings how to live. It is an argument both in aesthetics and in the metaphysics and epistemology of ethics.

Here is the human psyche, and there the world. What changes can we make in each so that the one will live as well as possible in the other? Let us suppose, plausibly but not uncontentiously, that this is the central question in ethics. Who is likely to be best able to answer it? On Plato's view, it is the person who has knowledge of the true, dialectically defensible, fully mathematized theory of the psyche and the world—the philosopher-king. He, then, is philosophy's champion in the ancient quarrel. Who is to defend poetry? Not surely just any actual poet. That would weight the contest too much in the philosopher's favour. But a poet who is as complete a poet as the philosopher-king is a philosopher—he would be a suitable adversary. Represented by Homer, "the pathfinder of tragedy" (598d8), as the philosopher-king is represented by Socrates, he is the adversary in Book 10. The point is not that Hesiod or Simonides or Aeschylus have not mastered dialectic. That is not worth arguing; no one has mastered dialectic. The point that the arguments of Book 10 are meant to drive home is that although dialectic is the science that enables one to see the world aright and to construct the best of all possible human societies, it is not what one needs to know in order to create great poetry or drama. The arguments are worth reviewing in this light.

The poet or dramatist writes for a nonspecialist audience. Hence he must employ a conceptual framework similar to theirs. Character, motive, plot—all must be drawn from folk psychology, not, say, from cognitive science, or neurophysiology, or whatever the true theory of the psyche turns out to be. This means that art represents people and their motives and actions not necessarily as they really are, but only as they seem to people without specialist training. The languages of art are not the language of truth. The scientist, or philosopher-king, is free of this constraint, for his is an audience of fellow specialists. The language of philosophy is the language of truth. This is the argument of 601a4-b4 and 603b9-605c4.

Poetry and drama, like all art, aim to provide a certain characteristic pleasure or satisfaction (606b3-5), which on Plato's view, and on Freud's as well, is related to repression. Art enables us to satisfy without reproach or shame the very desires we must repress in real life. These are characteristically appetitive desires, especially sexual ones. This might plausibly be taken to entail that the representation of ethically good people, like the representation of happy families, does not provide the kind of satisfaction art typically provides. So it is not knowledge of what good people are like that the poet needs. That, I take it, is the thrust of 604e1-605a6. If we suppose, as Plato does (485d6-7), that even artistic indulgence of repressed desires strengthens them and weakens the repressive mechanisms, we will see reason here to mistrust art in general (605b3-5, 606b5-8).

Finally, we must look at the poet himself, and why he writes. Plato is confident that no one would be satisfied merely to represent life if he knew how to live it well, or could teach others how to live it well (599b3-601a3). He does not explain why he thinks the poet's life is no better than third best. Perhaps he believes this is too obvious to need justification. But if we think again of the characteristic pleasure art provides, his view becomes intelligible, and again rather like a view of Freud's. A life devoted to making things that provide a fantasy satisfaction for unnecessary appetites could not rank very highly among lives.

Now, I do not want to say that these arguments should command our assent; we know too little about either art or the mind for that. But I do think there is much to admire in them. They make the philosophy of art continuous with ethics, politics, and the philosophy of mind, and that seems to me to be right.[28] The deep differences they identify between art and philosophy (at least as Plato conceives of it and its relations to science) are, I think, there. Art is, and must be, bound up with ordinary life and thought in a way that philosophy need not be. Art is related to pleasure, and to sex, in a way that philosophy, perhaps, is not.[29] Most important of all, even if they are inconclusive, Plato's arguments do, it seems to me, extend the right invitation to philosophers who think that art has something to teach us about how to live: develop a metaphysics, epistemology, psychology, and politics on the basis of which it will be clear that the knowledge a good poet or dramatist needs is relevant to ethics.[30] It is precisely as an invitation, indeed, and not as what Berkeley calls "the killing blow," that Plato himself seems to understand those arguments (607d6-e2).

4.14 FREEDOM

A person's needs, wants, and interests are in part determined by the natural lottery, in part by his education and upbringing, and in part by his actual circumstances. They also depend on his beliefs, which in turn depend to some extent on the same factors as his needs, wants, and interests themselves. His *real* interests are those he would form under optimal conditions—those in which his needs are satisfied, he is neither maltreated nor coerced nor the victim of false ideology, and he is as fully aware as possible of his actual circumstances, and the real alternatives to them. *Real* happiness is optimal satisfaction of real interests in the long term.

That was the story told in 1.12. Its relevance to the *Republic* should now be clear. For the Kallipolis has emerged as providing optimal conditions of the type in question. Each of its members has his needs satisfied, and is neither maltreated nor coerced nor the victim of false ideology. Each is educated and trained so as to develop a conception of the world, and his place in it, which is as close to the truth as his nature, fully developed with an eye to his maximal happiness, permits. Each has his ruling desires satisfied throughout life. Thus each develops his real interests, and is made really happy.

It sounds wonderful put like that. But that is not how the *Republic* feels. It feels authoritarian and repressive. Why? I think it is as much because of what we bring to the *Republic* as because of what we find there.

Partly, no doubt, because of where and when we live, we are inclined to presuppose that no amount of knowledge of the way the world is validates or underwrites a unique conception of the good.[31] Different conceptions are determined by what different individuals happen to want or prefer. And the state exists not to judge between these conceptions, but to allow each individual to realize his own conception as far as is compatible with others' realizing theirs to the same extent. In this way, the state at once respects the individuality of its members and treats them equally. An activity, institution, or issue is paradigmatically political for us if it pertains to disputes between people who may have different conceptions of the good, yet must coexist and have dealings with one another in the same community, or, more generally, in the same world.[32]

Individual freedom, on this broadly liberal conception, which we find in Locke and Hume,[33] is freedom to do what one wants, or—to bring in the good—freedom to live in accordance with that conception of the good which is ultimately rooted in one's own desires, preferences, or choices. And a state is free to the extent that it limits individual freedom only to guarantee equal freedom to all its members.

It is not surprising, then, that when in imagination we project ourselves into the Kallipolis we feel repressed and unfree. For given our actual desires and interests, and presupposing the liberal conception of freedom, *we* would be repressed and unfree there.

This conception of political freedom, however, is not the only one, and even if we leave aside worries about its metaphysical commitment to the distinction between facts and values, it is not clear that it is the best or most defensible conception. It may fail on its own terms: by seeking neutrality above all, the state may in fact undermine certain conceptions of the good which, even though they do not illegitimately limit the freedom of others, cannot easily survive in a neutral state. If, for example, the state has a market economy—either because many want it or because it, too, is thought to be neutral as regards conceptions of the good, allowing each conception to compete for allegiance in the open marketplace—then because of the extensive labour mobility necessitated by such an economy those who want stable neighbourhoods, extended families, close ties between the generations, or collective living are likely to find it very difficult to achieve their goals within the state. From their perspective the supposedly neutral state is biased against their conception of the good.[34]

But even if the liberal conception does not fail in its own terms, the foundations of freedom it supposes might be questioned. Freedom to do what we want, or *instrumental freedom*, is certainly important. But its importance, like that of the instrumental rationality of which it is a correlate, can be undermined by the desires on which it depends. If the desires we are free to satisfy are ones we would not have if we had engaged in a process of ideal deliberation, then being free to satisfy them is scarcely something worth caring about. If our desires themselves can mire us in heteronomy, instrumental freedom cannot be sufficient for real freedom or autonomy. This is essentially Kant's insight.

Perhaps, then, taking a clue from our discussion of theories of rationality, we should move away from instrumental freedom towards *deliberative freedom*. Perhaps the freedom we should be concerned about is the freedom to have and to satisfy only the desires we would choose to have if we were aware of the relevant facts, were thinking clearly, and were free from distorting influences. If we are persuaded to move in this direction, we can see at once that a state which guaranteed deliberative freedom might look and feel very repressive to someone concerned solely about instrumental freedom. It would very much depend on what his desires happened to be.

Since the costs of repression, in both psychic and political terms, are high, we can well imagine that an enlightened state, committed to deliberative freedom, would want to devote much of its resources to education and training, to insure that its members are as close to being deliberatively rational as possible. Such a state would already begin to look a little like the Kallipolis, and to share some of its priorities.

Even a state whose citizens enjoy complete deliberative and instrumental freedom, however, can seem to be defective from the point of view of freedom. For desires that are deliberatively rational may not be rational *überhaupt*. Brought up in a capitalist democracy, which does not provide optimal conditions for developing one's needs, wants, and interests, a person desires profit above everything else. And the more he deliberates under the aegis of that desire, the clearer it may become that his desire is perfectly rational.[35] Yet it may not be in his real interest to make profit his goal. But to discover this he would have to begin deliberating already possessed of desires other than those he actually has. His desire for profit is deliberatively rational, then, but not critically rational. Freedom to have and satisfy this desire is deliberative freedom not *critical freedom*, or the freedom to have and to satisfy only desires sanctioned by the critical theory of rationality. Critical freedom is a close relative of the notion of freedom we associate with Hegel.

But if deliberatively rational desires can somehow fail to be the best ones for a person to have, then the same considerations that caused us to abandon instrumentally free states for deliberatively free ones might cause us to abandon the latter in favour of states that guarantee complete critical freedom. And this would certainly bring us closer still to the Kallipolis. For like the Kallipolis, any critically free state would have to devote much of its resources to insuring that the actual interests of its citizens coincide as far as possible with their real interests. And that would require, not just extensive commitment to education and training in order to eliminate critically irrational desires and increase undistorted access to the real world, but extensive commitment to all branches of knowledge relevant to human beings and their interests. More than that, it would require political institutions that guarantee that knowledge thus gained would serve human good. If one cannot quite see producers, guardians, and philosopher-kings in all of that, one can can at least see their outlines.

In any case, it seems clear that the Kallipolis is intended to provide its members with as much critical freedom as their natures, fully developed in optimal conditions, permit.

It is not to harm the slave that we say he must be ruled, as Thrasymachus thought subjects should be, but because it is better for everyone to be ruled by divine reason, preferably within himself and his own, otherwise imposed from without, so that as far as possible all will be alike and friends, governed by the same thing. . . . This, I said, is clearly the aim of the law which is the ally of everyone in the polis; and it is also that of the rule of children, their not being free until we establish a constitution in them as in a polis, and until, caring for the best part of them with the best part of ourselves, we establish a similar guardian and ruler in them to take our place; only then do we set them free. (590d1–591a3; cf. 395b8–c2)

Even if we retain our liberal suspicion about the possibility of a science of values, we might still, by coming to see merit in the idea of critical freedom, also come to see the *Republic* in a new light—not as a totalitarian hymn to the benefits of repression and unfreedom, but as an attempt to design a polis whose members enjoy as much real happiness, and as much real or critical freedom, as possible.

FIVE

THE
PSYCHOPOLITICS
OF
JUSTICE

All the fruitful altruisms of nature develop in an egotistical manner and any
human altruism which is without egotism is sterile.   —PROUST

5.1 INTRODUCTION

An interlocutor raises the question, Why should I be just rather than unjust? The answer comes back: Because you want to be really happy, and
you cannot be really happy without being just; indeed, the closer you are
to being completely just, the closer you are to being really happy, and the
further you are from being completely just, the further you are from
being really happy. Rightly or wrongly, he accepts this as the appropriate
kind of answer. However, puzzled by Thrasymachean skepticism, he
wants to be shown that justice and happiness are related in this way, that
justice itself is a homoiomerous essential extensional component of happiness (1.11-13). The ensuing argument is long and complex, but its
rough overall form is readily discernible in the foregoing discussion:

    (1) X is a homoiomerous essential extensional component of happi-
        ness.

    (2) X is the property of being completely just (of having justice itself
        in one's psyche).

Therefore,

    (3) Justice itself is a homoiomerous essential extensional component of
        happiness.

Therefore,

    (4) Justice itself is more choiceworthy in terms of happiness than in-
        justice itself.

The interlocutor's attention now focuses on X. He wants to be convinced
that X is indeed the property with which he identifies being completely
just.

At this point, the sailing ceases to be plain. Because the interlocutor's ethical views may be the product of false ideology, it is unclear how they can have any bearing on the theory of justice. How can his views about what justice is determine what X can be? This is the *problem of ideology*. But if the interlocutor's ethical views have no bearing on the theory of justice, how can that theory be relevant to him? How can a theory that shows that X is an essential component of happiness be in any way relevant to *his* request for an explanation of how justice can guarantee happiness? That is the *problem of relevance*. If Plato is to avoid the charge that he has begged the question against Thrasymachus, or that what he has defended is not justice but something else—that his argument fails through irrelevance—it is vital that he have convincing solutions to both of these problems.[1]

What I propose to do, then, is to work through the *Republic* again with an eye to the theory of justice and the virtues, on the one hand, and to the problems of ideology and relevance, on the other. This will allow us to see Plato's theory of justice as a sequential line of thought, and to determine how successfully he achieves the goal of answering Glaucon.

5.2 CONVENTIONAL JUSTICE

The new investigation of justice in Book 2 begins with an argument from analogy.

> If our vision were poor and we were ordered to read small letters from a distance, and then someone told us that these same letters, only larger and on a larger surface, exist elsewhere, we'd account it a godsend, I think, to be allowed to read the latter first, and then examine the smaller, if, of course, they are really the same. (368d1-7)

But justice, like the letters, seems to exist both writ large in poleis and writ small in psyches. For "there is, we say, the justice of one man, and also the justice of a whole polis" (368e1-2). Consequently, we should first try to discover what justice is in the polis, and "only then look for it in the individual" (368e7-369a3). The argument, we should note, is not that we know that the small letters are the same as the large ones, so that we should first read the large ones, then the small ones. If it were, it would be incoherent. People who read the large-print edition of the *New York Times* do not need to read the regular edition as well. What is meant is that if there is a reason to believe that the large and small letters are the same, this acts as a control on our reading of each of them. We should start with the large letters, since these are easier to read. Our interpretation of them can then guide our reading of the small letters, suggesting hypotheses, which we can test against our reading of the small letters. This, in turn, may require us to modify our interpretation of the large letters, and so on. Only when this process is complete, and each set of letters has been investigated, can we be certain that either has been correctly identified. Hence, at the moment of transition from the investigation of political justice to that of psychic justice, we are told that we cannot "take it as final" (434d2) that justice is the proper functioning of the producers, guardians, and rulers, each class doing its own work in the polis (434c7-9), until "we find that this same form [eidos], when existing in the individual, is also agreed by us to be justice" (434d2-4).

Plato is not assuming that because we speak about the justice of a psyche and of a polis, we can be certain that justice is the same thing in each. That is something to be investigated, not taken for granted. Dialectic may begin with what we ordinarily say and think, but it does not always end up by underwriting it (2.9, 2.11, 5.3-4).

The search for justice should begin, then, in a polis. Socrates begins it not in just any polis, however, but in the Kallipolis. What is more, Glaucon and Adeimantus are confident that they will find it there: "I suppose that our polis, if indeed it is rightly founded, is completely good [teleōs agathēn]?—Necessarily so, he said.—Clearly, then, it is wise, courageous, moderate, and just.—Clearly" (427e6-12). We must now try to uncover the sources of their confidence.

At the end of Book 1, we are told the following story about work, virtue, goodness, and happiness. The fact that it is accepted by everyone, including Thrasymachus (352d2-354a9), attests to its conventional status. The work (ergon) of a thing is "that which can be done either only with it or best with it" (352e2-3). Its virtue (aretē) is that which alone enables it to do its work well, and be a good (agathon) rather than a bad (kakon) thing of its kind (353b2-d2). Part of the work of the psyche is to live (353d9). Therefore, a completely good psyche, which possesses all the appropriate virtues, will live well (353e7-11), and so be "blessed and happy [makarios te kai eudaimōn]" (354a1-4).

For poleis the story is exactly parallel:

(1) A completely good polis is one that possesses all the virtues of a polis.

(2) The virtues of a polis are those things that alone guarantee that it will do its work well.

(3) The work of a polis is to satisfy the needs and desires that cause it to come into being in the first place (369b5-c10).

(4) A completely good or completely virtuous polis is one that optimally satisfies the needs and desires of its members, thereby insuring that they are as happy as possible.

Hence, if justice is a virtue of a polis, it must be found in the Kallipolis. For the Kallipolis is designed to make all its members as happy as possible (4.4-9).

Now that we understand why justice must be somewhere in the Kallipolis, we may join in the search for it that occupies much of Book 4.

Because the Kallipolis is rightly founded, it is completely good (427e6-8). Because it is completely good, it is wise, brave, moderate, and just (427e10-11). For these are the virtues conventionally thought to be most important (433c4-e2; *Laws* 631c5-d2). Justice is in the Kallipolis, then, but where? Socrates proposes to find it by identifying wisdom, courage, and temperance directly, and identifying justice with whatever in addition to them is a virtue of a polis: "As with any four things, if we are looking for any one of them in a thing, then if we recognize it first, that will be enough, but if we recognize the other three first, that in itself will make the thing we are seeking known to us. For plainly it can be nothing other than what is left over" (428a2-6). By proceeding in this way, he can simultaneously identify justice and assay the relations that hold between the virtues. But his identification of justice will not depend entirely on this risky argument by elimination.

The first virtue to be identified is wisdom. The Kallipolis is wise because it is "well counseled" (428b3-4). And conventional ethical thought agrees, first, that good counsel is a kind of knowledge, "for it is because of knowledge, not ignorance, that people counsel well" (428b6-8), and, second, that the particular kind of knowledge in question is knowledge not of carpentry or of bronze manufacture, but of "how the polis as a whole would be best both in relation to itself and in relation to other poleis" (428d1-3). This knowledge—which we know to consist in knowledge of the good itself (2.11-12)—is located in the class of rulers, which is the smallest class (428d5-7): "Then it is because of its smallest part, and the wisdom that resides in it, in the part that leads and rules, that a polis established in accordance with [its] nature [*kata phusin*] is wise as a whole" (428e7-9). The polis as a whole is wise, then, because it is ruled by those who know what is best for it.

Courage—or a sort of courage, at any rate—is next.

But again it is not difficult to see courage itself, and the part of the polis in which it is situated, on account of which the polis is called courageous. . . . Who, I said, in calling a polis courageous or cowardly would look to anything else than that part of it that defends it and wages war on its behalf? . . . The polis is courageous then because of the part of itself that has within it the power always to preserve its belief about the things to be feared—that they are the very things which the lawgiver declared to be such in the course of the education. . . . I mean, I said, that courage is a kind of preserving [*sōtērian*] . . . the preserving of the belief inculcated by the law through one's education about what things and what kind of things are to be feared. And by preserving that belief under all conditions I mean preserving it in the face of pains and pleasures and desires and fears. (429a8-d1)

The power in question is located in the guardian class (429e7-430b4). It is not courage proper, however, that is identical to "the power to preserve through everything the true and lawful belief about what is to be feared" (430b2-4), but "political" courage (430c3-4).[2]

Plato does not explain why this is so; courage is not his topic (430c4-6). However, given what we already know, it is reasonably clear what he has in mind. The guardians will reliably have true belief about what is to be feared only if they are ruled by the philosopher-kings (2.11-12). Hence courage proper is something the polis possesses just in case its guardians have political courage *and* its rulers are wise (*Laches* 192b9-d11). It follows that although a polis can possess political courage even if it is not also wise, it cannot possess courage proper unless it is wise as well. By the same token, the polis cannot actually be wise unless it is also courageous. For if the guardians do not possess political courage, there is no guarantee that the rulers' wise decisions will be put into effect. Overcome by fear, the guardians may do something other than what is best. And this political equivalent of akrasia will prevent the Kallipolis from reliably doing the wise thing, from being reliably wise. But the combination of wisdom in the rulers and political courage in the guardians is courage proper. Wisdom and courage require one another; a polis is wise just in case it is courageous. This is the first of the structural relations between the virtues referred to earlier.

Moderation is the next of the four virtues to be identified.

Moderation, I said, is surely a kind of order and mastery of certain kinds of pleasures and desires, as people somehow try to indicate by speaking of someone being stronger than himself [*kreittō hautou*], and using other phrases that point us on the same trail. . . . But isn't this being stronger than oneself absurd? For the one who's stronger than himself would also be weaker than himself, and the weaker stronger.

For it is the same person who is referred to in all these expressions. (430e6-431a1)

To make sense of this conventional way of talking about moderation, which characteristically confuses moderation with its opposite, we have to think of the psyche as having more than one part:

> But, I said, it is plain to me that this expression wants to indicate that in the same person, as far as his psyche is concerned, there is something better and something worse, and that when that which is in its nature better is in control of that which is worse, he is said to be stronger than himself; that's why it is a term of praise. And when, because of bad upbringing or bad company, the larger worse part controls the smaller better, then this is subject to reproach, and the person in this condition is called weaker than himself and licentious. (431a3-b2)

Of these two alternative sorts of control, it is the former that is present in the Kallipolis. For there the desires of the many producers are controlled both by the true beliefs of the few guardians and by the wisdom of the fewer rulers (431c5-d2).

However, just as (political) courage is not just any kind of true belief about what is to be feared, of the sort that slaves or animals might chance to possess, but the kind induced by law and education (430b6-9), so the Kallipolis is not moderate simply because it is controlled in this way. In addition, the control must be based on consent. The producers, on the one hand, and the guardians and rulers, on the other, must agree about which of them should rule.

> Do you see now, I said, that we were correct to divine a while ago that moderation resembles a kind of harmony? . . . For, unlike courage and wisdom, each of which resides in a part, the one making the polis courageous, the other making it wise, moderation . . . stretches throughout the whole, making the strongest, the weakest, and those in between sing the same song, about wisdom, if you wish, or about strength, if you wish, or for that matter about numbers, wealth, or anything else. So that we would be quite right in saying that this unanimity is moderation—the agreement, that is to say, between the naturally better and worse as to which of the two must rule both in the polis and in each of them. (431e7-432a9)

In 4.10, we uncovered the basis of this agreement in the education and training the Kallipolis provides to its rulers, guardians, and producers.

Now if moderation, so understood, is to exist in the Kallipolis, the rulers, with the aid of the guardians and the consent of everyone, must control the producers. But this will not happen unless the rulers have wisdom and the guardians have political courage. For if the rulers are unwise, they will not be able to insure that everyone in the Kallipolis is maximally happy, and that will threaten consent. At the same time, if the guardians lack political courage, they will not reliably carry out the rulers' instructions, and that will threaten happiness and consent as well. However, it is also true that if the rulers are wise and the guardians are politically courageous, the producers will receive the kind of education and training necessary to insure that they consent to be ruled. Hence, if the Kallipolis is moderate, it is both wise and courageous, and if it is both wise and courageous, it is moderate. This is the second structural relation between the virtues to emerge.

Socrates begins his account of political justice with the conjecture, which he will eventually modify, that justice consists in obeying PS, the presciptive principle of specialization:

> Listen then, I said, and see whether I talk sense. For what we laid down in the beginning about what must be done concerning every-thing when we were founding our polis, this, I think, or some form of this, is justice. And what we laid down, and often repeated, if you remember, was that each person must perform one polis craft for which his nature was naturally best fitted. (433a1-6)

He cites three reasons to think that the conjecture is on the right track. First, conventional ethical thought seems to have a view of justice rather like this one. For "we have often heard others say, and often repeated ourselves, that to do one's own [*ta hautou prattein*], and not to be meddle-some [*mē polupragmonein*], is justice" (433a8-b1). Second, it is clearly a virtue of the Kallipolis that everyone obeys PS:

> And surely, I said, if we had to judge which of them will do our polis the most good by coming to be in it, it would be difficult to decide whether it is the sameness of belief between the rulers and ruled, or the preservation in the minds of the soldiers of the lawful belief about what is to be feared and what not, or the wisdom and guardianship of the rulers, or whether it is not, above all, the presence of this fourth thing in children and in women, in slaves and in freemen, in producers, rulers, and ruled that does the polis the most good—namely, that each one should do his own work and not be meddle-some. (433c4-d5)

Indeed, it is because everyone obeys PS that moderation, courage, and wisdom are a permanent presence in the Kallipolis: "It is this power that made it possible for these others to come into being, and that preserves them once they have come into being, for as long as it is there" (433b9-c1). Since the property the Kallipolis has because everyone in it does his own work is a virtue of it, but is not identical to wisdom, courage, or moderation, it must be justice. This, too, is a point of agreement with conventional ethical thought. For the latter classes justice among the four cardinal virtues of a polis (433c4-d5).

The third and final reason to think that justice has something to do with PS arises from reflection on the goals conventionally attributed to judicial justice:

> Look at it this way too, and see if you agree: will you order the rulers to judge lawsuits in your polis? . . . And will they have any other goal in rendering judgement than that no one have what is another's, nor be deprived of what is his own? . . . Because that is just? . . . Therefore, from this point of view too, the having and doing of one's own would be agreed to be justice. (433e3-434a1)

If a polis satisfies PS everyone in it will do and have what is his own, not another's. And if everyone in it does and has his own, not another's, it will be just.

Justice, however, is not identical to the property the Kallipolis has because its members satisfy PS. The reason for this is as follows. Injustice is conventionally believed to be "the greatest evildoing" that anyone could perpetrate against his polis (434c4-5). But violations of PS, even global violations of it, do no great harm to the Kallipolis (434a3-7; 4.3, 4.9). It follows that violations of PS need not constitute injustice, that being just is not the same as satisfying PS.

But justice is yet a matter of doing one's own.

> The meddling with one another of the three classes that there are, and exchange of work between them, is the greatest harm for the polis, and would be most correctly called the greatest evildoing. . . . Wouldn't you say that the greatest evildoing against one's polis is injustice? . . . So let's put it the other way around. The opposite of this—the money-making, guarding, and ruling classes doing their own, each doing its own work in the polis—would be justice and would make the polis just. (434b9-c10)

Justice is the property the Kallipolis has because its members satisfy, not PS, but PQS, the principle of quasispecialization (4.3). This is the property of being *properly ruled* (3.5).

If the Kallipolis is just, then only the producers must produce, only the guardians must guard, and only the rulers must rule. This being so, each will do its work as well as possible. The rulers will have knowledge of the good, the guardians will have lawful, education-induced true belief about what is to be feared, and the producers will agree that the rulers should rule and the guardians guard. Hence if the Kallipolis is just, it must also be wise, courageous, and moderate. By the same token, if it is wise, courageous, and moderate, it must be properly ruled—the rulers, guardians, and producers must do their own, and not meddle with the others. Therefore, it is also true that if the Kallipolis is wise, courageous, and moderate, it must be just. This is the third structural relation between the virtues referred to earlier.

The net consequence of these three structural relations is that a polis cannot have any one of the four cardinal virtues unless it has all of them. A polis has wisdom if and only if it has courage, it has courage if and only if it has moderation, it has moderation if and only if it has justice. Justice is not simply one virtue among many, then; it is all the cardinal virtues in one. It follows, given the conventional relations between virtue and happiness, that a polis cannot be happy unless it is just, and that the closer a polis comes to being completely just, the closer it will come to being completely virtuous and completely happy.[3] But the argument will not be successful unless it can be shown that "this same form, when existing in the individual, is also agreed by us to be justice" (434d2-4). So from the politics of justice we turn to its psychology.

There are two reasons to think that the psyche has three parts analogous to the three classes of producers, guardians, and rulers distinguished in the Kallipolis. The first is given in the following passage:

> Well, then, I said, isn't it necessary for us to agree that the very same forms [eidē] and ethical dispositions as are in the polis are also in each of us? Surely they didn't get there from anywhere else. It would be ridiculous for anyone to think that spiritedness has not come to be in the polis from those private individuals who are just the ones held to possess it . . . or that the same is not true of the love of learning . . . or the love of money. (435e1-436a3; cf. 544d6-e2; 5.4)

Poleis inherit their ethical properties from the psyches of some of their members. The second reason is provided by the argument for the tripartition of the psyche, which is itself based on conventional beliefs about psychological conflict (3.2). Together these make it reasonable to believe "that the same kind of parts as are in the polis are in each psyche, and that they are equal in number" (441c4-7).

"It necessarily follows," Socrates claims, that "everything that has to do with virtue" is the same in both (441d2-3). Wisdom, courage, moderation, and justice are the same powers in the psyche as in the polis, and they are interrelated in the same ways (441c9-443b2). The property the psyche has because it is ruled by reason is identical to the property the polis has because it is ruled by the philosopher-kings. Proper psychic rule is identical to proper political rule. But it is also identical to justice:

> If there are still any doubts in our psyche, we could reassure ourselves completely by applying vulgar standards [ta phortika].—Which ones?—For example, if we had to come to an agreement about whether this polis or the man who is like it by nature and training had embezzled gold or silver entrusted to him, do you think that anyone would suppose him to have done it rather than men of a different kind?—No one would, he said.—And he would be far from robbing temples, thefts, or betrayals, whether of friends in private life or of the polis in public life?—Far, indeed.—Further, he would in no way be faithless, either in the keeping of oaths or other agreements.—How could he be?—And, further, adultery, disrespect for parents, or neglect of the gods would be more in keeping with any other character than his.—With any other, he said. (442d10-443a11)

Hence proper psychic or political rule is justice, the same thing whether in psyche or in polis. Moreover, it is the complete virtue of both psyche and polis. A polis or psyche cannot be happy without being just, and the more just either of them is, the happier it is, and the more unjust it is, the less happy it is (444a10-445b7).

From the perspective of conventional ethical thought, then, justice has been identified and vindicated. But has it also been vindicated according to the terms set out by Glaucon? Has justice itself been shown to be a homoiomerous essential extensional component of happiness itself (1.9-13)? Glaucon himself seems ready to concede that it has:

> It now remains for us to inquire whether it is profitable to do just things, and fine deeds, and be just, whether one is known to be such or not, or whether it is rather profitable to do unjust things and be unjust, provided that one doesn't pay the penalty, and is not made better by punishment.—But Socrates, he [Glaucon] said, this inquiry seems to have become ridiculous, now that the two have been shown to be as we described them. It is generally believed that life is not worth living when the body's nature is corrupted, not even with every sort of food and drink and every sort of wealth and power; will it then be livable when the nature of that very thing by which we live is confused and corrupted, even if we can do whatever else we choose

except what would rid us of vice and injustice and enable us to acquire justice and virtue? (444e7-445b4)

But Socrates is not ready: "Ridiculous indeed, I said; but, all the same, now that we have reached the place from which we can see most clearly that these things are so, we must not give in to weariness" (445b5-7). We shall see why.

5.3 FROM CONVENTIONAL JUSTICE TO JUSTICE ITSELF

The argument of Book 4 purports to show that proper psychic and political rule are each of them justice on the grounds that they possess a number of the features that conventional ethical thought attributes to justice, including that of being complete virtues which guarantee happiness. If these are indeed Plato's grounds for believing that the properties in question are identical to justice, however, then it seems that he must be presupposing that conventional ethical thought has some true beliefs about justice, and that among these is the belief that justice is a complete virtue which guarantees happiness.[4] But if he is, then he is begging the question against Thrasymachus. He will solve the problem of relevance only to come to wreck on the problem of ideology.

The question is, then, whether Plato does simply presuppose that conventional ethical thought has some true beliefs about justice. And, of course, he does not. Conventional ethical thought is the thought of cave-dwellers—they are "like us" (515a5), remember—and Plato has an elaborate theory concerning the relationship between their views about the virtues (and about everything else) and the true views of dialectical-thought. It is because that theory has not yet been brought into play in Book 4 that Socrates refuses to say there just how he is able to identify the virtues in the Kallipolis: "So we've found, I don't know how [ouk oida], this one of the four virtues [wisdom], both it and its location in the polis" (429a5-6). It is because the theory will eventually explain how he identifies them that he begins his search for justice with a clear anticipation of the Cave analogy: "Indeed, I said, the place [the location of justice in the Kallipolis] is plainly inaccessible and full of shadows. It is certainly a dark place, in which it is difficult to distinguish things from one another" (432c7-8; cf. 520c1-6). So it is to the Sun, Line, and Cave we must turn to discover just what relationship holds between what conventional ethical thought takes to be justice and justice itself. Only when we know what that relationship is, will we be in a position to determine whether Plato can solve both the problem of relevance and the problem of ideology. Only then will we know whether conventional ethical thought's opinions about justice have any real substance.

From the point of view of reliably making money, it is actions, not thoughts or motives, that count. If people pay their debts, keep their promises, and avoid killing or stealing, then regardless of why they act in these ways, making money will be safeguarded from injustice (cf. 360b3-c3). This gives us some reason to think that money-lovers will identify the virtues primarily with properties of actions.

And this, I have suggested, is what Plato seems to have in mind. Cephalus and Polemarchus are money-lovers (1.12). Their ethical views are based on the authority of T-imitative poetry, which consists of imitations of "human beings performing compulsory or voluntary actions" (603c4-5). They identify justice with the property actions have when they are cases of giving "to each the things that are due to him" (331e3-4), cases of doing and having what is one's own, not another's (433a8-b1, 433c3-434a1). They identify injustice with the property actions have when they are cases of theft, or of breaking agreements, or of adultery, or of being disrespectful to parents, or of neglecting the gods—cases of taking what is another's, or not giving to someone what is due to him (331b1-4, 442e4-444a11).

Their identification is defective, however. The property of giving to each what is owed to him makes one action just, another unjust. It is just to return a weapon to a friend from whom you have borrowed it, everything else being equal. It is unjust to return a weapon to a deranged friend, who may hurt himself or another with it (331c1-9; 1.3). Hence the property in question is actually no more what the money-lovers think to be justice than it is what they think to be injustice.

But from the point of view of Plato's metaphysical, epistemological, and psychological theories, the money-lovers' misidentification is not arbitrary. Instead, it results in an intelligible and predictable fashion from the way their psyches are ruled. Money-lovers, being ruled by necessary appetites, identify the good with a mode of the good, with a structure of a polis in which they believe they would be maximally happy. They identify happiness with a mode of happiness, with reliably getting throughout life as much of the pleasure of making money as possible. And, in general, they identify F with a mode of F, with a substructure of a mode of the good (2.12, 3.6-7). They identify the virtues with modes of the virtues, with the properties they believe will guarantee them a life reliably filled with the pleasure of making money. That is why they think of justice as doing and having one's own (433e12-434a1), and believe that the just person will not steal, renege on a contract, commit adultery, or deprive the gods of what is theirs (442e4-443a10). That is why the money-loving oligarch enjoys a reputation for justice in his business activities (554c11-d3). But because the pleasure in question is not the most pleasant

kind, and because its pursuit leads to the frustration of rational and spirited desires, these identifications suffer from a distinctive kind of cognitive unreliability. They sometimes result in true judgements, sometimes
in false ones (2.8, 2.12).

Because the relation between how a money-lover's psyche is ruled and
the account he gives of justice is reliable and predictable in this way, it
imposes a constraint on what justice itself can turn out to be, of the sort
that a lens which distorts in a regular way imposes on what the original
of an image seen through it can look like. Justice itself must be something
that, seen reflected in actions from the perspective of folk-wisdom, is a
mode of justice—a property, such as giving to each what is his own, that
just actions often possess, and unjust actions sometimes possess. That is
the constraint that folk-wisdom's beliefs about justice impose on a theory
of justice.

Now if honour, rather than money, is one's ultimate goal, what matters is that the features that attract it should be identifiable, and the
method of inculcating them known. The honour-lover wants to be able
to discover how to acquire the traits that are always rewarded with social
approval, so that he can go about having them cultivated in himself. This
gives us some reason to think that honour-lovers will identify the virtues
primarily with properties of the laws and political institutions that are the
relatively stable repositories of social values.

Again this seems to be what Plato has in mind. Thrasymachus, who is
an honour-lover (1.12), identifies justice with the property laws and political institutions have when they are in the interest of the Stronger Rulers (1.5). And this property is a figure. For unlike qualities and modes it
is intelligible rather than visible—laws and institutions are abstract things.

The identification of justice with this property of the laws is also defective, however. It is empirically adequate, because justice is indeed the interest of the Stronger Rulers who have mastered the craft of Ruling. For
these, though Thrasymachus does not know this, are the philosopher-
kings. And their laws, and the institutions of the Kallipolis, are indeed
just. But the identification is dialectically indefensible. That is why the
property with which it identifies justice is a figure, not a form (2.11-12).
For if the laws are just only if they are made by Rulers, then it is the latter,
not the laws, that are the primary repositories of justice.

But, just as in the case of the money-lovers, the honour-lovers' misidentification of justice is not arbitrary, but the intelligible and predictable
outcome of their way of looking at the world (2.9). And because of this,
it, too, imposes constraints on what justice can turn out to be. Honour-
lovers identify the good with the figure of the good, with the structure of
the polis in which they believe they would be maximally happy. They

identify happiness with a figure of happiness, with getting as much of the pleasure of being honoured as possible throughout life (3.6-7). They identify the virtues with the properties they believe will guarantee them happiness so conceived. But because the pleasure of being honoured is not in fact the most pleasant kind, and because its pursuit leads to the frustration of rational desires, these identifications, too, suffer from a distinctive kind of cognitive unreliability. They can yield true beliefs about the visible or empirical world, but not about the intelligible one (2.12). And because the relation between how honour-lovers' psyches are ruled and the account they produce of justice is reliable and predictable, it follows that nothing can be a virtue unless, seen reflected in political institutions from the perspective of scientific-thought, it is a figure of a virtue. Nothing can be justice unless, seen in that way, it is the interest of the stronger. That is the constraint scientific-thought imposes on a theory of justice.

Finally, the wisdom-loving philosopher-kings, who alone see things as they are, undistorted by desire-induced fantasy, identify the good with the good itself, with the structure of the Kallipolis in which they know that they—and everyone else—will be maximally happy. They identify happiness with getting as much of the pleasure of knowing and learning the truth as possible throughout life. And they are right. For that pleasure is the most pleasant of all, and getting it involves satisfying all of their desires, not just some of them (3.6-7). They identify the virtues with the forms of the virtues, with the properties they believe will guarantee them happiness so conceived. They identify the forms of the virtues with properties of their own psyches. And, as we shall see, they are right about that too (5.4). But, in addition, they have a theory—the theory we have just been recalling—about how the world views of the money-lovers and honour-lovers are related to their own world view. Hence nothing can be a virtue unless when seen from the nondistorting perspective of dialectical-thought it is the form of a virtue, and is appropriately related to the modes and figures of that virtue. That is the constraint dialectical-thought imposes on a theory of justice.

Justice itself has now emerged in its true colours as a property, not primarily of actions or political institutions, but of psyches. And happiness itself has emerged in its true colours as getting as much as possible of the pleasure of knowing the truth throughout life. It is because the psyches of the philosopher-kings are just that they see the good itself. It is because they see the good itself that they understand why they are happiest being just and ruling in the Kallipolis. It is because they are just, and rule in the light of their knowledge of the good, that the institutions of the Kallipolis are just, promote the maximal happiness of the guardians, and are understood to have these properties by the guardians themselves. It is because the psyches of the guardians, shaped by those institutions, are reliably disposed to justice that the actions sanctioned as just in the Kallipolis promote the maximal happiness of the producers and are seen as doing so by the producers (5.4).

This degree of understanding of justice, which identifies it, not with its modes or figures, but with justice itself, is characteristic of the philosopher. In the *Republic* it is represented by Glaucon and Adeimantus and—above all—by the Socrates "made new and fine" (*Second Letter* 314c1-4) whom we meet after Book 1 (1.8, 1.12).

Plato does not simply presuppose, then, that the accounts of justice given by the money-lovers or honour-lovers are true. If he did, he would beg the question of ideology raised by Thrasymachus just as surely as Socrates does in Book 1—just as surely as anyone does who considers intuitions to be the primary evidence for an ethical theory (1.2, 1.5). Nor does he assume that these accounts can simply be ignored, that they impose no constraints on ethical theory. If he did, he would founder on the problem of relevance; it would not be clear what bearing his theory had on justice. The path to be followed by a successful theory is a narrow one, then. The problem of ideology seems to force it away from ordinary ethical thought. At the same time, the problem of relevance seems to force it back towards ordinary ethical thought.

It is this narrow path, which most philosophers have not appreciated the need to negotiate, that Plato found a way to follow. The money-lovers and honour-lovers do misidentify the virtues. But their misidentifications are a predictable consequence of their mind frames. Given the way their psyches are ruled, they must misidentify the virtues (and all other properties, for that matter) in precisely the way they do. Because of this, the virtues must be properties that will be misidentified by money-lovers and honour-lovers in that way. That is the constraint conventional ethical thought, of the sort exhibited by money-lovers and honour-lovers, imposes on ethical theory. So it is by constructing a theory of how the psyche works that Plato handles both the problem of relevance and the problem of ideology. The property he identifies with justice must, when appropriately reflected in actions or institutions, look like justice from the perspectives of the money-lovers and honour-lovers. That will solve the problem of relevance. But he does not presuppose that money-lovers and honour-lovers correctly identify justice, only that they misidentify it in a characteristic and predictable way. That circumvents the problem of ideology.

5.4 JUSTICE ITSELF

The principal components of conventional ethical thought's theory and defense of justice are these:

(1) Justice exists both in poleis and in psyches.

(2) It is doing and having one's own, not another's, and not being meddlesome. It guarantees that its possessor will not embezzle, steal, betray his friends or polis, break oaths or contracts, commit adultery, be disrespectful to his parents, neglect the gods, or, indeed, commit any conventionally unjust act.

(3) It is more choiceworthy for its own sake than injustice, because it is a complete virtue which alone guarantees happiness to its possessor.

Plato must show that justice itself—proper political or psychic rule—fits that image, that it will look like justice to conventional ethical thought. He must redraft the theory of conventional justice as a theory of justice itself, show that the property identified with justice itself stands in the right sorts of relations to conventional justice, and show that justice itself is a homoiomerous essential extensional component of happiness.[5] If he is successful, he will have solved the problems of relevance and ideology, established that proper psychic or political rule is justice, and explained to Glaucon and those like him why, even in the face of Thrasymachus' skeptical arguments, he should choose justice for its own sake over injustice. If, in addition, he can show that justice is more choiceworthy than injustice for the sake of its G-consequences, he will have shown that justice is a B-good (358a1-3), and have accomplished all that was undertaken in Book 2.

Since justice is a power (358b4-7), we do not have to resort to speculation in order to determine the conditions proper political and psychic rule must satisfy if they are to be identical. For if proper political rule is justice, then it too must be a power. And we know from 2.8 that Plato has clear and defensible views about the identity of powers, or, at any rate, of the relevant type of powers: "What is set over the same things and does the same work, I call the same power; what is set over something different and does different work, I call a different power" (477d2-5). Because proper political rule is complex, however, we need to compute what it is set over, and what work it does.

The Kallipolis is properly ruled just in case each of its three major constituent classes does its own work, and does not meddle in the work of the others. So the work proper rule does in the polis has as its essential components the work proper to the philosopher-kings, which is to rule, the work proper to the guardians, which is to guard under the direction of the philosophers, and the work proper to the producers, which is to produce under the joint direction of guardians and philosophers. Presumably, then, proper rule is set over the properties that the complete psychological powers of the philosophers, guardians, and rulers must be set over if they are to do their work as well as possible. On this showing, any power is identical to proper rule if and only if it has three constituent powers: one set over forms, which does the work of ruling; one set over figures, which does the work of guarding; and one set over modes, which does the work of producing. Hence what must be shown is that powers of this sort, and in this configuration, can exist in the psyche.

Each (embodied) psyche consists of appetite, aspiration, and reason (3.2). But, as we saw in 3.4, these parts just are instantiations of the complete psychological powers. Appetite (appropriately moderated by training in a craft) is an instantiation of folk-wisdom, which is a power set over modes. Aspiration is an instantiation of scientific-thought, which is a power set over figures. Reason is an instantiation of dialectical-thought, which is a power set over forms. Hence Plato's argument for the tripartite psyche, when seen in the light of the remainder of the *Republic*, also shows that powers set over modes, figures, and forms exist in the psyche.

These powers, however, do not gain access to the properties over which they are set in every psyche (3.4). It all depends on how the psyche in which they exist is ruled. In a psyche ruled by unnecessary appetites, appetite can gain cognitive access only to qualities, not to modes. In a psyche ruled by necessary appetites, appetite can gain access to modes, but not aspiration to figures, or reason to forms. In a psyche ruled by spirited desires, appetite can gain access to modes, and aspiration to figures, but not reason to forms. Only in a psyche ruled by rational desires can appetite gain access to modes, aspiration to figures, and reason to forms.

But even in a philosophic psyche, reason will not gain access to the good itself and its constituent forms unless that psyche has received the type of upbringing and education that is available only in the Kallipolis (496a11-497c3). Hence it is only in the psyche of the philosopher-king that the three powers both exist and have access to the properties over which they are set. It is only in his psyche, therefore, that folk-wisdom, scientific-thought, and dialectical-thought have the resources necessary to do their proper work. So, quite apart from the fact that the philosopher's psyche is the psychic analogue of the Kallipolis (442e3-6), there is compelling reason for Socrates to search—as he does in Book 4—for psychic justice in that particular psyche. Complete psychic justice exists nowhere else (580b8-c4).

But can these powers, even as they exist within the philosopher-king's psyche, reasonably be seen as doing work analogous to that performed by the corresponding social classes in the Kallipolis? In the case of reason, or the dialectical-thought it instantiates, the answer is straightforwardly yes. Reason rules the psyche in a way that is clearly analogous to the way in which the philosopher-kings rule the Kallipolis (3.5).

When we turn to appetite and aspiration, however, and the powers they instantiate, things look less promising. After all, the producers actually make shoes and till fields, the guardians actually fight battles and police the Kallipolis, but appetite and aspiration, especially the philosopher-king's appetite and aspiration, do not seem to do anything remotely like these things. Philosopher-kings neither produce nor guard, they just rule.

To see the error in this objection, we must reflect again on the work the producers and guardians actually do. The proper work of the producers is not simply to produce, but to produce *as directed by the guardians and philosopher-kings*. The proper work of the guardians is not simply to guard, but to guard *as directed by the philosopher-kings*. Hence the work of appetite, or of the folk-wisdom it instantiates, is to produce *as reason and aspiration direct* (442a4-b3; 3.5). And this means that a philosopher-king's appetite will not be directly productive. It will not cause him to engage in actually making shoes or tilling fields; rather, it will cause him to direct the productive activities of others in the Kallipolis, so that his appetitive desires, which are the forces that motivate appetite and folk-wisdom to produce, will be optimally satisfied. For this is the course of action that his reason judges to be best. In the same way, his aspiration, or the scientific-thought it instantiates, will not lead him into actually waging war or policing the producers. Instead, it will lead him to direct the guardians to do those things, so that his spirited desires, which are the motivating forces of aspiration and scientific-thought, will be optimally satisfied. For, again, this is what his reason judges to be best. Hence we should not be led to reject Plato's psychopolitical analogies by the superficial differences between what the philosopher-king's appetite and aspiration actually do and what the producers and guardians actually do. If we are careful to describe correctly what each does, we see that it is precisely by *not* producing and *not* guarding that appetite and aspiration do the same work in the philosopher-king's psyche that the producers and guardians perform in the Kallipolis by producing and guarding.

Plato has shown that proper psychic rule is identical to proper political rule, that his candidate for justice exists both in poleis and in psyches. But will that property look like justice to conventional ethical thought, to folk-wisdom and scientific-thought? When it is appropriately reflected in actions, or political institutions, will it fit the formulae that these constituencies use to define justice?

Designed by the reason-ruled philosopher-kings to have this very effect, primary education moderates both necessary and unnecessary appetites. It imbeds in spirited desires an ideal of the type that reason, which aims at the overall good of the psyche, judges to be best (3.4), thereby insuring that reason and aspiration are satisfied and frustrated in unison (3.5, 4.10). Reason, thus strengthened by aspiration, is then able to rule over weakened appetite, "which is the largest thing in each psyche and by nature most insatiable for possessions" (441e8-442b9). Now primary education is not value-neutral; it has obvious conventional ethical content. For what it presents as the ideal worthy of emulation and deserving of honour are gods and heroes who are moderate in their appetites, truth-loving, loyal, and courageous (4.5). It follows that the properly ruled psyche has moderated its appetitive desire for food, drink, sex, and money through appropriate training in youth, and is jointly ruled by reason, which believes that this sort of character is the best kind to have, and by aspiration, which aspires to have a character of that sort. Thus it would appear that a person whose psyche is properly ruled will pass muster as just from the perspective of conventional ethical thought (442d10-443a11)—that proper rule, when appropriately reflected in actions, will look like conventional justice. It remains to be seen whether this conclusion is warranted.

There is no doubt that Plato has done a good job of designing a psyche that is unlikely to act unjustly out of appetitive or spirited pleonexia—out of the desire for more and more food, drink, sex, and money without limit, on the one hand, or out of a desire for more and more honour, on the other. He has, therefore, guarded the philosopher-kings against many of the common causes of injustice and vice. But it is not so obvious that he has been equally successful in guarding them against all such causes. And if he has failed to do this, proper rule will not pass all of the vulgar tests that conventional ethical thought might reasonably set for his candidate for justice.[6]

Let us examine two different kinds of cases. In the first, what causes a philosopher-king to act unjustly seems not to be pleonexia of any kind. In the second, what causes him to act unjustly seems to be pleonexia of some sort, but not appetitive or spirited pleonexia. By seeing how Plato's theory can handle these cases, we will further deepen our understanding of it.

A takes an opportunity to benefit his friend by treating another unjustly. He gains nothing by it, not even increased affection from his friend (we may suppose that A cannot tell him what he has done because the latter would refuse to benefit from injustice). A's motive seems to be simply a disinterested desire to benefit a friend. A acts unjustly, but he does not seem to act out of pleonexia, or a desire for more and more of anything. Hence it seems possible for A to act unjustly out of friendship (or some other nonpleonectic motive) and, at the same time, to have a properly ruled psyche. And if this is possible, then it seems, unless there is something more to be said, that proper rule cannot be what conventional ethical thought calls justice.

This apparent counterexample, initially rather plausible, trades on neglect of the fact that if A has a properly ruled psyche, he is a wisdom-lover whose sole aim in life is long-term, stable acquisition of as much as possible of the pleasure of learning and knowing the truth. And once this fact is again in focus, we see that A cannot be both properly ruled and motivated by disinterested friendship in the way the counterexample requires. As an attack on Plato's account of justice, the counterexample fails. It presupposes something Plato's psychological theory excludes.

But because it does seem possible for a just person to be motivated by something other than a desire for the pleasure of knowing the truth, it might be that what the counterexample really points up is a flaw in the psychological theory underlying Plato's account of justice. For if a person motivated by disinterested friendship can be just, exhibiting his justice in part by refusing to act like A, then proper rule, though it may be a sufficient condition of being just, will fail to be justice by failing to be a necessary condition of being just. The real problem, according to this objection, is that Plato's account of justice is based on a theory of the psyche that does not fit the facts of human motivation.

This may well be so, of course. But it is not established by our finding it plausible to believe that a just person can be motivated by disinterested friendship, or by some other such motive. For what looks like disinterested friendship may, when all the facts about the psyche are in, always be a disguise for some other motive, such as the pleonectic desire to have the power of a god, or to secretly arrange the lives of our friends. What we need here is not intuition, or conventional judgements of plausibility, but an alternative theory to underwrite our views about motivation, as Plato's theory underwrites his. Without such a theory, counterexamples of this sort will make little impression in any Platonic quarter.

Because it seems that any attack on Plato's account of justice which appeals to a motive other than the desire for the pleasure of knowing the truth will suffer the fate of being deflected to his psychological theory in this way, it becomes attractive to try to undermine the account by appeal to that very desire itself. Plato has guarded his philosopher-kings against injustice caused by appetitive or spirited pleonexia, but what is to stop them from committing unjust acts out of *rational pleonexia*, out of a desire for more and more without limit of the pleasure of knowing the truth? If nothing is to stop them, then, again, conventional ethical thought will rightly object that proper rule, or its reflection in actions, cannot be what it calls justice.

What we are to imagine is something like the following. Each of the philosopher-kings wants to spend as much time doing philosophy and as little time actually ruling the Kallipolis as possible. We may suppose that justice requires that these desires be equally satisfied, that each philosopher-king should get to spend as much time philosophizing as is compatible with the others getting to spend the same amount. However, A sees a way to get more than his share. By altering the record books he can spend twice as much time philosophizing as his fellows. What is to stop him from doing it? What is to stop him from acting unjustly?

One might think that surrounded as he is by philosopher-kings who are his intellectual peers, fear of discovery would give A all the motive he needs to avoid fiddling the books. But this fact, if it is a fact, is of no use to Plato. If A avoids injustice only because he fears its bad G-consequences, then whatever justice is, even if it is proper rule, it cannot be something that A wants for its own sake. So if Plato has to have recourse to such fears in order to explain why A will not act unjustly, his project of showing that justice is a B-good, wanted for its own sake as well as its G-consequences, is in serious trouble (1.9-13). Fortunately for that project such desperate measures are not required.

We need to distinguish two kinds of practical questions. The first is, what sort of character is it best for someone to have, given the types of circumstances he is likely to find himself in? The second is, what is it best for him to do in the circumstances he is in? Obviously, the two are related: actions shape character; character to some degree determines actions. But they are also different, and, as we shall see, it is important to be clear about which of them is in view.

Through fifty years of education and training, A has come to know the good itself, and has concluded that the life of a philosopher-king is the best life practically possible, because it affords him more of the pleasure of knowing the truth than any other. It follows that a polis which instantiates the good itself must not only guarantee that all philosopher-kings receive as much as possible of the pleasure of knowing the truth, it must also insure that all of them receive the same amount of it. Otherwise knowledge of the good itself—knowledge of psychic and political structures—would not enable A to know that his life, which does not differ structurally from that of any other philosopher-king, is the most pleasant and happiest possible (a similar argument could be made in the case of the producers and guardians). So in thinking his own life best, A has come to think best a life in which he receives the same amount of the pleasure of knowing the truth as each of the other philosopher-kings.

Now A faces the second type of question. Should he fiddle the books in order to get more of the pleasure of knowing the truth than his fellows? To this question, however, he brings an already formed character. And it is out of this character, out of the desires and dispositions he actually has, that he will deliberate and act. Consequently, he will act in the light of his knowledge of the good itself; he will leave the books alone, settle for the same amount of the pleasure of knowing the truth as his fellows, and avoid injustice.

But is he not cheating himself out of some of his favourite pleasure by acting in this way? And does that not mean that being just is not the best option for him? It may well be that on a particular occasion A could get more pleasure by acting unjustly. But it certainly does not follow from this that there is a better option available to him than being just. To think so is to confuse choosing characters with choosing actions. In order for A to be able to act unjustly, he would have to have a character different from his actual one. We cannot develop a character and then act as if we did not have it. That is the point, and often a good part of the glory or tragedy, of having a character. But if Plato is right, any character which would allow A to act unjustly would result in his getting less, not more, of his favourite pleasure. Hence, even though A could in some circumstances do better by acting unjustly, he is still better off having a character that prevents him from acting in that way.

The desire for the pleasure of knowing the truth is a desire for the practical knowledge of how to live well or happily. That is why it culminates in knowledge of the good itself (2.15). That is why the natural object of a rational desire can be specified indifferently as *the pleasure of knowing the truth* or as *the good of the psyche as a complex whole* (3.6-7). Therefore, if proper rule is a homoiomerous essential extensional component of happiness, it cannot conflict with the desire for the pleasure of knowing the truth. It follows that there are no unnecessary rational desires. If—reverting to conventional terminology—justice is indeed a complete virtue, rational pleonexia is impossible.

All things considered, then, there is reason to believe that proper psychic rule reflected in actions will pass these sorts of vulgar or conventional tests. But will proper political rule also pass them? And will both types of rule pass the tests set by scientific-thought? It is convenient to answer these two questions together.

Proper rule guarantees that the political institutions necessary to combat pleonexia successfully, and to insure that everyone achieves what is most advantageous to him, will exist in the Kallipolis. It follows that these institutions will be advantageous to the stronger guardians (4.5). Moreover, the guardians will know this (4.1). Consequently, the institutions in question will instantiate a figure of justice. Proper rule, appropriately reflected in institutions, will look like justice to scientific-thought. But the same institutions also guarantee that no one will be deprived of the pleasure which, being best for him or most advantageous to him, is most his own (586e1-2), or be allowed to have any pleasure other than his own. And, like the guardians, the producers will know this. It follows that the actions sanctioned as just in the Kallipolis will instantiate a mode of justice—that proper rule, appropriately reflected in those actions, will look like justice to conventional ethical thought. A properly ruled polis will not sanction conventionally unjust actions. Proper rule is a sort of doing and having one's own, not another's.

Conventional ethical thought is committed to holding that justice is the complete political and psychic virtue, more choiceworthy for its own sake than injustice. If this is a reflection of a fact about justice itself, then justice itself must be a homoiomerous essential extensional component of happiness. It must be impossible to be happy without being properly ruled, and every step closer to rational rule must be a step closer to happiness.

Happiness has two aspects, content and form (3.7). Its content is pleasure; to be as happy as possible a psyche must be able to experience the most pleasant pleasure. Its form is, in part, a matter of desire structure; to be as happy as possible a psyche must be able to satisfy all of its desires, and frustrate none, throughout life. We have, then, two possible measures of happiness—one in terms of relative pleasantness of the pleasures enjoyed, the other in terms of satisfaction and frustration. On Plato's theory of the psyche, however, these two measures must coincide.

A psyche ruled by lawless unnecessary appetites, a tyrannical psyche, cannot satisfy any of its desires, whether appetitive, spirited, or rational. Consequently, it cannot experience any pleasure. Simply because of its desire structure it is frustrated and unhappy.

A psyche ruled by nonlawless unnecessary appetites, a democratic psyche, represses its lawless appetites by force. It exercises perceptual-thought and has access to the pleasures of food, drink, and sex, which are the least pleasant of all. But because it cannot experience the pleasures of being honoured or knowing the truth, its spirited and rational desires are frustrated. And because it cannot experience the pleasure of making money its appetites compete with one another for satisfaction. Hence, while it sometimes experiences the pleasure of eating (say), it does so at the expense of frustrating its other appetites.

A psyche ruled by necessary appetites, an oligarchic psyche, represses its unnecessary appetites. It exercises folk-wisdom and has access to the more pleasant pleasure of making money. Hence it can satisfy its necessary appetites. But because it cannot experience the pleasures of being honoured and of knowing the truth, its spirited and rational desires are frustrated, and because it forcibly represses its unnecessary appetites instead of moderating them through training and education, they remain as sources of frustration and akrasia.

A psyche ruled by spirited desires, a timocratic psyche, has managed to further repress its appetites. It exercises scientific-thought and has access to the more pleasant pleasure of being honoured. It can satisfy its spirited desires and its repressed appetites together. But because it cannot experience the pleasure of knowing the truth, its rational desires are frustrated, and because it forcibly represses its appetites instead of moderating them through education and training, they remain as sources of frustration and akrasia.

A psyche ruled by rational desires, a philosophic psyche, does not forcibly repress any of its desires, but moderates them through training and education. It exercises dialectical-thought and has access to the most pleasant pleasure, that of knowing the truth. It can satisfy all its desires in unison. It is properly ruled (3.5).

If this part of the argument is successful, it shows, on the basis of internal structural considerations alone, that a psyche cannot be happy unless it is properly ruled, and that every step away from proper rule is a step away from happiness, every step toward it a step towards happiness. The philosophic person is happier than the timocratic, the timocratic is happier than the oligarchic, the oligarchic is happier than the democratic, and the democratic is happier than the tyrannical.

But there is another part to the formal aspect of happiness besides desire structure, namely, polis structure (3.7). For whether our desires will be satisfied or frustrated depends not only on them but also on the polis, on the world. Hence we want to be satisfied that when this component of happiness is taken into consideration it will not disturb Plato's conclusions; we want to be satisfied that the world cannot make up in happiness what desire structure takes away. It is here that proper political rule reenters the picture.

In Book 8, Socrates picks up where he left off at the end of Book 4:

> You realize, of course, that there are of necessity as many forms [*eidē*] of character among men as there are forms of political constitutions.

Or do you suppose that constitutions are born "from oak or rock" and not from the characters or mores of the men who live in the poleis, which tip the scales and drag other things after them? . . . Then, if the forms of poleis are five, those of the individual psyches must be five also. (544d6–e5; cf. 445c9–10)

A person's psychological type is determined by the type of desires which rule in his psyche. Similarly, the constitutional type of a polis is determined by the character type of the people who rule in it.[7] The detailed argument in support of this view is the parade of five paired poleis and psyches that begins in Book 2 with the gradual account of the Kallipolis and the philosopher-kings and ends with the account of tyranny and the tyrant in Book 9.

But this is only one side of the coin. It is also true that people's characters, including that part of their characters which is due to nature, are—within the limits discussed in 2.14—shaped by the type of polis in which they are born and reared: "Sound rearing and education, when they are preserved, produce good natures; and sound natures, receiving such an education, grow up still better than those before them both in other respects and in the kind of children they produce, just as with other animals" (424a4–b1; cf. 377a4–d1, 401b1–402a6, 409a1–5, 441e8–442a2, 458e3–461e9). If this were not so, the elaborate educational and eugenics programmes established for the Kallipolis, which occupy so much of the *Republic*, would all be for nought. Hence a second reason that the virtues of polis and psyche are the same is that—again within the aforementioned limits—poleis determine the characters of their members.

The relationship between proper political rule and proper psychic rule is a reflection of this two-sided picture. The properly ruled Kallipolis cannot come into existence unless philosophers become kings or kings philosophers (473c11–e5). But it is equally true that philosophers cannot achieve complete proper rule outside the Kallipolis. Under other constitutions, the philosophic nature is "perverted and altered" (497b1–3), and fails to achieve its full potential for growth (497a3–5). However, "if it were to find the best political constitution, as it is itself the best, then it would be apparent that it is really divine" (497b7–c3; 2.11).

At first glance, it may seem that this is a paradoxical situation—the properly ruled Kallipolis cannot come into existence unless properly ruled philosophers become its kings, but properly ruled philosophers cannot come into existence except in a properly ruled Kallipolis. As is sometimes the case with such problematic situations, however, a bootstrapping maneuver offers an escape. And this is what Plato himself seems to envisage:

We were compelled by truth to say that no polis or constitution, and no man like them, will ever become complete [*teleos*], unless some necessity constrains those few philosophers who aren't vicious, those now called useless, to take charge of a polis, whether they want to or not, and the polis is compelled to obey them, or until a true passion for true philosophy flows by divine inspiration into the sons of those in power or of kings, or into the fathers themselves. (499b1-c2)

Philosophers whose psyches fall short of complete proper rule take over as kings of a polis (or kings who have the capacity to study philosophy take it up). They introduce the institutions that will appropriately modify the psyches of the members of the polis, including their own psyches. The result will be the joint realization of the properly ruled Kallipolis and the properly ruled philosophers necessary to be its kings. The complete man and the complete polis come into existence together.

Moreover, once they have come into existence, proper political rule helps sustain proper psychic rule. For in addition to shaping the philosopher's desire structure through education, the institutions of the Kallipolis also insure that the nonrational desires of others, whether inside or outside the Kallipolis (4.5), will not prevent him from doing what his reason determines to be best. This insures that his desires will always be optimally satisfied, so that frustration will not undermine or weaken proper rule.

The fact that psychic harmony and political harmony are symbiotically related in this way explains why "justice is the power which produces such men and such poleis as we have described" (443b4-5), namely, properly ruled ones. (Incomplete) proper rule in its kings produces (incomplete) proper rule in a polis, which, in turn, produces (complete) proper rule in both kings and polis. It also explains the otherwise mysterious claim that the person whose psyche is properly ruled, the philosopher-king,

> thinks and names a just and fine action one which preserves and helps to produce this condition [proper rule], and wisdom the knowledge which oversees this action; while he thinks and names an unjust action one which always undoes this condition, and ignorance the opinion which oversees it. (443e4-444a2)[8]

To be called fine and just by the philosopher-king, an action must be overseen by reason. This narrows the class of actions in question to two: those performed by the philosopher-king himself, and those sanctioned as just in the Kallipolis (590c2-d6). For these alone of relevant actions are overseen by reason. But if only the former are just, the Kallipolis will not be just; proper political rule will not be justice. Hence the latter class, which includes the former, must be the one intended. But these are the actions which constitute or realize the proper rule of the Kallipolis, a condition which, given the relation between proper political rule and proper psychic rule, "preserves and helps to produce" the proper psychic rule of the philosopher-kings.

Now, as we move away from the aristocratic Kallipolis, first to a timocracy, in which both rulers and polis are ruled by aspiration, then to an oligarchy, in which both are ruled by necessary appetites, then to a democracy, in which both are ruled by nonlawless unnecessary appetites, until we come to a tyranny in which both rulers and polis are ruled by lawless unnecessary appetites, we move away from a polis that so structures both desires and the world that the former are optimally satisfied in the latter to a polis which so structures desires and the world that the former are as frustrated as possible in the latter. We move away from a polis that contributes as much as possible to the proper rule and happiness of its members to one that contributes as much as possible to their improper rule and wretchedness. That is why the philosopher-king is closer to complete proper rule and closer to complete happiness than the philosophic person who leads a private life, while the tyrant is further from complete proper rule and complete happiness than the tyrannical person who leads a private life.

What a polis contributes to happiness is twofold, then. It partly determines desire structure and it partly determines desire satisfaction. But neither of these contributions changes a person's fundamental psychological type. An honour-lover will be an honour-lover in any polis that does not prevent him from developing his potential. Otherwise his polis simply makes a difference to how satisfied an honour-lover he will be. But this, though it certainly affects his happiness, cannot change his position in Plato's ranking of lives. A frustrated philosopher is still closer to true pleasure and true happiness than a satisfied honour-lover. A frustrated honour-lover is closer to them than a satisfied money-lover. And the same is true of the other psychological types as well. A polis can radically affect their absolute happiness but not their relative happiness. If this were not so, the relative pleasantness of pleasures, their relative closeness to purity and truth, would not be itself sufficient to decide the relative happiness of lives (3.6-7).

When we take into account the contribution that polis structure makes to happiness, then, we do nothing to alter Plato's ranking of lives. Regardless of the polis one is in, one cannot be happy without being properly ruled, and the closer one comes to being properly ruled the closer one comes to being happy. It follows that proper rule is a homoiomerous essential extensional component of happiness.

The principal, and by far the most interesting part of the long response to Glaucon's challenge is now complete. Proper political rule is proper psychic rule. Proper psychic rule is the doing and having of their own by reason, aspiration, and appetite. Proper political rule is the doing and having of their own by the philosopher-kings, guardians, and producers. Each insures that its possessor will perform no conventionally unjust actions. Each is a homoiomerous essential extensional component of happiness. It follows that proper rule is justice, and that justice is an essential extensional component of happiness, more choiceworthy for its own sake than injustice.

It remains to be shown that justice is a B-good, not only more choiceworthy for its own sake than injustice, but also more choiceworthy for its G-consequences. It is this part of Plato's theory that draws on the somewhat unprepossessing argument for the immortality of the psyche (3.8).

Because the psyche is immortal, there are two sorts of G-consequences, those which occur in this world and those which occur in the next (613e6-614a8). Those which occur in the next world depend only on the attitudes of the gods to justice and injustice (614a5-621d3), while those which occur in this world depend both on the attitudes of the gods (612e2-613b8) and on those of men (613b9-614a4).

As regards the latter class, we are told that the gods, being good and just (379b1-380c3) will love the just man and hate the unjust one, and that "as far as the gifts of the gods are concerned, all will happen as well as possible for the friend of the gods" (612e8-613a1). If things appear otherwise and the just person seems to languish, we must suppose either that he is being punished for some previous wrongdoing (613a1-2) or that "this will end well for him either during his lifetime or afterwards" (613a4-7). For "the gods never neglect a man who eagerly wants to be just and who, through the practice of virtue, tries to become as much like a god as a man can" (613a7-b1; cf. *Apology* 41c8-d2). But with the unjust the opposite is true (613b4). They may appear to flourish like the proverbial great bay tree, but in the end they suffer for their injustice.

Among men, too, it is justice that enjoys the good reputation. The just are chosen for public office, are able to make good marriages for themselves and their children, and enjoy many other advantages over the unjust (613c8-d5). The latter start well and deceive people at first, but in real life, as opposed to philosophical fantasy, they are caught and punished (613d5-e5).

The truth about this world is a matter of evidence and argument. The truth about the next world is a matter of myth. Traditional stories are our only source of information about the gods and Hades (382c10-d3, 427b2-c4; *Timaeus* 40d6-e4; 2.11). Hence it is no surprise that when we turn from the G-consequences of justice and injustice in this world to their G-consequences in the next, we are presented with a myth or story—the so-called Myth of Er.

After being "dead" for twelve days, Er, the son of Armenias, revived, and told what he had seen in the afterlife. The psyches of the dead appear before judges, who send just psyches up into the heavens, where for a thousand years they fare well, see beautiful things, and are rewarded tenfold for their good deeds, and who send unjust psyches down into the earth, where for the same number of years, or more in the case of some tyrants who have committed really terrible crimes, they suffer "ten times the pain they caused to each individual" (615b5-6). When psyches have completed this stage in their postmortal history, they proceed, via a series of stations in the cosmos, to a place where, in an order determined by lot, they choose their next sublunary life from a set of lives "far more numerous than the psyches present" (618a2-3). Some of these lives are those of men and women, others are lives of animals, but each is fully characterized from birth to death, so that all that happens in it can be seen by the psyches making their choice (618a3-b6, 619b2-d7). What kind of life a person chooses is in part a matter of chance—no more than a small selection of lives may remain by the time it is his turn to choose, although it is never the case that only bad lives remain, and a satisfactory life is always available (619b3-6). But "for the most part their choice depends upon the character of their previous life" (620a2-3). Those who have studied philosophy and are able "to distinguish the good life from the bad" (618c4-5) will be guided in their choice by the justice or injustice of the lives available. Those "who have been virtuous by habit without philosophy" (619c7-d1; cf. 430b6-9),[9] having neither knowledge nor experience of evil to guide them, choose to be tyrants. When the choice of lives is complete, and each has been made necessary and unchangeable by the fates, the psyches proceed to the parchingly hot plain of forgetfulness. There the unwise, overcome by a desire to quench their thirst, drink deeply from the waters of Oblivion, while the wise content themselves with shallower draughts. As a result, the unwise forget what will happen to the unjust after death, while the wise do not entirely forget, and so gain an additional motive to be just. At this point, they are ready for rebirth.

The moral of the story for those "who believe that the psyche is immortal and that it can endure all these evils and blessings" (621c2-3) is clear. If we practice "justice with wisdom," we will be happy not only in this incarnation, but in future incarnations, and in the thousand-year journeys which occur between. For such people, there is no doubt that the G-consequences of justice decisively outweigh those of injustice.

Others, unpersuaded that the psyche is immortal, agnostic about the gods or their attitudes to justice and injustice, and uncaptivated by the very captivating Myth of Er, will want to leave out of account all G-consequences except those which occur in this world. They will be less certain that the G-consequences of justice are always better than those of injustice. They will be unable to escape the reflection that one successful act of injustice can put a person on easy street for life. But that reflection simply confirms the soundness of Plato's overall strategy. It was his own clear awareness that justice could not be defended by appeal to G-consequences that led him to develop his defense of justice itself. It was that same awareness, we may be sure, that led him, when he turned to G-consequences, to weight things in his favour by bringing immortality and the gods into the picture.

Plato's argument is now complete. He has not demonstrated once and for all that proper rule is justice itself. Therefore, he has not demonstrated once and for all that justice is a B-good either. But neither did he set out to demonstrate these things. The path travelled in the *Republic* is, as we are now in a position to judge, a path for friends of the forms, a path littered with hypotheses that we are in no position to conclusively confirm, and any one of which we might reasonably question. But the *Republic* describes another path that is unhypothetical, a path we will be able travel only when, on the basis of an empirically adequate, dialectically defensible theory of everything, we come to know the *megiston mathēma*, the good itself (505a1-4). Until then, all we can do "is insist that there is some such thing to see" (533a1-6).

5.5 PLATO'S THEORY OF ETHICS

A theory of ethics must do three things. First, it must provide a *metaphysics* of ethics. It must identify the subject matter of ethics, what ethical judgements are about, what their truth conditions are. Second, it must provide an *epistemology* of ethics. It must explain how our cognitive apparatus interacts with that subject matter, how we discover facts about it. Third, it must provide *a theory of ethical motivation*. It must explain how that subject matter engages our conative apparatus, how it affects our will and our desires.[10] When we know what an ethical theory tells us on these heads, we know what sort of theory it is, where it belongs in the taxonomy of ethical theories. And when we know its place in that taxonomy, we know the major kinds of criticisms to which it is particularly open. In this section, I shall try to locate the ethical theory I have excavated from the *Republic* on the larger map of such theories.

Plato clearly thinks that ethics has a subject matter, that ethical judgments have truth conditions. He does not think that they simply express emotions or attitudes, or that they are a species of imperative. He is not a non-cognitivist. To judge that someone is just is to ascribe a property to him, the property of having a properly ruled psyche. The judgement is true if he has the property, false otherwise. Because ethical terms, such as 'just', 'wise', and 'temperate', refer to real, mind-independent properties, and ethical judgements possess an objective truth value, independently of our means of knowing it, Plato's theory is a species of ethical realism.[11] Because the properties in question are not nonnatural properties, of the sort with which G. E. Moore identified goodness, but properties belonging to the naturalistic theory of the psyche, Plato's theory is also a species of ethical naturalism. And because these properties are primarily properties of agents, not of their actions, his theory is agent-centred, not, like most contemporary ethical theories, act-centred.[12]

Now, the metaphysics of an ethical theory has obvious consequences for its epistemology. We can only discover, or plausibly be held to discover, facts about a certain sort of subject matter in a certain way. So it is a welcome relief that Plato does not think that we discover what justice is by intuition, by recollection of prenatal observation of a nonnaturalistic world, or by analyzing concepts or the meanings of words. For each of these is an implausible way to find out about naturalistic properties. Instead, he holds that we discover what justice is by developing a dialectically defensible, empirically adequate, unified theory of the world, including the psychological, social, and cultural parts of it. And this is a very plausible way to find out about naturalistic properties. Dialectical scientific holism fits well with realism and naturalism. The epistemology and metaphysics of Platonic ethics are made for each other.

But what is a virtue from the point of view of internal consistency and intelligibility may seem to be a vice from the point of view of truth. Naturalism, realism, and scientific holism in ethical theory face a barrage of familiar objections. Everyone has heard of the so-called naturalistic fallacy. My own sense, which I shall not try to justify, is that none of these objections is, or currently enjoys the reputation of being, conclusive, and that ethical naturalism is increasing, not decreasing, in respectability.[13] One objection, however, does seem to be particularly worth discussing. If ethics is naturalistic, realistic, and scientific, we would expect to see a convergence in ethical beliefs of the sort that we find among beliefs in physics or medicine. We would expect to be able to settle disputes about values conclusively by appeal to objective procedures. But this is not what we find; there seems to be no such convergence of ethical opinions, and no way to settle the bitterest ethical disagreements. Hence it seems unlikely that ethics is naturalistic, realistic, or scientific.

One response to this objection is available to any ethical realist. In ethics we are dealing with psychopolitical systems, which are vastly more complex, on the realist picture of them, than those discussed in physics or medicine. Yet these sciences were characterized by unsettleable disputes and lack of convergence for much of their history, and parts of them are still in that condition. In addition, ethical beliefs are even more open than physical or medical ones to the distorting influences of self-interest and ideology. For this reason they are correspondingly more liable to become the focus of disputes between interest groups, and correspondingly less liable to be influenced by reason or argument. Hence the existence of unsettleable disputes in ethics, and the lack of convergence among ethical beliefs, not only does not tell conclusively against ethical realism, it might with equal justice be held to tell in its favour.

But Plato has an additional distinctive response of his own to the objection. The beliefs and disputes the objection refers to are the beliefs and disputes of appetitive cave-dwellers. But it is an objective fact about such people, about their psychology, that they have access to nothing more cognitively reliable than qualities or modes. Hence it is not a surprise—indeed it is predicted by Plato's theory—that their ethical beliefs will fail to converge, and that many of their ethical disputes will be unresolvable. Realist theories need not stand mute in the face of attacks based on the failings or features of conventional ethical thought. They can counterattack, as Plato does, by offering a realist theory of those failings and features.

The third task for an ethical theory is to explain how the subject matter of ethics engages our will. It is here that consequentialism vies with deontology for our allegiance. It is by reference to them that Plato's theory must be located and characterized. My discussion will have two parts, corresponding to different ways of distinguishing these theories from each another.

Consequentialist theories, of which act-utilitarianism may serve as a particularly familiar example, claim that ethical facts engage our will through our desires. Thus egoistic act-utilitarianism holds that we have a reason to do, or to will to do, the just thing because as a consequence of doing the just thing more of our desires will be satisfied. The characteristic strength of such theories is that the mode of engagement they propose between ethical facts and our will is intelligible and straightforward—it makes good philosophical sense. The characteristic problem they face is that the variety of people's desires makes it difficult to see how ethical facts in particular can engage our will in that way. For it is evident that the demands of justice are categorical, that they do not depend on, and often conflict with, what we happen to want. If we follow justice we must sometimes frustrate our desires. If we follow our desires, we must sometimes act unjustly.

Deontological theories, of which Kant's is the most familiar, hold that ethical facts engage our will independently of our desires. Thus Kant claims that we have an objective reason, embodied in a categorical imperative, to will to do the just thing no matter what desires we happen to have. The characteristic strength of these theories is that the mode of engagement they propose between our will and ethical facts seems to be of the right sort to explain the categorical demands that justice makes on us, to get around the problem of the variety of our desires. Their characteristic weakness is that this mode of engagement is fundamentally mysterious. It is a measure of the mystery that Kant has to resort to the special resources of transcendental idealism, including the noumenal/phenomenal distinction, to "explain" how this sort of engagement is even possible.[14]

Both consequentialism and deontology attract, then, but neither satisfies completely. Indeed, neither satisfies in large part because both attract. What we want is a theory which proposes a mode of engagement between the will and ethical facts that is at once through our desires *and* categorical. And, to a large extent, this is what Plato's theory gives us.

On Plato's view, to be completely just simply is to be critically rational. And to be critically rational is to be motivated only by critically rational desires, or real interests. Consequently, there is no possibility of a rational person's desires conflicting with the demands of justice. His mode of engagement with ethical facts is, at least in that sense, categorical. It depends not on what he happens to want, but on what he must want if he is to be rational. At the same time, the just person is just because his desires are best satisfied by being just. Ethical facts engage his will through his (critically rational) desires. Hence Plato's theory might with some justification be held to give us the sort of theory we want—what we might call a naturalized deontology, a deontology with a Humean face.

However, there is a second way to draw the contrast between consequentialism and deontology. Consequentialist theories are teleological. They begin by developing a conception of the human good, of the ultimate end or *telos* of human endeavours, which makes no reference to justice, or as it is usually called in this context, *the right*, and then characterize the right as that which maximizes the good. Thus Mill identifies the good with happiness, and holds that "actions are right in proportion as they tend to promote happiness."[15] Teleological theories hold that the right engages our will by exploiting its prior engagement with the good. Deontological theories, on the other hand, are not teleological. They first develop a theory of the right which does not presuppose any final human purposes or ends or any determinate conception of the good, then allow for the pursuit of the good only within the limits determined by the right. Deontological theories hold that the right engages our will independently of its engagement with the good.

On this way of drawing the contrast, it is clear that Plato is a teleologist, not a deontologist. In his theory, it is the good, not justice and the other virtues, that is "the greatest object of study" (504d4-505b4). Justice, like everything else, is what it is because of its relation to the good itself. It is because we desire the good that our desires engage with ethical facts (2.11).

Now teleology, like naturalism, faces stock criticisms, one of which is alleged to be particularly devastating: teleological theories permit the teleological suspension of the ethical; they permit crucial individual rights to be violated, or important individual desires to be frustrated, in cases where this better achieves the good. If depriving an innocent individual of his liberty or even of his life maximizes the happiness of everyone else, then act-utilitarianism, for example, may justify incarcerating or killing him.[16]

To determine the real bite of this criticism, we need to distinguish two kinds of cases. In the first, the desires of the majority, which are satisfied by frustrating the important desires of some individual, are themselves very important. Unless a certain innocent person is put to death, one thousand other innocent people will be. In such cases, it is no clear defect in teleological theories if they justify, or permit, suspending or violating the individual's rights or frustrating his important desires. Indeed, it is very often urged as an objection to deontological theories that they *do not* justify sacrificing the individual in such cases.[17] In the second sort of case, however, the desires of the majority, which are satisfied by frustrating the rights or important desires of the individual, are not themselves very important. Unless an innocent individual is put to death, everyone else will have slightly less pleasure than they would otherwise have. If a teleological theory permits the sacrifice of the individual in this sort of situation, then that does seem to be a clear defect in it from the ethical point of view. So a utilitarian theory is in clear trouble if it allows the trivial goods of the majority to outweigh the serious good of an individual. But if it simply allows the serious good of the majority to outweigh the serious good of an individual, then either it is not in trouble at all, or it is not in very clear trouble.

This being so, I think that Plato's theory can make a good stand against the present objection on two different grounds. First, Plato is not an act-utilitarian. He does not think all just acts maximize happiness. Instead, he is what we might call a *character-utilitarian*.[18] He thinks that there is a utilitarian justification for being a just person, for having a properly ruled psyche, even if this sometimes results in our performing acts that do not maximize our happiness. So the fact that an act will maximize happiness does not mean that it will be just to perform it (5.4). And what is true of the individual is true of the polis. There is a utilitarian justification for the state's being structurally just, for its instantiating proper political rule. But it is not the case that acts are sanctioned as just in that polis if they maximize happiness. Hence the fact that violating an individual's rights, or frustrating his important desires, would maximize happiness does not make it just either for an individual or for the polis to do so. However, it seems certain that if the very survival of the polis were in question, and the considerable wisdom of the philosopher-kings could find no other way out, Plato would allow an individual to be sacrificed. But this is certainly not a case in which the serious desires of the individual are outweighed by the less serious desires of the majority. What is at stake in this case is the very survival of the just order itself.

The second ground I referred to is this. Plato's theory differs from many ethical theories in putting enormous weight on education and the shaping of desires. Hence he has less cause to worry about conflict between desires than they do. In the Kallipolis, everyone's desires are satisfied and frustrated in unison. We might have doubts about the success of the programme he advocates, but we cannot doubt that if it worked, it would insure that, except in very unusual circumstances, no individual would find that the serious desires of the majority could be satisfied only if his serious desires were frustrated. No doubt a rigid deontologist would not be content with only this level of protection for individual rights, but as I suggested, it is not clear that this is cause for serious worry.

A final issue is the precise nature of the desires that effect the engagement between ethical facts and the will. Here the relevant coordinates on the map of ethical theories are the various kinds of ethical egoism, on the one hand, and the various kinds of ethical altruism, on the other.

Ethical egoism has two subvarieties. Strong ethical egoism holds that ethical facts engage a person's will through desires for ends that do not have the satisfaction of anyone else's desires as essential components. Weak ethical egoism holds that ethical facts engage a person's will through desires for ends that may have the satisfaction of other people's desires as such components. Someone's desire for food is a strongly egoistic desire. But his desire for a happy marriage is weakly egoistic. Its satisfaction may, and typically will, have the satisfaction of his partner's desires as an essential component. In happy marriages, partners are satisfied in part by one another's satisfactions.

Altruism too has a weak and a strong variety. Weak altruism holds that ethical facts engage a person's will through desires for ends that may have the satisfaction of his own desires as essential components. Strong altruism holds that ethical facts engage the will through desires for ends that have only the satisfaction of other people's desires as such components. Someone's desire for a happy marriage is weakly altruistic. His desire that someone else's strongly egoistic desires be satisfied is strongly altruistic.

It is clear from this brief sketch that while strong egoism and strong altruism are mutually exclusive, weak altruism and weak egoism may go together. This opens up for ethical theory the pleasing possibility of an engagement with ethical facts that combines the self-benefits of egoism with the benefits to others of altruism. It is this possibility that Plato's theory exploits.[19]

The desire of a philosopher-king through which justice engages his will is a desire to live in a world whose structure guarantees him as much as possible of the pleasure of knowing the truth throughout life. And that desire, like the corresponding desires for the pleasure of making money or of being honored, through which ethical facts engage the wills of money-lovers and honour-lovers, is weakly egoistic. Its satisfaction has the satisfaction of other people's desires as an essential component. That is why the members of the Kallipolis love one another and experience their pleasures and pains in common (3.9, 4.10). The welfare of each member of the Kallipolis is symbiotically tied to the welfare of all the others. In pursuing his own happiness each is simultaneously pursuing the happiness of all the rest. Self-benefit and benefit to others coincide.

Nonetheless, it may seem that something is missing in all of this, that the fact that the philosopher-king's interest in the welfare of his fellows is mediated by his self-interest and his love for the good shows that he does not really love any of them for themselves. We might wonder, then, whether he should serve as our ideal, or whether we ought not cling instead to those things—interpersonal love may serve as our example—that we already think to be the greatest human goods.[20]

To discover what must be conceded to this objection, it is necessary to say something about love,[21] though what I shall say cannot, of course, be either exhaustive or conclusive. A good starting place is the idea, expressed by Aristotle, that to love someone is to want the good for him (*Rhetoric* 1380b35-1381a1; *Nicomachean Ethics* 1155b27-34). If we adopt it as our account of love, the philosopher-king loves his fellows. For he wants the good for them as strongly as he wants it for himself.

But should we adopt Aristotle's model? One reason to think not is the widely shared conviction that there is a quasi-Kantian element in love, a requirement that the lover respect the autonomy of the person he loves. To love someone is not simply to want the good for him; it is to want the good for him that he wants for himself, the good as he conceives it. But even on this model of love, the philosopher-king seems to love his fellows. For the good he wants for them is not the good as he conceives it, but the good as they conceive it. He wants a money-lover to be successful in getting the pleasure of making money, not the pleasure of knowing the truth.

Perhaps, then, there is more to loving someone than wanting the good for him as he conceives it. Maybe the attachment to his good must be independent of the lover's attachment to his own good. To love someone is to want him to have what he conceives as the good, whether it promotes the lover's own good or not. Lovers must be willing to make sacrifices for the one they love. If we adopt this model of love, the philosopher-kings do not love their fellows. For their love is egoistical love; they want the good for their fellows because it is biconditionally tied to their own good. However, we should not accept this model. According to it, what is important in love is that the lover wants the good of his beloved. But if that is so, the only reason to demand that love not be egoistical is that egoism might conflict with wanting the beloved's good. If this were guaranteed not to happen, however, as it is in the Kallipolis, then there is every reason to want love to be egoistical, since this would guarantee that the lover's devotion to the good of his beloved is as strong as his devotion to his own good.

Perhaps, then, our first step was misguided; perhaps we were wrong to focus on the good at all. Instead, the crucial thing in love may be the selfless, or relatively selfless, desire to further the beloved's end, whether it would in fact be good for him to achieve it or not. To love someone is to want him to have what he wants, even if getting it would be bad. Love involves respecting the loved one's liberty of spontaneity. But this model, too, has serious defects. Some of these are brought into focus if we take it as a model of self-love. For it would surely be a defect in self-love to have such an uncritical attitude to one's own desires. But it is equally clearly a defect in love of others to give their desires this sort of weight. What blinds us to this fact, what attracts us to this model, is, I think, the belief that the alternative to respecting someone's liberty of spontaneity is forcing him to submit to one's own. But this is a false belief. Desires can be changed by evidence, argument, and education as well as by coercion. And it is the rôle of the lover to try by these means to change for the better the desires of the one he loves (590e2-591a3).

We have not yet found a plausible model of love to underwrite the objection that the philosopher-kings do not care for or love their fellows. But the suspicion remains that they do not. So we must look further. Perhaps to love someone is not to want him to have either what he wants or the good, but rather to value him and cherish him because he is already good. On this model, which is also proposed by Aristotle, love is a response to already existing value (*Nicomachean Ethics* 1157b1-5). But we will do no better with it than with its predecessor. If love is a response to the good in someone, then, as long as egoism will not conflict with it, there is every reason to want it to be an egoistical response. If it can be an egoistical response, there is every reason to think that the philosopher-kings exhibit it to their fellows.

Perhaps, however, love is not a response to already existing value, but a bestowal of value. On this model, to love someone is to treat him as if he himself, in all his particularity, were valuable or good. The good does not determine his value; it is more as if he determined the content of the good. This model, though puzzling, seems to capture at least two ideas that many have thought essential to love: that love involves caring about or valuing someone *for his own sake*, and that love essentially involves *risk* for the lover. To care for someone as if he were the good is clearly to care for him for his own sake, but it is also to treat as the good what may not be the good at all, and that is clearly a risky business.

If this is our model of love, then a philosopher-king certainly does not love anyone. Egoistically attached to his own good, he would never make himself vulnerable to another in this way, never trust another with his happiness, never wantonly put his happiness at risk. Perhaps this is a defect in him, the defect we sensed at the beginning. But to show that it is a defect we need a defense, and not just an analysis, of love—a psychology, or psychopolitics, that shows why it is a good thing, and not rather a psychological disaster, to be capable of love. To think otherwise, to think that our intuitions are capable by themselves of substantiating our values, is to fail to take seriously the fact that our intuitions have a genealogy which puts their deliverances in question; it is to fail to take Thrasymachus or Plato seriously. Philosophers must see in philosopher-kings, not an invitation to dismissal *kata doxan*, or according to opinion, but an invitation to judgment *kat' ousian*, or according to the substance of the matter, a challenge to our intuitions that cannot be answered simply by appeal to those intuitions.

As always in philosophy, there is so much more to say that conclusions are out of place. Plato's overall theory—like the ethical theory which is a part of it—is contentious, filled with promising targets for further reflection and criticism. That is a feature it shares with every philosophical theory worth talking about. But it is defensible, at least to some degree, against initially compelling criticisms, and in all sorts of ways it points us in promising directions—by shaking our confidence in accepted dogma, by raising questions contemporary wisdom has ignored, and above all by showing us in detail how philosophy might achieve the "total grandeur of a total edifice." And these are features it shares with only the greatest theories.

NOTES

CHAPTER ONE

1. This portrait of Socrates is indebted to Irwin, *PMT*, pp. 37-101; Penner, "The Unity of Virtue"; Vlastos, "The Socratic Elenchus" and "Socrates' Disavowal of Knowledge."

2. Most commentators argue, to the contrary, that Book 1 is a standard Socratic dialogue; see Annas, *IPR*, pp. 16-58; Cross and Woozley, *PRPC*, pp. 1-60; Vlastos, "The Socratic Elenchus," p. 27 n. 2; White, *CPR*, pp. 8, 61-73.

3. Grote, *Plato and the Other Companions of Socrates*, vol. 3, p. 239, writes of this often overlooked passage:

> the dictum forbidding dialectic debate with youth . . . is decidedly anti-Sokratic. . . . It belongs indeed to the case of Meletus and Anytus, in their indictment of Sokrates before the Athenian dikastery. It is identical with their charge against him, of corrupting the youth, and inducing them to fancy themselves superior to the authority of established customs and opinions heard from their elders.

More recently, Nussbaum, "Aristophanes and Socrates on Learning Practical Wisdom," p. 88, has reaffirmed Grote's view:

> [T]he characterization of the practice found dangerous points unambiguously to Socrates. Only he accosted complacent citizens with the "What is X?" question; it was he who sought for general accounts of the *kalon*, the *dikaion* and the *agathon*; it was he who embarrassed and confused his interlocutors, throwing them into perplexity about the grounding of *nomos*. The double use of the word *elenchos* puts the identification beyond reasonable doubt. Plato charges his teacher (ironically, in his teacher's own *persona*) with contributing to moral decline by not restricting the questioning process to a chosen, well-trained few. Socrates is too optimistic about the potential of the ordinary man for understanding and moral growth. Plato, with Aristophanes [in the *Clouds*], believes that for the ordinary man questioning is destructive without being therapeutic.

I discuss Plato's reasons for restricting the elenchus to those who have successfully completed ten years' study of mathematical science in 2.13.

4. It is easy to be distracted by the rudeness of this comment from noticing the deep knowledge it reveals of Socrates' philosophical methods. For Socrates very often argues that justice, temperance, courage, and so forth, must be good, admirable, and self-beneficial on the grounds that they are genuine virtues. And he argues that they are genuine virtues by appealing to the conventional classification of them as virtues (1.4). Thrasymachus will later derail this type of argument by refusing to concede that justice is a genuine virtue. Socrates responds that he cannot then be refuted *kata ta nomizomena*, or "by appeal to conventional principles" (1.7, 2.13).

5. Many writers express opinions of the character Thrasymachus which suggest that they identify him with his historical namesake (on whom see Diels, *Die Fragmente der Vorsokratiker*, B85; Freeman, *Ancilla to the Pre-Socratic Philosophers*, pp. 141-142). Annas, *IPR*, p. 38, calls him "a hasty and confused thinker"; Cross and Woozley, *PRPC*, p. 47, describe the Ruler as "simply a quibble . . . and no answer to Socrates's dilemma"; Jowett, *The Dialogues of Plato*, vol. 2, p. 8, refers to Thrasymachus as "a mere child in argument." I think it is both risky and unnecessary to proceed in this way. It is risky because we have no way of knowing whether the historical Thrasymachus did argue in the way Plato's character does. It is unnecessary because even if he did argue in this way the important interpretative question is still why Plato put someone who argued in precisely that way in his dialogue, and why he reported that argument in precisely the way he did.

6. It is worth considering whether this view is really as silly as some of Thrasymachus' critics have suggested. The line of thought behind it is surely something like this. To call someone a physician (say) is implicitly to attribute to him a complex disposition to perform actions of the medical variety correctly. To call him a physician *at the moment of*, and *in regard to*, a particular medical act x is to cite x as a manifestation of that complex disposition. But if x is a botch or an error, it cannot be such a manifestation. Error manifests lack of skill, not skill. Thus we ought not call him a physician at the moment of, and in regard to, a medical error. The Thrasymachus lurking in all of us emerges when we say such things as "Call yourself a doctor? Butcher would be more like it." On this reconstruction, the notion of the Ruler relies on an account of dispositions according to which a determinately disposed item must manifest its disposition in the appropriate circumstances. This view may be mistaken, but it certainly is not silly.

It is also worth noting that Socrates does not have a monopoly on this way of thinking; it can be traced back to Homer. When a hero (*agathos*) fails to exhibit the appropriate heroic virtue, it takes divine interference—a miracle, so to speak—to explain it. Thus when Agamemnon's decision to take Briseus from Achilles turns out to have disastrous consequences for the Greeks it takes divine intervention (in the shape of *atē*, or blindness sent by Zeus) to explain it (see *Iliad* 18.85 ff.). How else could a hero possessed of wisdom have failed to do the wise thing? See Adkins, *Merit and Responsibility*.

7. It is possible to distinguish two views about Ruling. According to the first, a ruler is a Ruler at time t just in case he legislates in ways advantageous to himself at t. This allows a ruler to be only intermittently a Ruler. According to the second view, a ruler is a Ruler just in case he *always* legislates in ways advantageous to himself. This excludes the possibility of intermittent Rule. Cross and Woozley, *PRPC*, pp. 47-48, think that Thrasymachus adopts the former view. And they point out quite rightly that it leaves him open to serious objection:

> If a subject believes that obedience to a particular law would not serve the ruler's interest, he may be correct in believing so; he will have to choose between the two courses. And, if Thrasymachus means that a subject should not obey a law which does not serve the ruler's interest, on the ground that at the time of making the law the supposed ruler was not really a ruler, . . . then he is saying that it is for the subject to decide whether a law ought to be obeyed. The fact that the man who is the supposed ruler claims not to have made a mistake, and therefore to be the ruler, establishes nothing, for that claim itself may be mistaken. A situation in which the right to decide whether or not the laws are to be obeyed belongs to the subjects is hardly what Thrasymachus, with his general view of government, contemplated; if the subjects are the ones who have to decide whether the supposed ruler is in any piece of legislation *really* the ruler, it is they, not he, who are in control.

In my view, Thrasymachus means to adopt the second position, which is immune to this objection. Witness: "But each of these, insofar as he is what we call him, never [*oudepote*] makes mistakes, so that if you speak precisely . . . no [*oudeis*] craftsman makes mistakes" (340e1-3).

8. Strictly speaking, this is a fast move: (4*) follows from (3*) only if Ruling has the advantage of the Ruler as its aim or goal. Socrates will argue against this (341c4-343a2), but his argument is not a success (1.8). Moreover, Thrasymachus is able to support the inference by showing that some crafts—for example, cowherding and shepherding—do aim at their practitioner's advantage (1.7).

9. Notice that (A) must now be understood to be about Rulers. But according to Thrasymachus that is what he has intended from the beginning. Consequently, I have not relabeled it.

10. This does not mean, of course, that Thrasymachus does not accept (B) as a trivial consequence of (A). But (B) cannot be part of his argument for

(A). If (B) had attractions for Thrasymachus independently of the fact that it follows from (A), it could only be because he accepted

(B★) Justice is obedience to the law.

But in fact he rejects (B★). Kerferd, "Thrasymachus and Justice: A Reply," p. 14, argues for this as follows:

> Thrasymachus says that the subjects must obey what the ruler prescribes as law when the ruler is not making a mistake about his interests, not otherwise. He rejects the view of Cleitophon according to which he should obey the laws made by the ruler whether they actually prescribe what is in the interests of the ruler or not. He admits that actual rulers do make mistakes. It follows that in case of mistake, it is not just to obey the laws they make. This proves conclusively that justice does not consist in obedience to the law.

It follows that (B) is not a step in Thrasymachus' argument for (A).

11. An argument of this type can be found in Thucydides, *The Peloponnesian War* 3.82:

> In the various poleis these revolutions were the cause of many calamities—as happens and will continue to happen so long as human nature remains the same, with greater or less violence and varying in form, according as changes in circumstances impose themselves in individual cases. In times of peace and prosperity poleis and individuals alike follow higher standards, because they are not forced into a situation where they have to do what they do not want to do. But war is a teacher of violence; in depriving them of the power to easily satisfy their daily wants, it brings the passions of the majority of people down to the level of their actual conditions. So revolutions broke out in polis after polis, and in places where they occurred later the knowledge of what had already happened in other places caused still new extravagances of revolutionary zeal, these being expressed in more elaborate methods of seizing power and in unheard-of atrocities in revenge. To fit in with the change of events, words, too, had to change their usual meanings. What used to be described as a thoughtless act of aggression was now regarded as the courage that one would expect to find in a party member; to think of the future and to be cautious was just another way of being a coward; any suggestion of moderation was just an attempt to disguise one's unmanly character; to be able to grasp the whole of an issue was simply to be unfit for action. Fanatical enthusiasm was the mark of a real man, and to plot against an enemy behind his back was perfectly legitimate self-defense.

Later in the *Republic*, Plato himself presents a similar argument: the desires which change a psyche from being oligarchic to being democratic accomplish their task, at least in part, by changing the meanings of the terms the psyche employs in evaluating behaviour:

they [the desires in question] call reverence and awe folly, and cast it out beyond the frontiers as a dishonoured fugitive; they call moderation cowardliness, and spattering it with filth, they banish it; they teach that measured and orderly expenditure is boorish and mean, and join with many unbeneficial desires to throw it over the frontier. . . . And when they have thus emptied and purged the psyche of the victim that they have seized, which is being initiated in splendid rites, they proceed to lead insolence, anarchy, extravagance, and shamelessness home from exile wreathed and radiant and accompanied by a huge chorus, eulogizing them and calling them by fine names; they call insolence good education; anarchy, freedom; extravagance, munificence; and shamelessness, courage. (560c9-561a1)

In the *Theaetetus* 167c2-5, a similar line of thought is attributed to Protagoras:

My claim is, too, that wise and good politicians make beneficial things seem just to their poleis instead of harmful ones. If any type of thing seems just and fine to a polis, then it actually is just and fine for it, as long as that polis accepts it; but a wise and just man makes beneficial things be and seem just and fine to them, instead of any harmful things which used to be so for them.

Thus there is no anachronism involved in supposing Thrasymachus too to be arguing in this way.

12. MacIntyre, *After Virtue*, p. 128, writes about *pleonexia*: "*Pleonexia* is sometimes translated so as to make it appear that the vice which it picks out is simply that of wanting more than one's share. . . . But in fact the vice picked out is that of acquisitiveness as such. . . . Nietzsche translated *pleonexia* with insight as well as precision: *haben und mehrwollhaben*." My own discussion in 2.2-3 will bear out both his and Nietzsche's view.

Because he accepts the psychological theory that people by nature pursue pleonectic satisfaction, Thrasymachus—unlike Plato—has no room for the possibility that justice might be advantageous to both Rulers and Subjects. Rulers motivated by a desire for pleonectic satisfaction, who simply want more and more without limit, must benefit at the expense of their subjects.

13. That (6) and (A) appear to be inconsistent has been widely noticed. Those who believe that (A) is Thrasymachus' definition of justice claim that he intends to restrict (6) "to everyone except the ruler" (Barker, *The Political Thought of Plato and Aristotle*, p. 95). Those who think that (6) is his definition claim that he intends to impose this restriction on (A); see Annas, *IPR*, p. 46; Henderson, "In Defense of Thrasymachus," pp. 218-228; Kerferd, "Thrasymachus on Justice," pp. 19-27; Nicholson, "Unravelling Thrasymachus' Arguments in the *Republic*," pp. 210-232. Others claim that he intends to restrict both principles to "subjects of some superior" (Irwin, *PMT*, 289 n. 24). But

because the place of (6) in his argument for (A) has gone unnoticed the evidence for these Thrasymachean intentions has remained lacking.

14. Socrates' argument here merits brief analysis. It runs as follows:

(1) Crafts have been invented to satisfy the needs of things which, not being self-sufficient, cannot satisfy their own needs (341e3-6).

(2) Each Craft seeks the advantage of the class of non-self-sufficient things with which it is concerned (341e6-7).

(3) If Crafts themselves were not self-sufficient, each would need another, *ad infinitum.*

Therefore,

(4) No Craft needs another; all are self-sufficient (342b3-6).

Therefore,

(5) No Craft is included in the class of things with which that Craft is concerned (implicit).

Now,

(6) Crafts rule, and have power over, the things with which they are concerned (342c8-9).

Therefore,

(7) No Craft seeks its own advantage; every Craft seeks the advantage of the weaker thing which is ruled by it and subject to it (342c11-d1).

Therefore,

(8) No Ruler seeks his own advantage in Ruling; every Ruler seeks the advantage of the subject on whom he exercises his Craft (342e6-11).

Thus, on Socrates' view, Thrasymachus is wrong to infer that a Ruler cannot make mistakes about what is to his advantage from the fact that he cannot make any in exercising the Craft of Ruling. For it is not at *his* advantage that Ruling aims. However, as I point out in the text, (8) does not follow from (7); see White, *CPR*, p. 67. Moreover, (4) does not follow from (3). What does follow is that *some* Craft is self-sufficient. But that, of course, is too weak for Socrates' purposes.

15. I think that Socrates is wrong about Shepherding, and that Thrasymachus is right. The Shepherd aims at the good of his sheep at best incidentally. He fattens them not because it is good for them to be fat (although it may be good for them), but because fatter sheep fetch higher prices or are better to eat. He would still fatten them even if doing so made them wretched. Hence a Shepherd is not someone who "provides what is best for the object of [his Craft's] care" (345d1-3). That description does not capture his essence. Rather

he is someone who puts or keeps sheep in a condition that makes them best serve some interest of ours. Consequently, it does seem that the Shepherd aims at what is advantageous to himself (or his master), and not—except perhaps incidentally—at what is advantageous to his sheep.

16. Reeve, "Motion, Rest, and Dialectic in the *Sophist*," bears on this issue, as does the discussion of the rôle of the interlocutors in 1.12.

17. The authenticity of the *Letters* is a topic of dispute; see Raven, *Plato's Thought in the Making*, pp. 19-26. But if I am right, there is some reason to think that the following part of the *Second Letter* expresses a genuinely Platonic view: "It is impossible for what is written not to be disclosed. That is why I have never written anything about these things, and why there is not, and will never be, any written work of Plato's own. What are now called his, are the work of Socrates, but of a Socrates made new and fine" (314c1-4). It is important to notice that the works referred to here are those which embody the theory of forms (see 312e1-313c7). Hence it is only these dialogues, and not the earlier ones discussed in 1.2, that are the work of "a Socrates made new and fine."

18. The case for betrayal is argued at length, and with considerable passion, by Popper, *The Open Society and Its Enemies*, vol. 1, pp. 195-196:

> I cannot doubt the fact of Plato's betrayal, nor that his use of Socrates as the main speaker of the *Republic* was the most successful attempt to implicate him [in his attack on the "open society"]. . . . But since Socrates' faith [in the "open society"] was too strong to be challenged openly, Plato was driven to re-interpret it as a faith in a closed society. This was difficult; but it was not impossible. For had not Socrates been killed by the democracy [i.e., by an "open society"]? Had not democracy lost any right to claim him? And had not Socrates always criticized the anonymous multitude as well as its leaders for their lack of wisdom? It was not very difficult, moreover, to re-interpret Socrates as having recommended the rule of the "educated," the learned philosophers. . . . In this way Plato may have found that it was possible to give by degrees a new meaning to the teaching of [Socrates], and to persuade himself that the opponent whose overwhelming strength he would never have dared to attack directly, was an ally. This, I believe, is the simplest interpretation of the fact that Plato retained Socrates as his main speaker even after he had departed so widely from his teaching that he could no longer deceive himself about this deviation.

One of the many contentious presuppositions of this explanation is that the Socratic elenchus is an unequivocally good thing which any defender of democracy or "openness" should welcome. For the beginning of a brief against this psychologically naive view of the elenchus see Nussbaum, "Aristophanes and Socrates on Learning Practical Wisdom," pp. 43-97; Burnyeat, "Aristotle on Learning to Be Good," pp. 69-92. I take up the question of whether Plato is an enemy of the "open society" in 4.11 and 4.14.

19. Those (for example, Sachs, "A Fallacy in Plato's *Republic*," p. 41, n. 14) who claim that something is desirable for its own sake, on Plato's view, just in case it is productive of happiness (*eudaimonia*) cannot accommodate the examples of A-goods Glaucon gives here. For they are forced to conclude that enjoyment (*to chairein*) and pleasures (*hai hēdonai*) produce happiness. But we are told that these pleasures give rise to nothing except enjoyment. Thus they cannot produce happiness unless happiness is enjoyment. But if happiness is enjoyment, *it* cannot produce happiness. See Irwin, *PMT*, p. 325 n. 8; Mabbott, "Is Plato's *Republic* Utilitarian?" p. 61. These examples also pose problems for the view that A-goods and B-goods are components of happiness; see Crombie, *EPD*, vol. 1, p. 86; Grote, *Plato and the Other Companions of Socrates*, vol. 3, p. 131; Irwin, *PMT*, p. 184. For A-goods are wanted *for their own sake*. But even if happiness is wanted for its own sake, its components need not be (1.11). Moreover, happiness must not be a G-consequence of being just—it must not be something that can be stripped away from being just—if it is to figure in the defense of justice (1.10). But from the fact that being just is a component of being happy, it does not follow that one cannot be just without being happy. And if one can be just without being happy, being happy can be stripped away from being just (1.11). Finally, happiness that lacked a component would surely have to be incomplete or less than perfect. But it is implausible to think—or to saddle Plato with the thought—that no life could be completely happy that did not include each and every simple pleasure (although Aristotle, *Nicomachean Ethics* 1097b6-21, may have held something like this). However, the view that justice is a component of happiness is closer to the truth than the others (1.11).

It is also important to note that Glaucon's classification of goods has no immediate connection with choiceworthiness. A C-good may well be more choiceworthy (or better) than a competing A-good or B-good. Physical training is a C-good—no one wants it for its own sake. However, it is a means to psychic harmony which is an essential component of maximal happiness (410b10-412a8, 518c4-d1). Hence it is surely more choiceworthy than a competing A-good such as enjoying some simple pleasure. It also seems to be more choiceworthy than a B-good such as being able to smell. For any means to the attainment of something as valuable as psychic harmony must be more choiceworthy than a competing B-good which, like smell, a psychically harmonious person can do without. Hence, if physical training destroys someone's sense of smell, it seems that he should choose it anyway. Moreover, goods of the same class can differ in choiceworthiness. Knowledge and sight are both B-goods. But it seems that once someone has become a philosopher-king at the age of fifty (540a4-c2), he should not choose to preserve his sight at the cost of less time spent knowing or coming to know the truth about things. We might wonder, then, why Glaucon wants Socrates to show that justice is desirable for its own sake. Could it not be more choiceworthy than injustice simply by having more desirable G-consequences? We shall see in 1.10 that it could not. That is why Glaucon focuses on the question of whether justice is more desirable for its own sake than injustice; see Crombie, *EPD*, vol. 1, pp. 85-89; Murphy, *TIPR*, p. 8 n. 2; Sachs, "A Fallacy in Plato's *Republic*," p. 39 n. 9.

20. It is difficult to reconcile this passage with the view—defended by Annas, *IPR*, pp. 153-169, and Mabbott, "Is Plato's *Republic* Utilitarian?" pp. 61-65—that Socrates establishes that justice is desirable for its own sake in Book 4, and that after that point (for example, in Books 8 and 9) he is trying to show that it is also desirable for its G-consequences (see 5.2-3).

21. Because the psyche is "the very thing by which we live" (444a9-b1), the unjust life is lived by the person whose psyche is unjust, and the just life is lived by the person whose psyche is just. Hence it would be a mistake to think that in praising the unjust life, Glaucon is praising something other than injustice itself (at 353e10-11 Socrates transfers properties from psyches to lives without blinking an eye). If he were, he would not be praising injustice in the way that he wants Socrates to praise justice.

22. The first reference is to Homer, Hesiod, and the other poets who were the traditional teachers of virtue. The second is, surely, to Socrates himself, who teaches about virtue, not in verse or in elaborate prose speeches, but "in private conversation" (*Apology* 31c4-32a3).

23. At 348b8-350c11, Socrates and Thrasymachus agree that the perfectly unjust man will try to "outdo" (*pleonektein*) everyone.

24. Irwin, *PMT*, p. 186, argues that Glaucon is "hasty and careless in suggesting that a contract theorist has no reason to refuse Gyges' ring"; he might turn it down on the grounds that the unjust actions he would commit if he had it might "upset the system of justice" which benefits him. I think this criticism is unconvincing. Glaucon—that is to say, Plato—is neither hasty nor careless. For the benefit that the system confers on the just man is that of reducing his chances of being the impotent victim of injustice (358e3-359b5). But Gyges' ring will do that for him, and also allow him to do injustice with impunity. Since this is a better option than being just, a possessor of Gyges' ring has no reason to worry about being returned to a "state of nature," for he will there be one of the naturally strong men who have no incentive to be just—or to contract into a polis—in the first place.

25. It is partly for this reason that it is wrong to follow Annas, *IPR*, pp. 66-67, or Murphy, *TIPR*, p. 8 n. 2, in identifying G-consequences with *artificial*

consequences, that is, with those consequences, such as being honoured, which depend on other people's beliefs and attitudes. For Glaucon excludes G-consequences from the discussion both of justice and of injustice, but he does not exclude the artificial consequences of injustice.

26. Most agree with this broad assessment of Plato's aims; see Cooper, "The Psychology of Justice in Plato," pp. 155-157; Crombie, *EPD*, vol. 1, pp. 85-89; Gosling and Taylor, *The Greeks on Pleasure*, pp. 97-101; Grote, *Plato and the Other Companions of Socrates*, vol. 3, p. 126; Irwin, *PMT*, pp. 246-248; Nettleship, *Lectures on the Republic of Plato*, pp. 315-316; Vlastos, "Justice and Happiness in the *Republic*," pp. 111-112. But White, *CPR*, pp. 20-24, 43-54, for example, seems to dissent from it. He argues as follows: "Because it involves spending some time ruling, and thus not merely philosophizing, the task of the philosopher ruler necessarily involves some sacrifice of the individual good [happiness] of the person performing it" (p. 23). He concludes that Plato "does *not* claim that one gains a bit of happiness for every bit of justice that one acquires" (p. 23). However, precisely this is asserted at 472c4-d1 (quoted in 1.11). For further discussion relevant to White's position, see 2.11-12, 3.5-8, 4.9, 5.1-5.

27. See Aristotle, *Physics* 187a23-b7; Reeve, "Anaxagorean Panspermism," pp. 98-105.

28. Cf. Wiggins, "Deliberation and Practical Reason."

29. See Geuss, *The Idea of a Critical Theory*, pp. 45-54.

30. Neu, "Plato's Analogy of State and Individual: The *Republic* and the Organic Theory of the State," p. 238, writes: "Plato's political theory does not derive from an analogy which makes the state a monster individual with interests superior to and independent of those of ordinary citizens; it derives rather from a doctrine of objective interests discernible by those with special training and ability." He is one of the few commentators to notice that the Kallipolis has something to do with real interests.

31. See Williams, "Internal and External Reasons," pp. 101-113.

32. It is natural to wonder what benefit is intended here. Book 10 suggests the following answer. When the unconvinced arrive at the Spindle of Necessity they may, if they remember the argument of the *Republic*, avoid choosing unjust lives (618b6-619b1). This benefits them because just lives are happier both here and hereafter than unjust ones (5.4).

33. See Nozick, *Philosophical Explanations*, pp. 13-18.

Chapter Two

1. White, *CPR*, p. 215, claims that "the distinction is meant to classify appetites belonging to the third, appetitive part of the soul." I do not think he is right about this. At 581e2-4 (quoted in 2.2 below), the philosopher classes both the appetitive desire for money, and the spirited desire for honour as "really necessary" only because he must satisfy them in order to live. He cannot, while embodied (3.8), get rid of his appetitive and spirited desires altogether. But, through education in dialectic and polis management, he can moderate them so that they will be satisfied with those minimum amounts of money (food, drink, and sex) and honour that are necessary for life. And because he can moderate them in this way, he can experience the more pleasant pleasure of knowing the truth. It follows that appetitive and spirited desires which are less moderate than his, which are not satisfied by that bare minimum, are unnecessary desires for the philosopher. He can avoid them through training and education, and they "lead to no good, or indeed to the opposite" (559a3-6). The rôle of unnecessary spirited desires in Plato's theory is discussed in 4.8.

2. People who are by nature tyrannical or democratic, and cannot be trained or educated to abandon their lawless or nonlawless unnecessary appetites, have no place in the Kallipolis. "The ones whose psyches are naturally bad and are incurable they will kill" (410a3-4). Hence only one normal type corresponds to the three pathological types of appetitive people.

3. Kraut, "Reason and Justice in Plato's *Republic*," pp. 217-218, rejects the interpretation of this passage adopted in the text on the following grounds: "First, it is incompatible with the fact that the citizens of the ideal polis are tied to each other by feelings of affection. . . . Second, the passage in question states that the craftsman benefits from the philosopher's rule, but it is difficult to see how this is so, if we take the above interpretation." But his reasoning is unpersuasive. The rulers benefit the producers, first, by training and educating them to moderate their appetitive desires so that these really do best promote the producers' end in life, namely, the pleasure of making money (586d4-e2). It is this fact that minimizes, but does not obviate, the need for coercion in the Kallipolis. Second, the rulers benefit the producers by insuring the existence of a structure within which their desires will be reliably satisfied throughout life (3.8). The fact that the producers are enslaved to the rulers, or are in their power, would threaten to make them unfriendly to the rulers only if the latters' orders were constantly at odds with their own desires, or failed to further their own ultimate goals. But neither of these things is likely to occur in the Kallipolis. Education and training guarantee that the producers' desires are as the rulers think they should be. Knowledgeable rule, which aims at the producers' good, insures that the producers will reliably achieve the goals they most value. On the Platonic assumption that one loves something most when one believes that what is good for it is good for oneself, and that when it is

doing well the same is true of oneself (412d4-6), it seems reasonable to conclude that the producers will actually love the rulers. Kraut's own positive
interpretation is ably criticized by Irwin, *PMT*, pp. 329-330.

4. This is denied by Vlastos, "The Theory of Social Justice in the *Polis* in
Plato's *Republic*," pp. 29-37. He writes that it is Plato's view that "[t]he one
with low congenital endowment of intelligence" ought to be enslaved to those
who are intelligent enough to have access to forms. But this view confuses
having strong rational desires, which does distinguish the philosopher from
the money-lover and honour-lover, with being very intelligent, which does
not (519a1-b5).

5. *Phronēsis* and *nous* are often used interchangeably in the *Republic*. But
Plato does want to distinguish the complete psychological power exercised by
the philosopher (which is usually referred to as *nous*) from the power that enables a person of any psychological type to work out efficient means to his
ends (which is sometimes called *phronēsis*). Hence I shall translate either term
as "dialectical-thought" when the context suggests that it refers to the first
power, and as "intelligence" when the context suggests that it refers to the
second.

6. This passage makes it quite clear, in my view, that the theory of recollection (*anamnēsis*) is not being evoked at 518b6-d7, as has been suggested by Irwin, *PMT*, pp. 140, 218. The clever, wicked man sees just as sharply as the
philosopher, but he sees something different. Hence what is being compared is
the power of their vision, not their power to see (or recollect) a particular kind
of thing. It follows that the "blind eyes" referred to at 518b8-c2 are eyes that
cannot see anything, not eyes that cannot see (or recollect seeing) something
in particular—for example, prenatally encountered forms. The doctrine of recollection, and the reason that it is not found in the *Republic*, are discused in
2.13.

While this passage states no more than that people of different psychological
types can be equally intelligent, there is some reason to think that Plato holds
that *all* people are (in some sense) equally intelligent, and that all apparent differences in intelligence are to be explained in terms of differences in their ruling desires. For on Plato's cosmogonical views, and especially his views about
the origin of the psyche, all psyches are created equal in power by the Demiurge. They then have bodies made for them by lesser divinities (themselves
created by the Demiurge) and are sent to earth repeatedly until the rational
element in them triumphs over the other elements. The fullest version of this
story is to be found in the *Timaeus* (41b7-47e2), a dialogue very closely connected to the *Republic* in doctrine (2.11), but elements of it occur in the latter
as well (614b2-621b7).

7. It is for this reason that they are said to be "like us" (515a5). Since we
have not been brought up in the Kallipolis, we still have unnecessary appetites

in our psyches. But Irwin, *PMT*, p. 221, is wrong to think that anyone in the Kallipolis remains in this condition. Everyone there receives an education, either in a craft or in music and gymnastics, that releases him from the bondage of such appetites (4.4-6). And anyone who fails to benefit appropriately from this education is put to death (409e4-410a4; note 2 above).

8. I owe notice of this important passage to Morrison, "Two Unresolved Difficulties in the Line and Cave," pp. 216-217. But he detects only one kind of property in it, not the requisite two.

9. Although the commitment to modes and qualities in the *Republic* has not been noticed, many have argued that the *Republic* is committed to the existence of something like figures; see Adam, *PR*, vol. 2, pp. 68, 156-163; Hardie, *A Study in Plato*, pp. 49-65; Ross, *Plato's Theory of Ideas*, pp. 176-205; Wedberg, *Plato's Philosophy of Mathematics*. Moreover, no less an authority than Aristotle argues at length that Plato countenanced things of this sort—"the intermediates [*ta metaxu*]," as he calls them, perhaps following 511d4: "Further, besides the sensibles and forms he [Plato] says that there are the objects of mathematics, which occupy an intermediate position, differing from the sensibles in being eternal and unchangeable, from forms in being many alike, while the form is in each case unique" (*Metaphysics* 987b14-18). For further references, and helpful discussion, see Ross, *Aristotle's Metaphysics*, pp. lii-lxiv. In 2.9, we shall see that there is evidence in the *Republic* to support Aristotle's claim that while there is only one form of F, there are many figures of F. I think it is a point in favour of my interpretation that it gives intermediates a clear place in Plato's theories. For I think it unlikely that Aristotle, insensitive as he might be to the finer points of the doctrines of his predecessors, could be totally mistaken about so important a matter as this; see Burnyeat, "Platonism and Mathematics: A Prelude to Discussion."

10. The relevance of this question to the success of Plato's argument has been widely noticed; see Annas, *IPR*, p. 202; Crombie, *EPD*, vol. 2, p. 57; Fine, "Knowledge and Belief in *Republic* V," p. 129; Hintikka, "Knowledge and Its Objects in Plato," p. 15; Irwin, *PMT*, pp. 333-334.

11. *Agnoia* often means simply "not knowing." But since one who exercises *agnoia* forms beliefs that are *always false, agnoia* must, in the present argument, be *error*, the polar opposite of knowledge. For one who simply did not know might by chance form an occasional true belief (506b6-9).

12. Gosling, "*Republic* Book V: *ta polla kala* etc.," pp. 116-128, argues forcefully and clearly that " '*ta polla kala*' means not 'the many particular beautiful objects' but 'the many kinds of colour, shape, etc. commonly held to be beautiful' " (p. 116). A similar position is adopted by Adam, *PR*, vol. 1, p. 343, and by Crombie, *EPD*, vol. 1, pp. 102-103. The opposing view is defended by Allen, "The Argument from Opposites in *Republic* V," p. 330; Cross and

Woozley, *PRPC*, pp. 152-165; Nehamas, "Predication and Forms of Opposites in the *Phaedo*," pp. 466-467; Owen, "A Proof in the *Peri Ideōn*," p. 305; Vlastos, "Degrees of Reality in Plato," pp. 66-75; White, "J. Gosling on *ta polla kala*," pp. 127-132, and "The 'Many' in *Republic* 475a-480a," pp. 291-306. White is well answered by Gosling, "Reply to White," pp. 307-314.

13. The importance of this requirement has been noticed by a number of writers; see Gosling, "*Doxa* and *Dunamis* in Plato's *Republic*," pp. 120-121; Fine, "Knowledge and Belief in *Republic* V." But of the four interpretations of the principle that have been proposed, only the last succeeds in meeting it, and it is unacceptable on other grounds. The interpretations I refer to are these:

(1) The "degrees of existence" interpretation: *to pantelōs on* means "what completely exists"; see Cross and Woozley, *PRPC*, pp. 145-146, 162; Grube, *Plato's Republic*, p. 136 n. 15.

(2) The "degrees of reality" interpretation: *to pantelōs on [F]* means "what is fully, really, or genuinely F"; see Annas, *IPR*, pp. 198-199; Vlastos, "A Metaphysical Paradox" and "Degrees of Reality in Plato."

(3) The "degrees of truth" interpretation: *to pantelōs on* means "what is completely or fully true"; see Gosling, "*Doxa* and *Dunamis* in Plato's *Republic*," pp. 121-122.

(4) The "truth" interpretation: *to pantelōs on* means "what is true *simpliciter*"; see Fine, "Knowledge and Belief in *Republic* V," pp. 125-126.

(1) yields a principle that no sightseer would be likely to understand, let alone concede, and that not even a metaphysician would think obvious or uncontroversial. (2) is no better in this regard. Why should a sightseer concede that only what is fully, really, or genuinely F can be known? (3) is also controversial, and hard to understand. The sightseer, like most of us, would no doubt agree that only what is true can be known. But why should he concede that there are degrees of truth? (4), on the other hand, does give us an uncontroversial principle; in that respect it is unproblematic. The problems with it lie elsewhere. First, when it is said that each of the many Fs "is no more what one asserts it to be than it is not what one asserts it to be" (479a5-b11), the "truth" interpretation is forced to posit an unaccountable shift from the veridical sense of *esti*, which is allegedly involved in the problematic principle, to the predicative sense; see Fine, "Knowledge and Belief in *Republic* V," pp. 132-138. This is unattractive. Second, (4) does not explain why the principle refers to "what is *completely*" and what "*is in no way*." If the "truth" interpretation is correct, the rôle of these modifiers in the principle is an unsolved mystery. Third, the "truth" interpretation cannot adequately explain Plato's views about error (*agnoia*). We are told that *agnoia* is set over what is not (478c3-4). But if this means, as the "truth" interpretation suggests, that error is set over what is false, then it cannot explain why what is not (*to mē on*) is the same as nothing (*mēden*) (478b6-c9). Fine, p. 131, attempts to rescue the "truth" interpretation from this awkward predicament as follows:

Suppose I claim that justice is a vegetable. Plato might argue that my claim does not amount to a belief about justice at all; it displays total ignorance of justice. . . . It [478c3-4] claims that if what I say is not at all true of justice, it says nothing—that is, it says nothing true about justice. . . . Plato's claim is now only that totally false beliefs are assigned to ignorance . . . ignorance has as its contents only very false beliefs.

But this escape route is surely *ad hoc*. For the passage in question does not say that some claims about justice so radically miss the mark that they say nothing about it at all. And if it did say this, I cannot see any reason why the sight-seers and craft-lovers—or we ourselves—should go along with this claim.

14. It might be objected to this proposal that it treats *to on* and *to mē on* as incomplete expressions involving the predicative sense of *esti*, whereas the fact that they are not explicitly predicative suggests that they are meant to be complete expressions involving *esti* in its existential sense; see White, "The 'Many' in *Republic* 475a-480a," p. 293 n. 8. There are two reasons, beyond those provided by my general argument, not to be swayed by this objection. The first has been well stated by Gosling, "*Republic* Book V: *ta polla kala* etc.," pp. 123-124: " '*To on*' (*to pantelōs on*) and '*to mē on mēdamēi*' (477) are clearly incomplete expressions, to be filled out as '*to on kalon*' or '*to mē on dikaion*' according to context: this comes out at the conclusion of the passage (479) where *ta polla kala* are shown *einai kai mē* in that each *esti kai ouk esti kalon*." The second reason is that there are good grounds for thinking that Plato never isolated existential *esti*, but confined his investigations of being to predicative being; see Owen, "Plato on Not-Being"; Vlastos, "Degrees of Reality in Plato." On the various senses of the verb *eimi* ('to be'), see Kahn, *The Verb Be in Ancient Greek*.

15. See Armstrong, *A Theory of Universals*, pp. 101-131, especially p. 120.

16. In my view, this is the conclusion established by *Sophist* 237b7-241e6 (cf. 258c6-259a1).

17. This sort of account of knowing has recently been defended by Goldman, *Epistemology and Cognition*, pp. 42-57. I have adapted the example in the text from his earlier paper "Discrimination and Perceptual Knowledge," which defends a somewhat different account. Nozick, *Philosophical Explanations*, pp. 167-288, is also relevant.

18. See Goldman, *Epistemology and Cognition*, pp. 53-55.

19. *Phainetai* can be rendered as "appears" or as "seems to be" or as "is plainly or clearly." But only the latter alternative is appropriate here. For the argument is not that the many qualities and modes of F only appear (nonveridically) to be also not F—what is meant is that they actually are not F; see

Gosling, "Reply to White," pp. 308-309. However, Socrates is not himself committing any violations of the principle of noncontradiction—*he* is neither a sightseer nor a craft-lover (436b8-c1, 436e8-437a2; 3.2).

20. See Barnes, *The Presocratic Philosophers*, vol. 1, pp. 65-75; Irwin, "Plato's Heracleiteanism."

21. Cf. Adam, *PR*, vol. 1, p. 343, who writes perceptively: "The words refer to general rules, standards, canons, believed in by the multitude . . . who have on any single subject many such standards . . . mutually inconsistent and uncoordinated, because they do not know that *to kalon, to agathon* etc. are each of them *hen*." For further argument, see Gosling, "Reply to White," pp. 308-309.

22. This view receives some support, I think, from the following passage:

And again, are the many qualities or modes of the double [*ta polla diplasia*] plainly any the less halves than doubles [*hētton ti hēmisea hē diplasia phainetai*]?—Not one.—And likewise with qualities or modes of the big and the small, the light and the heavy, will any of them be more one of these things than it is its opposite?—No, he said, each of them will always partake of both. (479b3-8)

If we suppose that the sightseers and craft-lovers take a pair of objects A and B, where A is the half of B (or A is big or light compared to B), as their paradigm or standard for deciding whether one thing is half or double of another (or whether things are relatively speaking big or small, light or heavy), then we can understand, I think, why the qualities or modes of the double are not "any the less halves than doubles" (note the plural). If we say that x is (by definition) half of y just in case the lengths of x and y stand in the same relation as the lengths of A and B, then our definition or account of the half will also fit the double. For if A is the half of B, then B must be the double of A. If we try to modify this account in the obvious way, by introducing the notion of order, distinguishing the relation between A and B from that between B and A, we must remember that order, too, must be defined in terms of visible standards or paradigms. Hence we run into the same problem in defining it as we do in defining the light and the heavy, only now the problem has begun to look intractable.

23. It is instructive to compare Plato's requirements for epistemically adequate properties with the requirements for concepts adequate for logical purposes proposed by Frege; see *Translations from the Philosophical Writings of Gottlob Frege*, pp. 159-162.

24. This conclusion has obvious bearing on the vexed question of what forms there are. In several dialogues certain nondisputed (ND) predicates such as 'bee' (*Meno* 72a8-c4, 74d4-75a1), 'iron', 'silver' (*Phaedrus* 263a6-7), 'stick',

'stone' (*Alcibiades* 111a1-112d9), and 'finger' (*Republic* 523a10-e1) are contrasted with various disputed (D) predicates such as 'health' (*Meno* 65d12-e1, 72d4-e9), 'just' (*Alcibiades* 111e1), and 'big' and 'small' (*Republic* 523e3). There is wide agreement about the application of the former. But about the latter disputes arise. Some of these can be settled by appeal to agreed decision procedures; in other cases there is no agreed decision procedure (*Euthyphro* 7b6-d5). Many recent commentators have claimed that the dialogues argue only for the existence of separated forms corresponding to D predicates; see Fine, "The One Over Many," pp. 227-235; Irwin, *PMT*, pp. 144-157, 320 n. 38; Nehamas, "Predication and Forms of Opposites in the *Phaedo*"; Owen, "A Proof in the *Peri Ideōn*"; Strang, "Plato and the Third Man," pp. 194-198. I am unpersuaded by this claim, at least as far as the *Republic* goes. D and ND predicates are indeed contrasted at 523a5-525a5. But the aim is simply to find those studies that "lead to the exercise of dialectical-thought [*noēsin*]" and draw the psyche "towards substance [*pros ousian*]" (523a1-3). On the basis of sense-perception we can apply the ND predicate 'finger' to things without getting embroiled in obvious contradiction. Consequently, ND predicates do not lead to the exercise of dialectical-thought. But sense perception leads us to apply the D predicates 'big' and 'small' in obviously contradictory ways. Hence they do lead to the exercise of dialectical-thought. There is nothing in this to suggest that the predicates which spur us on to dialectic are the only ones to which forms correspond. Nor does Plato's theory have any room for such a restricted class of forms. He ties knowledge far too tightly to forms, and allows knowledge of too many things, for that to be true.

25. Despite this, many argue that Plato holds that knowledge of anything sublunary is impossible, that knowledge is only of transcendent forms; see Allen, "The Argument from Opposites in *Republic* V," p. 325; Cherniss, "The Philosophical Economy of the Theory of Ideas," pp. 20-27; Cross and Woozley, *PRPC*, pp. 134-195; Grube, *Plato's Republic*, pp. 136-137 n. 15; Hintikka, "Knowledge and Its Objects in Plato," pp. 9-12; Teloh, *The Development of Plato's Metaphysics*, pp. 117-119; White, *Plato on Knowledge and Reality*, p. 96. A view more like the one I defend has recently been advocated by Annas, *IPR*, pp. 210-215; Fine, "Knowledge and Belief in *Republic* V," p. 139; Irwin, *PMT*, p. 334. I return to this topic in 2.11.

26. My analysis has benefited from Adam, *PR*, vol. 2, pp. 115-116, 156-163. For brilliant discussion of the aporiai which beset various mathematical and philosophical accounts of unity, including the one mentioned in the text, see Frege, *The Foundations of Arithmetic*, section III.

27. Similar views are expressed by Adam, *PR*, vol. 2, p. 140; Murphy, *TIPR*, pp. 178-179; Nettleship, *Lectures on the Republic of Plato*, pp. 252-253; Robinson, *Plato's Earlier Dialectic*, pp. 160-162.

28. The views expressed in this paragraph have been substantially influenced by Robinson, *Plato's Earlier Dialectic*, pp. 146-179.

29. I think, therefore, that we can follow Ross, *Plato's Theory of Ideas*, p. 45, in thinking "that the four subsections are meant to stand for four divisions of being of increasing 'clearness' (509d9) or 'truth' (510a9)," without having to conclude that "[t]he equality of the middle subsections is an unintended, and perhaps by Plato unnoticed, consequence of what he does wish to emphasize."

30. It also follows, of course, that flutists do not know anything about their flutes, unless they chance to be dialecticians. Yet Socrates explicitly says here that flutists *in general* have such knowledge. Is he being careless? Is he contradicting himself? I do not think so. In my view, he is simply drawing on conventional beliefs about such things as flute playing and flute making to get across the general point that users, not makers, have knowledge, without being himself committed to the truth of those conventional beliefs.

31. A similar conclusion is suggested by the following passage from the *Cratylus*, which is very similar in thrust to the one under discussion:

> But who then is to determine [*gnōsomenos*] whether the proper form of the shuttle [*to prosēkon eidos kekridos*] is put in whatever sort of wood is used? The carpenter who makes it, or the weaver who uses it?—I should say that it is the one who uses it, Socrates.—And who uses the work of the lyre-maker? Will it not be the one who knows how to give directions about what is to be done, and who will know whether the work has been well done or not?—Clearly.—And who is he?—The one who plays the lyre.—And who will tell the boatmaker what to do?—The pilot.—And who will be best able to direct the lawmaker in his work whether here or in any other country, and will know whether it is being well done or not? Will it not be the user?—Yes.—And is not this the one who knows how to question [*ho erōtan*]?—Yes.—And also how to adjudicate the answers that are given?—Yes.—And the one who knows both how to question and to adjudicate you would call a dialectician?—Nothing else. (390b1-c12)

Consequently, this line of thought is in no way anomalous, or peculiar to *Republic* 10.

32. The parenthetical disjunction in this sentence is a product of the following line of thought. In the *Timaeus*, the Demiurge is described as looking to the forms in order to make as good a cosmos as possible (29e1-30a3). The good itself is not mentioned by name, but it is difficult to resist the thought that it is what the Demiurge looks to. This suggests that in that dialogue the good itself is the structure of the best cosmos, not simply of the best polis. Since the *Timaeus* (17c1-19b2) is closely related to the *Republic* we might reasonably conclude that the good itself is conceived in the same way in both

works. I do not see anything that prevents us from drawing this conclusion, but neither do I see see anything that compels us to draw it. Hence either the good is the structure of the Kallipolis or, being the structure of the best cosmos, it includes the structure of the Kallipolis as a substructure.

33. This accusation is developed at length by Annas, *IPR*, pp. 242-271. Cf. Irwin, *PMT*, pp. 242-243.

34. The existence of "bad" forms also shows that a currently popular account of the relation of forms to the good itself cannot be right. White, *Plato on Knowledge and Reality*, p. 101, expresses this account as follows:

> The Form of F, he [Plato] believes, is, as it were, an unqualified F, or something which is unqualifiedly F. But we know that he passes from this idea to thinking that it must therefore be a nondefective or, in this sense, a perfect F. . . . But his notion of goodness is such that he can think of the idea of a "perfect F" as close to, if not the same as, the idea of a "good F."

The same suggestion is made in Hare, "Plato and the Mathematicians," pp. 35-36. If it is adopted, the form of the bad will be perfectly bad, and hence good. If forms are self-instantiating (as many people believe), it follows that the form of the bad will be both good and bad. If forms are not self-instantiating (as I hold), then anything that instantiated the form of the bad would be perfectly bad, and would, therefore, instantiate the good itself. Violations of the principle of noncontradiction occur in either case.

35. This account of forms differs significantly from those currently favoured. The latter fall into two broad classes. In the first are those which identify forms with the meanings of general terms; see Gallop, *Plato: Phaedo*, pp. 96-97; Matthews and Cohen, "The One and the Many"; Nehamas, "Predication and Forms of Opposites in the *Phaedo*," p. 480; Ross, *Plato's Theory of Ideas*, pp. 24, 36, 225. In the second class are those which identify forms with properties or universals, where these are understood as being genuine, nonparticular features of reality discovered by science; see Fine, "The One Over Many," pp. 197-240. Clearly my view is closer to the latter than to the former. But it differs in identifying forms not (save *per accidens*) with the properties things actually happen to have, but with the properties they would have after the philosopher-kings have completed their world-transforming activities.

36. This passage has evoked two different types of response. Some take it to entail that there is a form corresponding to every group (however bizarre or arbitrary) to which a single name applies; see e.g., Annas, "Forms and First Principles," pp. 264, 277; Matthews and Cohen, "The One and the Many." Others find this interpretation, and the ontologically extravagant doctrine it attributes to Plato, hard to swallow. Smith, "General Relative Clauses in Greek," pp. 69-71, argues that the passage does not really state the doctrine at

all. He claims that it is properly translated: "For we are, as you know, in the habit of assuming [as a rule of procedure] that the Idea which corresponds to a group of particulars, each to each, is always one, in which case [or: in that case] we call the group, or its particulars, by the same name as the *eidos*." On his view, "all that is said is that if there is an Idea that Idea is indiscerptibly one, and must not be divided or multiplied." Fine, "The One Over Many," pp. 212-220, argues that before we can conclude that the passage (whether translated as Smith suggests or in the traditional way) commits Plato to the extravagant doctrine, we need to know how we are to understand *onoma*. She argues that Plato "has in mind a restricted usage of '*onoma*,' familiar from other contexts, such that 'n' is a name only if it denotes a real property or kind; names are restricted to what I shall call 'property-names,' to names denoting real properties or kinds" (p. 214).

Despite their ingenuity, I do not find either of these proposals plausible. The normal Platonic procedure is described in Book 6:

> I will, I said, when I have come to an understanding with you and re-minded you of the things we said before [at 475e6-476a7], and on many other occasions.—What things do you mean?—We speak of the many qualities and modes of the fine and the good [*polla kala kai polla agatha*], and we say that they are such, and so distinguish them in words. . . . And regarding the fine itself and the good itself, and similarly all the things which we then said were many, reversing ourselves, we postulate a unique form of each, believing that there is but one, and call it what each of them is in itself [*"ho estin" hekaston*]. (507a7-b7)

Since this description makes it clear that the assumption is that there is one form of F corresponding to each of the many qualities and modes of F, and not merely that if there is such a form it is "indiscerptibly one," we cannot follow Smith in Book 10. At the same time, this description does not use the term *onoma*. Hence Fine's stratagem does not apply to it. I conclude that Plato really did standardly assume that a single form corresponds to each quality and mode, and so to each general term. However, I do not think that it follows from this that he held the extravagant doctrine. 523e3-524c13, for example, clearly allows for the possibility that the big and the small, which are forms assumed to correspond to classes distinguished from one another in ordinary speech, might turn out, upon dialectical examination, to be not two opposed things but a single thing (2.9). This entails that not every class of things that share a name need have a distinct form corresponding to it (*Cratylus* 388e7-390e4). Assumptions are one thing; truths are another. Thus forms are assumed with ontological abandon, but the only ones there really are are those needed by dialectical-thought for its explanatory and reconstructive purposes. Ordinary language is the first word here, but it is not by any means the last word (5.2-3).

37. Many accept that the craftsman introduced at 596b6-8 has direct independent access to forms; see Adam, *PR*, vol. 2, p. 388; Annas, *IPR*, p. 336;

Cross and Woozley, *PRPC*, p. 274. But this would contradict the entire thrust of the *Republic* (2.8-9).

38. Some translators take this passage to be saying that the form of the bed is (predicatively) *ho estin klinē*; see Grube, Jowett, Shorey. Others take it to be identifying the form of the bed with *ho estin klinē*; see Chambry, Cornford. But neither interpretation is required by the Greek, and neither fits well with the use of this terminology at 507b2-7. There the form of F is what each of the many qualities, modes, or figures of F is in itself, not the form that is in itself what each of them is. As I read it, then, this passage does not embody the doctrine, familiar from the *Phaedo* and *Symposium*, that forms are self-instantiating. Nor, for the same reason, does the following passage:

> The god, either because he did not want to make more than one kind of bed which is in nature [*en tēi phusei*; sc. a bed], or because it was necessary for him not to do so, thus made only that one kind of bed which is in itself a bed [*ho estin klinē*]. Two or more of these have not been made by the god and never will be. . . . Because, I said, if he were to make only two, there would again appear a kind of which they would both possess the form [*to eidos echoien*], and it would be the one which is in itself a bed [*ho estin klinē*] and not the two. . . . The god knew this, I think, and wishing to be the real maker of the thing which is really a bed [*einai ontōs klinēs*] . . . made it in its nature one. (597c1-d3)

This passage does not tell us that only the form of the bed is in itself a bed, or really a bed. It tells us that the kind of bed the god makes is in itself a bed, and really a bed. The line of thought is this. There is only one kind of bed that instantiates the form of the bed (473a1-b2), this being the first bed. If, *per impossibile*, there were two kinds of beds that did this, they would, because of the relationship between forms and the good itself, instantiate the same form. Hence they would be one kind of bed, not two. For a contrary view, see Vlastos, "A Metaphysical Paradox," pp. 47-57, and "Degrees of Reality in Plato," pp. 58-75.

39. This phrase is usually translated in ways that suggest the bizarre idea that the first bed is a naturally occurring thing like a tree or a flower. In fact the phrase is a fairly common device for referring to forms; see *Republic* 476b6-8, 501b2-3; *Phaedo* 103b2-5; *Cratylus* 389a5-390a2; *Parmenides* 132d2; Adam, *PR*, vol. 2, p. 390; Gallop, *Plato: Phaedo*, pp. 94, 196-197.

40. On the difficulties of otherwise identifying this king, see Adam, *PR*, vol. 2, pp. 464-465.

41. At 518c9-d1 the good itself is called "the brightest of the beings [*tou ontos to phanotaton*]." This entails that the good is a being. Since, on my view being and substance are the same, it follows that the good is a substance. But this seems to contradict 509b9-10, which tells us that the good is "*beyond* sub-

stance in dignity and power." I doubt that there is any real difficulty here. If the good itself is the brightest of the beings, then it is beyond all *other* beings in brightness. I suspect that the phrase "beyond substance in dignity and power" simply means that the good is beyond *other* substances in dignity and power. Certainly someone may reject this view, and insist that being and substance are distinct. But he will then owe us an explanation both of the distinction itself and of the fact that it is not put to any further use in the *Republic*.

42. One might legitimately wonder why things in the world around us—even things that have not been affected by our world-transforming activities—instantiate modes. The *Republic* does not tell us. The *Timaeus*, however, which takes up where the *Republic* leaves off (17c1-19b2), is more forthcoming. In it the cosmos, and some of its contents, are said to be made directly by the Demiurge. But they are made neither *ex nihilo* nor according to a created paradigm. Rather the Demiurge, aiming, like all intelligent beings, to make everything good as far as possible (29e1-30a2), looks to the eternal forms (28c5-29c3), in order to shape already existing materials (primordial earth, water, air, and fire; 47e3-48e1, 52d2-53c3), in an already existing building site (space; 48e2-53c3). Among the things he makes in this way are human psyches (41d4-42d4) and a host of Homeric divinities (39e10-41a3), both of which are immortal as long as the Demiurge continues to will the good (39e10-41b6). To these created divinities the Demiurge assigns the task of populating the earth with living creatures:

> Three kinds of living creatures remain to be made [sea, air, and land animals; 39e10-40a2]—without them the cosmos would be unfinished; for it will not contain every kind of animal which it must contain if it is to be perfectly complete. But if they were made by me [the Demiurge], and received life at my hands, they would be equal to the gods; hence, in order that they be mortal, and the cosmos contain everything, you [divinities] shall make the animals, according to your natures, imitating [*mimoumenoi*] the power which I employed in making you. Of the part of them worthy of the name immortal and divine, which is the guide of all who are willing to follow justice and yourselves, I will sow the seed, and having made a beginning, I will hand the work over to you. You will weave together the mortal and the immortal, making and generating living creatures, giving them food and making them grow, and receiving them at death. (41b7-d3)

Thus the creation of the cosmos is a two-stage affair, part done by god himself, part by his divine ministers. This explains why so many of the things around us instantiate modes. The craftsmen who make them look to the things the Demiurge makes, not to forms themselves (e.g., 44d3-8). As a result, the things they make, like the carpenter's bed, are at two removes from truth and instantiate modes. If, as I am inclined to believe, the *Timaeus* is a late dialogue, then this continuity of doctrine suggests that Plato continued to hold the theory developed in the *Republic* throughout the remainder of his career. On the dating of the *Timaeus*, see Cherniss, "The Relation of the *Timaeus* to Plato's Later Dialogues"; Owen, "The Place of the *Timaeus* in Plato's Later Dialogues."

43. This view is advanced in a very insightful and imaginative paper, Cooper, "The Psychology of Justice in Plato." I reproduce the relevant argument. (i) The good itself is "a perfect example of rational order, conceived in explicitly mathematical terms" (p. 155). (ii) Each of the philosopher-kings "knows the good-itself and therefore whatever he values he values strictly in the light of a comparison between that thing and the good" (p. 155). (iii) But "the contemplation of the good, and in a lesser degree all other abstract scientific thought, since in these activities the impulse for rational order confronts less in the way of alien material to work upon, must be the most perfect earthly embodiments of good" (p. 155). (iv) It follows that the philosopher-kings "would prefer this kind of thinking to anything else" (p. 155). (v) But because a philosopher-king is "a devotee of *the* good, not *his own* good," what he most wants "is to advance the reign of rational order in the world as a whole so far as by his own efforts, alone or together with others, he can do this" (pp. 155-156). (vi) As a result, the philosopher-kings eschew the contemplative life and "deliberately and freely (520d6-7) choose a life for themselves that is less good than a more singlemindedly intellectual life, of which however they are individually capable" (p. 156). (vii) Hence, if the philosopher-kings' degree of eudaimonia is measured by comparison with that of the contemplative life, they "will settle for a less flourishing existence than they might have had" (p. 156). (viii) "This shows beyond any reasonable doubt that Plato's just man is no egoist, in any acceptable sense of the term. Not only does he not do everything out of concern for his own good, he never does anything for this reason. Even when he acts to benefit himself, recognizing that he does so, his reason for acting is that the good-itself demands it" (p. 157).

If (v) is true, devotion to the good itself requires the philosopher "to advance the reign of rational order in the world as a whole" at the cost of not advancing it as far as possible in his own life. The *Republic*, however, unequivocally denies this:

> As he [the philosopher-king] looks upon and contemplates things that are ordered and eternally the same, that neither do nor suffer injustice, but are all in an intelligible order, *he imitates them and tries to become as like them as he can.* Or do you think it possible to consort with something one admires without trying to imitate it oneself? . . . So the philosopher, who consorts with what is ordered and divine, *tries to become as ordered and divine himself as a person can.* (500c1-d1)

I conclude that the philosopher's devotion to the good does not require him to sacrifice his own good to that of the world as a whole. In fact, as I argue in detail in succeeding chapters, the philosopher achieves his own good precisely by ruling the Kallipolis—the only human community in which stable, long-term, happiness is available to individuals (473e4-5). Sections 2.11-12, 3.5-7,

4.9, and 5.2-5 contain material particularly pertinent to further assessing Cooper's views.

44. Annas, "Plato on the Triviality of Literature," p. 25 n. 16, writes: "one might add the whole Sun, Line, and Cave sequence in the *Republic*, where it is notoriously impossible to give a single overall interpretation that is both visually and philosophically coherent." Similar views are expressed or illustrated in Annas, *IPR*, pp. 242-271; Cross and Woozley, *PRPC*, pp. 196-238; Murphy *TIPR*, pp. 151-164; Raven, *Plato's Thought in the Making*, pp. 131-175; Robinson, *Plato's Earlier Dialectic*, pp. 180-183.

45. For clear expositions of the traditional theory, see Cherniss, "The Philosophical Economy of the Theory of Ideas"; Crombie, *EPD*, vol. 2, pp. 247-325; Ross, *Plato's Theory of Ideas*; Wedberg, *Plato's Philosophy of Mathematics*, pp. 26-44.

46. Given the emphasis on generality in Plato's accounts of recollection, I can see no reason to think that he supposes the paradox of inquiry to be a threat only to *a priori* knowledge; cf. Moravcsik, "Learning as Recollection"; Vlastos, "*Anamnesis* in the *Meno*," pp. 156-157; contrast White, *Plato on Knowledge and Reality*, p. 59 n. 35. My views on this part of the *Meno* have been influenced by Irwin, *PMT*, pp. 138-139.

47. I have benefited here from White, *Plato on Knowledge and Reality*, pp. 47-53.

48. My translations from the *Phaedo* are indebted to Gallop, *Plato: Phaedo*.

49. See Dorter, *Plato's Phaedo: An Interpretation*, pp. 60-62; Gallop, *Plato: Phaedo*, pp. 116-118.

50. See Ackrill, "*Anamnēsis* in the *Phaedo*: Remarks on 73c-75c," pp. 188-191.

51. As we shall see below, Aristotle believes that Platonic forms are self-instantiating. And he is not alone; see Teloh, *The Development of Plato's Metaphysics*, pp. 119-125; Vlastos, "The Third Man Argument in the *Parmenides*"; White, *Plato On Knowledge and Reality*, pp. 63-87. Others, however, deny that forms are self-instantiating; see Allen, "Participation and Predication in Plato's Middle Dialogues"; Nehamas, "Self-Predication and Plato's Theory of Forms"; Vlastos, "The Unity of the Virtues in the *Protagoras*."

52. For recent alternatives to the interpretation I defend, see Dorter, *Plato's Phaedo: An Interpretation*, pp. 52-60; Gallop, *Plato: Phaedo*, pp. 113-137; Gosling, "Similarity in *Phaedo* 73B *seq.*," pp. 151-161; Irwin, *PMT*, pp. 148-150;

Nehamas, "Predication and Forms of Opposites in the *Phaedo*," pp. 461-491, and "Plato on the Imperfection of the Sensible World," pp. 105-117.

53. Hardie, *A Study in Plato*, p. 73, claims that "[t]o say that a form is 'separate' is to say that there can be a form without there being particulars which exemplify it." Irwin, "Plato's Heracleiteanism," argues that separation is a matter of definability—the form of F is separate because it cannot be defined in terms of sensibles. Others seem to conceive of separation in spatial terms.

54. The best exploration and defense of this interpretation is in Fine, "Separation."

55. Indeed, as Fine points out in "Separation," p. 57, the forms are said to be *chōris* in only two places in Plato's writings. The first is in the *Sophist*: "You speak of becoming, on the one hand, and of substance, on the other, dividing them separately [*chōris*], I suppose" (248a7-8). The second is in the *Parmenides*: "But, as I said just now, if someone first distinguishes the forms separately [*chōris*], themselves in themselves . . ." (129d6-8). And neither of these passages can involve existential separation. For the separation they speak of is clearly a symmetrical relation, whereas existential separation is asymmetrical.

56. If the doctrine of recollection is abandoned in the *Republic*, then the *Republic* must be later than the *Phaedrus*. For recollection is still accepted in the latter dialogue (248e2-249d3). But it is generally—albeit not universally (see Guthrie, *A History of Greek Philosophy*, vol. 4, pp. 396-433)—believed that the *Phaedrus* is later than the *Republic*. The question is, then, whether this belief is well founded.

Many suppose that the method of collection and division discussed in the *Phaedrus* (265d3-266c1) is the same as the method used in such late dialogues as the *Sophist, Statesman,* and *Philebus,* and assign the *Phaedrus* a later date than the *Republic* (which does not mention collection and division by name) on this basis; see Hackforth, *Plato's Phaedrus*, pp. 134-135; Nussbaum, " 'This Story Isn't True': Poetry, Goodness, and Understanding in Plato's *Phaedrus*." But this reasoning is not compelling. For the method of collection and division mentioned in the *Phaedrus* belongs to an overall conception of dialectic which includes the doctrine of recollection as a prominent part, and this is not the case with the method used in the late dialogues. For recollection is as absent from them as it is from the *Republic*.

The other evidence for dating the *Phaedrus* later has been usefully summarized by Hackforth, *Plato's Phaedrus*, pp. 2-7. (1) It "can hardly be accidental" that most stylometric analysts place the *Phaedrus* "between the *Republic* and the late six" (p. 3). (2) Even if the comparison of the soul to a charioteer could be understood without a knowledge of Book 4 of the *Republic*, "it is unlikely that Plato would have put it before the public for the first time in this symbolic form" (p. 4). (3) 249b1-3 seems "to allude to the curious mixture of determination by lot and chance with which souls are confronted in the Myth of Er."

This allusion is "one of the strongest evidences of the priority of the *Republic*" (p. 4). (4) The proof of the immortality of the psyche given in the *Phaedrus* (245c5-246a2) is more satisfactory than the one given in the *Republic* and "rests on a conception of the soul's nature, as that which moves itself, which is preserved in Plato's latest work (*Laws* X), but is apparently unknown to the *Phaedo* and *Republic*."

Assertions (2) and (3) are both weakened, in my view, by the fact that we do not know the intended audience for Plato's dialogues, nor what was common knowledge among them. (2) is, in any case, implausible. The image of the charioteer is completely *intelligible* without knowledge of Book 4. The latter gives us an argument for thinking of the psyche as tripartite, but we do not need the argument to understand the image. Moreover, the fact that the *Phaedrus* contains no argument for the tripartite psyche suggests that Plato does not yet have an argument, not that he is presupposing knowledge of an argument he has developed elsewhere. For his dialogues are usually self-contained. Nor is (4) very convincing. The argument for immortality given in the *Republic* relies on a doctrine about the effects of the vices on the psyche that makes it particularly well suited to a dialogue about justice and injustice (3.8). Moreover, the fact that we find the argument wanting does not mean that Plato did. Nor does the fact that he did not present an argument that we like better show that he was not aware of that argument (3.2). We are left, then, with stylometry. It must be accorded some weight, certainly. But its findings here are sufficiently indecisive to be of little use on their own.

I turn now from defense to counterattack. First, the form of the fine plays the same sort of rôle in the *Phaedrus* as it does in the *Symposium*; see Irwin, *PMT*, pp. 164-176. In the *Republic*, however, the form of the fine does not play this rôle. Indeed, it is scarcely mentioned. Instead, the good itself has become central. Those who accept the orthodox view that the *Symposium* is earlier than the *Republic*, and who simultaneously claim that the *Phaedrus* is later, owe us an explanation of this apparent doctrinal reversal. Second, it is widely recognized that Plato did abandon the doctrine of recollection at some point prior to the late dialogues. If the *Republic* is later than the *Phaedrus* we can explain why and where he abandoned it, and how he solved the problem it had been introduced to solve. But if the *Phaedrus* is later, we cannot do any of this.

All things considered, then, in my view we should revise the orthodox dating of the *Phaedrus*. It is earlier than the *Republic*, not later.

57. Cf. Annas, *IPR*, pp. 312-313.

58. The passage containing them has been described as "the most obscure and controversial in the whole of Plato's works" (Grube, *Plato's Republic*, p. 197; see Adam, *PR*, vol. 2, p. 264).

59. There is a very full discussion of this so-called marriage number in Adam, *PR*, vol. 2, pp. 264-312; vol. 1, pp. xlviii-l, contains a survey by Rees of important corrections of Adam's account.

60. Many translations create the impression that the antecedent of the relative pronoun *has* is *arithmos geōmetrikos*; see Chambry, Cornford, Grube, Jowett, Shorey. But this is excluded by the number and gender of the pronoun, which, being feminine plural, must have *geneseōn* as its antecedent.

61. See, e.g., Hacking, *Representing and Intervening*; McDowell, "Virtue and Reason"; Murdoch, *The Sovereignty of Good*; Rorty, *Philosophy and the Mirror of Nature*.

CHAPTER THREE

1. The text does not always have the Greek word *meros* where translations feature its English equivalent 'part'. But since *meros* is often used in connection with appetite, aspiration, and reason (e.g., 442b11, 442c5, 444b3, 462d1, 462d4, 583a1, 586e5), there is little reason to doubt Plato's commitment to the view that they are *parts* of the psyche. It would be a mistake, however, to become obsessed with a word, especially a syncategorematic word like 'part'. One must look instead to the doctrine it is intended to express. And as we shall see in 3.4-6, the doctrine that the psyche has parts makes impeccable psychological sense. It would also be a mistake to become obsessed with the number three. It is quite clear from 443d7 that the psyche may have more than three parts. But for Plato's principle purposes it is usually necessary to distinguish only three; see Grube, *Plato's Thought*, p. 135.

2. Robinson, "Plato's Separation of Reason from Desire," is wrong to claim that PO conflicts with the view, expressed at 479b9, that each of the many Fs, where F is a mode or quality, is no more F than it is not F. A large part of Plato's reason for rejecting modes and qualities as unfit for epistemic purposes, and introducing forms in their place, is that modes and qualities violate PO while forms do not. He is not committed to any violations of PO; the sightseers and craft-lovers are (2.8).

3. There are useful discussions of formal objects in de Sousa, "The Good and the True," and in Kenny, *Action, Emotion and Will*, pp. 187-202.

4. It might be objected that because someone can thirst for something he falsely believes to be drink, it is not *drink* that is the natural object of thirst, but *what is believed to be drink*. But this would be a mistake. Plato is interested in *referential* psychological relations, which relate a psyche to a property independently of how that property is characterized or described, not in *attributive* ones, which only relate a psyche to something "under a description." That is why his list of relations includes both psychological and nonpsychological examples. Suppose now that *x* is one of those candles that look like a glass of beer, and that thirsty A takes it for beer, and tries to drink it. Does A referentially thirst for *x*? Surely he does not. What he thirsts for is, one might say,

the beer he believes x to be, or x under the false description "beer." And this is an attributive thirst. So it is wrong to think that people referentially thirst for real things that are not drink, although they can be said to attributively thirst for them. Hence the natural object of thirst is drink. In my view, Plato is wise to ignore, as he invariably does, the problems of intensionality in discussing psychological relations. For one should begin with normal cases, in which the psyche is successfully related to the world, and only then try to fit in the pathological cases, where, because of false beliefs, lack of information, or some other reason, that relation fails. This approach to psychological relations is defended in Wilson, *Emotion and Object*. The distinction between referential and attributive psychological attitudes is taken from Quine, "Quantifiers and Propositional Attitudes."

5. These criticisms of the argument for psychic division are clearly set out in MacIntyre, *A Short History of Ethics*, pp. 36-37.

6. See Hobbes, *Leviathan*, pp. 118-119.

7. See Penner, "Thought and Desire in Plato," which contains a very subtle treatment of its topic. I remain unconvinced, however, by the defense Penner offers Plato against the objection. Penner sets up a case in which appetite's desire for a drink conflicts with its desire to stay warm. Then he sets out an argument that uses this conflict to try to divide appetite. The bracketed entities are "possible states of affairs" (p. 109).

(1) Appetite desires to drink.

(2) Appetite desires to stay warm.

(3) In this situation [to drink] = [to get this glass of water and then to drink it] = [to not stay warm in bed] = [to not be warm].

Substituting these identicals in (1), we get

(4) Appetite desires to not be warm.

Conjoining (2) and (4) gives us

(5) Appetite desires to be warm and appetite desires to not be warm.

By applying PO we get the conclusion,

(6) Appetite has (at least) two parts, one of which desires to be warm, the other of which desires to not be warm.

Now, according to Penner, the illegitimate move in this argument occurs when (4) is derived on the basis of (1) and (3): "[I]t seems to me plausible to suppose that Plato would have regarded it as a necessary condition for substituting equivalents after 'desires' that the *author* of the desire (be it a person, an embodied soul, or part of a soul) know or believe that the equivalents in question are equivalents" (p. 110). But Penner does not think that Plato would allow that appetite is capable of such advanced cognitive feats (p. 110). Hence the argument fails to establish that Plato is committed to the divisibility of appetite. This defense is unconvincing for two reasons. First, Plato would not accept that appetite is too cognitively limited to gain access to the substitutions necessary to arrive at (4). Appetite can, after all, set complex tasks for reason to perform and act on the results (553d1-7). Second, the defense works only if appetite's desires are attributive rather than referential. For if they are referential, there are no substitutions to be performed. Hence the defense will not work against the sort of example I discuss in the text.

8. The idea of compromise formation was suggested to me by the following discussion in Parfit, *Reasons and Persons*, p. 298:

> We can imagine a world in which fusion was a natural process. Two people come together. While they are unconscious, their two bodies grow into one. One person then wakes up. . . . Any two persons who fuse together would have different characteristics, different desires, different intentions. How could these be combined? The answers might be these. Some of these features will be compatible. These would co-exist in the one resulting person. Some will be incompatible. These, if of equal strength, would cancel out, and, if of different strengths, the stronger would become weaker. These effects might be as predictable as the laws governing dominant and recessive genes.

This is a dramatic example. But compromise formation is in fact a commonplace of folk psychology.

9. In a subtle discussion of this passage, Nehamas, "Plato on Imitation and Poetry in *Republic* 10," pp. 64-65, writes:

> For what is it that this logically imperfect principle [PO] divides? And into what does it divide it? I find the obvious answer, that the soul is divided into reason and appetite once again, difficult to accept. For one thing this would involve the attribution of thinking to appetite. And though this is not a serious difficulty, the suggestion raises the more difficult question of what appetite has to do with perceptual error and illusion. Why should our desire tell us that the immersed stick is bent? . . . Since in our present passage the calculating part of the soul is said to have two opposing beliefs (602e4-6), it must be the calculating part itself that is further divided. Our principle does not allow us to introduce a distinct object, appetite, and attribute to it one of the two conflicting beliefs.

Now Nehamas is surely right that anyone who thinks, as I do, that a conflict in beliefs is being used here to divide the psyche into reason, or "the best part of the psyche" (603a4-5), on the one hand, and appetite or another of "the inferior parts within us" (603a7), on the other, must explain how it is that appetite can think or form beliefs, and how it is that desire can tell us "that the immersed stick is bent." And in 2.12 and 3.4-7 I have tried to do just that.

However, I do not agree that 602e4-6 says that reason has opposing beliefs. Reason "believes in accord with" measurement (603a1-5). It is also to reason that "opposites are apparent about the same things at the same time" (602e5-6). But we are never told that reason believes in accord with these appearances. On the contrary, it is not reason but one of "the inferior parts within us" that believes "against measurement" (603a1-8), and so in accord with the appearances.

10. For discussion of this view, see Foley, "Is It Possible to Have Contradictory Beliefs?"

11. Translations are based on Taylor, *Plato: Protagoras*.

12. This is noticed by Davidson, "How Is Weakness of the Will Possible?" pp. 22-23, who argues that "self-evident" principles of action seem to entail that weak-willed actions cannot occur.

13. I agree with Santas, *Socrates*, pp. 196-199, that Socrates is attacking an explanation of the possibility of akrasia rather than trying to show directly that it is impossible.

14. Taylor, *Plato: Protagoras*, pp. 180-181, objects that this substitution is illegitimate because it takes place in an opaque, intensional context. I do not find this objection compelling. After all, Socrates' argument is addressed to the hedonistic many who believe that the good is pleasure and that evil is pain. Hence they believe that x is worse than y just in case x is less pleasant than y. And if they believe that, the substitution is in good order. This line of response is suggested by Santas, *Socrates*, p. 319 n. 14.

15. See Santas, *Socrates*, pp. 208-209, for convincing supporting argument.

16. See Murphy, *TIPR*, pp. 28-29.

17. This description is actually applied to the oligarchic polis, not (explicitly) to the oligarchic psyche. Psyche and polis, however, are closely analogous (435a5-b2, 553a1-4), and the polis takes its stamp from "the characters of the people in the poleis, which, tipping the scale, draw other things along with them" (514d7-e2; 2.14). Consequently, I think it safe to transfer the description from polis to psyche.

18. Penner, "Thought and Desire in Plato," p. 113, writes: "Plato had no logical or psychological arguments for going beyond two parts of the soul; and . . . he probably succeeded in partially blinding himself to this fact because of the political momentum he acquired from his creatures, the guardians." Similar views are expressed by Hardie, *A Study in Plato*, pp. 141-143, and by Robinson, *Plato's Psychology*, pp. 44-46.

19. Aristotle defines anger as follows: "Anger is a desire [*orexis*], accompanied by pain, to take what is believed to be or appears to be revenge [*timōrias phainomenēs*] because of what is believed to be or what appears to be an insult [*dia phainomenēn oligōrian*]" (*Rhetoric* 1378a30-32). Many recent philosophers give similar accounts; see Kenny, *Action, Emotion and Will*, pp. 187-194.

20. This conception is explored in Finley, *The World of Odysseus*, especially pp. 74-141. Adkins, *Merit and Responsibility*, is also relevant.

21. See Irwin, *PMT*, pp. 193-194.

22. See de Sousa, "The Rationality of Emotions."

23. See Mill, *Utilitarianism*, pp. 35-36.

24. See Cross and Woozley, *PRPC*, pp. 264-266.

25. See Gosling and Taylor, *The Greeks on Pleasure*, pp. 320-330. On Don Giovanni, see Williams, "Don Giovanni as an Idea." On Ajax, see Winnington-Ingram, *Sophocles: An Interpretation*, pp. 11-56.

26. Some commentators have argued that *lupē* should not be translated as 'pain' on the grounds that pain is not the opposite of pleasure; see Urmson, "Pleasure and Distress," pp. 209-210. As a philosophical thesis this view may have some merit. But as a claim about English it does not seem to have very much. The second thing the *Oxford English Dictionary* tells us about pain is that it is "the opposite of pleasure."

27. Urmson, "Pleasure and Distress," p. 213, criticizes this argument:

[I]t is clear that *algein* is having an unpleasant, even painful sensation and must be contrasted with having a pleasant feeling, while *hēsuchia* must be the absence of a feeling of either sort. Clearly these are three mutually exclusive possibilities. But does anyone ever confuse the absence of a pleasant feeling with the presence of an unpleasant feeling or the absence of a pain with a pleasant feeling? I doubt it. What they find, and say, is that in the circumstances the absence of feeling, pleasant or unpleasant, is pleasant; the *hēsuchia* is pleasant as being what it is. There is no error or illusion involved at all, so no ground for stigmatizing the pleasure as unreal.

But Plato's point is misrepresented by this response. For he is arguing that people mistakenly *define* pleasure as the absence of pain because they find the absence of pain to be pleasant when it follows upon pain. He is not arguing that they wrongly find this state to be pleasant. His argument is about the nature of pleasure, about what pleasure is, about what account of it is true. That is why pleasures that are neither preceded nor followed by pain are relevant to his case.

28. There is a fuller discussion of these mixed psychological, or non-body-based, pleasures at *Philebus* 47e1-50e7.

29. *Philebus* 51e8-52b8 returns to this problem. See Gosling, *Plato: Philebus*, pp. 122-123.

30. Gosling and Taylor, *The Greeks on Pleasure*, pp. 122-123, have objected to this argument as follows:

> Pleasure is the replenishment of desire and only that which truly replenishes a desire is truly pleasant. Now everything is set up for showing the philosopher's superiority, since the objects of his pursuit are the only ones to give genuine replenishment. Unfortunately, there is a fatal ambiguity in this notion of replenishment. Suppose we take it, as the original account requires, that the pleasure consists in the replenishing. Then it ceases when the replenishment is complete. In that case, if the philosopher's desires can be genuinely satisfied, that means that the so-called process of replenishing genuinely and once and for all replenishes. But then as life goes on and a philosopher acquires full understanding he will be wise, and . . . in that case he will no longer desire wisdom. Since these desires/lacks are now satisfied there is no further replenishing of them to occur. So the more successful a philosopher is, the sooner his life will cease to be pleasant. This considerably weakens the argument that his life will be pleasanter. Alternatively, one might take the pleasure/replenishment equation to mean that pleasure consists in being in possession of that whose absence would constitute a natural lack—in having what one wants. This would certainly secure the conclusion that the successful philosopher's life was pleasant, and even, by underlining "being in possession," that it alone was truly pleasant. The cost, however, would be to cut off one's ties with the original account and leave one with the unsatisfactorily negative view that pleasure consisted in the absence of lacks, a view hardly consistent with the distinction made at 583c-584a [between pain, pleasure, and *hēsuchia*, which is neither]. Furthermore, this second view is highly implausible when applied to the pleasure of quenching one's thirst, and the others with which the original account started.

But this objection does not carry complete conviction. Even if Plato did identify pleasure just with the process of being filled, he could still argue that the philosopher is more truly engaged in that process than the money-lover. For the philosopher is being filled with things that would, were he to go on long enough, eventually truly fill the lack that is his desire to know everything. He is being truly filled, or on his way to being truly full. But the money-lover is not being truly filled. For he is not on his way to being truly full. Moreover, there is a great deal to know, and knowledge requires dialectical defensibility (2.9). Hence it is plausible to think that the process of filling up with knowledge can continue uncompleted, and relatively uninterrupted, throughout life. Therefore, if the process of filling is pleasure, the philosopher is more truly pleased than the money-lover. However, I suspect that Plato thinks of *both* the process of filling *and* the state of being full as pleasant, and I have so represented him in the text. The use of the present infinitive, "being filled [*plērousthai*]," in the definition of pleasure at 585d11 strongly suggests that Plato thinks of the process of filling as pleasure. For if he had wanted to identify pleasure simply with the state of being full, he would almost certainly have used the aorist infinitive. On the other hand, the argument that the philosopher is more truly filled because what he is filled with is always and unalterably what it is puts it beyond reasonable doubt that Plato also thinks of the state of being filled as pleasant. (Notice, in this regard, that we are told not that pleasure and pain are psychic movements, which would suggest that pain and pleasure are processes, but that their "coming to be" [583e9-10] is a psychic movement.) On this view, both filling and being full will be pleasant, both emptying (beyond a certain point) and being empty will be painful. But if Plato does think of pleasure and pain in this way, can he still make out his distinction between pleasure, pain, and *hēsuchia*? I think he can. He clearly thinks of being truly pleased as moving up from a middle state, and being pained as moving down from it. Perhaps, then, moving down from full to the middle state is neither pleasant nor painful. Surely such a view has some folk-psychological plausibility. One is emptying from the moment one has finished eating, but one does not feel hungry until a certain degree of emptiness has been reached.

31. See Adam, *PR*, vol. 2, pp. 358-359.

32. See Gosling, *Pleasure and Desire*; Kenny, *Action, Emotion and Will*, pp. 127-150; Ryle, *The Concept of Mind*, pp. 103-106, and *Dilemmas*, pp. 54-67.

33. Some commentators deny that Plato intends these proofs about pleasure to bear directly on happiness; see Cross and Woozley, *PRPC*, pp. 262-269; Murphy, *TIPR*, pp. 207-223. Gosling and Taylor, *The Greeks on Pleasure*, p. 99, justly comment: "If Plato intended to separate his proofs of the greater pleasantness of the philosophic life from the proof of the greater *eudaimonia* of the just life, then he has certainly done his best to conceal that intention by his manner of introducing the second proof." I might add that if we do not preserve the connection between goodness, pleasure, and happiness, explored in 3.7, Plato's entire argument begins to totter. For this connection is crucial to his epistemology and metaphysics (2.12), and to his theory and defense of justice (5.2-3).

34. See Cooper, "Plato's Theory of Human Motivation," pp. 16-17.

35. I see no reason to follow Grube, *Plato's Republic*, p. 252 n. 16, in taking this to imply that, for example, wood can be destroyed *only* by rot. Certainly the argument for immortality requires nothing so obviously implausible.

36. One reason why L2 needs a *ceteris paribus* clause is that when we are not under the influence of a strong desire we can arrange for its later frustration. Knowing that when my desire for a cigarette strikes it will prove irresistible, I burn all the available cigarettes. Hence, when the desire strikes, it will not be satisfied in action. In this way I may eventually cease to be a smoker altogether. As George Eliot puts it in *Daniel Deronda*: "We are not always in a state of strong emotion, and when we are calm we can use our memories and gradually change the bias of our fear, as we do our tastes." Without this ability, limited as it is, we would not, in my view, be capable of freedom.

37. Both quotations are from Hume, *A Treatise of Human Nature*, p. 416.

38. The deliberative theory has recently been defended by Brandt, *A Theory of the Good and the Right*.

39. Hume, *A Treatise of Human Nature*, p. 120, notices this phenomenon, but he gives it no place in his finished theory.

40. See Parfit, *Reasons and Persons*, pp. 117-126.

CHAPTER FOUR

1. Adam, *PR*, vol. 2, p. 34, suggests that the reference here might be to 423e4-424a2, "although the reference is hardly justified." I think it is much more likely that the reference is to 412a4-10.

2. Crombie, *EPD*, vol. 1, pp. 89-90, describes the First Polis as a "false start." Annas, *IPR*, p. 78, writes, "we have to conclude, though reluctantly, that Plato has not given the first city a clear place in the *Republic*'s moral argument." I am indebted to Nettleship, *Lectures on the Republic of Plato*, pp. 70-71, in which the relevance of the division of desires to the First Polis is noticed.

3. Not, notice, a good *sailor*, even though the navy saved the Athenians from the Persians at Salamis. The navy was too democratic, and, perhaps, too implicated in Athenian expansionism, for Plato's tastes. That is why the neophyte guardians are not to imitate "those who row in triremes, or their timekeepers, or anything else connected with ships" (396a8-b4; see *Laws* 706a4-707c7, for an even stronger statement).

4. See Adam, *PR*, vol. 1, p. 205.

5. Some commentators think that Plato is unclear about who is to receive primary education. Irwin, *PMT*, pp. 330-331 n. 6, writes: "Plato insinuates that the training [primary education] will extend beyond the guardians, but he never says so." Murphy, *TIPR*, pp. 78-79, quotes with approval Aristotle's comment that "on these matters the text is not explicit nor are its implications easy to discover" (*Politics* 1264a11-13). Others are confident that primary education (or some parts of it) is intended for all citizens. Cornford, *The Republic of Plato*, p. 154 n. 1, writes: "The elementary education . . . will be open to all citizens, but presumably carried further (to the age of 17 or 18 . . .) in the case of those who show special promise." And, in a similar vein, Vlastos, "Justice and Happiness in the *Republic*," p. 137, writes: "That this [the musical part of primary education] is directed to all the citizens, not only to the philosophers-to-be, is certain." Still others claim that primary education is intended for future rulers and guardians only. This has been most forcefully argued in Hourani, "The Education of the Third Class in Plato's *Republic*," to which my own discussion is indebted.

6. After a review of the evidence, Dover, *Greek Popular Morality in the Time of Plato and Aristotle*, p. 45, produces the following cautious gloss:

> Until persuaded otherwise by arguments which I have not yet encountered, I make the assumption that the poor Athenian was normally willing to apply the expression *kalos kagathos* to any man who had what he himself would have liked to have (wealth, a great name, distinguished ancestors) and was what he himself would have liked to be (educated, well-dressed and well-groomed, with the physique and poise of a man trained in fighting, wrestling and dancing).

But whether *kalos kagathos* is being used in that sense here, or as a label for the aristocracy, as at 568e7-569a7, it is surely not supposed that the producers should try to imitate such people.

7. A number of commentators have argued that because he allows for the promotion of some of the children of producers to neophyte guardian status, Plato must be covertly assuming that all such children start out receiving primary education. Cornford, *The Republic of Plato*, pp. 63-64: "No explicit provision is made for their [the producers'] education; but unless they share in the early education provided for the Guardians, there could hardly be opportunities for promoting their most promising children to a higher order." Murphy, *TIPR*, p. 78: "Plato . . . holds that everyone should be classified according to his merits, and unless children of the lower class at any rate begin with the others in common classrooms and on common playing-fields, the machinery of selection becomes rather indefinite." But this argument is not convincing. Because rulers, guardians, and producers for the most part breed true to type (see 415a7-8), not many producer offspring are likely to be promoted. Since primary education can start as late as the age of ten, without irremediable bad

effects (see 540e5-541a7; 4.5), the rulers and guardians will have plenty of time to spot the few likely candidates who, given the physical prerequisites of guardians alone, are likely to stand out from the rest.

8. Vlastos, "Justice and Happiness in the *Republic*," pp. 137-138, has argued against this:

> it [the musical part of primary education] is explicitly designed to inculcate *sōphrosunē*, a virtue required of all three classes. So all are subject to what Plato calls "musical" *paideia*: a process which employs not only music itself and the other arts, but manipulates everything in the social environment (down to games and haircuts) to stock the growing mind with the right beliefs and, what is more, with the right emotive charges, so that what one comes to call "just" one will feel irresistibly attractive and its contrary disgustingly ugly. Thus the internal controls will be secured and a condition of soul induced which is emphatically called "harmony" in anticipation of the later use of this metaphor in the definition of temperance and justice.

I agree that music is designed to inculcate a certain sort of moderation—music-induced or *musical* moderation, as I shall call it. But I do not agree that Plato thinks that musical moderation is required of producers. Nor do I agree that the virtue of moderation, properly so called, is required of all three classes. The closest the text comes to asserting that musical moderation is required of the producers is at 389d7-e2: "And again our youth [*tois neaniais*] will need moderation. . . . And are not these the most important features of moderation for the majority [*sōphrosunēs plēthei*]—to obey the rulers, and oneself to rule over the pleasures of food, drink, and sex?" But—appearances to the contrary—only future guardians (who are the majority of the rulers and guardians) are under discussion. For throughout Book 3, "the youth" is used simply as a stylistic variant of "the guardians-to-be." This is made particularly clear in the following passage: "Now, after music, our youths [*hoi neaniai*] must be trained in gymnastics. . . . And we said that they [*our guardians*; 398e6-7] must avoid drunkenness. For it is more improper for a guardian [*phulaki*] than for anyone else to be a drunkard and not to know where on earth he is" (403c9-e6). Hence the text does not assert that musical moderation is required of producers. Nor does the account of moderation commit Plato to this. A polis is moderate just in case "the desires of the inferior many are controlled by the desires and intelligence [*phronēseōs*] of the fewer and better" (431c10-d2), and "the same opinion exists among the rulers and the ruled as to who must rule" (431d9-e2). Hence moderation exists neither exclusively in the ruling class nor exclusively in the ruled, but in the two taken jointly (see 431e4-432a9). Consequently, moderation is possessed not by each class taken in isolation, but by the polis of which each is a part.

9. This principle may be a special case of the principle of qualification discussed in 3.2.

10. White, *CPR*, pp. 22-24, argues that, because it involves some time spent ruling rather than full-time philosophizing, the life of the philosopher-king involves sacrifice of self-interest. Cooper, "The Psychology of Justice in Plato," pp. 156-157, argues on the same basis that the philosopher-kings "deliberately and freely (520d6-7) choose a life for themselves that is less good than a singlemindedly intellectual life." What both overlook is that the mixed life of ruling and philosophizing is the best possible life reliably available to a wisdom-lover. The life of pure philosophy is too high for a human being. A similar view is, I think, part of the Platonism of Aristotle (see *Nicomachean Ethics* 1176a30-1178b33). But this is itself a controversial issue.

11. Vlastos, "The Theory of Social Justice in the *Polis* in Plato's *Republic*," pp. 29-30, sees this clearly:

> But when Plato speaks of the manual worker as the intellectual's *philos* it is love, not mere friendship, that he means—love according to Plato's understanding, sustained by solidarity in the pursuit of happiness and excellence, since each gives indispensable support to the other's quest: If they did not have each other, both would fail: the philosopher, for he would then have to divert precious time to meaningless drudgery; the manual worker too would fail, and more disastrously, for without direction from above his life would be bestial: he would be ruled "by the brood of beasts within him." So only by pooling their disparate resources, fixed ineluctably for each by nature, can either of them have the chance to find the best life for himself and make the best that can be made of himself. If the worker has even a glimmering of this truth, how could he resent the deprivation of rights which casts him in the role of slave to "the best man"? How could you fail to respond with love to one who stands by you to share with you day by day his "divine" gift of reason?

But Vlastos underestimates the degree of awareness the producer, or manual worker, must have for friendship or love to exist between him and the philosophers and guardians. A glimmer of the truth is not enough. What is required is that the producer have a sufficient understanding of the Kallipolis, and his place in it, to enable him to form, and rationally sustain, the belief that he is better off in his own terms in the Kallipolis than he would be in any other polis. This is not something the producers can come by casually. It is something their education must guarantee.

12. Annas, *IPR*, p. 107, understands the distinction in this way.

13. Vlastos, "The Individual as the Object of Love in Plato," pp. 15-16, cites 407c7-e2 to support the following claim:

> Consider what would happen in this utopia if someone through no fault of his own were to cease being a public asset. One of the philosophers, let us say, becomes permanently disabled and can no longer do his job or any

other work that would come anywhere near the expected level of productive excellence. . . . What may he then claim, now that he may no longer ground his claims on the needs of his job, but only on the value of his individual existence? As I read the *Republic*, the answer is: Nothing. . . . If men are to be loved for their productiveness and for no other reason, why should there be breach of love in the refusal of medical treatment to the unproductive?

Vlastos' position is criticized by Irwin, *PMT*, pp. 342-344 n. 28. My own response will be clear from what follows in the text (see 5.5).

14. However, an Athenian father, unlike a Roman one, did not have the right to actively put his child to death; see MacDowell, *The Law in Classical Athens*, pp. 91-92.

15. See Tooley, "Abortion and Infanticide."

16. This evidence is discussed in Vlastos, "Does Slavery Exist in Plato's *Republic*?" As I shall argue in the text, however, his claim that "the case for the affirmative must be reckoned conclusive" (p. 146) is overly optimistic.

17. The chances that a female infant would be exposed, though not exactly calculable, were almost certainly higher than the chances that a male would be exposed; see Ste. Croix, *The Class Struggle in the Ancient Greek World*, p. 103, and associated notes.

18. This brief, and obviously incomplete, portrait of how Athenian women were treated in law and custom is based primarily on Gould, "Law, Custom and Myth: Aspects of the Social Position of Women in Classical Athens." I have also learned from Dover, *Greek Homosexuality*, and *Greek Popular Morality in the Time of Plato and Aristotle*, pp. 95-102, 205-216; Keuls, *The Reign of the Phallus*; MacDowell, *The Law in Classical Athens*, pp. 84-108; Pomeroy, *Goddesses, Whores, Wives and Slaves*, pp. 57-119.

19. This is argued convincingly by Ste. Croix, *The Class Struggle in the Ancient Greek World*, pp. 100-101:

In many societies either women in general, or married women (who may be regarded in principle as monopolising the reproductive function), have rights, including above all property rights, markedly inferior to those of men; and they have these inferior rights as a direct result of their reproductive function, which gives them a special role in the productive process and makes men desire to dominate and *possess* them and their offspring. In such societies it is surely necessary . . . to see the women, or the wives (as the case may be), as a distinct economic class, in the technical Marxist sense. They are "exploited," by being kept in a position of legal and economic inferiority, so dependent upon men (their husbands in the first place, with their male kin, so to speak, in reserve) that they have no choice but to perform the tasks allotted to them, the compulsory character of which is not in principle lessened by the fact that they may often find real personal satisfaction in performing them. . . . In Classical Athens I would see the class position of a citizen woman as largely determined by her sex, by the fact that she belonged to the class of women, for her father, brothers, husband and sons would all be property owners, while she would be virtually destitute of property rights, and her class position would therefore be greatly inferior to theirs.

20. Cf. Annas, *IPR*, p. 183: "Moreover, we should notice that even in the *Republic* the proposals are limited to Guardian women; Plato sees no need to improve the lives of the producer-class women, who can make no distinctively useful contribution to the common good." Okin, "Philosopher Queens and Private Wives: Plato on Women and the Family," p. 359, also adopts this view.

21. In the *Timaeus* the inferiority of women is explained in terms of the theory of reincarnation:

Human nature being of two kinds, the superior kind was of such and such a nature, and would be called male. Now when they [human psyches] should be implanted in bodies, as is necessary, and be always gaining or losing part of their bodily material, then these would be the necessary consequences: first, sense perception that is innate and common to all, and that arises out of violent affections; second, desire mingled with pleasure and pain; and besides these fear and anger, and all the emotions that are naturally allied to them, and their opposites as well. And if they master these, they will live justly; but if they are mastered by them, unjustly. And the one who has lived his appointed time well shall return again to live in his native star, and have a life that is happy and congenial. But the one who failed to attain this, at the second birth he would be changed into having a woman's nature. And if in that condition, he does not desist from evil, he shall be changed every time into some form of beast. (42a1-c4; see 90e6-91a1)

And this same account seems to be presupposed in the *Laws*: "For it is not, as one might suppose, only the half that is affected if one overlooks the disorderliness of things concerning women; in fact to the degree that woman's nature is inferior in virtue to man's, by so much would the harm more approach being double" (781a6-b4). The idea seems to be this. Because a female nature is one incarnation further away from the disembodied starting point than a male nature, women are naturally twice inferior to men in virtue. Hence, if women are not properly trained and educated, they will be worse than untrained and uneducated men. If they are properly trained and educated, however, some women will become just and be superior to men who fail to be just. This theory does not emerge in the *Republic*, but it is compatible with the views expressed there.

22. Annas, "Plato's *Republic* and Feminism," though it makes many completely fair points, gives a distorted picture because it overlooks these facts. Her arguments are ably criticized in Lesser, "Plato's Feminism."

23. Cf. Annas, *IPR*, pp. 335-354: Book 10 "adds new and unexpected points about poetry" and "appears gratuitous and clumsy, and it is full of oddities"; Cornford, *The Republic of Plato*, p. 321: "The attack on poetry in this Part has the air of an appendix, only superficially linked to the preceding and following context"; Else, *The Structure and Date of Book 10 of Plato's Republic*, p. 21: "the impression we get at the beginning of Book 10—an impression which remains undiminished after repeated readings—is of an abrupt hiatus"; Nettleship, *Lectures on the Republic of Plato*, p. 341: "The first half of Book X is disconnected from the rest of the *Republic*, and the transition to the subject of art and poetry, which is here made, is sudden and unnatural."

24. The translations of Chambry, Cornford, and Grube suggest that tragic poets are assumed to be T-imitators at 597e6-8. But this is not what the passage actually says. The correct translation is as follows: "This will then be true of the tragedian, *if indeed* [*eiper*] he is an imitator; he is naturally third from a king and the truth, and so are all other imitators." The antecedent of the conditional remains to be established; its truth is not being presupposed.

25. Annas, "Plato on the Triviality of Literature," p. 5 represents these arguments as trading on a false analogy between poetry and *trompe l'oeil* painting:

> The account of painting that made the painter into a mindless copier of appearances is carried over to poetry (598d7) and applied to Homer and the tragedians. The point to be taken over is that the artist, in whatever medium, produces without *knowledge* of his product. . . . But does the claim about the artist's lack of knowledge carry over from painting to poetry? It does not, because of the very narrow way in which the painter's activity has been described. Homer cannot be said to copy the appearances of things in anything like the way that the illusionistic painter does. What corresponds to holding up the mirror, or capturing the perspective of the way a bed looks from one particular angle of vision? There seems to be no analogy at all.

A similar view is defended by Else, *The Structure and Date of Book 10 of Plato's Republic*, p. 33, and by Nehamas, "Plato on Imitation and Poetry in *Republic* 10," p. 55. But I do not think it can be sustained. Socrates uses painting as an uncontentious example of T-imitation. He claims that because people can be deceived by illusionistic painting, their claim that poets know what they are talking about cannot be taken at face value (598d7-599a4). He then argues, without appealing to painting at all, that tragic poetry is at three removes from the truth (599a6-601a3). On this basis, he claims that poets do with words, meters, and rhymes what painters do with colours, namely, deceive those "without knowledge, who judge by words" (601a4-b5). So there is no illegitimate transfer of conclusions from illusionistic painting to poetry. The only argument that actually trades directly on the analogy with painting is 601b9-602b8, and it is characterized as being only "likely" (603b9-c2). Annas is quite right, however, that the crucial point the argument is meant to establish is that poets have no knowledge of their ethical subject matter. But once that is clear, most would concede this point even without argument. For given what Plato thinks is required for knowledge (2.8-9), it is uncontentiously true that no poet has knowledge about the virtues, or indeed about anything else.

26. Nehamas, "Plato on Imitation and Poetry in *Republic* 10," which contains one of the best discussions of these questions, reaches a conclusion of relative despair: "We still have to face the conflict between Books 3 and 10: The former seems to allow imitative poetry, the latter to forbid it. This conflict, I am afraid, cannot be ultimately eliminated; but it is not as stark and glaring as it has often seemed to be" (p. 51). Many recent writers echo these sentiments. Annas, "Plato on the Triviality of Literature," p. 22: "any attempt to harmonize Books 3 and 10 must be deeply misconceived"; Urmson, "Plato and the Poets," p. 129: "We can represent the argument of Book 10 as resuming that of Book 3 only by doing gross violence to one or the other or both." The more optimistic answer defended by Tate, " 'Imitation' in Plato's *Republic*" and "Plato and Imitation," and Cross and Woozley, *PRPC*, pp. 278-281, is ably criticized in the other papers mentioned in this note.

27. A number of writers have argued that *mimēsis* "as it was traditionally applied to poetry, speaking, and dancing meant primarily *acting like* someone else" (Nehamas, "Plato on Imitation and Poetry in *Republic* 10," p. 58). Cf. Havelock, *Preface to Plato*, pp. 57-60 n. 22.

28. A contemporary philosophy of art which respects this continuity is developed in Wollheim, *Art and Its Objects* and *On Art and the Mind*.

29. Murdoch, "Philosophy and Literature," pp. 230-235, is worth quoting in this regard:

Literature is read by many and various people, philosophy by very few. Serious artists are their own critics and do not usually work for an audience of "experts." Besides, art is fun and for fun, it has innumerable intentions and charms. Literature interests us on different levels in different fashions. It is full of tricks and magic and deliberate mystification. Literature entertains, it does many things, and philosophy does one thing. . . . Literary modes are very natural to us, very close to ordinary life and to the way we live as reflective beings. . . . I think philosophy is very counter-natural, it is a very odd unnatural activity. Any teacher of philosophy must feel this. Philosophy disturbs the mass of semi-aesthetic conceptual habits on which we normally rely. . . . Literature could be called a disciplined technique for arousing certain emotions. . . . I would include the arousing of emotion in the definition of art, although not every occasion of experiencing art is an emotional occasion. The sensuous nature of art is involved here, the fact that it is involved with visual and auditory sensations and bodily sensations. If nothing sensuous is present no art is present. This fact alone makes it quite different from "theoretical" activities. Moreover, much art, perhaps most art, perhaps all art is connected with sex, in some extremely general sense. (This may be a metaphysical statement.) Art is close dangerous play with unconscious forces.

Some of these ideas are further developed in *The Sovereignty of Good*.

30. Nussbaum, *The Fragility of Goodness*, represents Aristotle as taking up this invitation.

31. Cf. Popper, *The Open Society and Its Enemies*, vol. 1, pp. 62-67. There is an interesting exploration of the rôle of the fact/value distinction in liberal criticisms of Plato in Versenyi, "Plato and His Liberal Opponents."

32. For a brief and forceful defense of this conception of the state, see Dworkin, "Liberalism."

33. In *An Essay concerning Human Understanding*, p. 238, Locke writes: "Liberty is . . . an Idea belonging to . . . the Person having the Power of doing, or forebearing to do, according as the Mind shall chuse or direct." An almost identical definition appears in Hume, *An Enquiry concerning the Human Understanding*, p. 95.

34. This criticism has recently been developed in Connolly, *Appearance and Reality in Politics*, especially pp. 94-101.

35. See Cohen and Rogers, *On Democracy*, pp. 47-87.

CHAPTER FIVE

1. The problem of relevance was first noticed by Sachs, "A Fallacy in Plato's *Republic*," who argues that Plato's failure to solve it "wrecks the *Republic*'s main argument" (p. 35). The following contain responses to Sachs' arguments: Irwin, *PMT*, pp. 208-212; Kraut, "Reason and Justice in Plato's *Republic*"; Vlastos, "Justice and Happiness in the *Republic*."

2. See Cooper, "The Psychology of Justice in Plato," pp. 152-153.

3. It is instructive to compare this argument about the relations between the virtues to Aristotle's discussion of the relations between practical wisdom (*phronēsis*) and the virtues in *Nicomachean Ethics* 1143b18-1145a11. According

to the latter, there is a kind of virtue one can have even if one is not practically wise, namely, "natural virtue [*hē phusikē aretē*]." (Plato's "political courage" is an example of such virtue.) But for "full virtue" practical wisdom is required. (In Plato's terms, the polis cannot be fully or properly courageous unless it is wise.) But, at the same time, it is impossible to be practically wise without being virtuous. The natural virtues can exist in separation from one another, but the full or proper virtues cannot. (In Plato's terms, the polis is wise if and only if it is just, moderate, and courageous.)

4. Sachs, "A Fallacy in Plato's *Republic*," claims that if Plato is to avoid a "fallacy of irrelevance" (p. 35), and show that proper psychic rule ("p-justice") is justice, he must establish the following biconditional relation between p-justice and justice as it is conventionally or vulgarly conceived ("v-justice"):

(i) If someone is p-just, he must be v-just

and

(ii) If someone is v-just, he must be p-just (p. 46).

Vlastos, "Justice and Happiness in the *Republic*," pp. 114, 135-136, agrees with Sachs that Plato must establish both (i) and (ii). Kraut, "Reason and Justice in Plato's *Republic*," p. 207, thinks that it is enough if Plato can establish (i). Irwin, *PMT*, pp. 208-212, 331-333 nn. 29-33, argues that Plato need not establish even (i). He thinks that it is enough if a p-just man "will be innocent of the more flagrant acts of theft, murder, lying, adultery, promise-breaking, and so on," and if at "various points . . . p-justice is recognizably the virtue referred to in ordinary beliefs about virtue" (p. 209). Despite their differences on this matter, all four agree, then, that Plato will not have shown that p-justice is justice unless he can establish that

(iii) If someone is p-just, then he must be *to some degree* v-just—he must avoid at least the most flagrant v-unjust actions.

And, of course, this presupposes that some conventional ethical beliefs about justice are true. But if Plato simply presupposes this, as the commentators themselves do, he is in serious trouble—as we are about to see.

5. The strategic similarity between Plato's argument and Kant's is worth noting. The First Section of the *Grounding for the Metaphysics of Morals* is devoted to showing that an analysis of "the moral cognition of ordinary human reason" (p. 15; cf. p. 5) reveals the categorical imperative to be its underlying principle. This is the analogue of Plato's argument in Book 4. But this does not by itself justify the categorical imperative:

worse service cannot be rendered morality than that an attempt be made to derive it from examples. For every example of morality presented to me must first be judged according to the principles of morality in order to see whether it is fit to serve as an example, i.e., as a model. But in no way can it authoritatively furnish the concept of morality. (p. 20)

This is the analogue of the problem of ideology. The remaining two sections of the *Grounding* then try to underwrite the categorical imperative without appealing to conventional ethical beliefs. "[T]he principles [of morals] should be derived from the concept of a rational being in general, since moral laws should hold for every rational being as such" (p. 23). The task of showing that the categorical imperative can be so derived falls to "the metaphysics of morals" in the Second Section. One more task remains, namely, that of showing that the concept of a rational being is satisfiable, that it is possible to act autonomously, or in accord with the categorical imperative (p. 38), that "freedom is something actual in ourselves and in human nature" (p. 51). This task, which falls to "a critique of pure practical reason," occupies the Third Section. The argument of these sections is analogous to Plato's theory of justice itself.

6. There is a good discussion of the difficulties facing a theory of justice that portrays injustice as the result of pleonexia in Williams, "Justice as a Virtue."

7. Plato's commitment to this view is noticed and discussed by Williams, "The Analogy of City and Soul in Plato's *Republic*," pp. 200-206.

8. Irwin, *PMT*, p. 210, takes this passage to be claiming that each particular just action must produce proper rule in the agent who performs it, and rightly objects that this is an implausible doctrine:

> For some clearer test of the co-reference of "p-justice" [proper rule] and "justice," we need to know what actions can be expected of a p-just man. Plato's answer is strange. He identifies justice with psychic health; like the other virtues in *Republic* IV it is a state of a person not defined in behavioural terms. Just actions are taken to be parallel to healthy, health-preserving actions; they produce a condition of justice in the soul (443e4-444a2, 444c10-d11), and all admirable actions produce psychic virtue (444d13-e5). Now Plato might argue that some just actions produce p-justice because we become just by doing just actions. . . . But his claim that promotion of psychic health is necessary to make an action just (443e4-6) seems to misuse the analogy with health; no doubt a healthy medicine is productive of health, but healthy appetites and complexions are not productive, but indicative of health. . . . It seems much more promising to claim that the just man's just action expresses his p-justice than to insist that it must always produce or maintain it.

However, I do not think that Irwin's interpretation can be right. For Plato is trying to characterize not the just actions of the properly ruled person only, but just actions in general, and these must, for reasons we shall see in the text, include all actions sanctioned in the Kallipolis. Hence Plato cannot hold that just actions in general express proper rule, although there is nothing to prevent him from holding that the just actions of a properly ruled person do so. Nor do I think that Plato is arguing by analogy with health here, although he is clearly doing so in the other passage Irwin mentions (444c1-e2). But it is not clear that even there he misuses the analogy. For healthy *actions*, as opposed to healthy complexions, need not express health. An unhealthy person can perform healthy actions. Moreover, he can perform them without being made healthy by them. But healthy actions must, I think, be *of the sort* which help produce or maintain health in those with the requisite natural resources. There is no reason, then, to interpret the claim that "doing just things produces justice" (444c10-d1) to mean that *each particular just action* produces justice in an agent. For that would not only make just actions disanalogous to healthy ones, but it would conflict with the basic tenet of Plato's psychology that no amount of just action will produce proper rule in the psyche of someone who is by nature a money-lover or an honour-lover. What is being claimed, if I am right, is that just actions are of the sort that produce proper rule in those with the appropriate natural resources. And this does make just actions genuinely analogous to healthy actions.

9. Even though this group includes someone who "lived his life under an ordered constitution [*tetagmenēi politeiai*]" (619c6-7), I do not think that it includes the producers and guardians of the Kallipolis. Although the producers and guardians—with the exception of the officers, who may have studied dialectic (4.8)—do not themselves formally study philosophy, their polis is steeped in it. And they themselves have been made friends of justice by their education. Moreover, if they were included in the present class, it would not be in their true long-term interests to live in the Kallipolis. For they would pay in their next incarnation for their happiness in this one.

10. This way of looking at ethical theories was suggested to me by Scanlon, "Contractualism and Utilitarianism."

11. See, e.g., Dummett, "Realism" and "Platonism."

12. See Annas, *IPR*, pp. 157-169.

13. See Railton, "Moral Realism"; Sturgeon, "Moral Explanations"; Wollheim, *The Thread of Life*, pp. 197-225. Railton's theory is especially close to Plato's.

14. See Kant's *Grounding for the Metaphysics of Morals*, Third Section. Our free noumenal will is engaged simply by the motive of duty, by the perception of an objective or categorical reason. But our phenomenal will needs a phenomenal motive to get it going. The motive Kant provides is *Achtung*, or awe at the moral law. But *Achtung*, though Kant tries desperately to prove otherwise in a series of fascinating footnotes (p. 14 n. 14, p. 24 n. 3, p. 59 n. 3), seems to be a desire or inclination. So even Kant ends up with a theory in

which ethical facts engage our phenomenal will through our desires. It is only our noumenal will that avoids this fate, and about it we can know nothing except that we must have it if we are to make sense of moral motivation as Kant portrays it.

15. Mill, *Utilitarianism*, p. 7.

16. See, e.g., Rawls, *A Theory of Justice*, pp. 22-27.

17. See Scheffler, *The Rejection of Consequentialism*.

18. See Adams, "Motive Utilitarianism."

19. See Irwin, *PMT*, pp. 254-280.

20. A similar objection has been raised against Kant; see Williams, "Morality and the Emotions," especially pp. 226-227; Vlastos, "The Theory of Social Justice in the *Polis* in Plato's *Republic*," pp. 38-39. Wolf, "Moral Saints," also raises relevant issues in an interesting way.

21. In constructing the various models of love considered I have drawn on the following works: Irwin, *PMT*, pp. 268-274; Kosman, "Platonic Love"; Singer, *The Nature of Love*, vol. 1; Vlastos, "The Individual as Object of Love in Plato."

BIBLIOGRAPHY

Ackrill, J. L. "*Anamnēsis* in the *Phaedo*." In *Exegesis and Argument*, ed. E. N. Lee, A.P.D. Mourelatos, and R. M. Rorty, pp. 177-195. New York: Humanities Press, 1973.

Adam, James, ed. *PR* = *The Republic of Plato*. 2 vols. Cambridge: Cambridge University Press, 1969.

Adams, Robert Merrihew. "Motive Utilitarianism." *Journal of Philosophy* 73 (1976): 467-481.

Adkins, A.W.H. *Merit and Responsibility*. Oxford: Clarendon Press, 1960.

Allen, R. E. "The Argument from Opposites in *Republic* V." *Review of Metaphysics* 15 (1961): 325-335.

———. "Participation and Predication in Plato's Middle Dialogues." In *Studies in Plato's Metaphysics*, ed. R. E. Allen, pp. 43-60. London: Routledge and Kegan Paul, 1965.

Annas, Julia. "Forms and First Principles." *Phronesis* 19 (1974): 257-283.

———. *IPR* = *An Introduction to Plato's Republic*. Oxford: Clarendon Press, 1981.

———. "Plato on the Triviality of Literature." In *Plato on Beauty, Wisdom and the Arts*, ed. Julius Moravcsik and Philip Temko, pp. 1-28.

———. "Plato's *Republic* and Feminism." *Philosophy* 51 (1976): 307-321.

Armstrong, D. M. *A Theory of Universals*. Cambridge: Cambridge University Press, 1978.

Barker, Ernest. *The Political Thought of Plato and Aristotle*. New York: Russell and Russell, 1959.

Barnes, Jonathan. *The Presocratic Philosophers*. 2 vols. London: Routledge and Kegan Paul, 1979.

Bloom, Allan, trans. *The Republic of Plato*. New York: Basic Books, 1968.

Brandt, R. B. *A Theory of the Good and the Right*. Oxford: Clarendon Press, 1979.

Brandwood, Leonard. *A Word Index to Plato*. Leeds: Maney, 1976.

Burnet, John, ed. *Platonis Opera*. 5 vols. Oxford: Clarendon Press, 1900-1907.

Burnyeat, Myles. "Aristotle on Learning to Be Good." In *Essays on Aristotle's Ethics*, ed. A. Rorty, pp. 69-92. Berkeley and Los Angeles: University of California Press, 1980.

———. "Platonism and Mathematics: A Prelude to Discussion." In *Metaphysik und Mathematik*, ed. A. Graeser. Bern, 1987.

Chambry, Emile, trans. *Platon, La République*. 3 vols. Paris: Budé, 1932.

Cherniss, H. F. "The Philosophical Economy of the Theory of Ideas." In *PI*, ed. Vlastos, pp. 16-27.

———. "The Relation of the *Timaeus* to Plato's Later Dialogues." In *Studies in*

Plato's Metaphysics, ed. R. E. Allen, pp. 339-378. London: Routledge and Kegan Paul, 1965.

Cohen, Joshua, and Rogers, Joel. *On Democracy*. Harmondsworth: Penguin, 1983.

Connolly, W. E. *Appearance and Reality in Politics*. Cambridge: Cambridge University Press, 1981.

Cooper, John M. "Plato's Theory of Human Motivation." *History of Philosophy Quarterly* 1 (1984): 3-21.

———. "The Psychology of Justice in Plato." *American Philosophical Quarterly* 14 (1977): 151-157.

Cornford, F. M., trans. *The Republic of Plato*. New York: Oxford University Press, 1941.

Crombie, I. M. *EPD* = *An Examination of Plato's Doctrines*. 2 vols. London: Routledge and Kegan Paul, 1962.

Cross, R. C., and Woozley, A. D. *PRPC* = *Plato's Republic: A Philosophical Commentary*. London: Macmillan, 1964.

Davidson, Donald. "How Is Weakness of the Will Possible?" In *Essays on Actions and Events*, pp. 21-42. Oxford: Clarendon Press, 1980.

de Sousa, Ronald. "The Good and the True." *Mind* 68 (1974): 534-551.

———. "The Rationality of Emotions." In *Explaining Emotions*, ed. A. Rorty, pp. 127-151. Berkeley and Los Angeles: University of California Press, 1980.

Diels, Hermann, ed. *Die Fragmente der Vorsokratiker*. Berlin: Weidmann, 1951.

Dorter, Kenneth. *Plato's Phaedo: An Interpretation*. Toronto: University of Toronto Press, 1982.

Dover, Kenneth. *Greek Homosexuality*. Cambridge: Harvard University Press, 1978.

———. *Greek Popular Morality in the Time of Plato and Aristotle*. Berkeley and Los Angeles: University of California Press, 1974.

Dummett, Michael. "Platonism." In *Truth and Other Enigmas*, pp. 202-214. Cambridge: Harvard University Press, 1978.

———. "Realism." In *Truth and Other Enigmas*, pp. 145-165. Cambridge: Harvard University Press, 1978.

Dworkin, Ronald. "Liberalism." In *Public and Private Morality*, ed. Stuart Hampshire, pp. 113-143. Cambridge: Cambridge University Press, 1978.

Else, Gerald F. *The Structure and Date of Book 10 of Plato's Republic*. Heidelberg: Carl Winter, 1972.

Fine, Gail. "Knowledge and Belief in *Republic* V." *Archiv für Geschichte der Philosophie* 60 (1978): 121-139.

———. "The One Over Many." *Philosophical Review* 89 (1980): 197-240.

———. "Separation." *Oxford Studies in Ancient Philosophy* 2 (1984): 31-87.

Finley, M. I. *The World of Odysseus*. New York: Viking, 1978.

Foley, Richard. "Is It Possible to Have Contradictory Beliefs?" *Midwest Studies in Philosophy* 10 (1986): 327-355.

Foot, Philippa. *Virtues and Vices*. Berkeley and Los Angeles: University of California Press, 1978.

Freeman, Kathleen. *Ancilla to the Pre-Socratic Philosophers*. Cambridge: Harvard University Press, 1977.

Frege, Gottlob. *The Foundations of Arithmetic*, trans. J. L. Austin. Oxford: Blackwell, 1959.

———. *Translations from the Philosophical Writings of Gottlob Frege*, trans. P. T. Geach and Max Black. Oxford: Blackwell, 1966.

Gallop, David, trans. *Plato: Phaedo*. Oxford: Clarendon Press, 1975.

Geuss, Raymond. *The Idea of a Critical Theory*. Cambridge: Cambridge University Press, 1981.

Goldman, Alvin I. "Discrimination and Perceptual Knowledge." *Journal of Philosophy* 73 (1976): 771-791.

———. *Epistemology and Cognition*. Cambridge: Harvard University Press, 1986.

Gosling, J.C.B. "*Doxa* and *Dunamis* in Plato's *Republic*." *Phronesis* 13 (1968): 119-130.

———. *Plato*. London: Routledge and Kegan Paul, 1973.

———, trans. *Plato: Philebus*. Oxford: Clarendon Press, 1975.

———. *Pleasure and Desire*. Oxford: Clarendon Press, 1969.

———. "Reply to White." *Canadian Journal of Philosophy* 7 (1977): 307-314.

———. "*Republic* Book V: *ta polla kala* etc." *Phronesis* 5 (1960): 116-128.

———. "Similarity in *Phaedo* 73B *seq*." *Phronesis* 10 (1965): 151-161.

———, and Taylor, C. C. W. *The Greeks on Pleasure*. Oxford: Clarendon Press, 1982.

Gould, John. "Law, Custom and Myth: Aspects of the Social Position of Women in Classical Athens." *Journal of Hellenic Studies* 100 (1980): 38-59.

Grote, George. *Plato and the Other Companions of Socrates*. 3 vols. London: Murray, 1865.

Grube, G.M.A., trans. *Plato's Republic*. Indianapolis: Hackett, 1974.

———. *Plato's Thought*. London: Methuen, 1935.

Guthrie, W.K.C. *A History of Greek Philosophy*. Vol. 4. Cambridge: Cambridge University Press, 1975.

Hackforth, R., trans. *Plato's Phaedrus*. Cambridge: Cambridge University Press, 1972.

Hacking, Ian. *Representing and Intervening*. Cambridge: Cambridge University Press, 1983.

Hardie, W.F.R. *A Study in Plato*. Oxford: Clarendon Press, 1936.

Hare, R. M. "Plato and the Mathematicians." In *New Essays on Plato and Aristotle*, ed. Renford Bambrough, pp. 21-38. London: Routledge and Kegan Paul, 1965.

Havelock, Eric A. *Preface to Plato*. Cambridge: Belknap Press, 1982.

Henderson, T. Y. "In Defense of Thrasymachus." *American Philosophical Quarterly* 7 (1970): 218-228.

Hintikka, Jaakko. "Knowledge and Its Objects in Plato." In *Patterns in Plato's Thought*, ed. J.M.E. Moravcsik, pp. 1-30. Dordrecht: Reidel, 1973.

Hobbes, Thomas. *Leviathan*. Ed. C. B. Macpherson. Harmondsworth: Penguin, 1968.

Hourani, G. F. "The Education of the Third Class in Plato's *Republic*." *Classical Quarterly* 43 (1949): 58-60.

———. "Thrasymachus' Definition of Justice in Plato's *Republic*." *Phronesis* 7 (1962): 110-120.

Hume, David. *Enquiries concerning the Human Understanding and concerning the Principles of Morals*. Ed. L. A. Selby-Bigge. Oxford: Clarendon Press, 1902.

———. *A Treatise of Human Nature*. Ed. L. A. Selby-Bigge. Oxford: Clarendon Press, 1967.

Irwin, T. H. "Plato's Heracleiteanism." *Philosophical Quarterly* 27 (1977): 1-13.

———. *PMT = Plato's Moral Theory: The Early and Middle Dialogues*. Oxford: Clarendon Press, 1977.

Jowett, Benjamin, trans. *The Dialogues of Plato*. 2 vols. Oxford: Clarendon Press, 1953.

Kahn, Charles. *The Verb Be in Ancient Greek*. Dordrecht: Reidel, 1973.

Kant, Immanuel. *Grounding for the Metaphysics of Morals*. Trans. James W. Ellington. Indianapolis: Hackett, 1983.

Kenny, Anthony. *Action, Emotion and Will*. London: Routledge and Kegan Paul, 1963.

Kerferd, G. B. "Thrasymachus and Justice: A Reply." *Phronesis* 9 (1964): pp. 12-16.

———. "Thrasymachus on Justice." *Durham University Journal* 9 (1947-1948): 19-27.

Keuls, Eva C. *The Reign of the Phallus*. New York: Harper and Row, 1985.

Kosman, L. A. "Platonic Love." In *Facets of Plato's Philosophy*, ed. W. H. Werkmeister, pp. 53-69. Assen: Van Gorcum, 1976.

Kraut, Richard. "Reason and Justice in Plato's *Republic*." In *Exegesis and Argument*, ed. E. N. Lee, A.P.D. Mourelatos, and R. M. Rorty, pp. 207-224. New York: Humanities Press, 1973.

Lesser, H. "Plato's Feminism." *Philosophy* 54 (1979): 113-117.

Locke, John. *An Essay concerning Human Understanding*. Ed. Peter H. Nidditch. Oxford: Clarendon Press, 1979.

Mabbott, J. D. "Is Plato's *Republic* Utilitarian?." In PII, ed. Vlastos, pp. 57-65.

MacDowell, Douglas M. *The Law in Classical Athens*. Ithaca: Cornell University Press, 1978.

MacIntyre, Alasdair. *After Virtue*. Notre Dame: University of Notre Dame Press, 1981.

———. *A Short History of Ethics*. London: Routledge and Kegan Paul, 1966.

Matthews, Gareth B., and Cohen, S. Marc. "The One and the Many." *Review of Metaphysics* 21 (1968): 630-655.

McDowell, John. "Virtue and Reason." *Monist* 62 (1979): 331-350.

Mill, J. S. *Utilitarianism*. Ed. George Sher. Indianapolis: Hackett, 1979.

Moravcsik, Julius. "Learning as Recollection." In *PI*, ed. Vlastos, pp. 52-69.

———, and Temko, Philip, eds. *Plato on Beauty, Wisdom and the Arts*. Totowa, N.J.: Rowman and Littlefield, 1982.

Morrison, J. S. "Two Unresolved Difficulties in the Line and Cave." *Phronesis* 22 (1977): 212-231.

Murdoch, Iris. *The Fire and the Sun: Why Plato Banished the Artists.* Oxford: Clarendon Press, 1977.

———. "Philosophy and Literature: Dialogue with Iris Murdoch." In *Men of Ideas*, ed. Brian Magee. New York: Viking, 1978.

———. *The Sovereignty of Good.* London: Routledge and Kegan Paul, 1970.

Murphy, N. R. *TIPR = The Interpretation of Plato's Republic.* Oxford: Clarendon Press, 1951.

Nehamas, Alexander. "Plato on Imitation and Poetry in *Republic* 10." In *Plato on Beauty, Wisdom and the Arts*, ed. Julius Moravcsik and Philip Temko, pp. 47-78.

———. "Plato on the Imperfection of the Sensible World." *American Philosophical Quarterly* 12 (1975): 105-117.

———. "Predication and Forms of Opposites in the *Phaedo*." *Review of Metaphysics* 26 (1973): 461-491.

———. "Self-Predication and Plato's Theory of Forms." *American Philosophical Quarterly* 16 (1979): 93-103.

Nettleship, R. L. *Lectures on the Republic of Plato.* London: Macmillan, 1967.

Neu, Jerome. "Plato's Analogy of State and Individual: The *Republic* and the Organic Theory of the State." *Philosophy* 46 (1971): 238-254.

Nicholson, P. P. "Unravelling Thrasymachus' Arguments in the *Republic*." *Phronesis* 19 (1974): 210-232.

Nozick, Robert. *Philosophical Explanations.* Cambridge: Harvard University Press, 1981.

Nussbaum, Martha C. "Aristophanes and Socrates on Learning Practical Wisdom." *Yale Classical Studies* 26 (1980): 43-98.

———. *The Fragility of Goodness: Luck and Ethics in Greek Tragedy and Philosophy.* Cambridge: Cambridge University Press, 1986.

———. " 'This Story Isn't True': Poetry, Goodness, and Understanding in Plato's *Phaedrus*." In *Plato on Beauty, Wisdom and the Arts*, ed. Julius Moravcsik and Philip Temko, pp. 79-124.

Okin, S. M. "Philosopher Queens and Private Wives: Plato on Women and the Family." *Philosophy & Public Affairs* 6 (1976-1977): 345-369.

Owen, G.E.L. "The Place of the *Timaeus* in Plato's Later Dialogues." In *Studies in Plato's Metaphysics*, ed. R. E. Allen, pp. 313-338. London: Routledge and Kegan Paul, 1965.

———. "Plato on Not-Being." In *PI*, ed. Vlastos, pp. 223-267.

———. "A Proof in the *Peri Ideōn*." In *Studies in Plato's Metaphysics*, ed. R. E. Allen, pp. 293-312. London: Routledge and Kegan Paul, 1965

Parfit, Derek. *Reasons and Persons.* Oxford: Clarendon Press, 1984.

Penner, Terry. "Thought and Desire in Plato." In *PII*, ed. Vlastos, pp. 96-118.

———. "The Unity of Virtue." *Philosophical Review* 82 (1973): 35-68.

Pomeroy, Sarah. *Goddesses, Whores, Wives and Slaves: Women in Classical Antiquity.* New York: Schocken, 1975.

Popper, Karl. *The Open Society and Its Enemies.* Vol. 1. Princeton: Princeton University Press, 1971.

Quine, W.V.O. "Quantifiers and Propositional Attitudes." In *The Ways of Paradox*, pp. 183-194. New York: Random House, 1966.

Railton, Peter. "Moral Realism." *Philosophical Review* 95 (1986): 163-207.

Raven, J. E. *Plato's Thought in the Making.* Cambridge: Cambridge University Press, 1965.

Rawls, John. *A Theory of Justice.* Cambridge: Harvard University Press, 1971.

Reeve, C.D.C., "Anaxagorean Panspermism." *Ancient Philosophy* 1 (1981): 89-108.

———. "Motion, Rest, and Dialectic in the *Sophist.*" *Archiv für Geschichte der Philosophie* 67 (1985): 47-64.

———. "Socrates Meets Thrasymachus." *Archiv für Geschichte der Philosophie* 67 (1985): 246-265.

Robinson, Richard. *Plato's Earlier Dialectic.* Oxford: Clarendon Press, 1953.

———. "Plato's Separation of Reason from Desire." *Phronesis* 16 (1971): 38-48.

Robinson, T. M. *Plato's Psychology.* Toronto: University of Toronto Press, 1970.

Rorty, Richard. *Philosophy and the Mirror of Nature.* Princeton: Princeton University Press, 1980.

Ross, W. D., ed. *Aristotle's Metaphysics.* 2 vols. Oxford: Clarendon Press, 1953.

———. *Plato's Theory of Ideas.* Oxford: Clarendon Press, 1953.

Ryle, Gilbert. *The Concept of Mind.* Harmondsworth: Penguin, 1966.

———. *Dilemmas.* Cambridge: Cambridge University Press, 1966.

Sachs, David. "A Fallacy in Plato's *Republic.*" In *PII*, ed. Vlastos, pp. 35-51.

Ste. Croix, G.E.M. de. *The Class Struggle in the Ancient Greek World.* Ithaca: Cornell University Press, 1981.

Santas, Gerasimos. *Socrates.* London: Routledge and Kegan Paul, 1979.

Scanlon, Thomas. "Contractualism and Utilitarianism." In *Utilitarianism and Beyond*, ed. Amartya Sen and Bernard Williams, pp. 103-128. Cambridge: Cambridge University Press, 1982.

Scheffler, Samuel. *The Rejection of Consequentialism.* Oxford: Clarendon Press, 1982.

Shorey, Paul, trans. *Plato: The Republic.* Cambridge: Harvard University Press, 1956.

Singer, Irving. *The Nature of Love.* Vol. 1: *Plato to Luther.* Chicago: University of Chicago Press, 1984.

Smith, J. A. "General Relative Clauses in Greek." *Classical Review* 31 (1917): 69-71.

Strang, Colin. "Plato and the Third Man." In *PI*, ed. Vlastos, pp. 184-200.

Sturgeon, Nicholas. "Moral Explanations." In *Morality, Reason and Truth*, ed. David Copp and David Zimmerman, pp. 49-78. Totowa, N.J.: Rowman and Allanheld, 1985.

Tate, J. " 'Imitation' in Plato's *Republic.*" *Classical Quarterly* 22 (1928): 16-23.

———. "Plato and Imitation." *Classical Quarterly* 26 (1932): 161-169.

Taylor, C.C.W., trans. *Plato: Protagoras.* Oxford: Clarendon Press, 1976.

Teloh, Henry. *The Development of Plato's Metaphysics*. University Park, Pa.: Pennsylvania State University Press, 1981.

Tooley, Michael. "Abortion and Infanticide." In *The Rights and Wrongs of Abortion*, ed. Marshall Cohen, Thomas Nagel, and Thomas Scanlon, pp. 52-84. Princeton: Princeton University Press, 1974.

Urmson, J. O. "Plato and the Poets." In *Plato on Beauty, Wisdom and the Arts*, ed. Julius Moravcsik and Philip Temko, pp. 125-136.

———. "Pleasure and Distress." *Oxford Studies in Ancient Philosophy* 2 (1984): 209-221.

Versenyi, L. "Plato and His Liberal Opponents." *Philosophy* 46 (1971): 222-237.

Vlastos, Gregory, "*Anamnesis* in the *Meno*." *Dialogue* 4 (1965): 143-167.

———. "Degrees of Reality in Plato." In *PS*, pp. 58-75.

———. "Does Slavery Exist in Plato's *Republic*?" In *PS*, pp. 140-146.

———. "The Individual as the Object of Love in Plato." In *PS*, pp. 3-34.

———. "Justice and Happiness in the *Republic*." In *PS*, pp. 111-139.

———. "A Metaphysical Paradox." In *PS*, pp. 43-57.

———. *PS* = *Platonic Studies*. Princeton: Princeton University Press, 1973.

———. "Socrates' Disavowal of Knowledge." *Philosophical Quarterly* 35 (1985): 1-31.

———. "The Socratic Elenchus." *Oxford Studies in Ancient Philosophy* 1 (1983): 27-58.

———. "The Theory of Social Justice in the *Polis* in Plato's *Republic*." In *Interpretations of Plato*, ed. Helen North, pp. 1-40. Leiden: Brill, 1977.

———. "The Third Man Argument in the *Parmenides*." In *Studies in Plato's Metaphysics*, ed. R. E. Allen, pp. 231-263. London: Routledge and Kegan Paul, 1965.

———. "The Unity of the Virtues in the *Protagoras*." In *PS*, pp. 221-265.

———, ed. *PI* = *Plato: A Collection of Critical Essays*. Vol. 1. New York: Doubleday, 1971.

———, ed. *PII* = *Plato: A Collection of Critical Essays*. Vol. 2. New York: Doubleday, 1971.

Wallace, James D. *Virtues and Vices*. Ithaca: Cornell University Press, 1978.

Wedberg, Anders. *Plato's Philosophy of Mathematics*. Stockholm: Almqvist and Wixell, 1955.

White, F. C. "J. Gosling on *ta polla kala*." *Phronesis* 23 (1978): 127-132.

———. "The 'Many' in *Republic* 475a-480a." *Canadian Journal of Philosophy* 7 (1977): 291-306.

White, Nicholas. *CPR* = *A Companion to Plato's Republic*. Indianapolis: Hackett, 1979.

———. *Plato on Knowledge and Reality*. Indianapolis: Hackett, 1976.

Wiggins, David. "Deliberation and Practical Reason." In *Essays on Aristotle's Ethics*, ed. A. Rorty, pp. 221-240. Berkeley and Los Angeles: University of California Press, 1980.

Williams, Bernard, "The Analogy of City and Soul in Plato's *Republic*." In *Exe-*

gesis and Argument, ed. E. N. Lee, A.P.D. Mourelatos, and R. M. Rorty, pp. 196-206. New York: Humanities Press, 1973.

————. "Don Giovanni as an Idea." In *W. A. Mozart: Don Giovanni*, ed. Julian Rushton, pp. 81-91. Cambridge: Cambridge University Press, 1981.

————. *Ethics and the Limits of Philosophy*. Cambridge: Harvard University Press, 1985.

————. "Internal and External Reasons." In *Moral Luck*, pp. 101-113. Cambridge: Cambridge University Press, 1981.

————. "Justice as a Virtue." In *Essays on Aristotle's Ethics*, ed. A. Rorty, pp. 189-200. Berkeley and Los Angeles: University of California Press, 1980.

————. "Morality and the Emotions." In *Problems of the Self*, pp. 207-229. Cambridge: Cambridge University Press, 1973.

Wilson, J.R.S. *Emotion and Object*. Cambridge: Cambridge University Press, 1972.

Winnington-Ingram, R. P. *Sophocles: An Interpretation*. Cambridge: Cambridge University Press, 1980.

Wittgenstein, Ludwig. *Philosophical Investigations*. Oxford: Blackwell, 1953.

Wolf, Susan. "Moral Saints." *Journal of Philosophy* 79 (1982): 419-439.

Wollheim, Richard. *Art and Its Objects*. Cambridge: Cambridge University Press, 1980.

————. *On Art and the Mind*. Cambridge: Harvard University Press, 1974.

————. *The Thread of Life*. Cambridge: Harvard University Press, 1984.

GENERAL INDEX

Achilles, 187
Achtung, 319-320
Ackrill, J. L., 298
Adam, James, 287, 290, 291, 294, 295, 300, 307, 308
Adams, Robert Merrihew, 320
Adeimantus: the defense of justice he does not want, 25; a philosopher, 41, 249
Adkins, A.W.H., 277, 305
Aeschylus, 32, 229
agnoia. See error
A-goods, 24, 33, 282-283
Ajax, 146, 187
akrasia, 131-135, 239; Socrates' views on, 5; in the *Republic*, 134
Alcibiades, 193
Allen, R. E., 287, 291, 298
altruism, 269-270
anamnēsis. See recollection
Anaxagoras, 31
anger, 305; components of, 137; natural object of, 130-131; a spirited desire, 129-131
Annas, Julia, 275, 276, 279, 283-284, 285, 288, 291, 293, 294, 298, 300, 308, 311, 313, 314-315, 316
antiforms, 68-69; complete nonresemblers, 64-65; *Undingen*, 64
appetite, 43, 163; apparent conflict in, 124-125; cognitive components of, 139-140; core conception of, 135; and folk-wisdom, 140; nature of its rule in the psyche, 141-142; unified source of motivation, 151-153
appetites, 138; good-independent, 135-136; lawless unnecessary, 162; necessary, 44, 135-136, 162-163; nonlawless unnecessary, 162; part-good-dependent, 135-136; unnecessary, 44-45, 162, 178

appetitive-part-good-dependent desires, 136, 152-153
aretē. See virtue
Aristotle, 84, 154; on anger, 305; on practical wisdom and the virtues, 316-317; on primary education, 309; on separation of forms, 105-107; on substance, 106-107
Armstrong, D. M., 289
Asclepius, 213-214
aspiration, 44, 163, 304; cognitive components of, 139-140; core conception of, 135-137; nature of its rule in the psyche, 141-142; and scientific-thought, 140; a unified source of motivation, 151-153
auxiliaries, 182

Barker, Ernest, 279
Barnes, Jonathan, 290
bed, 85-86; first, second, third, 86-87
being, 64-65, 92, 106, 110-112; complete being (what is completely), 62-65; existential or predicative, 92, 228-229; identical to substance, 92
Bentham, Jeremy, 151
Berkeley, George, 231
B-goods, 24, 33, 282-283
Book 1 (*Republic*), 3; rôle in the argument, 22-23
Brandt, R. B., 308
Burnyeat, Myles, 281-282, 287

Cave, 50-52; and education, 51
cave-dwellers, 245; bound, 51, 56; unbound, 51, 56-57
Cephalus: his account of justice, 6; character of, 6; and the elenchus, 7, 9; moderation of, 5; a money-lover, 5, 246; problem he poses for Socrates, 6-7; similarities to Socrates of the *Apology*, 6-7

money-lovers, 176-178; relation to Kallipolis, 178

flux, 67

Foley, Richard, 304

folk-wisdom, 56-58, 100, 164; yields true opinion about the visible, 98

formal object. *See* natural object

forms, 52, 54, 294, 295; access to, 86, 108, 294-295; "bad" forms, 84-85, 293; cognitive reliability of, 104-105; completely instantiated by particulars, 110-113; complete resemblers, 64-65; constituents of the good, 84-85, 92-93; not identical to sensibles, 105; immutability of, 67-68; intelligible rather than visible, 67; as meanings of general terms, 293; objects of direct perception, 104, 108; objects of recollected knowledge, 103; neither real nor intentional properties, 116-117; relational, 110-113; self-instantiation of, 103-104, 108, 295, 298; separation of, 108, 299; simplicity of, 105, 108; traditional theory of, 100-107; structures of pleasure-world constituents, 100; uniqueness of, 67, 295; what each of the many Fs is in itself, 93; what there are forms of, 85-86, 290-291, 293-294; what things would instantiate in the best of all possible worlds, 85

fortuna, 169

freedom: critical, 233; deliberative, 232-233; instrumental, 232; in the Kallipolis, 231-234

Freeman, Kathleen, 276

Frege, Gottlob, 290, 291

Freud, Sigmund, 115, 169, 230

friendship. *See* love

Future of an Illusion, The (Freud), 146

Gallop, David, 293, 295, 298

G-consequences, 24, 29-31

geometrical number, 113-114

Geuss, Raymond, 284

Glaucon, 3, 26; the defense of justice he wants, 25-26; his division of goods, 24-25; as philosopher, 41, 249; why he takes over from Thrasymachus, 39-41

Goldman, Alvin I., 289

good-independent desires, 135

good itself, 81-100, 205; beyond substance, 94-95, 295-296; brightest of the beings, 295-296; and dialectic, 76-77; cause of figures, modes, and qualities, 57; goal of philosophic education, 194-195; and happiness, 158-159; how it causes us to know, 90-91; how knowable things derive their being and substance from it, 91-94; and pleasure, 158-159; structure of cosmos, 292-293; structure of Kallipolis, 84; structure of a pleasure-world, 99-100

goods, Glaucon's division of, 24-25, 33

Gosling, J.C.B., 284, 287, 288, 289, 290, 298, 305, 306-307

Gould, John, 312

Grote, George, 275, 282, 284

Grube, G.M.A., 291, 295, 300, 301, 308, 314

guardians, 178-186, 195-197; education and training, 179-181; happiness in Second Polis, 184-186, 200; lifestyle of, 184; natures, 179; soldier-police, 178-179. *See also* complete guardians; honour-lovers; officers; privates

Guthrie, W.K.C., 296

Gyges' ring, 27

Hackforth, R., 299-300

Hacking, Ian, 301

happiness, 153-159, 164; components of, 34-35; and desire structure, 257-258; a formal goal, 154-158; and the good itself, 158-159; and pleasure, 158-159; as pleonectic satisfaction, 34-35; and polis structure, 158, 258-262; real, 36; a substantial goal, 153-154; and work and virtue, 237-238

Hardie, W.F.R., 287, 299, 304

Hare, R. M., 293

Havelock, Eric A., 315

hedonism, and *akrasia*, 132-133, 154

Hegel, G.W.F., 116, 233

Henderson, T. Y., 279

Heraclitus, 67

Hesiod, 229, 283

hēsuchia. *See* psychic calm

Hintikka, Jaakko, 287, 291

Hobbes, Thomas, 123, 302

Homer, 223-226, 229, 276-277, 283

INDEX LOCORUM